Comrades against Imperialism

In this book Michele L. Louro compiles the debates, introduces the personalities, and reveals the ideas that seeded Jawaharlal Nehru's political vision for India and the wider world. Set between the world wars, this book argues that Nehru's politics reached beyond India in order to fulfill a greater vision of internationalism that was rooted in his experiences with anti-imperialist and anti-fascist mobilizations in the 1920s and 1930s. Using archival sources from India, the United States, the United Kingdom, the Netherlands, Germany, and Russia, the author offers a compelling study of Nehru's internationalism, and contributes a necessary interwar history of institutions and networks that were confronting imperialist, capitalist, and fascist hegemonies in the twentieth-century world. Louro provides readers with a global intellectual history of anti-imperialism and Nehru's appropriation of it, while also establishing a history of a typically overlooked period.

Michele L. Louro is an Associate Professor of History at Salem State University, Massachusetts, where she specializes in Modern South Asia, the British Empire, and World History.

D0555356

Global and International History

Series Editors

Erez Manela, Harvard University
John McNeill, Georgetown University
Aviel Roshwald, Georgetown University

The Global and International History series seeks to highlight and explore the convergences between the new International History and the new World History. Its editors are interested in approaches that mix traditional units of analysis such as civilizations, nations and states with other concepts such as transnationalism, diasporas, and international institutions.

Titles in the Series

Antoine Acker, *Volkswagen in the Amazon: The Tragedy of Global Development in Modern Brazil*

Christopher R. W. Dietrich, *Oil Revolution: Anti-Colonial Elites, Sovereign Rights, and the Economic Culture of Decolonization*

Stefan Rinke, *Latin America and the First World War*

Nathan J. Citino, *Envisioning the Arab Future: Modernization in U.S.-Arab Relations, 1945–1967*

Timothy Nunan, *Humanitarian Invasion: Global Development in Cold War Afghanistan*

Michael Goebel, *Anti-Imperial Metropolis: Interwar Paris and the Seeds of Third World Nationalism*

Stephen J. Macekura, *Of Limits and Growth: The Rise of Global Sustainable Development in the Twentieth Century*

Comrades against Imperialism

Nehru, India, and Interwar Internationalism

MICHELE L. LOURO
Salem State University

CAMBRIDGE
UNIVERSITY PRESS

CAMBRIDGE
UNIVERSITY PRESS

University Printing House, Cambridge CB2 8BS, United Kingdom

One Liberty Plaza, 20th Floor, New York, NY 10006, USA

477 Williamstown Road, Port Melbourne, VIC 3207, Australia

314-321, 3rd Floor, Plot 3, Splendor Forum, Jasola District Centre, New Delhi - 110025, India

79 Anson Road, #06-04/06, Singapore 079906

Cambridge University Press is part of the University of Cambridge.

It furthers the University's mission by disseminating knowledge in the pursuit of
education, learning and research at the highest international levels of excellence.

www.cambridge.org
Information on this title: www.cambridge.org/9781108410403
DOI: 10.1017/9781108297615

First published 2018
First paperback edition 2019

A catalogue record for this publication is available from the British Library

ISBN 978-1-108-41930-7 Hardback
ISBN 978-1-108-41040-3 Paperback

Cambridge University Press has no responsibility for the persistence or
accuracy of URLs for external or third-party internet websites referred to in
this publication, and does not guarantee that any content on such websites is,
or will remain, accurate or appropriate.

For my boys, Logan and Evan

Contents

List of Figures   *page* viii
Acknowledgments   x
Note on Text and Transliteration   xiv
List of Abbreviations   xv

Introduction: Nehru and the Interwar World   1

PART I MOBILIZING AGAINST EMPIRE, 1927–1930

1   A "Real" League of Nations: The Brussels Congress, 1927   19
2   The Making of the League against Imperialism, 1927   65
3   Internationalizing Nationalism in India, 1928–1929   103
4   Anti-Imperialism in Crisis, 1929–1930   140

PART II AFTERLIVES OF ANTI-IMPERIALISM

5   Nehru's Anti-Imperialism after 1930   181
6   Peace and War, 1936–1939   214
7   The War and the Fate of Anti-Imperialist
    Internationalism   256

Bibliography   284
Index   299

Figures

1.1 The plenary session of the Brussels Congress, 1927.
Nehru is seated in the second row, on the left-hand side
nearest the center aisle. *Das Flammenzeichen vom Palais
Egmont: offizielles Protokoll des Kongresses gegen koloniale
Unterdrückung und Imperialismus, Brüssel, 10–15 Februar
1927*. Berlin: Neuer Deutscher Verlag, 1927   *page* 20

1.2 Delegates at the Brussels Congress (1927).
Willi Münzenberg is first on the left and Nehru is next to
him. Contrary to descriptions in other publications, the
woman next to Nehru is not his daughter, Indira, who would
have been ten years old. Instead, the two comrades in the
middle were part of a delegation of Indians based in London
including Tarini Sinha (center). Edo Fimmen is on the far
right. *Das Flammenzeichen vom Palais Egmont: offizielles
Protokoll des Kongresses gegen koloniale Unterdrückung
und Imperialismus, Brüssel, 10–15 Februar 1927*. Berlin:
Neuer Deutscher Verlag, 1927   34

1.3 The Presidium of the Brussels Congress, 1927. Left to right:
Jawaharlal Nehru, George Lansbury, Edo Fimmen, General
Lu Chung Lin, and Liau Hansin. *Das Flammenzeichen vom
Palais Egmont: offizielles Protokoll des Kongresses gegen
koloniale Unterdrückung und Imperialismus, Brüssel,
10–15 Februar 1927*. Berlin: Neuer Deutscher Verlag, 1927   42

1.4 The General Council elected at the Brussels Congress, 1927.
Liau Hansin is first from left (back row), Roger Baldwin
is second from left (back row), Mohammad Hatta is sixth
from left (back row), Reginald Bridgeman is seventh from
left (back row), Willi Münzenberg is third from left (front

row), Edo Fimmen is fifth from left (front row), and Nehru is eighth from left (front row). *Das Flammenzeichen vom Palais Egmont: offizielles Protokoll des Kongresses gegen koloniale Unterdrückung und Imperialismus, Brüssel, 10–15 Februar 1927*. Berlin: Neuer Deutscher Verlag, 1927   52

4.1 The Honorary Presidium and Executive Committee of the League against Imperialism. The Berlin secretariat published this document as a flyer announcing the Second World Congress of the LAI. It featured the founding members of the LAI from the Brussels Congress. Courtesy of Universal History Archive/Getty Images   145

4.2 Chatto and James Maxton just before the Frankfurt Congress in Cologne, Germany, in January 1929. Horst Krueger Scholar Estate Archive, Leibniz-Zentrum Moderner Orient, Berlin, Germany. Photo credit: Ali Raza   151

7.1 Chatto in Leningrad. Photo undated (after 1932). Horst Krueger Scholar Estate Archive, Leibniz-Zentrum Moderner Orient, Berlin, Germany. Photo credit: Ali Raza   261

Acknowledgments

This book is the product of thinking about Nehru and his world for more than a decade. In this time, I have accumulated many intellectual debts. The project began as a master's thesis at Miami University, Ohio, under the supervision of Judith Zinsser, whose encouragement and guidance prompted me to begin this research journey. Even earlier, Barbara Ramusack's course at the University of Cincinnati inspired me to study Indian history. Howard Spodek at Temple University agreed to supervise my dissertation, and I am tremendously thankful for his mentorship, wisdom, and friendship, without which this book would not be possible. My other committee members – Lynn Hollen Lees, Richard Immerman, and Thomas Metcalf – enriched the ideas presented in my dissertation and prepared me for the work of revising it into a book.

Several institutions generously funded my research. Foremost, the US Fulbright student program allowed me to spend a year researching in India. Thanks to Mushirul Hasan and Lakshmi Subramaniam, then at Jamia Millia Islamia, for serving as my Fulbright supervisors in New Delhi, 2008–2009. In addition, the project was sustained by smaller grants from the Center for the Study of Force and Diplomacy (CENFAD) at Temple University, the Center for Humanities at Temple (CHAT), and the School of Graduate Studies at Salem State University. The College of Arts and Sciences and the Department of History at Salem State University also provided financial assistance for short research trips and conference presentations.

Numerous archivists and librarians also facilitated my research. I thank the staff at the Nehru Memorial Museum and Library, National Archives of India, P. C. Joshi Archives at Jawaharlal Nehru University, British Library, People's History Museum (UK), Hull University Archives, Seeley G. Mudd Manuscript Library at Princeton University, New York

Public Library, European Reading Room at the Library of Congress, the Horest Krüger Scholar Estate at Leibniz-Zentrum Moderner Orient, and the International Institute of Social History (IISH). Special thanks to the Horest Krüger Scholar Estate at Leibniz-Zentrum Moderner Orient in Berlin for providing permission to reproduce several images from their collections.

This book has been shaped significantly by several colleagues working on various themes relevant to South Asia and the interwar world: Carolien Stolte, Ali Raza, Franziska Roy, Maia Ramnath, and Benjamin Zachariah. We met in the archives in New Delhi, traveled the world presenting together at various academic conferences, and became lifelong friends. Back in 2009, we made our first academic presentations together at a research symposium at Temple University, "India and the World," which was sponsored and supported by the Center for the Study of Force and Diplomacy (CENFAD) and its fearless leader, Richard Immerman. This event made possible our many subsequent conversations about interwar internationalism and South Asia in Madison, Bonn, and Lisbon, which culminated in the publication *The Internationalist Moment: South Asia, Worlds, and Worldviews* (2014). These experiences, and the comradeship of this internationalist group, informed many of the ideas presented here.

I could not have found a more supportive and collegial community than at Salem State University. In particular, I am grateful for the support of Brad Austin, Bethany Jay, Andrew Darien, Dane Morrison, Avi Chomsky, and Tanya Rodrigue. I am also appreciative that two department chairs, Donna Seger and Christopher Mauriello, advocated for course release time and travel funding necessary to complete this book. Special thanks also to Elizabeth Kenney, Jeff Theis, and Nancy Schultz, who put together various writing groups that provided encouragement, feedback, and accountability when I needed it most. I had the privilege of sharing and discussing my research with a talented group of students. Kelsey J. Utne stands out as a student who encouraged me to articulate my points more clearly. My conversations with Rosie Segil also sharpened my views about Nehru after 1939. Finally, the preparation of the manuscript benefited from the editing skills of Julia Bennett, while Amy Kellet assisted in the translation of German documents relevant to the project.

The revising of this book also benefited from several important workshops. The early guidance from Philip Oldenburg, Geraldine Forbes, and Susan Wadley during the American Institute of Indian Studies dissertation-to-book workshop was tremendously helpful.

The Princeton Institute of International and Regional Studies Exploratory Workshop on Nonalignment and International History, organized by Brad Simpson and James Parker, proved invaluable to my thinking about the relationship between the interwar and postcolonial world. Finally, the international conference, "South Asia and the Long 1930s: Appropriations and Afterlives," held at Leiden University and organized by Nira Wickramasinghe, Sanjukta Sunderason, and Carolien Stolte, was instrumental to my thinking about the later chapters of this book.

The book also evolved thanks to the many conversations I had with colleagues at conferences and in informal settings. This list is hardly exhaustive: David Fahey, Dan Labotz, Mary Kupiec Cayton, Elizabeth Kolsky, Petra Goedde, William Hitchcock, Harvey Neptune, Benjamin Talton, Abigail Perkiss, Kelly Shannon, Jay Sylvestre, Mrinalini Sinha, David Engerman, Duad Ali, Erez Manela, Susan Pennybacker, Fredrick Cooper, Jane Burbank, Vijay Prasad, Sana Tannoury-Karam, Durba Ghosh, Lucy Chester, Marc Jason Gilbert, Maria Framke, Anand Yang, Klaas Stutje, Anupama Rao, Rachel Ball-Philips, Michael Goebel, Christopher Lee, Ani Mukherji, and Sugata Bose. This book improved substantially thanks to the careful reading of Heather Streets-Salter, Lincoln Paine, and Robert Rakove. Of course, it goes without saying that I alone am responsible for any errors and omissions in this book.

Friendships in the United States, India, and Europe sustained the many years of research abroad and write-up at home. I am grateful especially for the support of Jen Faber, Jim Ambruske, Kelly Shannon, Abigail Perkiss, Kate Scott, Jason Sylvestre, Rebecca Grapevine, David Alverez, Eric Colvard, Cailin Shannon, Jaspreet Kaur, Suzanne Schwartz, Aditi Mallick, Michelle Pierce, Louise Swiniarsk, Christine Roecker, and Michelle Terry.

My thanks to Cambridge University Press, especially series editor Erez Manela, who believed in this project and guided it from book proposal to acceptance. Thanks as well to Deborah Gershenowitz, Kristina Deusch, and Abigail Neale at Cambridge and the other series editors, John McNeill and Aviel Roshwald, who supported my project and stewarded it through the final stages.

Finally, tremendous thanks is due to my family. My mother, Marie Doughman, instilled in me the courage to attempt anything and to pursue it with confidence and persistence. She also picked up and moved hundreds of miles from her hometown in Ohio to Massachusetts in order to watch my young children while I finished the book. I only hope I can be as instrumental in the lives of my children as she has been in mine.

My father, Michael Langford, has been no less influential in my life. I am thankful for his unconditional support, even though we may not always agree in terms of our views of politics and the world. In fact, our disagreements forced me to sharpen my arguments and substantiate my claims with stronger evidence. My brother, sister, and stepmother have also been a source of encouragement and inspiration. My sister, Jessica, made this book possible by spending a summer with my kids during the write-up of the final chapters. I've only seen a preview of my sister's own talents as a teacher, and I have no doubt that the world will be a better place thanks to her compassion and commitment to education.

My last and greatest thanks go to my husband, Luis, and my boys, Evan and Logan. Many years ago, Luis supported my decision to leave our home and embark on a journey to India that separated us for nearly a year. It was not what he bargained for when he married me, and it was not always easy, but I thank him for his patience and understanding. Over the years, his companionship, beginning with the long walks with our dog, Buddy, and later play time with our two boys, has been a source of tranquility even when I was overwhelmed with teaching, research, and writing obligations. Along the way, my two children, Evan and Logan, arrived and enriched my life beyond the archive in ways that I couldn't have imagined. I continue to be inspired by their curiosity, kindness, and fearlessness. My world is a better place since their arrival.

Note on Text and Transliteration

Because this book is about recovering the history of the interwar period on its own terms, I've tried wherever possible to use the transliteration of the time. The most notable example is the spelling of the Kuomintang Party (rather than Guomindang Party). In some cases, however, I've made an exception for well-known actors such as Mao Zedong (rather than Mao Tse-tung).

Abbreviations

ACLU	American Civil Liberties Union
AICC	All-India Congress Committee
AIFTU	Amsterdam International Federation of Trade Unions
AIR	*Anti-Imperialist Review*
AITUC	All-India Trade Union Congress
ALIF	American League for India's Freedom
BAWC	British Anti-War Council
BJP	Bharatiya Janata Party
BTUC	British Trade Union Congress
CAGF	Comité contre la Guerre et le Fascisme (Committee against War and Fascism)
CCP	Chinese Communist Party
CNRA	Chinese National Revolutionary Army
CPGB	Communist Party of Great Britain
IASB	International African Service Bureau
ICPP	International Committee for Political Prisoners
IL	India League (London)
ILO	International Labor Organization
ILP	Independent Labour Party (Great Britain)
INC	Indian National Congress
IPC (see also RUP)	International Peace Campaign
ITUC-NW	International Trade Union Committee of Negro Workers
KMT	Kuomintang Party (alternative spelling: Guomindang Party)
LACO	League against Colonial Oppression
LAI	League against Imperialism
LAWF	League against War and Fascism
LP	Labour Party (Great Britain)
LSI	Labour and Socialist International
NACASD	North American Committee to Aid Spanish Democracy

NKVD	Narodnyi Komissariat Vnutrennikh Del (People's Commissariat for Internal Affairs)
RSS	Rashtriya Swayamsevak Sangh (Universal Rally for Peace)
RUP	Rassemblement universel pour la paix
WIR	Workers International Relief
WPP	Workers' and Peasants' Party (India)

INTRODUCTION

Nehru and the Interwar World

In 1927, more than 170 delegates from across the world joined together in Brussels for the inaugural meeting of the League against Imperialism (LAI). This little-studied organization sought to coordinate the efforts of anti-imperialists across the interwar world and especially in the colonies. The chairman of the congress, George Lansbury of the British Labour Party, best captured the meeting's message by calling upon his comrades from Asia who were entrenched in anticolonial struggles: "Do not be fooled by the cry of mere nationalism ... Get your national ownership, get your national control, that is right and proper, but do not stop there because if you do you will have only gone half way." Instead, Lansbury emphasized that "nationalism is *to be blended* with internationalism, because until it is, until the world is built on the foundation of *international comradeship* ... all our labour is in vain."[1] Among the audience of notable Asian leaders was a budding anticolonial nationalist from India, Jawaharlal Nehru, who came to be profoundly influenced by Lansbury's message. After 1927, Nehru frequently argued that India's "nationalism is based on the most intense internationalism."[2]

This book reconstructs the history of Nehru's engagement with anti-imperialist "comradeship" and the special "blend" between internationalism and nationalism. The story begins in 1927, when Nehru arrived in Brussels and joined the LAI. As a result, he established lasting connections with many interwar activists abroad, both communists and noncommunists, who also sought a collective mobilization against imperialist powers and capitalist classes. The LAI

---

[1] George Lansbury, "Speech at the Brussels Congress," February 13, 1927, File G29-1927, All-Indian Congress Committee Papers, Jawaharlal Nehru Memorial Museum and Library, New Delhi, India (hereafter AICC) (emphasis added).

[2] Nehru, Press Statement made in Brussels, February 9, 1927, *Selected Works of Jawaharlal Nehru*, vol. 2 (New Delhi: Orient Longman, 1972), 270 (hereafter cited as *SWJN*). Citations are from the first series published in 1972 unless otherwise noted.

joined Nehru with other anticolonial nationalists, socialists, communists, civil liberties reformers, pacifists, and antifascists. Although Nehru left the LAI in 1930, this book traces how anti-imperialist internationalism continued to inform his conceptualization of India and the wider world throughout the later years of the interwar period and beyond. Later in the 1930s, anti-imperialism became a struggle not only against capitalism and imperialism, but also against fascism and war. This led Nehru to the International Peace Campaign (IPC) in 1936. He also made the case that India's anticolonialism was linked to antifascist and anti-imperialist struggles in places such as China, Nicaragua, Abyssinia, Egypt, Republican Spain, and the Gold Coast (or present-day Ghana).

Nehru's politics were never confined to the nation after 1927; rather, for him, the nation was only the partial fulfillment of a broader vision of internationalism rooted in his experiences with anti-imperialist mobilizations in the interwar years. For Nehru, anti-imperialism came to mean the "blend" of Indian anticolonial nationalism and the diverse political projects represented in the anti-imperialist movement. I return to Lansbury's notion of "blending" frequently in this book to demonstrate the flexibility and heterogeneity of ideas that came to be part of the anti-imperialist movement and Nehru's appropriation of it. Nehru accepted Lansbury's argument that national sovereignty was "only half way" to achieving the goals of anti-imperialist "comradeship," and worked to "blend" Indian nationalist and internationalist objectives. His internationalist engagements enabled Nehru to develop lifelong partnerships and political projects in the name of anti-imperialism.

Nehru remains a mercurial figure in Indian historiography, and this book contends that this perception is primarily because we have yet to understand the pre-eminence of anti-imperialist internationalism in his life and work before 1947. This reinterpretation of Nehru encourages a history of political activism in India beyond the dominant narratives of Indian nationalism.[3] Tony Ballantyne and Antoinette Burton rightly argue that histories of empire remain "insular," while historiography of

---

[3] Scholars such as Maia Ramnath and Kama Maclean argue persuasively that Indian anticolonial resistance in the interwar years was more diverse and complicated than historians have recognized. See Maia Ramnath, *Haj to Utopia: How the Ghadar Movement Charted Global Radicalism and Attempted to Overthrow the British Empire* (Berkeley: University of California Press, 2011); and Kama Maclean, *A Revolutionary History of Interwar India: Violence, Image, Voice and Text* (New York: Oxford University Press, 2015).

anticolonial nationalism is "equally inward-looking."[4] Studies of colonial India and leaders such as Nehru are no exception. Scholarship on Nehru continues to privilege his local and national politics, largely due to the overwhelming concentration of micro-histories rooted in area studies and subaltern studies scholarship. Many scholars have situated Nehru's British education and elite upbringing as the foundation of his Indian nationalist politics. Consequently, Nehru emerges as a central figure to blame for what subaltern scholars such as Ranajit Guha have called the "failure of the nation to come into its own."[5] The few existing biographical works that consider Nehru beyond the frames of the nation have done so as an anecdotal footnote to the larger narrative of his anticolonial nationalist activities in India.[6]

This book attempts to restore Nehru to his proper place in the world of the 1920s and 1930s.[7] As biographer Benjamin Zachariah has aptly

---

[4] Tony Ballantyne and Antoinette Burton, *Empires and the Reach of the Global*, published in *A World Connecting, 1870–1945*, edited by Emily S. Rosenberg (Cambridge, MA: Belknap Press of Harvard University Press, 2012), 423.

[5] Ranajit Guha, "On Some Aspects of the Historiography of Colonial India," in *Selected Subaltern Studies*, edited by Ranajit Guha and Gayatri Chakravorty Spivak (New York: Oxford University Press, 1988), 43.

[6] There are many biographies on Nehru and collected volumes of his writings before and after independence, although the volume of scholarship still pales in comparison to books on Gandhi. Scholars rely on the classic text, Sarvepalli Gopal, *Jawaharlal Nehru: A Biography* (Oxford: Oxford University Press, 1989). Other works include Michael Brecher, *Nehru: A Political Biography* (New York: Oxford University Press, 1959); B. R. Nanda, *Jawaharlal Nehru: A Rebel and a Statesman* (New York: Oxford University Press, 1995); Judith Brown, *Nehru: A Political Life* (New Haven: Yale University Press, 2003); and Benjamin Zachariah, *Nehru* (London: Routledge Press, 2004). Of these, only Zachariah's work considers Nehru's internationalism in any depth.

[7] Three important works in 2006 launched a burgeoning subfield of South Asia and the world: Mrinalini Sinha, *Specters of Mother India: The Global Restructuring of an Empire* (Durham: Duke University Press, 2006); Sugata Bose, *A Hundred Horizons: The Indian Ocean in the Age of Global Empires* (Cambridge, MA: Harvard University Press, 2006); and Durba Ghosh and Dane Keith Kennedy, eds., *Decentering Empire: Britain, India, and the Transcolonial World* (Hyderabad: Orient Longman, 2006). In their wake, a number of texts study various aspects of South Asia and the world in the colonial period: Sugata Bose and Kris Manjapra, eds., *Cosmopolitan Thought Zones: South Asia and the Global Circulation of Ideas* (New York: Palgrave Macmillan, 2010); Maia Ramnath, *Haj to Utopia*; Nico Slate, *Colored Cosmopolitanism: The Shared Struggle for Freedom in the United States and India* (Cambridge, MA: Harvard University Press, 2012); Manu Goswami, "Colonial Internationalisms and Imaginary Futures," *American Historical Review* 117, no. 5 (2012): 1461–1485; Ali Raza, Franziska Roy, and Benjamin Zachariah, eds., *The Internationalist Moment: South Asia, Worlds, and World Views, 1917–1939* (Los Angeles: SAGE Publications, 2014); Stephen Legg, *Prostitution and the Ends of Empire: Scale, Governmentalities, and Interwar India* (Durham: Duke University Press, 2014); Kris Manjapra, *Age of Entanglement: German*

suggested, Nehru believed that "the idea of the nation was problematic" because "the nationalist is only important until you are free." Instead, Zachariah stressed that Nehru was more interested in the "larger questions" beyond political independence.[8] Zachariah's biography on Nehru is one of the only works that considers in any depth the Indian leader's internationalism. This book seeks to study Nehru's preoccupation with the world and the "larger questions" he sought to answer. However, it is not a biography in the sense that it seeks to recount the entirety of his life. Rather, it emphasizes the most significant aspects of the interplay between Nehru's internationalist and nationalist projects. For Nehru, Indian nationalism and internationalism were never oppositional, and this book argues that the meaning of Indian anticolonial resistance developed not only in relation to people within Indian borders, but also in relation to the world beyond India.

Much of this rich history of interplay between national and international has been lost or silenced by scholarship that seeks to either displace or transcend the nation entirely. In doing so, international and national histories have become dichotomous and frequently situated at odds with one another. Instead, this book supports Glenda Sluga's argument that there was a "long, intimate, conceptual past shared by the national and the international as entangled ways of thinking about modernity, progress and politics."[9] I argue that the interwar period was a critical moment

---

and *Indian Intellectuals across Empire* (Cambridge: Harvard University Press, 2014); Sana Aiyar, *Indians in Kenya: The Politics of Diaspora* (Cambridge, MA: Harvard University Press, 2015); and Seema Alavi, *Muslim Cosmopolitanism in the Age of Empire* (Cambridge, MA: Harvard University Press, 2015).

[8] Benjamin Zachariah, quoted in Sandip Roy, "Freeing Nehru from the Gandhis: A 50th Anniversary Tribute," *Firstpost*, May 27, 2014. URL: www.firstpost.com/politics/freeing -nehru-from-the-gandhis-a-50th-anniversary-tribute-1544599.html (accessed April 19, 2017).

[9] Glenda Sluga, *Internationalism in the Age of Nationalism* (Philadelphia: University of Pennsylvania Press, 2015), 3. The argument that anticolonial nationalism for the colonized emerged in relation to internationalism was made even earlier, by Brent Hayes Edwards, "The Shadow of Shadows," *positions* 11, no. 1 (Spring 2003): 11–49. See also Erez Manela, *The Wilsonian Moment: Self-Determination and the International Origins of Anticolonial Nationalism* (New York: Oxford University Press, 2007); Cemil Aydin, *The Politics of Anti-Westernism in Asia: Visions of World Order in Pan-Islamic and Pan-Asian Thought* (New York: Columbia University Press, 2007); Michael Goebel, *Interwar Paris and the Seeds of Third World Nationalism* (New York: Cambridge University Press, 2015); Noor Khan *Egyptian-Indian Nationalist Collaboration and the British Empire* (New York: Palgrave Macmillan, 2011); Rebecca E. Karl, *Staging the World: Chinese Nationalism at the Turn of the Twentieth Century* (Durham: Duke University Press, 2002); and Jeffrey James Byrne, *Mecca of Revolution: Algeria, Decolonization, and the Third World Order* (New York: Oxford University Press, 2016).

when international solidarities against imperialism were not only possible but also desirable for those seeking to capture the nation-state from European colonial powers. Nehru's story is a perfect example, as his participation in anti-imperialist networks and meetings were a catalyst for extending his political and intellectual horizons beyond the local and national arenas to places as distant as Jakarta, Canton, Cairo, New York, and Moscow. At the same time, his nationalist politics and ideas were connected to this wider world and informed his understanding of India.

Another point worth noting is that interwar anti-imperialism was global rather than solely European. Until recently, anti-imperialism and anticolonialism have been used interchangeably and rarely interrogated as a historically constructed set of ideas and practices rooted in a particular moment and place.[10] I argue here that anti-imperialism during the interwar years became an idiom in which multiple advocates came together to debate, construct, and circulate across the world. Nehru was a mediator and contributor in this process, and he negotiated the meaning and terms of anti-imperialism with comrades worldwide. Over time, he appropriated the ideas embedded in anti-imperialist discourse and reconfigured them to fit conditions in India. In making these claims, this book furthers the endeavors by recent scholars of global intellectual history, who have enabled us to rethink the circulation of ideas and overturn assumptions that they moved from the West to "the rest."[11]

Interwar anti-imperialism came to shape Nehru's worldview in profound ways. Nehru began to construct a global geography of anti-imperialism, defined as an imagined mapping of an anti-imperialist world with pivotal nodes to the East (China), to the West (Egypt), and to the North (Soviet Russia), and, on the other hand, an imperialist world comprised of European imperialists and American capitalists. Nehru located the key to world progress in the encounters and cooperation between anti-capitalist and anti-imperialist forces worldwide. A reading

---

[10] Noor Khan recently argued that anti-imperialism was a global framework of resistance, while anticolonialism denotes a more localized resistance to a colonial power within a given territorial unit of empire. See her *Egyptian-Indian Nationalist Collaboration*, 2–3.

[11] Samuel Moyn and Andrew Sartori, eds., *Global Intellectual History* (New York: Columbia University Press, 2013); and Cemil Aydin, *The Idea of the Muslim World: A Global Intellectual History* (Cambridge, MA: Harvard University Press, 2017). For debates about Indian nationalism as a derivative of the western epistemology, see Partha Chatterjee, *Nationalist Thought and the Colonial World: A Derivative Discourse?* (Minneapolis: University of Minnesota Press, 1993); and his *The Nation and Its Fragments: Colonial and Postcolonial Histories* (Princeton: Princeton University Press, 1993).

of this history illuminates the interwar years as formative to his later assumptions about India's neighbors, such as China and Egypt, as well as the future super powers: the Soviet Union and the United States. Finally, the anti-imperialist worldview provided for an anti-war agenda, as it demanded that anti-imperialists defend their counterparts worldwide – in the colonies and the Soviet Union – against imperialist aggression and war.

THE INTERWAR WORLD

While this book focuses on Nehru, it is equally a story about the interwar world that he engaged. The flexibility and heterogeneity of interwar politics, particularly in uniting communists and noncommunists or anti-capitalists with anti-imperialists, is best articulated by one of Nehru's closest comrades within the LAI, Roger Baldwin, who was a civil liberties advocate within the USA and internationally. Baldwin once wrote of the LAI and other interwar projects that:

> Peace, democracy, anti-imperialism and civil liberties claimed my interest sufficiently to induce going along with any movement that seemed to me genuinely to promote them ... It seems remarkable, looking back on the period, that no criticism from liberal quarters was directed at us non-Communists who took part [in united-front movements].[12]

Baldwin's reflection tells us two things. First, he demonstrates that many internationalists in the interwar years were less attentive to differences in orthodoxies or party politics; instead, they constructed inclusive and accommodative solidarities for "freedom" that transcended political, social and geographic boundaries. Second, as Baldwin eloquently adds, the differences between disparate members of such movements were easily overlooked in the interwar years, yet were difficult to reconcile in retrospect. Such retrospective or teleological views most often characterize interwar movements through the lens of communist and noncommunist tensions rather than as sites of solidarity and collaboration. That most institutions for anti-imperialism, peace, and civil liberties eventually fragmented along the fault lines of communism and noncommunism in the context of World War II and the Cold War forced Baldwin, in hindsight, to regret his "misplaced faith" in the "incongruity" inherent in

---

[12] Roger N. Baldwin, *Reminiscences of Roger Nash Baldwin*. Oral History taken by Harlan B. Phillips, Oral History Research Office, Columbia University, December 1953–January 1954 (microfilm), 354.

such interwar mobilizations. His only solace was that he shared this "misplaced faith" with "distinguished company all over the world," and specifically comrades such as Nehru.[13]

Nehru and Baldwin were drawn to organizations that transcended the boundaries of political activism and connected their local concerns to a wider world. Their story necessitates a rethinking of the basic categories of historical analysis for the interwar period. As historians, we have been trained to identify our historical figures through the lens of geography or political groups rather than recognizing the intersections between socialism, communism, nationalism, pacifism, and civil liberties worldwide. Such categories were highly unstable during the interwar period. What was so unique about the 1920s and 1930s was the ability to move across and within such categories and to rethink solidarities beyond the rigid frameworks afforded by strict orthodoxies or institutionalization. Nehru joined international movements of the period that were remarkably fluid and attracted a broad spectrum of activists.

The internationalist milieu of the interwar period was unique. Early histories of the interwar years have emphasized the great powers as the primary subjects of analysis, although this is changing as international historians have recently revisited the period.[14] There certainly were earlier antecedents in the prewar years, but the interwar moment witnessed an unprecedented proliferation of internationalist institutions and ideas.[15] The Great War and the Bolshevik Revolution had done much to destabilize and challenge the old world order of the late nineteenth century, and politicians and activists participated in an emerging discourse on the imagined futures of a new world of greater equality, justice, and

---

[13] Ibid.

[14] The classic text on the interwar years remains E. H. Carr, *International Relations between the Two World Wars, 1919–1939* (London: Macmillan, 1947). More recent scholarship on the interwar years has focused on the impact of the League of Nations on the colonial world. See Susan Pedersen, *The Guardians: The League of Nations and the Crisis of Empire* (New York: Oxford University Press, 2015); Erez Manela, *Wilsonian Moment*; and Daniel Laqua, ed., *Internationalism Reconfigured: Transnational Ideas and Movements between the World War* (New York: IB Tauris, 2011).

[15] Akira Iriye argues that the quantity and membership of international organizations surged in the interwar period. See his, *Cultural Internationalism and the World Order* (Baltimore: Johns Hopkins University Press, 1997). The argument for a unique interwar moment is laid out in Ali Raza, et al., *The Internationalist Moment*. For prewar internationalism, see Harald Fisher-Tine, "Indian Nationalism and the 'World Forces': Transnational and Diasporic Dimensions of the Indian freedom movement on the Eve of the First World War," *Journal of Global History* 2 (2007): 325–44.

peace.[16] Mobilization for national sovereignty, working class rights, suffrage, civil liberties, pacifism, disarmament, and anti-racism grew dramatically in the 1920s and 1930s as a consequence of the war's failure to change global and local inequalities. These new platforms hosted debates about the past and the future of the world; about the staying power of imperialism, racism, and capitalism; and about the tensions between nations, empires, and colonies.

Activists and revolutionaries from the colonial world were among the many who found these interwar spaces an opportunity to make claims for sovereignty and statehood to a global audience. The immediate postwar generation was inspired by the "Wilsonian moment" and the avenues afforded by the League of Nations.[17] However, when the League proved more of a tool for imperialist expansion, anticolonial activists sought other platforms, notably ones inspired by communism and trade unionism.[18] In the later 1920s, the Bolshevik Revolution and international communism became a great beacon of hope for many discontented nationalists and leftists from the colonies. The revolution introduced an internationalist model that sought to destroy the capitalist system through world revolution. Famous Indian exiles such as M. N. Roy found their way to communism and Moscow in the 1920s, while a burgeoning community of leftists in India sought inspiration and sometimes direction from Moscow, especially after the founding of the Communist Party of India in 1925.[19]

Nehru's entry into the international politics of anti-imperialism began in this distinctively "Leninist moment." In 1920, Lenin persuaded the Comintern to pursue a united-front alliance with bourgeois nationalist movements in the colonies as a means to encourage anti-imperialist revolution first, and class revolution later. The flexibility afforded by the Comintern's united-front years informed the making of anti-imperialism

---

[16] Goswami, "Colonial Internationalisms and Imaginary Futures."

[17] Manela, *Wilsonian Moment.*

[18] On Indian trade unionism and internationalism, see C. M. Stolte, "Bringing Asia to the World: Indian Trade Unionism and the Long Road towards the Asiatic Labour Congress, 1919–1937," *Journal of Global History* 7, no. 2 (2012): 257–278. On India and international communism, see Sobhanlal Datta Gupta, *Comintern and the Destiny of Communism in India: 1919–1943: Dialectics of Real and a Possible History* (Bakhrahat: Seribaan, 2006). The classic text on this subject is Gene D. Overstreet and Marshall Windmiller, *Communism in India* (Berkeley: University of California Press, 1959).

[19] See, for example, Kris Manjapra, *M. N. Roy: Marxism and Colonial Cosmopolitanism* (Delhi: Routledge India, 2010).

as a "blend" between communist and noncommunist projects. By the time Nehru joined the LAI in 1927, the Comintern was actively recruiting noncommunists from the colonies and looking upon the anti-imperialist movement as progressively moving toward the overthrow of the capitalist and imperialist world.[20]

While it was closely linked to international communism, I argue that interwar anti-imperialism warrants its own history. Some scholars have identified the LAI in particular as a communist-dominated institution.[21] However, this characterization neglects the robust participation and leadership by a wide range of anti-imperialists, especially noncommunists, who worked through and beyond the boundaries of party politics.[22] Instead,

[20] There has been new and interesting work on the global networks created by international communism as well. See Holger Weiss, ed., *International Communism and Transnational Solidarity: Radical Networks, Mass Movements, and Global Politics, 1919–1939* (Leiden: Brill, 2017).

[21] This argument is made by Fredrik Petersson in his published dissertation, *Willi Münzenberg, the League against Imperialism, and the Comintern, 1925–1933* (Lewiston: Queenston Press, 2013); and his "Anti-Imperialism and Nostalgia," in Weiss, ed., *International Communism and Transnational Solidarity*.

[22] Aside from Petersson's work on the Comintern, scholarship on the LAI has been slow to develop and remains rather thin. For brief but informative overviews of the LAI, see *Dictionary of Labour Biography*, vol. VII, ed. by Joyce M. Bellamy and John Saville (London: Macmillan Press, 1984), 40–49; Jean Jones, *The League against Imperialism*, Socialist History Occasional Pamphlet Series (Lancashire: The Socialist History Society and the Lancashire Community Press, 1996); and Robert J. C. Young, *Postcolonialism: An Historical Introduction* (Malden: Blackwell Publishing, 2001), 176–177. Nehru's relationship to the LAI is treated briefly in Gopal, *Nehru*, 52–58; Milton Israel, *Communications and Power: Propaganda and the Press in the Indian Nationalist Struggle, 1920–1947* (Cambridge: Cambridge University Press, 1994), 256–263; and Nirode K. Barooah, *Chatto: The Life and Times of an Indian Anti-Imperialist in Europe* (Oxford: Oxford University Press, 2004), 246–282. For an overview of the inaugural Brussels Congress, see Vijay Prashad, *The Darker Nations: A People's History of the Third World* (New York: New Press: distributed by W. W. Norton, 2007), 16–30. Other scholars have picked up various aspects of the organization. For the Comintern perspective, see Petersson, *Willi Münzenberg*. For the intersectionality of race and anti-imperialism in Britain, see Susan D. Pennybacker, *From Scottsboro to Munich: Race and Political Culture in 1930s Britain* (Princeton: Princeton University Press, 2009). For a short history of the LAI in Paris, see Michael Goebel, *Anti-Imperial Metropolis: Interwar Paris and the Seeds of Third World Nationalism* (New York: Cambridge University Press, 2015). For the African diaspora and the LAI, see Holger Weiss, *Framing a Racial African Atlantic: African American Agency, West African Intellectuals, and the International Trade Union Committee of Negro Workers* (Leiden: Brill, 2014). For a study of European colonial intelligence and the LAI, see Daniel Brückenhaus, *Policing Transnational Protest: Liberal Imperialism and the Surveillance of Anticolonialists in Europe, 1905–1945* (New York: Oxford University Press, 2017), 139–168.

this book supports Michael Goebel's argument that the Comintern and LAI provided a "platform for claims-making for anti-imperialists," and that these connections "unleashed [their] own dynamic" beyond the history of communism.[23] In a similar vein, this book tells a new story, not from the perspective of Moscow, but rather from those such as Nehru, who sought broadly conceived alliances across the communist divide in an attempt to challenge the global hegemonic power of capitalism and imperialism. Their story cannot be explained fully by the history of the Comintern, nor can one adequately understand Nehru's allegiances to it without considering the overlapping and flexible nature of these solidarities – in particular, the ways anti-imperialism brought together communists and noncommunists throughout the 1920s and 1930s, even when Moscow sent directives to split the ranks along party lines.

Much of these collaborative interconnections, so central to the anti-imperialist movement, have been neglected and lost as historiographical fields have developed around nationalism, international communism, socialism, and pacifism as separate categories with distinctive trajectories after World War II. We cannot fully understand the significance of the anti-imperialist institutions and solidarities of the interwar world without taking into account these intersecting histories. This book moves beyond teleological readings of the interwar year from the present, which neglect the overlap of anticolonial nationalism and communism, and instead encourages us to rethink conventional narratives of interwar history.

This book also dovetails and complements important research unearthed by those writing about new and unconventional narratives of black internationalism in the 1920s and 1930s. Susan Pennybacker's study of the antiracist solidarities that intersected in Britain in the 1930s emblemizes this kind of rigorous scholarship. She writes against the historiographical silos that separate the histories of those activists deeply invested in articulating a "vision for an interracial world culture." She offers a richly researched discussion of the ways in which American protests against the Jim Crow South brought together an unlikely alliance of liberals, communists, socialists, and anticolonial nationalists in Britain.[24] Unsurprisingly, three of the five activists in her book also came to be part of the anti-imperialist movement and were some of

[23] Goebel, *Anti-Imperial Metropolis*, 177. His treatment of the LAI is informative although brief and limited to the Brussels Congress and a few points about the French LAI after 1927.
[24] Pennybacker, *From Scottsboro to Munich*, 5.

Nehru's closest associates in the interwar years. Similar narratives are explored by Brent Hayes Edwards in his study of black internationalism across the Francophone and Anglophone world.[25] He finds incongruities, or "paradoxes," within black internationalism that were "translated" across the movement. In many ways, these translations are what Nehru and others in this book would have recognized as "blending" the many ideologies within the anti-imperialist movement.

At the same time, Nehru's story is not about race and internationalism. Certainly, the circles of anti-imperialism and Pan-Africanism overlapped extensively, and as much as those of anticolonial nationalism and communism. However, Nehru's appropriation of anti-imperialism as an idea and a set of practices was never informed by the discourse of race. His commitment to internationalism was based upon the struggle for Indian independence, the anticolonial struggle in Asia and Africa, and the struggle of workers for social equality and justice once all colonies achieved political sovereignty. In his many speeches on the meaning of anti-imperialism and the relationship between India and the world, the language of race was not part of his rhetoric, nor was racial oppression a critical aspect of his vision of global struggle. Rather, nation and class were the primary dimensions of his anti-imperialism.

While much of this book considers the possibilities for solidarity afforded by the interwar moment, it also grapples with the limits and contradictions embedded within anti-imperialism. Nehru failed to reconcile the critical differences between the political projects for an Indian nation-state and the mobilization of the working classes. These tensions were readily overlooked in the interwar years but difficult to reconcile after World War II and the arrival of political independence for India and many other nation-states soon after. Inevitably, the capture of the nation-state for Nehru meant that his role as an elite, bourgeois nationalist would place him at odds with his communist, trade unionist, and even socialist counterparts within the anti-imperialist movement.

For Nehru, anti-imperialism in India meant the "blend" of political independence with socialism. This amalgamation of nationalism with socialism symbiotically linked the anti-imperialist and anti-capitalist

---

[25] Brent Hayes Edwards, *The Practice of Diaspora: Literature, Translation, and the Rise of Black Internationalism* (Cambridge, MA: Harvard University Press, 2003); and for history focused on the late 1930s to the post-World War II period, see Penny Von Eschen, *Race against Empire: Black Americans and Anticolonialism, 1937–1957* (Ithaca: Cornell University Press, 1997).

struggles within India. He resolved the tensions between class and nation by arguing that national independence in India was the fundamental, although only partial, fulfillment of anti-imperialism, while socialism within the subcontinent would usher in a new era of freedom and equality by challenging capitalism. His counterparts within the anti-imperialist movement, particularly many hard-line communists, found Nehru's commitments to national independence and socialism problematic. At the same time, he worked within an Indian National Congress that was diverse and often hostile to the ideas about socialism and anti-imperialism that Nehru advocated. Often, Nehru's anti-imperialist internationalism placed him at odds with his comrades abroad and at home.

Equally formidable for Nehru were the ways in which internationalism – as a vehicle for making-meaning, forging solidarities and creating global spaces of protest – came into conflict with the anticolonial nationalist objective to capture the nation-state. Internationalism transcended not only party politics, but also the very states that anticolonial nationalists sought to claim sovereignty over. Defining more precisely the internationalism of the anti-imperialist project in relation to the imperatives of the state and interstate system is necessary here. Nehru and his comrades identified themselves as internationalists, and they spoke of internationalism as their project. But what did internationalism in the interwar period mean? I argue that internationalisms are projects much like nationalisms. There is no scarcity of literature on nationalism as a project seeking to assimilate citizens into a shared spatial and cultural imaginary within a set of territorial borders.[26] Internationalism, too, aims to construct and deploy a discursive imagined community with a common historical experience, language, and goal, although it is based on an extra-territorial framework that is inclusive of but not limited to the nations and nationalism. In the case of Nehru, nationalism was often framed as a "stage" to an internationalism that would bring freedom, peace, and social justice to the colonies and worldwide. It encouraged the active repression of difference among constituent members and the breaking down of boundaries between states, colonies, and empires. This internationalism was an imagined community

---

[26] Benedict Anderson, *Imagined Communities: Reflections on the Origin and Spread of Nationalism* (London: Verso, 1983). Of course, anticolonial nationalist expressions were diverse and not solely a derivative of the Western model, a critique rightly made by Partha Chatterjee in his *The Nation and Its Fragments*. I argue here for recognizing both nationalism and internationalism as constructed communities contingent to time, place and perspective.

that sought solidarity for the excluded, the stateless, and the "oppressed peoples of the world."[27]

Internationalism must also be understood in contradistinction to interstate relations. The latter, often misleadingly referred to as internationalism, reflects the interaction of *states* across the world. Modern states constituted in the mid-nineteenth century, as Charles Maier contends, operated under a world order defined by the Treaties of Westphalia (1648), in which the idea of sovereignty "emerged with a dual thrust." It was an "inward" sovereignty over a territorial unit and an "outward" recognition by other states of its legitimate statehood.[28] Maier argues that this "outward" sovereignty has been conditioned by interstate "competition, if not open warfare," and was "premised on insecurity."[29] The negotiations and relations between states, then, necessitate a different set of approaches, practices, and ideas. Rather than a homogenizing project of internationalism in which difference is overlooked and accommodated for a broad and heterogeneous community of anti-imperialists, the interstate platforms recognize difference, negotiate state interests, and establish normative relations between nation-states as distinct, geopolitical units with the idea that "competition" and "warfare" were central aspects of such relations.[30] In making this distinction, the League of Nations offers a clear model for interstate relations during the interwar period, one Nehru and most anti-imperialists opposed in the late 1920s and early 1930s because it reinforced the primacy of states over the more flexible solidarities of their movement.[31]

---

[27] Brussels Congress Manifesto, reprinted in "The Brussels Congress against Imperialism and for National Independence" and distributed to League members. Box 8, Folder 2, Roger Nash Baldwin Papers, Seeley G. Mudd Manuscript Library, Princeton University, Princeton, New Jersey (hereafter Baldwin Papers).

[28] Charles S. Maier, *Leviathan 2.0*, published in *A World Connecting, 1870–1945*, edited by Emily S. Rosenberg (Cambridge, MA: Belknap Press of Harvard University Press, 2012), 35. See also the earlier work by Prasenjit Duara on the constitution of nation-states in relation to a world of nation-states in the East Asian context: *The Global and Regional in China's Nation-Formation* (New York: Routledge, 2009).

[29] Ibid., 33. There is some debate over the timing of the rise to prominence of the nation-state. While Maier situates it much earlier, Fredrick Cooper argues that a world of nation-states became normative only in the 1960s after the political decolonization of Africa. See his *Colonialism in Question: Theory, Knowledge, History* (Berkley: University of California Press, 2005).

[30] I am indebted to conversations with several colleagues about the distinction between the interstate and the international: Maia Ramnath, Ali Raza, Franziska Roy, Carolien Stolte, and Benjamin Zachariah. Our discussions became the basis of Raza, et al., *Internationalist Moment*.

[31] This is where I differ with scholars of the League of Nations, such as Akira Iriye, Glenda Sluga, and Susan Pedersen, in that they consider the Geneva-based institution as the

This distinction is critical in rethinking the ways in which anti-imperialist internationalism was incompatible with the interstate system. This tension can be located in the transition from anti-imperialism to antifascism and peace in the 1930s. When Nehru sought to forge internationalist solidarities with antifascists and advocates of peace, primarily through the IPC, he was forced to join hands with those who advocated for the League of Nations as the sole guardian of peace and stability worldwide. In this moment, on the eve of World War II, Nehru's internationalism found expression in a movement dependent on the interstate system and the primacy of nation-states that often openly supported the status quo and imperialism. This incompatibility between anti-imperialist internationalism and the IPC provides interesting clues for thinking about late interwar history and the inconsistencies created by internationalist modes of thinking when situated within interstate structures worldwide.

The difference between the interstate and the international became more pronounced after Indian independence in 1947 and in Nehru's attempts to build Afro-Asian solidarity in the 1950s. There has been a scholarly tendency to celebrate interwar anti-imperialism, and especially the LAI, as the precursor to the Asian-African Conference in Bandung (1955).[32] In his opening remarks at the Bandung Conference, Indonesian President Sukarno evoked the historical legacy of the LAI as the forerunner to the much later Bandung Conference.[33] In studies from this perspective, communist involvement is downplayed and anticolonial solidarities are foregrounded, while the LAI is taken out of the interwar context entirely and given a new teleological reading from the vantage point of 1955 and after.[34] While continuities exist in both the interwar and postcolonial

premier forum of interwar internationalism. But the League of Nations focused on interstate diplomacy and "collective security" between nation-states.

[32] The connection between the LAI and Bandung is made in several works: Prashad, *The Darker Nations*; Christopher J. Lee, ed., *Making a World after Empire: The Bandung Moment and Its Political Afterlives* (Ohio University Press, 2010); Tony Ballantyne and Antoinette Burton, *Empires and the Reach of the Global*; Goebel, *Anti-Imperial Metropolis*.

[33] President Sukarno, "Opening Address" (presented at African and Asian Conference, Bandung, Indonesia, April 18, 1955), *Selected Documents of the Bandung Conference* (New York: Distributed by the Institute of Pacific Relations, 1955).

[34] Fredrik Petersson makes a similar case by arguing that the LAI belongs as much to the global history of interwar international communism as to the nostalgic collective memory of postcolonial decolonization. This book differs in that the history of the LAI must be situated within broader internationalist histories of the interwar years, which were not the exclusive domain of international communism. See Petersson, "Anti-Imperialism and Nostalgia."

movements, I argue here that one cannot adequately understand interwar anti-imperialism, or its importance to Nehru and India, without situating it within the internationalist milieu of the late 1920s.

This book moves away from celebrating Bandung as a triumph of a global anti-imperialist struggle that began in the interwar period. Rather, it asks critically how this earlier history of anti-imperialist solidarity shaped and impacted Nehru's views of India and the third world. His formative experiences in the interwar period certainly informed Nehru's preconceptions about places such as the United States, Soviet Union, Egypt, China, and Indonesia. Yet, anti-imperialism as a way of thinking about commonalities, metaphors, and solidarities beyond political and state borders was highly incompatible with the interstate dynamics of the world after World War II. New heads of states across the global south came to places like Bandung to negotiate difference and establish normative interstate relations rather than forge internationalist solidarities.

Finally, a reframing of Nehru's past has some immediate ramifications for Indian history and contemporary political discourse. The current ruling political party in India – the Bharatiya Janata Party (BJP) and its ancillary organizations – have long considered Nehru "anti-national" for his sympathies with Muslims and his hostility to the Rashtriya Swayamsevak Sangh (RSS) and Sangh Parivar after the assassination of Gandhi. Nehru's history in the interwar period no doubt challenges this criticism, for it takes India as a starting point but borrows eclectically from an internationalist idiom that shaped political ideas and moved people around the world. Nehru both informed it and was shaped by it. This book does not, however, consider internationalism to be "anti-national," but rather points to the rare and unique qualities of Nehru's political imagination – in particular, the idea that the nation was always shaped by the world and the world was always shaped the nation. The recognition that the nation and the world are not mutually exclusive could go a long way in thinking beyond the narrow and antagonistic nationalisms being advocated not only in India today, but also across the world.

This book is organized into two parts. Part I consists of four chapters that recount the story of Nehru's engagement with the LAI. The first chapter focuses on the inaugural meeting of the LAI in Brussels (1927), while the second explores his ongoing service in building the LAI as an institution capable of "blending" the diverse projects within the movement. Chapter 3 considers Nehru's return to India and his efforts to internationalize the nationalist movement. Collectively, these chapters demonstrate the significance of anti-imperialist internationalism to Nehru's conceptualization of India and the interwar world.

The fourth chapter considers the crisis point in Nehru's relationship with the League by examining the Second World Congress of the LAI in Frankfurt (1929), where many communist members attempted to purge noncommunists from the movement. Communists operated under directives from Moscow to abandon united-front alliances. This chapter argues that Nehru and his comrades resisted the pressure from Moscow for months beyond the Frankfurt Congress, and only in 1930, when the INC wavered on the question of independence, did Nehru and the LAI split ranks.

Nehru's formal relationship with the League ended in 1930, although he continued to collaborate with former LAI comrades on anti-imperialist projects inspired by the organization's mission outlined in Brussels. Opening Part II, Chapter 5 traces Nehru's re-engagement with the LAI in London and his introduction to Pan-Africanists who were involved in the movement. Chapter 6 offers a study of Nehru's travels to Egypt and China and his work with peace organizations in the late 1930s. These chapters argue that Nehru's worldview and international networks expanded rather than receded in the 1930s as he came to see anti-imperialism as interconnected with antifascism. At the same time, his commitment to the latter led him to interstate platforms that were highly incompatible with interwar internationalism.

The final chapter reveals the fate of anti-imperialist internationalism in the run-up to and aftermath of World War II. Many of Nehru's comrades were forced into hiding or died in the war, while those who survived were never able to remake the "blend" of anti-imperialism emblematic of the interwar period. The chapter concludes with some reflections on the continuities and discontinuities between interwar and postcolonial internationalisms with a focus on Nehru and the Bandung Conference. Instead of inaugurating the third world project rooted in the ideas of the interwar period, the Bandung Conference must be seen as a closure. Nehru recognized in Bandung that the internationalist solidarities he sought to forge in the interwar years were no longer tenable in the postcolonial and Cold War world.

PART I

MOBILIZING AGAINST EMPIRE, 1927–1930

I

A "Real" League of Nations

The Brussels Congress, 1927

In May 1927, a featured article in the *Modern Review*, a Calcutta-based English-language publication, celebrated the Brussels Congress against Colonial Oppression and Imperialism and for National Independence. It characterized the event as "unique," for it was the "first time in history that the representatives of the working class and of subject peoples assembled under the same roof to express the message of the enslaved: 'Brothers! Your suffering is my suffering. Let us unite, for we have nothing more to lose but our chains and a world to gain.'"[1] In the case of the representatives from the colonies, including delegates such as Jawaharlal Nehru of the Indian National Congress (INC), all shared a common experience of imperialist oppression across the world: "All had had their 1857's and their Amritsars – many times over. All had their Ordinance Laws and Penal Codes, their suppression of speech, press and assembly." The article continued:

In the stories told in a dozen different languages, in the reports or facts and conditions, we saw that imperialism is the most deadly enemy of human life. Is there any wonder, then, that at palace Egmont [venue of the Congress], peoples with different languages and culture, different shades of opinion, found themselves amongst men and women who instinctively understood and that they could work in such harmony?[2]

Such prevailing perceptions of the Brussels Congress as an unprecedented meeting to construct "harmony" among "peoples with different languages and culture" and "different shades of opinion" emerged from the proceedings and inspired many people across colonial India. This was a powerful and inclusive moment of anti-imperialist

[1] Bakar Ali Mirza, "The Congress against Imperialism," *Modern Review* (May 1927), File DBN/25/3, Papers of Reginald Francis Orlando Bridgeman (1884–1968), Hull University Archives, United Kingdom (hereafter cited as Bridgeman Papers).
[2] Ibid.

FIGURE 1.1 The plenary session of the Brussels Congress, 1927. Nehru is seated in the second row, on the left-hand side nearest the center aisle. *Das Flammenzeichen vom Palais Egmont: offizielles Protokoll des Kongresses gegen koloniale Unterdrückung und Imperialismus, Brüssel, 10–15 Februar 1927.* Berlin: Neuer Deutscher Verlag, 1927

activism that connected experiences of colonialism in India, in this case the 1857 uprising and Jallianwala Bagh massacre in Amritsar, to similar stories "told in a dozen different languages" about British aggression in China, Dutch imperialism in Indonesia, and American interventionism in Mexico. Solidarity was not only intercolonial, as the article reported; the Brussels Congress, as it came to be known, worked across ideological and political party boundaries, too. Leaders of working-class movements – communists, socialists, and trade unionists – and the "subject peoples" in the colonies were "brothers" in the struggle against imperialism. The effusiveness for solidarity in Brussels inspired the delegates to establish the LAI, an institution whose goal was to coordinate a sustained and widespread campaign against imperialist powers and capitalist classes of the interwar world. As the *Modern Review* article concluded, the LAI "could be called a League of Nations in a truer sense than the one that deliberates on behalf of the Great Powers at Geneva."[3]

The significance of the Brussels Congress moment to the colonial world, and especially India, has been poorly understood and rarely studied.[4]

---

[3] Ibid.

[4] The Brussels Congress and LAI archival record is scarce and scattered. German police and Nazi raids of the LAI's Berlin-based headquarters (1931–1933) destroyed much of the institutional archive. Existing sources have been collected at the International Institution of Social History or preserved in the personal papers of individual members, the colonial intelligence records, or the Communist International files. The LAI published the most extensive summary of the Brussels Congress in German: *Das Flammenzeichen vom Palais*

The lacuna is in part due to the lack of sources on the Brussels Congress and LAI before the recent opening and digitization of the Communist International (Comintern) papers.[5] Communist agents collected copious records of the event and the development of the LAI. The most comprehensive study of the Brussels Congress and LAI based on these Comintern sources is by Fredrik Petersson, whose work is an excellent starting point for considering the perspective of communists involved.[6] However, the emphasis on communist sources may lead one to assume that noncommunists played almost no role in the movement. This was not the case. As this chapter demonstrates, Nehru and other noncommunists were significant to the shape of the proceedings and the constitution of the anti-imperialist movement in the late 1920s. In addition, the Comintern demonstrated only a minor interest and investment in the Brussels Congress, enabling it to develop with a degree of autonomy from Moscow, while noncommunists were welcomed and later given important roles in the proceedings.

The Brussels Congress captivated Nehru's political imagination and accentuated the interplay of nationalism and internationalism in his conceptualization of India and the wider world. He described the event as one of "first class importance" and recommended the INC associate with the LAI as an "organization which might play a big role in the future."[7] After Brussels, Nehru's letters and publications to Indian and international audiences underscored the need to think internationally and avoid the "dangers of narrow-minded nationalism."[8] Such rhetoric has led many scholars to characterize Nehru as an "internationalist," although few have unpacked the precise meanings of his internationalism or situated it within his Brussels Congress and LAI experiences.[9]

Egmont. Offizielles Protokoll des Kongresses gegen koloniale Unterdrückung und Imperialismus Brüssel, 10.–15. Februar 1927: Hrsg. von der Liga gegen Imperialismus und für nationale Unabhängigkeit (Berlin: Neuer Deutscher Verlag, 1927). For a discussion of the historiography on the LAI, see footnote 22 in the Introduction.

5   The Comintern files, opened in 1991, are located at the Russian State Archives for Social and Political History (RGASPI). From 1996 to 2004, a multinational project began with the aim of translating finding aids from Russian and digitizing a substantial part of the archive. In 2004, the digitized files were released to several major repositories in the United States and Europe. The files cited here are from the Library of Congress, European Reading Room (hereafter cited as RGASPI).

6   Petersson, Willi Münzenberg.

7   Nehru, "Report on Brussels Congress," February 19, 1927, SWJN, vol. 2, 287.

8   Nehru, "On the Indian Situation," published originally in Aaj on March 2, 1927, reprinted in SWJN, vol. 2, 297.

9   Most specialists of Nehru focus on his local and all-India activities. See, for example, Judith Brown, Nehru: A Political Life (New Haven: Yale University Press, 2003). While

There were many internationalist projects during the interwar years, and Nehru's internationalism reflected a set of central principles that he first encountered in Brussels. Foremost, the Brussels Congress offered a clarion call for solidarity between proletarian and anticolonial struggles. It accepted the premise first articulated by V. I. Lenin (1870–1924): that imperialism was the highest stage of capitalism and that the struggle against imperialism and capitalism were two sides of the same coin. Since 1920, the international communist approach to the colonial question was based on Lenin's directives to establish contact with bourgeois nationalist movements in the colonies as a means to encourage anticolonial revolution first and class revolution later. The united-front approach afforded flexibility and appealed to a diverse constellation of socialists, communists, trade unionists, civil liberties reformers, pacifists, Pan-Africanists, and anticolonial nationalists seeking to construct a common platform for a global struggle against imperialist powers and capitalist classes.

The Brussels Congress also challenged the historical and geographical conceptions of the late nineteenth- and early twentieth-century world. It rejected the "civilizing mission" evoked by European colonial regimes to legitimate their sovereignty over much of Asia and Africa. This widely accepted discourse represented Europe as historically more developed and civilized, while at the same time justified colonial expansion as a means to "civilize" their colonial subjects. The Brussels Congress overturned such Eurocentric notions about historical development and progress by arguing that the working classes and the colonized across the world were the only agents who could usher in a new era of equality, progress, and civilization. Moreover, the blueprint for progress was not found in Europe, but in the Soviet Union. It was the "great experiment" underway in the Soviet Union that inspired the hopes and dreams of many delegates at Brussels, and the congress discourse represented the Soviets as anti-imperialist comrades to the oppressed peoples of the colonial world. The agenda for Brussels and the LAI was therefore the creation of anti-imperialist solidarity between the Soviet Union, nationalists in the colonies, and international communists and socialists worldwide. Taken together, these guiding principles in Brussels, which challenged many of

---

Sarvepalli Gopal's *Jawaharlal Nehru* and Benjamin Zachariah's *Nehru* (London: Routledge Press, 2004) attempt to situate Nehru in the international context of the colonial and postcolonial periods, the broad scope of biography has not allowed for a more detailed examination of the Nehru and LAI story beyond the Brussels Congress meeting.

the political and historical foundations of the capitalist and imperialist world, bolstered a new vision for internationalism based on anti-imperialism.

Nehru's encounter with anti-imperialist internationalism in Brussels served as a catalyst in a number of ways. It convinced Nehru to accept the basic premise that progress in India and worldwide depended on the solidarity of working class and anticolonial movements. This recognition led Nehru to become a strong advocate for socialism in the late 1920s and after. This chapter demonstrates that his commitments to socialism began in Brussels, a point that contends with assumptions that Nehru's socialist ideas stemmed from his years in England as a student in the early twentieth century. Rather, the archival record reveals that Nehru's earliest engagement with questions about class, as well the connection between socialism and nationalism, emerged from his experiences in Brussels and the later LAI.

The Brussels Congress also expanded Nehru's vision for anticolonial resistance beyond the confines of India or even the British Empire, as he came to see nationalism and anti-imperialist internationalism as mutually interdependent. As a consequence, Nehru developed an anti-imperialist worldview – a mental mapping of a Manichean world divided along the fault lines of capitalism-imperialism on one hand, and anti-capitalism and anti-imperialism on the other. Of course, the British Empire eclipsed all capitalist-imperialist forces in Nehru's India-centered perspective, but other European imperialists and even American capitalists came to be the antagonists of his worldview. Meanwhile, anticolonial nationalists, socialists, communists, and sympathetic leftists formed his geographical imaginary of an anti-imperialist world. In particular, Nehru envisioned solidarity with China and the Soviet Union as fundamental to anti-imperialism in India. Ultimately, the Brussels Congress went a long way in forming Nehru's earliest views of other colonies, Europe, and the future superpowers of the Cold War.

A final and interrelated point this chapter makes is that, for Nehru, anti-imperialist internationalism came to mean the connections and coop-eration among the myriad individuals resisting the symbiotic forces of capitalism and imperialism. His personal encounters and meetings with counterparts in other colonies and countries were critical here, and Nehru began to identify comrades in Brussels who ultimately became significant to his networks against empire throughout the interwar years and beyond. As much as the Brussels Congress was a discursive space for resistance to Eurocentric worldviews, this chapter also underscores its significance as a contact zone and site of encounter. In other words, the Brussels Congress moment became more than a discursive shift for Nehru in that it also offered a meeting ground for like-minded comrades to develop lifelong partnerships against imperialism that were not simply imagined.

NEHRU'S JOURNEY TO BRUSSELS, 1926–1927

In his autobiography, Nehru remembered his European travels in the late 1920s as a time of great transformation. He remarked: "I was going back to Europe after more than thirteen years – years of war, revolution, and tremendous change. The old world I knew had expired in the blood and horror of the War and a new world awaited me."[10] His observation captured a widely held sentiment during the immediate postwar decade about the destructive nature of the Great War and the "new world" emerging in its wake. The global scope of the war and its weapons – fruits of industrial technology harnessed for military purposes – wreaked unprecedented devastation and death across the world. The war also toppled powerful and historic empires, while serving as the catalyst for the overthrow of the Russian Tsar and the world's first communist revolution. In the years that followed the Great War and the peace settlement in Paris, a broad constellation of politicians, activists, revolutionaries, and reformers flocked to European centers in the hopes of shaping the world anew. Nehru's engagement with international politics began in this moment of uncertainty about the "new" world that was emerging in the 1920s.

The "old world" Nehru referenced was antebellum Europe, where he lived in the heart of the British Empire for his education and legal training from 1905 to 1912. Born into a Brahman family in 1889, Nehru enjoyed a privileged upbringing and lifestyle, like many of the emergent and upwardly mobile middle class in British India. The Nehrus were among this small, urban-based, and Western-educated class taking up jobs within colonial society as lawyers, journalists, and physicians. Nehru's father, Motilal, became a wealthy and successful lawyer in Allahabad, and he was a prominent politician and moderate representative of the INC. Motilal planned for his son to receive the best education accessible for British Indians. In the fall of 1905, he sent his son to Harrow, a premier boarding school in Northwest London. Nehru passed his coursework without remarkable distinction, and he began studies at Trinity College,

---

[10] Jawaharlal Nehru, *An Autobiography with Musings on Recent Events in India* (London: John Lane, 1936. Reprint, New Delhi: Penguin Books India, 2004), 156.

Cambridge in 1907. His small circle of friends consisted mostly of other Indian students, and especially two of his cousins, who were also students in Britain. It was his father's great hope that Jawaharlal would join the Indian Civil Service (ICS), an elite and prestigious cadre of colonial administrators. Nehru's less than stellar performance in school, however, meant that he failed to qualify for the ICS entry exam. Young Nehru ultimately finished his legal training and passed the bar examinations in London in 1912 before returning to India that same year.

There was little evidence that Nehru had any serious engagement with anticolonial politics during this period.[11] This was not for lack of opportunity. In the years when Nehru was in Britain, Indian students had developed robust groups dedicated to debating questions about constitutional reforms and sovereignty for India. Remarkably, Nehru left no evidence of his impressions on either the radical or moderate leaning Indians in Britain. What little we know about young Nehru's political views were confined to his correspondence with his father, who had taken a more active role in the INC during this period. Nehru often criticized his father's moderation within the Indian nationalist movement, although he conceded that his father knew far more about these matters and backed away from conflict.[12] Instead, the predominant themes in Nehru's letters home were his struggles to learn scripture, Latin, and science, as well as his disinterest in marriage – an issue taken up often in his father's correspondence.

Nehru also had many opportunities to engage with socialism and socialists in this period; however, he admittedly had little interest in the prewar left, and socialists in particular.[13] In his letters home, Nehru made only one fleeting reference to socialism. In October 1907, he wrote to his father about his attendance of a lecture by George Bernard Shaw. Nehru admitted that socialism was not of interest to him; instead, he was "more interested in the man [Shaw] than the subject of the lecture."[14] The lecture prompted no further reflections on the application of socialism to Britain or India. This is striking given the significance of socialism to his later conceptualization of India and the world after his introduction to the anti-imperialist movement in 1927.

---

[11] Gopal, *Nehru*, 10.
[12] Nehru's correspondence with his father is published in the first volume of *SWJN*. For this reference, see Jawaharlal Nehru to Motilal Nehru, January 30, 1908, *SWJN*, vol. 1, 44.
[13] Nehru, *Autobiography*, 172.
[14] Jawaharlal Nehru to Motilal Nehru, October 24, 1907, *SWJN*, vol. 1, 35.

Instead, Nehru's earliest political awakening began in India rather than Britain. The war had a tremendous impact on the Indian political landscape.[15] In wartime, the British had deployed over a million Indian soldiers, a contribution that reaffirmed India's importance to the empire. This raised Indian expectations for greater political autonomy after the war. In addition, Indian soldiers returned home to tell horror stories about the violence of the "civilized" powers of Europe, which shook the foundations of the "civilizing mission" espoused in the nineteenth century. The Jallianwalla Bagh massacre in 1919, in which the British army, under the direction of General Reginald Dyer, opened fire on an unarmed crowd of Indian men, women, and children, further tarnished the image of benevolent colonial rule and ushered in a new era of discontent across the subcontinent. In the aftermath of war and the Jallianwalla Bagh massacre, the advent of Mohandas Gandhi's leadership at the helm of the INC launched an unprecedented mass protest against the British in India from 1920 to 1922.

Nehru's politicization took place at this moment of growing nationalist agitation. He met Gandhi in 1916, and the two began to forge a lifelong (although often contentious) partnership against the British raj. In the early 1920s, Gandhi became a father-figure and political mentor to Nehru, and biographers rightly characterize Nehru, during this period, as a loyal and obedient "disciple" of Gandhi.[16] Nehru's more radical anticolonial critiques emerged when he first served on the INC's investigating commission for the Jallianwalla Bagh massacre and later participated in Gandhi's Non-Cooperation movement. Nehru's charismatic appeal and ability to draw large crowds of supporters had earned him a reputation within the INC during this formative period of the 1920s. In all of these events, however, Nehru conceptualized colonial oppression and resistance in a local and national framework, although his internationalist experiences in Europe from 1926 to 1927 were about to change this.

The Great War also transformed the international landscape of the 1920s in profound ways. The Paris Peace Settlement (1919) set the precedent for the international meetings and conferences that were so central to the international sphere of debate in the 1920s. Described by Erez Manela as the "Wilsonian Moment," the immediate aftermath of the Great War and

---

[15] For a thorough analysis of this period in India, see the introduction to Sinha, *Specters of Mother India*.
[16] Gopal, *Nehru*, 30–37.

the peace settlement was a time of optimism for anticolonial activists in India and elsewhere who were inspired by the American president's call for self-determination and a liberal international order.[17] However, as the peace talks progressed, it became increasingly clear to anticolonial nationalists worldwide that the leaders in Paris, including Wilson, had not intended for the postwar peace and rhetoric of self-determination to extend to the colonies in Asia and Africa. The British government barred the INC-elected delegate, Bal Gangadhar Tilak (1856–1920), from attaining a visa to attend the meetings. Instead, the colonial government handpicked two loyalist delegates to represent India.

The League of Nations further disillusioned once hopeful anticolonial nationalists by protecting European imperial interests rather than national self-determination. The League established the mandate system and commission to determine the fitness for self-rule of former colonial territories of the dismantled Ottoman and Austro-Hungarian empires. In practice, it worked as a tool for imperial expansion rather than liberation. Former Ottoman territories were cannibalized and left to the imperial designs of France and Britain. The status of India within the League of Nations was complicated as well. The original League of Nations Charter granted India full membership, equal in status with other sovereign nations and British self-governing dominions. As with the Paris delegation, the Indian representatives in the League of Nations, although members with the same privileges as representatives of independent nations, were chosen by the colonial government and often supported the official stance of the British raj, not the interests of Indian nationalists.[18]

Nehru's disappointment in the Geneva circles was evident early on, in his writings from Europe in 1927. He resided in Geneva throughout much of his European stay while attending to his sick wife, Kamala, who was receiving treatment for chronic tuberculosis. As Kamala's prognosis improved, Nehru frequently attended League of Nations meetings and experienced firsthand the exclusion of colonies such as India from Geneva's international community. This exclusion troubled Nehru so much that he wrote an article in January 1927 for the *Review of*

---

[17] Manela, *The Wilsonian Moment*.

[18] Older works debate the international status of India in the League of Nations, arguing that their inclusion was a ploy by Britain to gain more power. See D. N. Verma, *India and the League of Nations* (Patna: Bharati Bhawan, 1968); and Vangala Shiva Ram and Brij Mohan Sharma, *India and the League of Nations* (Lucknow: Upper India Publishing House, 1932).

Nations defending India's claim to nationhood as no different from European rights to national sovereignty.[19] In it, Nehru rhetorically asked why India desired freedom. First, he argued that India was a member of the League of Nations, but the British government controlled its representation. Second, India was treated like a "political pariah" within the empire, and specifically at the Imperial Conferences in the metropole, such as the Imperial War Conference (1917–1918).[20] Third, Indians were treated poorly across the empire in places such as Kenya and South Africa. But most importantly, Indians had been stripped of their rights and sovereignty at home, while British policies impoverished the subcontinent and imprisoned or exiled the brightest members of its society. The striking feature of this piece, written on the eve of the Brussels Congress, was Nehru's overwhelming sense of India's exclusion from the most significant international conferences and institutions of the day.

In search of alternative platforms for India in the "new" world of postwar Europe, Nehru ventured beyond his Swiss headquarters and met activists in Germany, France, Belgium, the Netherlands, and Britain. Since the early twentieth century before the Great War, networks of Indians headquartered in Berlin, Paris, Geneva, Moscow, New York, San Francisco, and Tokyo had produced and disseminated anti-imperialist propaganda, recruited sympathizers from the international community, and even concocted conspiratorial plots to arm revolutionaries in India.[21] The growth of such activities outside the South Asian subcontinent had pushed the British government to develop a new department for colonial intelligence, the Indian Political Intelligence (IPI) Bureau, to track the movement of Indian revolutionaries, terrorists, and nationalists abroad.[22] The files, recently opened for scholarly inquiry, are voluminous and include surveillance of exiles of the empire and well-known travelers such as Nehru and Gandhi, among others.

---

[19] Nehru, "The Psychology of Indian Nationalism," reprinted in *SWJN*, vol. 2, 259–70.

[20] Ibid., 268. The Imperial War Conference was an empire-wide meeting in London to discuss the joint war effort. Conveners invited India, although Indian delegates experienced exclusion from the decision-making process.

[21] Ramnath, *Haj to Utopia*, and Fischer-Tiné, "Indian Nationalism and the 'World Forces,'" 325–44.

[22] Indian Political Intelligence Files, 1912–1950 Oriental and India Office Collections, British Library, Microfilm edition (Leiden: IDC Publishers, 2000). The IPI files are comprised of 624 microfiches: 767 files on 57,811 pages tracking the movement of South Asians outside the Indian subcontinent. The files were released to scholars in 1996.

For South Asians, Berlin eclipsed other European cities as a haven for politically active expatriates and exiles.[23] An American observer visiting Berlin in 1927 characterized the city as the European "centre for political activity of Oriental peoples, chiefly against English Imperialism."[24] During World War I, in fact, the German Foreign Office welcomed anti-British and anti-French activists and employed Indian expatriates in schemes to incite revolts among Indian soldiers in the Middle East and to ship weapons to India to disrupt or at least distract the British wartime effort. The alliance worked well in wartime; however, Indian expatriates found themselves in a peculiar place after the war. The Weimar state saw these communities less as anti-British allies and more as undesirable residents without clearly defined citizenship within Germany or the British Empire. Still, before the rise to power of Hitler and the Nazi regime in the 1930s, Indian expatriates in Berlin continued to operate with some degree of autonomy.

Berlin was a hotbed of political activity for socialists and communists as well. Postwar ferment and unrest characterized Germany more than other countries in Europe. The victors at the Paris Peace Settlement assigned Germany sole blame for the Great War and demanded immense reparations. At the same time, the German monarchy abdicated at the end of the war and in its place emerged the Weimar Republic (1918–1933), a state run by an elected parliament (*Reichstag*). Inflation, overwhelming wartime debts, and a weak state had sown discontent among Germans and paved the way for socialists and communists to garner a strong support base in the 1920s. Although the German Communist Party and the German Social Democrats launched caustic attacks against one another, both were equally critical of the diminished place of Germany in the world, as well as the weakness of the Weimar state and economy. The rising power of the German Communist Party, until the emergence of Hitler and the Nazi Party in 1933, convinced Moscow that the Weimar state would be the next government toppled by communist revolution. Berlin served as an especially important meeting space for South Asian

---

[23] There are some recent works on Indians in Germany in this period. See Joanne Miyang Cho, Eric Kurlander, and Douglas T. McGetchin, eds., *Transcultural Encounters between Germany and India: Kindred Spirits in the Nineteenth and Twentieth Centuries* (London: Routledge, 2013); and Kris Manjapra, *Age of Entanglement: German and Indian Intellectuals across Empire* (Cambridge: Harvard University Press, 2014).

[24] Roger Nash Baldwin, report written for the International Committee for Political Prisoners dated February 13, 1927, Box 11, Folder 9, Baldwin Papers.

expatriates to encounter communists, socialists, and leftists. There they developed a common framework and shared platform for anticolonialism and anti-capitalism. Moscow welcomed anticolonial nationalists from the colonies and encouraged them to join international communism and the common struggle against capitalism and imperialism. For much of the united-front years (1920–1928), Berlin provided an ideal contact zone for such collaborations.

One of Berlin's most politically active Indian exiles, Virendranath Chattopadhyaya, introduced Nehru to these radical circles of interwar Germany.[25] Of the Indian expatriates Nehru encountered throughout his nearly two-year European sojourn, he most enjoyed the company of Chattopadhyaya and admired his work and vision.[26] Slightly senior to Nehru, Chatto, as his colleagues called him, came from a wealthy Bengali family living in Hyderabad that included his sister Sarojini Naidu, an influential Gandhian nationalist and poetess. Chatto's existence in Europe is emblematic of the transnational existence of many Indian exiles and expatriates of the interwar years. He first traveled to London in 1902 to take the ICS exam, but after failing it twice he began studying law and taking a more active role in Indian expatriate political circles in Britain. When Chatto joined the infamous India House, a London-based militant organization of Indian expatriates and students, his life moved in a different direction, away from service within the empire and toward a more revolutionary critique of the British in India. In 1910, members of the India House were implicated in the assassination of a British official, and colonial authorities issued warrants for the arrest of most members. This forced Chatto into exile, settling first in Paris, from 1910 to 1914, then permanently in Berlin, with a brief interlude in Stockholm from 1917 to 1921. In Berlin, Chatto emerged as a chief agent of the German Foreign Office during the Great War by attempting to incite rebellion and mutiny among Indian soldiers stationed in Baghdad, Kabul, and the Suez Canal. Chatto even attempted, albeit unsuccessfully, to transport arms to revolutionaries in India. His efforts established him as one of the most influential Indians in Berlin, and British intelligence carefully documented his every move.

The years immediately following the Great War were difficult ones for Chatto. Weimar Germany was not particularly sympathetic to the

---

[25] Archival sources on Chatto's life are scattered across many archives, and only one biography of him exists: Nirode K. Barooah, *Chatto: The Life and Times of an Indian Anti-Imperialist in Europe* (Oxford: Oxford University Press, 2004).

[26] Nehru, *Autobiography*, 162.

groundswell of exiles and revolutionaries from the British and French empires. Chatto complained about the heavy surveillance of British intelligence agents and even accused some of trying to poison him. Eventually, he sought support and financial assistance from the Soviet Union. He arranged for a delegation of Berlin Indians to travel to Moscow in May 1921 and make a case for Soviet support of the Indian nationalist cause. Spending four months in Moscow, Chatto encountered high-ranking Soviets, and spoke before the Third Congress of the Comintern in July. But rivalry between Chatto and M. N. Roy, the Comintern's chosen representative for Indian affairs since 1920, divided the Indian anticolonial nationalists and revolutionaries in Moscow and Berlin. Chatto sought to work with the nationalist movement in India, while Roy argued that the Comintern ought to concentrate on building and strengthening an Indian Communist Party. Despite the Comintern's united-front policy, Roy persuaded the Comintern of his credentials to lead Soviet policies toward India, and Chatto returned to Berlin in late 1921 without Moscow's blessing or money. M. N. Roy also left Moscow for Berlin, in 1928, to propagate his ideas about communism and India.

By the time Nehru met Chatto in Berlin in 1926, the latter had been working with German communists and especially Willi Münzenberg, a propagandist who ran a Berlin-based relief organization with communist ties, the Workers International Relief (WIR).[27] Like many in Berlin and throughout Europe, Münzenberg's interest in the colonial question was rooted in the events taking place in China during the 1920s. In May 1925, British authorities killed thirteen protesters in Shanghai. The response in China and internationally was immediate. A surge in student unrest and strikes in China underscored the discontent across much of the region. The shooting also provided impetus for a series of "Hands Off China" campaigns in Berlin, London, and elsewhere.[28] The success of Berlin's China campaign in bringing together German communists and anti-imperialist groups had prompted Münzenberg

---

[27] The classic text on Münzenberg is a biography written by his partner, Babette Gross. For the English version, see her, *Willi Münzenberg: A Political Biography* (East Lansing: Michigan State University Press, 1974). He is studied extensively in Pennybacker, *Scottsboro to Munich*, and Petersson, *Willi Münzenberg*. See also Sean McMeekin, *The Red Millionaire: A Political Biography of Willi Münzenberg, Moscow's Secret Propaganda Tsar in the West* (New Haven: Yale University Press, 2005); and Stephen Koch, *Double Lives: Stalin, Willi Münzenberg, and the Seduction of the Intellectuals* (New York: Enigma Books, 2004).

[28] For a history of the China campaigns in Britain, see Tom Buchanan, *East Wind: China and British Left, 1925–1976* (New York: Oxford University Press, 2012).

to develop the League against Colonial Oppression (LACO) in February 1926. It brought together a vibrant community of expatriates from the colonial world, communists, and intellectuals in Berlin. The inaugural meeting of LACO was the first time Chatto met Münzenberg and other Indians, including A. C. N. Nambiar and Suraj Kishun, who represented Indian anticolonialism. Significant numbers of Syrian expatriates were in attendance, while a large number of members of the Chinese Kuomintang Party (KMT) in Berlin came to be active in LACO. Overall, the meeting encouraged greater contact between European communists, socialists, and activists involved in the anticolonial movement. In addition, a consensus emerged on the necessity for a more representative international congress to discuss a worldwide campaign against colonialism. This final priority paved the way for the Brussels Congress.

The relationship between the Comintern and Münzenberg's projects (WIR, LACO, and the Brussels Congress) requires further explanation. Willi Münzenberg intended to use all three as vehicles for the expansion of communism into the colonial world, and he worked closely with the Comintern and the German Communist Party in his activities. In principle, the Comintern supported Münzenberg's plans for the Brussels Congress and created a special commission in Moscow to oversee the project in March 1926.[29] Nevertheless, the Comintern's special commission did little to support Münzenberg, and from March to July 1926 failed to send a single directive as plans progressed. When directions from Moscow did arrive in July, the Comintern recommended the Brussels Congress be postponed. Only with the insistence of Münzenberg did the meeting convene in early 1927. Comintern funds were slow to arrive as well, while much of the initial costs were procured by Münzenberg's other organization, WIR, and his contacts from Mexico and China.[30] In this context, the Brussels Congress developed somewhat organically in Berlin and at a distance from Moscow.

---

[29] Documents on this commission are located in the Comintern papers. References are organized in the following manner: Fond/Opis/Delo/List, and the League against Imperialism papers are found in Fond 542. For the documents on the early commission, see the lists in File 3 (Delo).

[30] The money trail is difficult to trace. Petersson suggests that Münzenberg's WIR fronted the money and a Comintern agent reimbursed him in Brussels. On the other hand, Nehru reported that the Chinese KMT delegation and the Mexican delegation paid for the event. See Nehru, "Report on Brussels Congress," 278–97 and Petersson, *Willi Münzenberg.*

Nehru's arrival in Berlin coincided with final preparations for the Brussels Congress. There is little doubt that the architects of the Brussels Congress saw INC participation as a coveted prize. Comintern correspondence with organizers in Berlin reveals a keen interest in Nehru's attendance, so much so that dates would be rearranged to accommodate his travel plans.[31] Nehru also shared with his Berlin colleagues an enthusiasm for the possibility of an international platform more inclusive of Indian participation and with an emphasis on the colonial question. Nehru first wrote about the Brussels Congress to his father in November 1926, and he asked him to persuade the All-Indian Congress Committee (AICC), the administrative unit of the INC, to appoint a large and representative delegation to the meeting. In January, the AICC Secretary sent a mandate to Nehru to be the sole spokesman of the INC in Brussels. The document offered no directives from the INC, although it included a draft for fifty pounds sterling for Nehru's travel expenses.[32] With little more direction outside the one-line appointment letter, Nehru boarded a train and embarked on a journey to Brussels in February 1927 that would change profoundly his political and intellectual understanding of India and the world.

THE BRUSSELS CONGRESS: THE MAKING OF A "REAL" LEAGUE OF NATIONS

The Brussels Congress harnessed the frustrations of many like Nehru who arrived in European cities such as Geneva only to be disillusioned by the lack of engagement with the colonial question and the exclusion of Asians and Africans from the "Wilsonian" promises of the early interwar years. Organizers channeled this collective disillusionment across the colonies into an enthusiasm for the Brussels Congress and the newly created League against Imperialism – a name carefully chosen to mock the League of Nations. Willi Münzenberg made this connection clear in his remarks during the proceedings: "The presence of delegations of the greatest organizations of the movement for colonial emancipation and the organizations of the working class of the imperialist countries, at this congress, demonstrates that the first steps toward the formation of a real League of Nations have been made, not in Geneva, but here in

---

[31] For evidence of Nehru's importance to the Comintern's interest in the Brussels Congress, see 542/1/7/27, RGASPI.

[32] Indian National Congress Secretary to Nehru, January 6, 1927, File G21-1926, AICC.

FIGURE 1.2 Delegates at the Brussels Congress (1927). Willi Münzenberg is first on the left and Nehru is next to him. Contrary to descriptions in other publications, the woman next to Nehru is not his daughter, Indira, who would have been ten years old. Instead, the two comrades in the middle were part of a delegation of Indians based in London including Tarini Sinha (center). Edo Fimmen is on the far right. *Das Flammenzeichen vom Palais Egmont: offizielles Protokoll des Kongresses gegen koloniale Unterdrückung und Imperialismus, Brüssel, 10–15 Februar 1927.* Berlin: Neuer Deutscher Verlag, 1927

Brussels."[33] Given Nehru's own search for a fitting international platform to raise the colonial question for India, Münzenberg's sentiments were welcomed wholeheartedly, and he later wrote to the INC that there was "a germ of truth" in the effusive optimism for the LAI expressed by his German colleague.[34]

The success of the Brussels Congress was evident from the beginning. It was well attended by more than 170 delegates, while 37 colonial territories were represented.[35] Messages of support arrived from Albert Einstein of

[33] Report, "The Brussels Congress against Imperialism and for National Independence," published by the League against Imperialism Secretariat, Berlin (1929), Box 8, Folder 2, Baldwin Papers. Münzenberg delivered his speech in German, and although the translation of "league" may have been altered in the English reprint, the deliberate comparison of Geneva's League of Nations to the representative nature of the newly created League against Imperialism was clear in his and other speeches in Brussels.

[34] Nehru, "Report on Brussels Congress," 287.

[35] Sources vary on the exact numbers. Approximately 170 delegates attended, representing 134 organizations from 37 countries. A published list of delegates can be found in File 2, League against Imperialism Archives (1927–1931), International Institute of Social History (IISH), Amsterdam, Netherlands (hereafter IISH).

Germany, Ernst Toller of Poland, Romain Rolland of France, Upton Sinclair of the United States, Maxim Gorki of Russia, and Victor Margueritte of French Algeria. Other messages came from political figures including Mohandas K. Gandhi of India, Clara Zetkin of Germany, and Madame Sun Yat-Sen of China. Over the five days, a spirit of solidarity emerged from the Congress. The final session culminated with the unanimous decision to create an institution, the League against Imperialism, to continue the coordination of the anti-imperialist movement.

In keeping with the spirit of solidarity between nationalists, socialists, and communists, the first session provided an equal balance of each to demonstrate the representative nature of the congress. Three were well-known European labor leaders, two of whom were from the British labour movement: S. O. Davies of the British Miners Association warmed up the eager crowd, while Fenner Brockway, a member of the British Independent Labour Party and editor of its flagship journal, *Labour Leader*, offered the concluding remarks of the first session. The other was a Belgian socialist, Albert Marteux. Two professed communists also spoke during this session. French writer and communist Henri Barbusse made a passionate speech calling the delegates of Brussels "soldiers of emancipation."[36] The other speaker was Sen Katayama, co-founder of the Japanese Communist Party and member of the Comintern, who appealed for unity between the working class and nationalist movements of the East. Katayama's appearance in the first sessions was noteworthy because he attended the Brussels Congress as an agent of the Comintern. He also carried with him directives from Moscow to covertly shape the course of the proceedings and send back detailed reports to the Comintern.[37]

Aside from Katayama, most communists operated in the shadows of the Brussels Congress. This had been a clear directive from Moscow to Münzenberg in July: "While influencing and directing the entire work of the League, the Communist Faction should try to remain as much as possible in the background, so that neither the League nor the Congress is too obviously identified with the Communists."[38] Rather, Comintern agents held secret meetings with Münzenberg to chart the course of the

---

[36] A summary of speakers and speeches is located in "Revolutionary Movements in the Colonies," *International Press Correspondence* 16 (1927): 328–331. Labour History Archive and Study Center (People's History Museum), File 183, Manchester, United Kingdom.

[37] Confidential report from Sen Katayama to Comrade Petrof (ECCI, Moscow), February 24, 1927, 542/1/7/131, RGASPI.

[38] ECCI to Münzenberg, July 2, 1926, 542/1/3/15, RGASPI.

proceedings. According to Katayama's report to the Comintern, a "Small Bureau [of communists] met constantly and secretly, I support [*sic*] none knew the existence of such a Bureau that has been directing the Congress and everything that might come up on the Congress was discussed and decided at the Small Bureau beforehand and carried out later by the Presidium or by a commission."[39]

These covert operations of the "small bureau" did not go unnoticed, however, and Nehru commented on the presence of Comintern agents in his report to India on the Brussels Congress. He was certain that the Berlin organizers were in touch with the Comintern in Moscow, and he speculated that communist party members purposely distanced themselves from the event "because they thought that too close an association might frighten away many people."[40] The presence of communists did not deter Nehru, but in fact intrigued him, especially in thinking about the great experiment underway in Soviet Russia. He thought collaboration with international communism could benefit and strengthen anticolonialism at home. He particularly appreciated not only the worldly expertise of Russians, but also their ability to circulate widely and efficiently propaganda campaigns to mobilize communists across the globe. But Nehru also commented on the dangers of the Soviets using the LAI as a tool for expansion: "Personally I have the strongest objection to being led by the nose by the Russians or anyone else. But I do not think there is much danger of this so far as we are concerned."[41]

Alongside communists and socialists, the opening session highlighted the struggles of the colonized in three key arenas – China, India, and Mexico. Liau Hansin of the Central Executive Committee of China's Kuomintang Party spoke on behalf of China, and José Vasconcelos, former education minister (1921–1924) of Mexico and later presidential candidate in the 1929 national elections, spoke about American imperialist interventions in Mexico and Latin America more broadly. Alongside Liau and Vasconcelos, Nehru was the third anticolonial representative, and he spoke on behalf of India. The emphasis on China, India, and Mexico underscored the premise that imperialism was not simply political colonization of a territory, as in the Indian case, but that capitalist-imperialist expansion took place in nominally independent countries such as China and Mexico. The Brussels Congress resolution on imperialism was clear on its definition of two kinds of "exploited colonial

---

[39] Katayama to ECCI, February 24, 1927, RGASPI.
[40] Nehru, "Report on the Brussels Congress," 289.   [41] Ibid.

territories." The first were "completely subjected countries which are governed by the motherland through its colonial bureaucracy," while the second were "nominally independent countries, but which have been brought into actual dependence upon the imperialist powers through treaties forced upon them, and which represent a state of equal exploitation."[42]

China was the pre-eminent concern at Brussels. The Chinese representatives far outnumbered all other delegations from outside Europe and included communists, trade unionists, and members of the Kuomintang Party Executive. Most of these delegates were Chinese travelers and expatriates already in Europe; nonetheless, they represented major organizations in China. The timing of the Brussels Congress is significant, too. In China, internal tensions and unrest were growing among workers, peasants, landlords, warlords, and nationalists of the KMT. During the same month as the Brussels Congress, the British Parliament in London began deliberating over the best means to intervene in China to quell unrest, in order to ensure the safety of British investments and national interests in the region. Moreover, Chinese trade unionists, Soviet-trained communists, and KMT forces under Chiang Kai-sheik had been working on the basis of a fragile alliance against warlords and foreigners. This united front in China emerged as the exemplary model for the solidarities that the delegates in Brussels hoped to create. Nehru even commented on this in his opening address to the delegation: "The noble example of the Chinese nationalists has filled us with hope, and we [Indian nationalists] earnestly want as soon as we can to be able to emulate them and follow in their footsteps."[43] In retrospect, the concentration on China would be a significant miscalculation for the Brussels Congress and the later LAI – not to mention the Soviets and Stalin – whose collective hopes for a nationalist and communist united front would be dashed only a few months later, in April 1927, when Chiang Kai-shek turned on Chinese communists and split ranks.

As the "jewel" in Britain's crown, India's importance to the Brussels Congress was second only to China. In the formative plans, the Berlin organizers extended an invitation to Gandhi, although he politely declined. Planners also reached out to Indian trade unionists and

---

[42] "Resolution on Imperialism," (copy) February 10–15, 1927, Brussels Congress against Colonialism and Imperialism, File G21-1926, AICC.
[43] Nehru, "Speech at Brussels Congress," February 10, 1927, reprinted in *SWJN*, vol. 2, 276.

developed a correspondence with S. H. Jhabwala, a Bombay trade unionist. Jhabwala was eager to support the Brussels Congress and LAI even
though Indian trade union organizations did not send a delegation.[44]
It was the arrival of Nehru in Berlin that broadened the Indian representation beyond a small number of students and exiles already in Europe.
The organizers moved quickly to secure Nehru's attendance, and he
accepted an invitation to attend special meetings ahead of the congress
in order to provide input on the construction of sessions. In the formal
proceedings, he drafted several resolutions, chaired a session, and earned
a coveted place on the executive council of the LAI.

It was no small task for Nehru to represent the Indian anticolonial
struggle as a cohesive movement in February 1927. Factionalism overtook
the INC in the 1920s after Gandhi called off the Non-Cooperation
Campaign (1920–1922). Deep divisions emerged over the plan for future
action. Many INC leaders who had given up successful careers and posh
lifestyles for *swaraj* in 1920 found Gandhi's abrupt and unilateral aban-
donment of the campaign in 1922 a bitter pill to swallow. Lacking direction
for several years, the INC splintered into two factions. The Swaraj Party
sought re-entry into the provincial legislatures as a means to wreck the
colonial state from within the existing system. Legislative council members
did so by creating deadlocks and exposing the colonial state as a repressive
regime. Opposing the Swaraj Party, the "no-changers" argued for the
continuation of Gandhi's program of boycotting British institutions,
including the legislatures, while also preparing for another non-
cooperation movement through grassroots constructive programs.
Gandhi managed to bring the swarajists and no-changers together within
the INC fold after his release from prison in November 1924, but the two
camps continued to work separately. When Nehru left India, as he later
recalled in his autobiography, he welcomed the break from the internal
politics of the INC: "I wanted an excuse to go out of India ... My mind was
befogged, and no clear path was visible; and I thought that, perhaps, if I was
far from India I could see things in better perspective and lighten up the dark
corners of my mind."[45] The Brussels Congress would be the remedy for
Nehru's search for a new and "clear path."

In Brussels, Nehru made two formal statements on the Indian situation:
one to the press on the eve of the congress, and one to the delegation at the

---

[44] For a brief account of these early contacts between Jhabwala and the LAI, see 542/1/18/7,
RGASPI.
[45] Nehru, *Autobiography*, 155.

opening session. In both, Nehru positioned India at the forefront of the world struggle against imperialism and considered the ways India shaped anticolonial movements elsewhere. He argued, "India is a world problem and as in the past so in the future other countries and peoples will be vitally affected by the condition of India."[46] In his presentation, he stated that the British not only depended on Indian resources and labor to manage the empire, but also that Britain's imperial expansion into Africa, and Egypt in particular, was a maneuver to ensure safe passage of goods between the metropole and its "crown jewel." Nehru concluded, "What it will be in the future, if and when India becomes independent, I cannot say, but certainly the British Empire would cease to exist."[47] Consequently, India's independence would be the catalyst for a new era of a world freed from imperialist and capitalist chains.

This Indian-centric perspective also focused on the issue of Indian soldiers and manpower used to serve British imperial interests worldwide. Nehru observed that it had been very disheartening to meet his fellow comrades from the colonized world and realize that the most common encounters many had with India had been with Indian soldiers and police officers manning the British Empire. By 1927, Indian soldiers worked in the service of the British Empire in China, Egypt, Abyssinia, Mesopotamia, Arabia, Syria, Georgia, Tibet, Afghanistan, and Burma. Nehru was especially concerned about the use of Indian troops to intervene in the internal affairs of China on behalf of British imperial interests, remarking,

It has been a matter of shame and sorrow to us that the British Government should venture to send Indian troops to China in an attempt to coerce the Chinese ... imperialism is trying to utilise one subject country to coerce another but in spite of her weakness India is not so weak today as to permit herself to be employed as a pawn in the imperialist game.[48]

Here, again, India was central to the functioning of imperialism around the world, and thus the Indian nationalist movement was pivotal to anti-imperialist internationalism.

Alongside India and China, Mexico served as the third site highlighted at the Brussels Congress. It is noteworthy that in 1927 Mexico was an independent state. The Mexican delegate, Vasconcelos, had positioned Mexico as the natural leader of a Pan-American resistance to the shadowy hand of US imperialism. He argued that local capitalists suppressed the

---

[46] Nehru, "Press Statement in Brussels," February 9, 1927, reprinted in *SWJN*, vol. 2, 270.
[47] Nehru, "Speech at Brussels Congress," 275.
[48] Nehru, "Speech at Brussels Congress," 271.

masses in Latin America, while US imperialists pillaged their Southern neighbors "through robbery, through bravery, through cruelty and through cleverness."[49] Nehru listened to the speeches of other delegates from Mexico, Cuba, Puerto Rico, Peru, Venezuela, and Colombia, who characterized the "American Dollar Empire as the common problem of us all, because it is an empire, which takes tribute from the whole world."[50]

The remaining sessions of the Brussels Congress stretched out over the next five days and opened the floor to delegates from Egypt, Indonesia, South Africa, Algeria, Tunis, Morocco, Persia, Indo-China, Syria, Korea, the United States, France, Germany, Italy, and Britain. In all instances, speakers either pointed to the atrocities of imperialism and capitalism in their respective homes, or professed their support for workers and national emancipation movements in the colonies. Other delegates engaged in transnational discussions about Pan-African, Pan-American, and Pan-Asian solidarities. The "Negro" solidarities were significant among the many connections forged in Brussels. This resulted in a resolution passed by the delegation and modeled after a similar one drafted at the Fifth Annual Convention of the Negro Peoples of the World in New York in 1926. It called for the collective "emancipation of the oppressed African peoples from all imperialist subjugation and exploitation."[51]

The colonial delegates and working-class representatives dominated the proceedings, but there was space for delegates to speak about other preoccupations peripheral to anti-imperialism. Among these were the growing concerns about fascism and war. Two pacifist delegates spoke about the dangers of another world war, one that would be global in scale and more destructive than the Great War. In addition, a lone delegate, Guido Miglioli of the Catholic People's Party in Italy, drew attention to fascist Italy as a new and dangerous ally of imperialism. The peace and antifascist pillars were not central to Brussels, but their appearance foreshadows the direction that the anti-imperialist campaign would take later in the 1930s as the international context rapidly changed, a point examined in Chapters 5 and 6.

Overall, the Brussels moment was significant for several reasons. First, it provided analogies that linked localized anticolonial struggles across the

---

[49] José Vasconcelos, "Speech at Brussels Congress," February 10, 1927, File 39, LAI, IISH.
[50] Manuel Gomez, "Speech at Brussels Congress," undated, File G29-1927, AICC.
[51] For copies of "Negro" resolutions, see Files 54 and 55, LAI, IISH. See also, Holger Weiss, *Framing a Radical African Atlantic: African American Agency, West African Intellectuals and the International Trade Union Committee of Negro Workers* (Leiden: Brill, 2014).

world to a universalized sense of oppression at the hands of imperialists. An impressive assortment of ephemera in the form of printed speeches and resolutions circulated in Brussels as well. In total, the delegation introduced twenty-six resolutions on the anti-imperialist struggle, although only ten resolutions were presented to the congress and unanimously approved. The rest were sent to the executive council of the newly formed LAI for approval. Among the ten presented and passed, four focused on India, three of which Nehru drafted personally. The remaining resolutions focused on specific examples of the atrocities, massacres, and injustices of European and American imperialism. Two resolutions dealt with the responsibility and role trade unions and activists in Europe had in supporting anticolonial movements and workers in the colonies. Secondly, it provided a model for international conferencing and meetings that could accommodate a diverse variety of activists within the framework of a broad movement against capitalism-imperialism and all of its manifestations. This was a rather optimistic moment for many constituent members, who had come to find new possibilities for anticolonial resistance. Finally, speeches aside, the Congress offered a platform to begin to define a more specific agenda and set of principles for anti-imperialist resistance and mobilization.

ANTI-IMPERIALISM DEFINED AND DEBATED

The chairman of the Brussels Congress, George Lansbury of the British Labour Party, offered perhaps the most eloquent and grandiose language to capture the event's idealism. Even before his speech, he called onto stage and joined hands with a Chinese representative as a symbolic expression of solidarity. The audience erupted into applause. His speech that followed impressed upon the audience that the Brussels Congress was a meeting that came "only occasionally in the history of the whole race; that is, you are proclaiming the union of the black, yellow and white." He added, "it is the unity of the human race that we are after – united in the bonds of economic freedom, working to produce not for imperialist nations, not for capitalism, but for the service of all the children of men."[52] In addition to breaking down racial and economic boundaries, Lansbury made a special appeal to his comrades in the colonies entrenched in anticolonial struggles for nationalism: "Do not be fooled

[52] George Lansbury, "Speech at the Brussels Congress," February 13, 1927, File G29-1927, AICC.

FIGURE 1.3 The Presidium of the Brussels Congress, 1927. Left to right: Jawaharlal Nehru, George Lansbury, Edo Fimmen, General Lu Chung Lin, and Liau Hansin. *Das Flammenzeichen vom Palais Egmont: offizielles Protokoll des Kongresses gegen koloniale Unterdrückung und Imperialismus, Brüssel, 10–15 Februar 1927.* Berlin: Neuer Deutscher Verlag, 1927

by the cry of mere nationalism ... Get your national ownership, get your national control, that is right and proper, but do not stop there because if you do you will have only gone half way." Instead, Lansbury emphasized that "Nationalism is to be blended with internationalism, because until it is, until the world is built on the foundation of international comradeship ... all our Labour is in vain."[53]

The conceptualization of anti-imperialist comradeship as a special "blend" of nationalism and internationalism among anti-imperialists was at the crux of the Brussels Congress message. It spoke to the possibilities of solidarity across racial divides of "black, yellow and white," as well as the geographical boundaries of nations, colonies, and empires. Even so, there also existed diverse interpretations of the path to build a collective anti-imperialist resistance and to blend national and international projects. For Labour Party leaders such as George Lansbury, anti-imperialist comradeship meant the "blend" between international socialism and trade unionism with anticolonial struggle in the colonies. It necessitated a strong appeal for

[53] Ibid.

workers in imperialist countries to consider the colonial question in relation to their class struggle, while at the same time urging nationalist leaders in the colonies to embrace the proletariat cause for colonial laborers. Alternatively, Münzenberg and other communists in Brussels hoped to use the LAI as a vehicle to draw anticolonial nationalists into the orbit of international communism and Moscow. By introducing the principles of communism in Brussels, Münzenberg believed he could win the hearts and minds (or at least sympathies) of his colonial colleagues. For Nehru and many other nationalists from the colonies, however, the anti-imperialist movement offered an alternative discourse, network, and set of contacts to internationalize the colonial question. The class question became significant to Nehru, but political independence took precedence.

Brussels especially demonstrated that it was possible to overlook party differences and doctrine in order to forge solidarity across the anti-imperialist world, and a remarkable consensus emerged around the main principles of anti-imperialist comradeship formulated at the proceedings. These principles were most clearly articulated in the "Congress Manifesto." Münzenberg and other Comintern agents drafted the text during a secret meeting outside the regular sessions of the congress, and many of its principal ideas were informed by international communism. The manifesto was a six-page document, and it arrived in front of the delegation for consideration and approval at the last minute during the final day of the proceedings. It had been hastily, although unanimously, approved. Nehru remarked on the conditions behind its ratification in his report to the INC: "A number of enormous manifestos were rushed through the Congress at the last moment when there was no time to consider them. One of these, called the Congress Manifesto ... is more or less Marxian and although personally I have no very great objection to it, the manner of its being rushed through was objectionable."[54]

Despite its questionable origins, the manifesto represented the central pillars of the anti-imperialist movement rooted in the Brussels Congress. It might best be characterized as a reimagining of the world from an anti-imperialist lens. This worldview necessitated a discursive shift in the narrative of world history, and, in this case, a rejection of the civilizing mission emanating from European imperial histories and epistemologies.[55] Such late nineteenth-century models of history

[54] Nehru, "Report on Brussels Congress," 287.
[55] For a broader argument on the impact of the Great War on challenging the foundations of the civilizing mission, see Michael Adas' essay in *Making a World after Empire:*

represented Europeans as the carriers of civilization to the backward colonies and even races of the world. Of course, social Darwinism and racism underpinned such assumptions of Europeans as more civilized than their colonized counterparts in Asia and Africa. One of the manifesto's central theses turned the civilizing mission on its head: "The emancipation of the oppressed colonial peoples, vassals and those subjugated by violence, will not diminish the great accomplishments and possibilities of the material and spiritual culture of mankind but will increase them on a scale never yet experienced."[56]

Moreover, the anti-imperialist logic went beyond subverting the "civilizing mission" by offering a contradistinctive history and model for progress and civilization based on the Soviet Union. According to the manifesto, the great experiment in Soviet Russia represented a new path for greater social equality for the working class, and also a global model that rejected European imperialism and capitalism worldwide. In doing so, Soviet Russia emerged from the proceedings as a stalwart of anti-imperialism and a friend to nationalists in the colonies. The manifesto celebrated Soviet Russia, as it "lights up like a torch the path of the struggle for freedom of the oppressed and enslaved nations."[57] The Brussels Congress, accordingly, was a momentous event inaugurating anti-imperialist solidarity between Soviet Russia and nationalists from the colonial and semi-colonial world.

The specter of the "war danger" provided the main impetus for anti-imperialist solidarity. This pillar of anti-imperialism foreshadowed a future world war pitting anti-imperialists against their imperialist-capitalist antagonists. As Franziska Roy and Ali Raza have argued elsewhere, the interwar years witnessed a proliferation of mobilizations and paramilitary volunteer associations, which sought to prepare youth for a future war in places outside of the well-documented cases of fascist Italy and Germany.[58] Such imagined war dangers often were not indicative of

---

The Bandung Moment and Its Political Afterlives, ed. Christopher Lee (Athens: Ohio University Press, 2010).

[56] "Congress Manifesto," Brussels Congress against Colonial Oppression and Imperialism, February 10–15, 1927, File 10, p. 6, LAI, IISH.

[57] "Congress Manifesto," 3.

[58] See Ali Raza and Franziska Roy, "Paramilitary Organisations in Interwar India," *South Asia: Journal of South Asian Studies* 38:4 (2015). For an important discussion on imaginary futures and anticolonial resistance, see Manu Goswami, "Imaginary Futures and Colonial Internationalisms," *American Historical Review* 117:5 (2012), 1461–85. This is part of a special issue on the power of imagining the future, and essays by David Engerman and Matthew Connelly also offer relevant discussions.

the realities or future outcomes of world geopolitics, and mostly had contingent and localized concerns. The manifesto's "war danger" also borrowed significantly from the Soviet Union's "war scare" of 1927.[59] Propounded by Stalin and his supporters, the "war scare" amplified anxieties that a British-led coalition of powers were mobilizing for another military intervention against the Soviet Union. Many within the Comintern called upon communists worldwide to defend the Soviet Union and prepare for war against Britain.

The anti-imperialist war danger in Brussels modified the Comintern's "war scare" thesis to fit a broader narrative of a world threatened by British imperialism in the colonies as well as the Soviet Union. It argued that imperialists worldwide were already engaged in "colonial wars" in pre-eminent sites of anticolonial resistance, in places such as China, India, and Mexico, as well as other enclaves in Morocco, Turkey, Syria, Egypt, Sudan, and the Dutch East Indies. Inevitably, according to the document, imperialists would launch a "new crusade" in Soviet Russia because "in the eyes of the imperialist world there is no greater crime than moral solidarity with the liberation movements of an Asiatic nation."[60] This amalgamation of anticolonial struggle with the perceived threat of Britain to the Soviet Union embedded in the "war scare" created a global battleground for anti-imperialism.

The manifesto underscored the pre-eminence of China and India as the immediate battlegrounds for the anti-imperialist struggle. It was most attentive to the situation in China. According to the manifesto, "British diplomacy is constantly, indefatigably and energetically busy drawing other imperialist powers into an armed conflict with China."[61] The document also reminded readers about the ongoing colonial oppression in India and specifically called attention to the Jallianwalla Bagh massacre in Amritsar. It rhetorically asked: "Who in India has forgotten with what brutality an unarmed crowd on the market-place of Amritsar, of which the gates had been closed, was fired upon? Who has forgotten that General O'Dyer received an honorable distinction from the adherents of the brutal proceedings?"[62]

Finally, the war danger also reinforced the mapping of a world divided along the boundaries of imperialism and anti-imperialism. This

---

[59] For a discussion of the war scare and Stalin's mistrust of Britain, see Kevin McDermott and Jeremy Agnew, *The Comintern: A History of International Communism from Lenin to Stalin* (New York: St. Martin's Press, 1997), 71 and 198–199.
[60] "Congress Manifesto," 4–5.   [61] Ibid., 4.   [62] Ibid., 3.

dichotomy is most clear in the manifesto's articulation of the importance of the war danger and the inevitable conflict between the two opposing forces: "The imperialist powers buy and sell whole nations and populated continents like cattle." Thus, "always and everywhere, we see the same picture – on the one side dozens and hundreds of millions who strive for independence and freedom and on the other side small but powerful minorities of exploiters who strive to secure extra-profits in underhand ways of privileged trade, by export of capital and by monopolist control of the most important raw material."[63] The imperialist-capitalist drive for more colonies was already responsible for the Great War. Despite the war's carnage, the imperialist system survived, and the capitalist-imperialist antagonists "clung like limpets to the booty" in their colonies.[64] The hope for the future, then, rested in the hands of the anti-imperialists. The manifesto concluded that only "the oppressed and enslaved nations, which are representing the overwhelming majority of mankind, like the proletariat, can conquer the world, the world of the future."[65]

Although consensus emerged over these central pillars of anti-imperialism, the Brussels Congress moment was not without tension and debate. It was the resolutions associated with Nehru that provided terrain for the earliest struggles over the power to define the language of anti-imperialism. Nehru stood out in the proceedings as the only delegate to draft three resolutions of the ten adopted in Brussels. He was the signatory on a fourth. All of those he drafted pertained to the anti-imperialist movement: one on conditions in India, the second on anti-imperialist solidarity between India and China, and the third on the presence of Indian troops in Mesopotamia. The final resolution to which he was a signatory was drafted by the British delegation, and dealt with the cooperation between Indian, Chinese, and British anti-imperialists. All were unanimously adopted, and the Brussels delegation agreed to send greetings and news of the resolutions to the INC and the Chinese government in Hankow.

Despite the fact that all of the resolutions were approved, the multiple revisions these documents went through reflected the robust debate over the language and discourse anti-imperialism that continued throughout the meetings and afterward. In the resolution on British, Indian, and Chinese solidarity, several versions existed and had been debated mainly by the different Labour leaders from Britain. The original draft called for

[63] Ibid., 5.   [64] Ibid.   [65] Ibid., 6.

a "severance of the British connection" with India and China rather than the final draft's aim for "complete independence."[66] The alteration took place when the British delegation objected to the original wording, "severance of the British connection," because it implied that India and China would reject any diplomatic relations with Britain. Nehru admitted that these debates were entirely between the British delegates, and so far as India was concerned, "the change made no difference."[67] Revisions to the Indian and Chinese resolution provided another source of ongoing debate. The resolution called for the objective of "attaining the complete independence of India and China by carrying on a joint ['united' was removed and replaced by 'joint'] struggle against British imperialism."[68] The removal of the phrase "united struggle" likely signaled an attempt to distance the resolution from the language of the united front that international communists deployed in the 1920s. An even more significant revision to the document appeared later in the files of the Comintern. The resolution, in Nehru's handwriting, had been edited in Moscow, and "joint struggle" was replaced with "soviet struggle." Thus, the final version of the objective aimed at "attaining the complete independence of India and China by carrying on a soviet struggle against British Imperialism."[69]

Nehru likely never saw his resolution after the Comintern's reworking. The initial copies of resolutions were not edited in this manner, and an official report on the resolutions of the Brussels Congress was not published by the LAI in English until 1929, in the form of a small pamphlet which included abstracts of speeches and full transcripts of only two documents, the "Congress Manifesto" and the "Resolution of Trade Union Delegates." Between 1927 and 1929, Nehru complained frequently to the LAI secretariat that there had not been a publication on the Brussels Congress by the LAI for circulation in India. There is no doubt that the Comintern revisions would not have been welcomed by Nehru and certainly not by many of his INC colleagues. In the context of Brussels, however, the changing dimensions of the document demonstrate the debate over the meanings, language, and priorities of the anti-imperialist movement among a variety of voices from India, Britain, and Soviet Russia.

Even as tensions appeared early on, such divisions between delegates were easily overlooked in the Brussels moment, even if they

---

[66] Nehru, "Report on the Brussels Congress," 284.   [67] Ibid.
[68] Nehru, Resolution on India and China, undated, 542/1/10/4, RGASPI.   [69] Ibid.

would be hard to reconcile after the initial enthusiasm for the proceedings diminished. The possibilities for anti-imperialist collective action in the late 1920s enabled delegates to work across their ideological differences and find common ground for their movement. All rested on the fundamental principles outlined in the manifesto, including the united-front alliances between proletariat and nationalists in the colonies; the anti-imperialist geography of the world; and the urgency presented by the war danger in China, India, Soviet Russia, and other colonies. In the immediate aftermath of the Brussels Congress, Nehru began to articulate these central pillars of anti-imperialism in his burgeoning conceptualization of India and its relationship to the wider world of the 1920s.

ANTI-IMPERIALISM AND INDIA: WORLDVIEWS, GEOGRAPHIES, AND COMRADES

A mere four days after the Brussels Congress concluded, Nehru bundled together a package of documents from the proceedings and sent them to the secretary of the INC Working Committee in New Delhi. The most significant and revealing document was the report on the Brussels Congress, a 32-page handwritten account of the proceedings from Nehru's perspective.[70] It represented both the transformative impact of the meetings on Nehru, as well as his immediate reflections on anti-imperialist internationalism in the wake of the congress. The supporting documents included the Congress Manifesto; copies of many speeches and resolutions, including the ones Nehru drafted for India; an incomplete list of delegates and agenda items; a handwritten list of names and addresses of Asian delegates for the INC to contact; and a copy of a report on the proceedings published in Britain's *The Labour Leader*. This package was the first of several Nehru sent from Europe in 1927 demonstrating the importance of the ideas and encounters, rooted in the Brussels Congress moment, which shaped Nehru's formulation of an anti-imperialist worldview for India.

Unlike the other documents in the package, which Nehru instructed the INC secretary to distribute widely, the report on the Congress was

---

[70] Nehru, "Brussels Congress Report," handwritten with list of enclosed documents, February 19, 1927, File G-29, AICC. The report is reprinted as "Report on the Brussels Congress," *SWJN*, vol. 2, 278–297.

marked "confidential – not for publication."[71] In it, Nehru's report made a clear case for the INC to associate with the LAI. At the same time, the report also represented his immediate and more candid reflections on the people and ideas that had circulated in Brussels. The report differed significantly from his official speeches in Brussels, which focused primarily on India as a pivotal site for the anti-imperialist campaign. To his audience of INC colleagues, Nehru had to argue that world problems were significant to India. He made this argument by appropriating for India many aspects of the Brussels Congress message, while at the same time linking these issues to the local and all-Indian politics of the day. In this way, the report reflected Nehru's special "blend" of Indian nationalism and the anti-imperialist internationalism of the Brussels Congress.

Among the most significant points Nehru made was the necessity to consider the anticolonial struggle of the INC in relation to the working-class movement in India and abroad. Repeating a familiar argument from the Brussels discourse, Nehru made a case that "imperialism and capitalism go hand in hand and back up each other and neither will disappear till both are put down."[72] Nehru argued that the LAI was useful for coordinating forces against capitalism and imperialism, and India could only benefit from this coordination. He also echoed and expanded upon Lansbury's call to the colonies to "blend" nationalism and internationalism. He began by pointing out that "nationalism of a narrow variety" had been the "main pillar" of imperialists, but that "the problem in oppressed countries is somewhat different and nationalism automatically and rightly takes precedence of all other sentiments." He added that the socialists in the LAI agreed in principle on the pre-eminence of nationalism in the colonies, but "they point out that in such countries nationalism might be given a broader basis more in consonance with the tendencies of the age, that it might derive its strength from and work specially for the masses, the peasants and other workers."[73] In a rather dramatic shift, Nehru added for the first time in his writings his acceptance of socialism: "Personally, I agree with this contention because I accept in its fundamentals the socialist theory of the State."[74]

---

[71] Nehru, "Brussels Congress Report," File G-29, AICC.
[72] Nehru, "Report on the Brussels Congress," *SWJN*, vol. 2, 287. The remaining discussion of the report is drawn from the printed copy in *SWJN*.
[73] Ibid., 287.   [74] Ibid.

The report revealed a radical transformation of Nehru's understanding of the working-class questions in India and the world. He had not considered or advocated for socialism before February 1927. Even a few months before the Brussels Congress, Nehru observed the 1926 general miners' strike in England, but his letters to India on the strike offered little commentary on working-class issues in the metropole or their implications for Indian workers. When he wrote to colleagues in India in October 1926 to discuss the lessons of the strike, Nehru was most concerned with the methodology of strikes as non-violent means to challenge the British state rather than the demands of the working class or the trade unionist critique of British capitalism and imperialism.[75]

The report made clear that Nehru's engagement with socialism began in Brussels. In his speeches at the Congress, he already articulated a more concrete connection between the local conditions in India and the larger, international struggle against class exploitation that his newly found comrades were eager to stress. Nehru attributed the divisions within Indian society and its catastrophic poverty to the means by which the British capitalists ruled India – by propping up exploitative princes, landowners, and Indian capitalists. The "real injury that the British have done to India," according to Nehru, "is the systematic way in which they have crushed the workers and peasants of India, and made India what she is today."[76] The comparison between his earlier neglect of working-class issues as late as 1926 and his Brussels commentary is striking and offers clear evidence of a radical shift, at least in his rhetoric.

In his report to the INC, Nehru also articulated a warning about the war danger that echoed the Brussels Congress as well, although his warning pointed to immediate and localized concerns for India. His report argued that the future of anti-imperialist resistance, in India and worldwide, depended on the events in China first and India second. This, too, represented a shift from his speeches about the centrality of India to world problems. Instead, Nehru's report argued that a great conflict between China and Britain would inevitably spill over into Soviet Russia. Based on this domino-theory logic, war between China and Britain on the one hand, and China and Russia on the other, would spread to the North-West Frontier of India as another principal battleground. Nehru concluded that the INC must be prepared to resist and obstruct designs to mobilize

---

[75] The absence of an engagement with socialism and trade unionism is clear in his letter to the Hindustani Seva Dal, October 1926, *SWJN*, vol. 2, 247–249.
[76] Nehru, "Speech at Brussels Congress," *SWJN*, vol. 2, 273.

Indian resources and manpower for the British imperialist struggle against anti-imperialist allies such as China and Russia: "We cannot remain aloof ... else our best laid plans will break down and we will find ourselves suddenly faced with crises for which we are wholly unprepared or even stampeded into a war for the support of the very system against which we are contending."[77]

Overall, his points about India and the world, rooted in the Brussels Congress discourse, enabled Nehru to begin formulating a global geography of anti-imperialism. This imaginary mapping of the world from an anti-imperialist lens became critical to the ways Nehru conceptualized India and its relationship to the wider world. His first attempt to map the Indian worldview in many ways resembled the geography constructed in Brussels – that of a world divided along the fault lines of imperialism and anti-imperialism. Soviet Russia, Asia, Africa, and Latin America were pitted against the imperialist-capitalist powers of Europe and the United States. The specific nodal points in this geography, however, varied greatly among Brussels delegates, and Nehru's report began to develop a mapping of anti-imperialist sites most significant to India. For Nehru, Soviet Russia, China, Indonesia, and Egypt provided the most critical and pragmatically important partners in the struggle against imperialism. In other words, his mapping reflected Indian nationalist interests vis-à-vis the anti-imperialist world, and it prioritized comrades that most readily had connections to colonial India in terms of proximity or imperialist networks of labor and goods.

Nehru's geography of anti-imperialism was more than pragmatic, however, and it came to be informed by the comrades he met in Brussels, too. Encounters and the establishment of personal networks were equally important to Nehru's formulations of India and the anti-imperialist world. As the earlier sketch of the proceedings suggested, Nehru met many figures representing a diverse array of political and social movements, and his report to the INC also reflected his formative impressions of his new colleagues. In his final analysis of the delegation he met in Brussels, Nehru's appraisal of potential comrades for India was based upon a mix of pragmatism and personal encounters with fellow anti-imperialists. In other words, Nehru's anti-imperialist worldview depended as much on personalities as it did on their strategic and geopolitical importance to India.

---

[77] Nehru, "Report on the Brussels Congress," 293.

FIGURE 1.4 The General Council elected at the Brussels Congress, 1927. Liau Hansin is first from left (back row), Roger Baldwin is second from left (back row), Mohammad Hatta is sixth from left (back row), Reginald Bridgeman is seventh from left (back row), Willi Münzenberg is third from left (front row), Edo Fimmen is fifth from left (front row), and Nehru is eighth from left (front row). *Das Flammenzeichen vom Palais Egmont: offizielles Protokoll des Kongresses gegen koloniale Unterdrückung und Imperialismus, Brüssel, 10–15 Februar 1927.* Berlin: Neuer Deutscher Verlag, 1927

COMRADES FROM THE COLONIAL WORLD

The primary sites of anti-imperialist comradeship for India, according to Nehru, were in the colonial world, and especially in Asia. As it had at the Brussels Congress, China occupied the pre-eminent place in Nehru's report, although his assessment of Chinese delegates was not entirely favorable. The Chinese presence far outnumbered that of any other delegation aside from the Germans, and the representation included the Kuomintang Party (KMT), the Canton Government, and Chinese trade unions. Among them, Liau Hansin was a clear leader, and Nehru likely spent time with him in Brussels and at subsequent LAI meetings throughout 1927. Officially, Liau represented the Kuomintang Party Executive Committee in Berlin, although he had been in Germany under the directives and patronage of the Comintern. He also received a monthly salary from Moscow.[78] After Brussels, Liau served as one of the LAI secretaries

---

[78] For details of Liau Hansin and the LAI, see Petersson, *Willi Münzenberg*, 328–334.

for a short time before resigning in January 1928. Nehru described Liau and his Chinese colleagues as "young and full of energy and enthusiasm," yet "not remarkably able."[79] He added that "before the Congress was over people were rather tired of listening to Chinese orations, which were not remarkable for their lucidity."[80] Little is mentioned in his confidential report of the private dinner party Nehru hosted for the Chinese delegates, although these more intimate settings had not encouraged him to say anything impressive about the Chinese delegates either.[81]

Despite his unmemorable encounters with Chinese representatives, Nehru outlined a plan for closer contact with India's anti-imperialist neighbor based on the importance assigned to China in Brussels. In particular, Nehru recommended a Chinese information bureau, headed by a representative from China, to be established in Calcutta to collect and disseminate news and propaganda. The INC and the KMT, as well as the All-India Trade Union Congress (AITUC) and the Chinese trade unions, should send representatives to their counterparts' annual meetings. Nehru also thought it desirable to send Indian students to China to study and further develop contacts between the two countries. Nehru recognized in these plans the problem of travel restrictions imposed by the colonial state, especially for Indians to travel to China, but "even if Government prevented our representatives from leaving India it would have a good effect."[82]

More passionate appeals for his Indian colleagues to recognize the urgency of the crisis in China followed in the months to come. In April, Nehru sent a short article for publication in the flagship journal of the Hindustani Seva Dal, a volunteer organization for Hindus with ties to the INC. Nehru identified China as the most urgent world crisis and argued that India had a role to play in assisting its neighbor by sending volunteer medical corps as an expression of goodwill and sympathy. The crux of the article emphasized the common bonds of comradeship shared by India and China: "China is holding out her hand of comradeship to India. It is for us to grasp it and to renew our ancient and honourable association and thereby ensure the freedom and progress of both these great countries, which have so much in common."[83] Clearly, Nehru deployed the

[79] Nehru, "Report on the Brussels Congress," 280.   [80] Ibid.
[81] The INC paid Nehru's expenses. This included his travel, a dinner with Chinese delegates, and a tea party for Asian delegates. "Note on Accounts," Nehru to Secretary of the AICC, April 9, 1927, File G29-1927, AICC.
[82] Nehru, "Report on Brussels Congress," 295.
[83] Jawaharlal Nehru, "The Situation in China and India's Duty," The Volunteer, April 1927, reprinted in SWJN, vol. 2, 326–328.

language of comradeship and a shared experience of imperialist oppression and anti-imperialist resistance. The appeal also drew upon some assumptions about the two Asian countries already made popular in India by the Greater India Society in Calcutta. The premise of Greater India, as Carolien Stolte has demonstrated, was the historical argument that Asia, before the advent of imperialism, had been interconnected by the peaceful exchange of people, goods, and ideas.[84] India, in particular, had been a peaceful hegemon in the region by spreading its religious and cultural influence throughout East and Southeast Asia. Only with imperialism were these progressive and peaceful networks disrupted and the ancient bonds of Asia dismantled by the greed and violence of European colonial rule. While organizations such as the Greater India Society produced a discourse on India's pre-eminent role in fertilizing the rest of Asia, variant models suggested that China and India, as powerful and large states of the ancient world, both had a dominating cultural influence over the rest of Asia. Nehru's fresh encounters with China and the Chinese informed some of these pre-existing ideas about "ancient and honourable bonds," but it was also informed by a view that both countries also had an obligation to lead anti-imperialism in Asia in the 1920s.

Nehru's views of India and China were an integral part of the larger vision of Asianism that he began to articulate in the wake of the Brussels Congress. The construction of Asia as a regional geography has been the focus of recent scholarship, and here again Stolte's work makes clear that multiple mappings and meanings of Asia coexisted during the interwar years.[85] In Brussels, a Pan-Asian framework emerged from both a desire among such delegates for Asian solidarities and a desire of the organizers to promote such regional affinities. At the insistence of Katayama, the Comintern agent, Nehru agreed to host a tea party for Asian delegates. He used INC funds for the event, which offered a more intimate setting outside the proceedings for delegates to consider better communication networks and a possible institution that could coordinate regional and intercolonial interests.[86] The smaller meeting did much to define

---

[84] Carolien Stolte, *Orienting India: Interwar Internationalism in an Asian Inflection, 1917–1937* (PhD Diss., University of Leiden, 2013).

[85] See Stolte, "Orienting India," and also Cemil Aydin, *The Politics of Anti-Westernism in Asia*. For a Chinese perspective, see Rebecca Karl, *Staging the World*.

[86] For Katayama's assistance in the Asian meeting, see the "Confidential report from Sen Katayama to Comrade Petrof (ECCI, Moscow)," February 24, 1927, 542/1/7/131, RGASPI; for Nehru's expenditures, see "Note on Accounts," Nehru to Secretary of the AICC, April 9, 1927, File G29-1927, AICC.

a geography of anti-imperialist Asia as a broad and inclusive mapping that stretched from Egypt to South and East Asia. Among the delegates mentioned in Nehru's report were those representing China, the Dutch East Indies (Indonesia), Korea, Annam, Persia, Syria, and Egypt. Nehru expressed doubt at the possibility of creating of an institution to connect with his Asian counterparts given that "various parts of Asia are more inaccessible to each other than they are to Europe and at present moment Europe is the best meeting ground for Asiatic nationalities."[87] Nevertheless, he was committed to improved communication networks and, along with the INC report, Nehru forwarded to India the names and contact details of his comrades in Asia so that India could "try to visit the other countries and put ourselves in touch with the national organizations there."[88]

Of all the Asian delegates, the Indonesians left a profound impression on Nehru. His main contact in Brussels was Mohammed Hatta, a high-profile Indonesian student who served as the chairman for an anticolonial organization in Holland, Perhimpunan Indonesia (PI), and the editor of *Indonesia Merdeka (Free Indonesia)*.[89] Hatta is perhaps most notable for his later ascendance in Indonesian politics, culminating in his role as Sukarno's Vice-President (1945–1956). Much later, Hatta characterized his time with Nehru, beginning in Brussels, as the beginning of a "close and affectionate relationship over the years."[90] His oral history also recalls their collaboration within the LAI as an important precursor to the Bandung Conference in 1955. Nehru, too, came to appreciate the Indonesian situation and to envision a shared history of anticolonial resistance for India and Indonesia. Nehru found the Indonesian delegates "more interesting" than the Chinese. He mused that although most Indonesian representatives were Muslims, their names were derived from Sanskrit. Moreover, he noted, "Their customs, they told us, were still largely Hindu in origin, and many of them bore a striking resemblance

---

[87] Nehru, "Report on the Brussels Congress," 290.
[88] The list of addresses and names is located in a handwritten note in File G29-1927, AICC. His comments are from Nehru, "Report on the Brussels Congress," 290.
[89] For Indonesian connections to the LAI, see Klaas Stutje, "Indonesian Identities Abroad: International Engagement of Colonial Students in the Netherlands, 1908–1931," *Low Countries Historical Review* 128, 1 (2013): 151–172, and "Behind the Banner of Unity Nationalism and Anticolonialism among Indonesian Students in Europe, 1917–1931" (PhD Thesis, University of Amsterdam, 2016).
[90] Mohammed Hatta, interviewed by B. R. Nanda, September 1972, interview transcript 121, Nehru Memorial Museum and Library (NMML) Oral History Collection, NMML, New Delhi, India.

to the higher caste Hindus."[91] That his encounters with Indonesians confirmed this in both their appearance and their explanations of Indonesian culture had only reaffirmed Nehru's ideas about the unilateral expansion of Indian culture into Southeast Asia in ancient times. It also remains noteworthy that this was the only aspect of the Indonesian delegation that Nehru shared in his report.

Egypt retained a special place in Nehru's burgeoning conception of Asia. He argued that Egypt shared with Asia a "common bond" uniting the "Asiatic elements," although he neglected to define or elaborate on the meaning of such a "bond."[92] In situating Egypt within Asia, Nehru's mapping was both pragmatic and connected to his encounters with Egyptians. Most importantly, Nehru considered Egypt to be oriented more toward the Indian Ocean world than toward the African world because of its importance to India. Egypt's Suez Canal was the gateway to South Asia for Britain, and it played a pivotal role in the functioning of the empire. Nehru's integration of Egypt into his early schemes at Brussels for a Pan-Asian vision reveals the importance of an Indian-centric world-view rather than any conceptualization of regional or even linguistic affinities of the modern world.

In Brussels, Nehru met Hafiz Ramadan Bey, who was the main delegate from Egypt. At the time (1927), Egypt was another nominally indepen-dent state with a constitutional monarchy, although the British presence in the region and unfair treaties made by Britain had limited the freedoms of Egyptians. Hafiz Ramadan Bey served as a member of the Egyptian Parliament and represented the Egyptian Nationalist Party (Watanist Party). His statement in the proceedings underscored Egypt as another example of British imperialist oppression: "Despite this pseudo-independence, Great Britain has still its iron heel in the shape of its military forces, pressed on the neck of Egypt and does not intend to sacrifice the least of the interest of British imperialism in favour of the vital interest of the Egyptian people."[93] No doubt Nehru connected his Egyptian comrade's experiences of imperial oppression with his own interpretation of the British in India.

Nehru also included Western Asia or the present-day Middle East in this vision of anti-imperialist regionalism, although his representations of

---

[91] Nehru, "Report on the Brussels Congress," 280.
[92] Nehru, "Report on the Brussels Congress," 290.
[93] Pamphlet, "The Brussels Congress," League against Imperialism Secretariat, Berlin. Box 8, Folder 2, Baldwin Papers.

these countries and even the rest of the colonial world were informed by racialized stereotypes and generalizations. He described Western Asia and North Africa in the following way: "Arabs from Syria and North Africa" were "typical fighting men, who understood independence and fighting for it and little else, and were wholly untainted with the slave mentality of more intellectual races."[94] The racial homogenization of vastly diverse populations within a category of "fighting" peoples lacking "intellectual" qualities was a rather disparaging caricature. Likely, Nehru had either not been impressed by such delegates or had little time to speak with them, although this is not clear in the archival sources. Certainly, in relation to Egypt, the rest of North Africa and Western Asia had less strategic importance to colonial India, and this factored into Nehru's analysis as well.

Nehru's impressions of delegates from the rest of Africa and Latin America were even more dubious and informed by race. He described the "negro" delegates as those who "varied from the inkiest black to every shade of brown."[95] He offered a rather empathetic although brief account of his comrades of African descent: "they all bore traces of the long martyrdom which their race had suffered, more perhaps than any other people, and there was a want of hope in the dark future which faces them."[96] Aside from this brief commentary, Nehru failed to deeply engage with the "negro" issues and had limited interactions with Africans or the African diaspora. This necessitates some scrutiny. There was an impressive presence of Pan-Africanists and African delegates who came to Brussels from South Africa, Sierra Leone, Senegal, Morocco, Algeria, Tunis, and the United States. In Brussels, there was a concerted effort among the African delegates to meet separately with their African-American counterparts from the United States, who represented the National Association for the Advancement of Colored People (NAACP) and the American Negro Labor Congress.[97]

Nehru's lack of attentiveness to anti-imperialism in Africa reflected two things. First, his pragmatic structuring of anti-imperialism prioritized Asia over other regions of the world at the expense of a deeper engagement with Africa or the Pan-Africanists. Second, this privileging was underscored by the structure of the proceedings and private meetings in

---

[94] Nehru, "Report on the Brussels Congress," 280–281.   [95] Ibid.   [96] Ibid.
[97] Delegates passed a resolution for greater cooperation among Pan-Africanists and created a separate commission to examine the "Negro question." See "The Brussels Congress," Box 8, Folder 2, 21–22, Baldwin Papers.

Brussels. Sessions and resolutions were built around regional affinities – Asia, Africa and the African diaspora, Latin America, and Europe. The appearance of Africa in Nehru's anti-imperialist worldview would begin much later and only after the Italian invasion of Abyssinia in 1935, an event that placed North Africa on nearly everyone's anti-imperialist radar. It also coincided with Nehru's first encounters with like-minded and high-profile Pan-Africanists in London, including Jomo Kenyatta and George Padmore in 1936, a point addressed in Chapter 5.

Nehru made special mention of South Africa, a place with which India shared a long history of anticolonialism ever since Gandhi had launched his first political campaigns there (1893–1914). Gandhi wrote about and published widely his experiences of racial discrimination in South Africa, and conditions there had become well known among India's political elites. Nehru drew upon some pre-existing knowledge about South Africa and racism to make this statement in the report: "In these days of race hatred in South Africa . . . it was pleasing to hear the representative of the White workers giving expression to the most advanced opinions on the equality of races and of workers of all races."[98] That the white and "negro" South Africans worked together in Brussels was a point of praise for Nehru in his report, and he later earmarked the speeches of two South Africans – J. T. Guemede (Natal Native Council) and Daniel Coraine (South African Trade Union Congress) – as being of great interest for Indian publication.[99]

SOVIETS, COMMUNISTS, AND SOCIALISTS

Much like the Brussels Congress geography, Nehru's worldview appreciated the importance of the European left and Soviet Russia as bulwarks against imperialism. This was especially the case for the Soviet Union, which Nehru recognized as a bastion of anti-imperialism after the Brussels Congress. Nehru regretfully admitted in his report that he never met a Russian, but "the knowledge I have gathered from indirect sources about their activities and their intimate knowledge of external politics amazed me."[100] To illustrate, Nehru mused that, "the British politician whose job it is to know thoroughly the countries he rules probably knows far less about them than the Russian experts."[101] This admiration from

---

[98] Nehru, "Report on the Brussels Congress," 281.
[99] Nehru to Rangaswami (INC), March 16, 1927, File G29-1927, AICC.
[100] Nehru, "Report on the Brussels Congress," 289.   [101] Ibid.

afar was strengthened by a consensus in Brussels that Soviet Russia was a friend to anticolonial nationalists. According to Nehru, Soviet Russia and India shared a common foe: British imperialism. He appealed to the INC in this vein: "In so far as we are up against British imperialism we must recognize that Soviet Russia is also much against it."[102] Beyond sharing a common enemy, however, Nehru did not elaborate on communist doctrine or ideologies underpinning the Soviet regime or international communism. Indeed, his earliest impressions from Brussels in no way offered evidence of any engagement with communist ideology. Rather, they demonstrated Nehru's impressions of Russia as ones tempered by his view of the country as an anti-imperialist comrade instead of a communist nation-state.

Nehru's primary contacts with communists were with the Berlin anti-imperialists responsible for organizing the Brussels Congress. Foremost among these contacts was Chatto, who had connections with and knowledge of the communist movement in both Germany and Soviet Russia. Nehru encountered only two Indian expatriates who impressed him during his European sojourn in the late 1920s: one of them was Chatto, and the other was M. N. Roy. Roy did not attend Brussels, although he served on the Comintern's advisory committee for the congress. Chatto did attend, and quickly rose through the ranks of the LAI. By 1928, he was appointed the chief secretary of the institution. In 1927, it was not clear to most of his contemporaries whether Chatto was a committed communist or whether his links to Münzenberg and the Comintern were of a pragmatic nature. Only one biography of Chatto exists, and its author, Nirode K. Barooah, casts him as an Indian revolutionary first, who saw communism as a means to connect the colonial question to broader movements of the interwar world. Nehru agreed with this assessment: "Chatto was not, I believe, a regular Communist, but he was communistically inclined."[103] At the same time, the Comintern greatly distrusted Indian exiles in Europe, seeing them as opportunists and not true revolutionaries. A letter from Moscow to Münzenberg warned: "It is necessary to act very carefully in establishing relations with emigrant groups in Europe."[104] Another letter dated several months later named Chatto specifically as one to watch.[105] Chatto, however, sought communist party membership in August 1927, eventually becoming deeply entrenched in international

---

[102] Ibid.   [103] Nehru, *Autobiography*, 162.
[104] ECCI to Münzenberg, May 29, 1926, 542/1/3/10–11, RGASPI.
[105] ECCI to Münzenberg, July 2, 1926, 542/1/3/15–17, RGASPI.

communism and moving closer to the Soviet political agenda in the years to come.[106] Ultimately, as the Nazi Party ascended to the helm of Germany in the 1930s, Chatto left Berlin for the Soviet Union.

The Brussels Congress encounters also strengthened Nehru's contacts with the British left and convinced him of their commitment to Indian anticolonialism.[107] The British delegation to the Brussels Congress was one of the largest representations of any European country outside of Germany. It included a number of Labour Party (LP), Independent Labour Party (ILP), and Communist Party of Great Britain (CPGB) representatives. Among the notable were Lansbury, the Brussels Congress chairman and LP Member of the British Parliament; Fenner Brockway, secretary of the ILP; and Harry Pollitt, secretary of the CPGB. Trade unionists such as S. O. Davies also played a significant role in Brussels. Conspicuously absent was an English-based Indian communist named Shapurji Saklatvala, who could not attend because he was touring India at the time of the Brussels Congress. It was in India where Saklatvala was incidentally involved in a fiery exchanging with Gandhi over the course the INC should take in the future. For Saklatvala, Gandhi's politics were too moderate, gradual, and out of touch with the working-class movements. Once Saklatvala returned to Europe, however, he joined the LAI.

A more obscure British delegate, Reginald Bridgeman, would prove to be an important actor in the anti-imperialist movement and a key figure in Nehru's personal networks well into the 1930s.[108] Bridgeman had become an active anti-imperialist through his early experiences and travels as a foreign diplomat during and immediately after World War I. Stationed in Tehran (1921–1922) as part of the British Legation, Bridgeman ruffled the feathers of the British Foreign Office when he developed amicable relations with the Soviet Minister, Theodore

---

[106] He wrote to M. N. Roy notifying him of his applications to both the Communist Party of Germany and the Communist Party of India. Chatto to M. N. Roy, August 26, 1927, reprinted in *Indo-Russian Relations, 1917–1947: Select Documents from the Archives of the Russian Federation*, Part I, ed. Purabi Roy, Sobhanlal Das Gupta, and Hari Vasudevan (Calcutta: The Asiatic Society, 1999).

[107] For overviews of the British left and anti-imperialism in the 1920s, see Stephen Howe, *Anticolonialism in British Politics: The Left and the End of Empire, 1918–1964* (New York: Oxford University Press, 1993), 27–81; and Nicholas Owen, *The British Left and India: Metropolitan Anti-Imperialism, 1885–1947* (New York: Oxford University Press, 2007), 136–196. Neither attribute much attention or significance to the LAI.

[108] For a concise biographical sketch of Bridgeman and the LAI, see *Dictionary of Labour Biography*, vol. 7, ed. Joyce M. Bellamy and John Saville (London: Macmillan Press, 1984), s.v. "Reginald Bridgeman," 40–49.

Rothstein. His stay in Tehran, coupled with trips to India before and after his appointment, transformed Bridgeman into a lifelong anti-imperialist. Although his roots in anti-imperialism were grounded in Persia and India, Bridgeman's first anti-imperialist campaign was his work with the British-based Chinese Information Bureau in 1925. Like his counterparts in Germany, including Münzenberg, Bridgeman worked for the Chinese cause by organizing the dissemination of propaganda in Britain. The bureau offered Bridgeman excellent practice for his later role as the secretary of the British national section of the LAI, a role he would hold until 1933 when he became the secretary of the international LAI until 1937. The connections between Bridgeman and Nehru were not immediate, although the Englishman's central place in the British section would place the two comrades in more frequent contact in years to come.

AMERICAS AND AMERICANS

Thanks to the Brussels Congress, Nehru demonstrated for the first time an interest in matters in the Western hemisphere, and especially in US imperialism. This point necessitates more attention, since most historians and biographers wrongly suggest that Nehru had not considered in any depth the role of the United States in world affairs before the Cold War. His Brussels Congress experience in 1927 tells a different story, and he made this an important point in his reports to India: "Most of us, specially [sic] from Asia, were wholly ignorant of the problems of South America, and of how the rising imperialism of the United States, with its tremendous resources and its immunity from outside attack, is gradually taking a strangle hold to Central and South America."[109] To his Indian colleagues, Nehru added, "we are not likely to remain ignorant much longer for the great problem of the near future will be American imperialism, even more than British imperialism."[110] Despite the interest in the Americas piqued by the congress, no Latin American delegates came to play a significant role in Nehru's encounters and personal networks, although his keen awareness of American imperialism rooted in the Brussels moment continued to inform his worldview throughout the interwar period and beyond.

One American delegate stood out among anti-imperialists in Brussels. Roger Nash Baldwin became Nehru's most dependable contact in the United States during the late 1920s. Baldwin came from New York and

[109] Nehru, "Report on the Brussels Congress," 281.   [110] Ibid.

attended the Brussels Congress as a representative of the International Committee for Political Prisoners (ICPP), an international arm of the American Civil Liberties Union (ACLU). Baldwin's career in the ACLU is better known.[111] He helped found the ACLU in 1920 to protect the legal rights of US citizens. Under his leadership, the ACLU provided legal counsel to defendants in some of the most high-profile court cases in the United States, including the Scopes Trial (1925) over the right to teach evolution in schools. After World War II, Baldwin became an important international champion of human rights, and he was called upon to assist in the postwar establishment of civil liberties unions in Japan, Germany, and Austria. Baldwin's international work during the interwar years primarily focused on the ICPP, although he visited Soviet Russia and wrote a book about their civil liberties in the 1920s. His keen interest in India's independence movement predated Brussels and began during World War I when he was imprisoned as a conscientious objector. He met Indian political exiles while serving his year-long term. The Indians in prison during the Great War were accused of circulating seditious litera-ture about Britain, the American wartime ally. After his release, from 1920 onwards, Baldwin worked with Indian independence organizations in New York, and his later encounter with Nehru at the Brussels Congress in 1927 strengthened his commitment to and contacts with the INC.

Through the course of the meetings at Brussels, Nehru and Baldwin began cultivating a professional partnership that would have lasting con-sequences for both. Beyond the general concern of anti-imperialism, the two delegates considered the issue of political prisoners in India and what Baldwin and the ICPP might do to help. Baldwin had already sought to contribute financially to a fund for Indian political prisoners before 1927, but he had yet to find the proper channel to do so. Although Nehru did not mention Baldwin personally in his report, he wrote a special letter from Brussels on February 11, 1927, to the INC general secretary to introduce Baldwin as "one of the most courageous and effective workers in the United States."[112] Nehru asked the INC to facilitate a process in which Baldwin and the ICPP and ACLU could contribute funds to protect the civil liberties of political prisoners in India. He added in conclusion, "I have no doubt that you and the Congress will cordially welcome American help, not merely because of its monetary value but specially

---

[111] Robert C. Cottrell, *Roger Nash Baldwin and the American Civil Liberties Union* (New York: Columbia University Press, 2000).
[112] Jawaharlal Nehru to Rangaswami Iyengar, February 11, 1927, *SWJN*, vol. 2, 277.

[sic] because it is an expression of the goodwill of friends in America."[113] During the decades after Brussels, Baldwin and Nehru developed a close professional and personal relationship, exchanging ideas, information, and impressions of the changing world around them.[114]

CONCLUSION

The Brussels Congress opened up new international spaces from which to contest empire, and it profoundly shaped the ways Nehru conceptualized anticolonial resistance in India and worldwide. The proceedings specifically challenged the fundamental premises of European hegemony in the prewar and interwar world. It debunked the civilizing mission by arguing that the colonized and the Soviet Union would only enrich the spiritual and material development of the world. It articulated a desirability for leaders of the working class, of both communist and socialist allegiances, to join in solidarity with nationalists in the colonies and others suffering at the hands of capitalist classes and imperialist powers. It recast the threat of war, emblematic of the anxieties of many during the interwar period, as a danger posed by imperialists and one that needed to be met with a coordinated anti-imperialist resistance. Finally, and perhaps most profoundly important to Nehru, the anti-imperialist discourse remapped the world along the fault lines of capitalism-imperialism. The colonies in Asia, Africa, and Latin America would be joined by the anti-imperialist partnership of the Soviet Union. This geography of anti-imperialism continued to inspire the hopes and aspirations of a generation of anticolonial activists such as Nehru for years to come.

The Brussels Congress ultimately widened Nehru's conceptualization of anticolonial resistance, as well as expanded his address book of comrades he could call upon for guidance and support. Nehru's experiences enabled him to consider the struggle in India as interconnected with other movements for working-class equality and political independence. His geography of anti-imperialist resistance came to include activists from places as diverse and distant as China, Indonesia, Egypt, Mexico, the United States, and Soviet Russia. It also included connections to the Indian diaspora in Berlin and metropolitan partners on the British left. On the other hand, the Brussels Congress provided a working knowledge

---

[113] Ibid.
[114] Roger Baldwin, "Reflections of Jawaharlal Nehru," undated 1967, Box 7, Folder 30, Baldwin Papers.

of imperialism beyond the confines of India and the British Empire, and it also offered a strong criticism of the United States as an imperialist adversary for India to fear.

Nehru could draw upon his anti-imperialist worldview and networks of comrades throughout the ebbs and flows of the Indian nationalist movement. Such ideas and networks would also evolve over time as the international arena of politics changed dramatically in the late 1920s and 1930s. But before Nehru returned to India to make use of his broader understanding of Indian nationalism and the anti-imperialist world, he spent several months traveling across Europe in the service of a new international institution: the LAI. Nehru's League experiences would sharpen and strengthen his burgeoning worldview, while also catapulting him to the upper echelons of the LAI's leadership in the months after Brussels.

2

The Making of the League against Imperialism, 1927

In the months after the Brussels Congress and before his departure for India in December 1927, Nehru traveled the European continent in the service of the LAI. As an executive committee member, Nehru was a key architect of the LAI. He took part in two executive committee meetings in Amsterdam (March) and Cologne (August), and made several informal visits to the provisional secretariats in Berlin and Paris to oversee the organization of the headquarters. By the time of his departure from Europe, Nehru had left an indelible mark on the construction of the LAI. On his role in the LAI, he remarked: "We have occasionally to take risks in building a big organization. Let us take them and not be afraid of them. So far as I am concerned I shall always be glad to be of every service to [the League]."[1]

The "risks" in building the LAI in 1927 were many, and Nehru's optimistic appraisal reflected his growing commitment and "service" to anti-imperialist internationalism in the wake of the Brussels Congress. In the weeks and months after Brussels, the LAI faced a dire financial crisis, internal conflict between socialists and communists, and heavy colonial surveillance by European governments. Despite this turbulent beginning, Nehru and his comrades hung their aspirations and hopes on the possibilities for solidarity and collective action that the LAI promised. By the time Nehru sailed from Europe to India, he had become one of the LAI's strongest voices in the colonial world.

This chapter examines Nehru's years in Europe to demonstrate several significant points. First, throughout 1927 Nehru offered the LAI financial and administrative guidance that was unrivaled by any other colonial representative. The British attributed great significance to Nehru's anti-imperialist work and tracked it closely. The official stance on the LAI,

[1] Nehru to Chatto, December 11, 1927, File 16, Chattopadhyaya Papers, P.C. Joshi Archives, Jawaharlal Nehru University, New Delhi, India.

according to British intelligence reports, was unmistakable: "There can be no question that the League aims at upsetting the existing form of government in India, as elsewhere, its very name is in itself a sufficient indication of its object."[2] Because of his League connections, the intelligence agents concluded in early 1928 that Nehru, "more than any other leader ... may be considered responsible for the comparatively close liaison established during the last few years between the Congress [INC] and political groups abroad."[3]

Additionally, Nehru's endeavors for the LAI in 1927 – in Berlin, Paris, Amsterdam, Cologne, and Moscow – crystallized his burgeoning anti-imperialist worldview rooted in the Brussels Congress. While the inaugural meeting in Brussels offered a transformative moment of encounter for Nehru, his months serving the LAI in Europe produced a more nuanced conceptualization of the relationship between India and the world: one which built upon the formative ideas in Brussels about international comradeship, the link between nationalism and the struggle of the proletariat, and Nehru's notion of an anti-imperialist geography of the world. These ideas were strengthened by engagements with the smaller group of comrades within the executive committee, as well his travels and interactions with anti-imperialists across Europe. The LAI even facilitated Nehru's brief trip to the Soviet Union in late 1927. Most notably, Nehru strengthened personal and professional relationships with comrades in the LAI, such as Chatto and Baldwin, while he also met for the first time Madame Sun Yat-Sen, who would serve as his primary contact in China. These comrades would become significant sources of inspiration for Nehru as he returned to India to engage in a prolonged and difficult anticolonial struggle in the late 1920s and after.

At the same time, his experiences on the executive committee of the LAI also offered Nehru profound lessons about the "risks" and limitations of collective action against imperialism. There emerged clear contradictions and tensions inherent within a movement that homogenized and universalized anti-imperialism despite the fundamental and doctrinal differences between its constituent members. In particular, Nehru personally witnessed debates between socialists and communists in the LAI that led to visceral attacks against one another. Such fragile alliances between socialists and

---

[2] "Refusal of a passport to Mme. Sun Yat Sen," File L/P&J/12/268, Indian Political Intelligence files on the League against Imperialism, Asia, Pacific and Africa Collections, India Office Records (hereafter IPI).

[3] "Visit of Pandit Jawahar Lal Nehru," File L/P&J/12/292, IPI [author's emphasis].

communists in the name of anti-imperialism would be challenged as the enthusiasm from Brussels waned and the discussions about institution-building began. In the case of the British national section of the LAI, alliances between LP leaders and communists quickly fell apart. Nehru had been an observer to the early meetings of the British LAI and beheld firsthand the divisive politics of working-class movements in the metropole. Even so, as this chapter concludes, his conceptualization of international anti-imperialism grounded in the LAI maintained a pre-eminent place in Nehru's worldview despite his knowledge of the limitations and risks inherent in such a movement.

THE INSTITUTIONALIZATION OF ANTI-IMPERIALISM

The executive committee of the LAI met for the first time in Amsterdam at the end of March 1927. On the eve of the meeting, Nehru wrote to his colleagues in India that the Amsterdam proceedings would go a long way in building a permanent organization and structure for the LAI. He hoped that the LAI, like the Brussels Congress, would be "really representative and not dominated by a particular clique."[4] His letter reflected a widely held concern that the LAI might become "merely a tool to further the objects" of the Communist International since its organizers in Berlin were party members. Nehru was hopeful this was not the case and stressed to the INC that the LAI accommodated communists, socialists, and anticolonial nationalists. He concluded, "The Executive Committee has all interests represented and it will be difficult to convert it into a mere off-shoot of the Communist International." He added that the "presence of Lansbury as chairman also indicates that the cooperation of the non-communist elements is considered essential."[5]

A "really representative" and careful balance of "all interests" was no simple task for the LAI in 1927. While the Brussels Congress had been an important site to develop common anti-imperialist platforms, despite critical and often fundamental differences among delegates, the institutionalization of the movement was a much more complicated matter. Already in March, Willi Münzenberg and his Berlin colleagues began plotting for greater power for communists within the LAI. In a letter to Moscow, Münzenberg revealed his plans for "strict control" over the LAI

---

[4] Letter to Rangaswami Iyengar and INC Working Committee, March 26, 1927, *SWJN*, vol. 2, 315.

[5] Ibid.

by establishing the secretariat under his supervision in Berlin and employing secretaries who were Comintern agents on Moscow's payroll.[6] Labor and socialist leaders within the LAI were not unaware of the communist ambitions of Münzenberg and his Berlin colleagues, and the former's cooperation remained tenuous in the months after Brussels.

Certainly, Münzenberg and others had designs for greater power within the LAI; however, the strong presence and leadership of noncommunists such as Nehru within the executive committee, and their critical contributions to the startup of the LAI, diminished the opportunity for "strict control" by communists. Much of this history of the LAI has been lost by narratives that focus solely on communist sources in Berlin and Moscow.[7] However, the sources from Nehru and other noncommunists reveal a more complex story of the LAI and its possibilities for solidarities that transcended the political and geographic borders of anti-imperialist internationalism.

The early months of the LAI were noteworthy for two reasons. First, the meetings and negotiations within the executive committee ensured communist and noncommunist parity. Executives such as Nehru charted a path for an institution that was flexible, inclusive, and non-partisan. Thus, this period of institution-building represents a moment when the trajectory of the LAI was up for grabs and not simply dominated by communists from the start. Secondly, Nehru emerged from this preliminary stage of institution-building as a significant leader in his own right. His agency in the making of the LAI was critical during the first turbulent months of the institution's existence.

At the Amsterdam meeting in March, Nehru joined a diverse cohort of colleagues. The Brussels delegation elected the executive committee and officers, who collectively represented a careful balance of socialists and communists alongside their counterparts from the colonies. High-profile socialists such as George Lansbury of the British LP and Edo Fimmen of the Amsterdam International Federation of Trade Unions (AIFTU) authenticated this balance. The representatives from the colonial world included Nehru as well as Mohamed Hatta of Perhimpunan Indonesia, Liau Hansin of the Executive of the KMT and Comintern, Chan Kuen of Chinese Trade Union Association, and Manuel Ugarte of the Argentine

---

[6] Münzenberg to Secretary of the Comintern, March 11, 1927, 542/1/7/159–160, RGASPI (German).

[7] The only study of the LAI that extends its history beyond the Brussels Congress is Petersson, *Willi Münzenberg*. It is a useful starting point, but the emphasis on communist sources neglects the important role of non-communists such as Nehru who hardly figure in his analysis.

nationalist movement. The communist members within the executive committee included the Brussels Congress founder, Willi Münzenberg; Henri Barbusse of the French Communist Party; and Alfons Goldschmidt of the International Workers' Aid. A further addition to the committee was Roger Baldwin of the ACLU, who served as a substitute representative for elected committee member Lamine Senghor, a Senegalese nationalist and brother of the more famous Léopold Sédar Senghor, later the president of postcolonial Senegal.[8] Lamine Senghor was a delegate to Brussels, but, after the congress and the wide circulation of his speeches there, the French authorities arrested him in Paris, where he remained at the time of the Amsterdam meeting.

The executives first had to consider the immediate and urgent task of procuring funds to launch the LAI. Münzenberg spent lavishly on the Brussels Congress, and the LAI treasury began with a negative balance thanks to the debts he accumulated in February. The situation was so dire that the first executive meeting took place at Fimmen's private residence to avoid further expenditures. A letter by Münzenberg to the Comintern articulated the dilemma. He complained that "the entire [LAI] office [was] now only a single man." He added, "We have even had to adjust the copies of important materials, because we could not even muster 100 marks for these purposes."[9] Münzenberg pleaded for more cash from the Comintern to repay debts from Brussels and supply fresh funds for the LAI, but, as historian Fredrik Petersson notes, the Comintern's responses to his requests, from February until June 1927, were characterized by "silence and lack of money from Moscow."[10] Instead, the noncommunist members of the executive committee, not the Comintern, kept the LAI afloat in the initial months of financial uncertainty.[11] Nehru even ensured that the INC contributed 100 pounds sterling, a hefty donation for the time, to the LAI in 1927 and again in 1928.[12]

---

[8] On Lamine Senghor, see Edwards, *The Practice of Diaspora.*
[9] Münzenberg to Secretary of the Comintern, March 11, 1927, 542/1/7/159–160, RGASPI (German).
[10] Petersson, *Willi Münzenberg*, 364.
[11] Roger Baldwin contributed $1,000, while Fimmen and Goldschmidt contributed $500 each. The KMT and Egyptian members promised more funds as well, although it is unclear whether the LAI received them. For financial details, see Nehru, Note to the Working Committee, April 4, 1927, *SWJN*, vol. 2, 316–323; and Minutes of the Executive Council Meeting of the League against Imperialism, March 29–30, 1927, 542/1/12/3–6, RGASPI.
[12] Beyond institutional contributions, Nehru also convinced the INC to pay his European travel expenses in connection with the League against Imperialism. See his correspondence with the INC general secretary Rangaswami Iyengar, File 127(ii) 1927, AICC.

The early agenda items in Amsterdam were ones easily agreed upon and included protests against imperialism in China and Nicaragua, as well as against French metropolitan repression of anti-imperialist activism in Paris. In particular, the executive committee issued telegrams to the French president protesting Lamine Senghor's arrest and to the US president protesting American military occupation of Nicaragua.[13] The situation in China, however, dominated the early sessions. Only days before the Amsterdam meeting, news arrived in Europe of another military skirmish between the British and American navy vessels and the Chinese National Revolutionary Army (CNRA), led by Chiang Kai-shek and supported by the KMT and Chinese communists. The CNRA captured the city of Nanjing, a treaty port with dense populations of Britons and Americans, while the looting of foreign consulates and residences followed. British and American navies responded by bombarding the city to protect foreign interests and lives. Hostilities ended on March 27, just two days before the Amsterdam meeting commenced. Liau offered a briefing on the "Nanjing incident," although he admitted that reliable information from China was slow to arrive. Lansbury promised that the British LP had already mobilized a protest campaign in parliament and demonstrations throughout London against the latest conflict. The LAI executives collectively resolved to send a telegram of protest to Britain.[14]

There is little doubt that China retained the spotlight of the LAI's early anti-imperialist program. Münzenberg acknowledged this fixation by arguing in the Amsterdam meeting that China was unquestionably "the center of the colonial liberation movement and our [LAI] action."[15] The primary focus for the LAI's further work was the support for an anti-imperialist conference in Hankou, China. The conference had been devised by the Brussels delegation, and despite the recent military skirmish in China, the LAI pressed onward with plans for the meeting. According to the executive committee minutes, the most urgent matter was to ensure that India and other Asian colonies would send strong delegations to Hankou.[16] Nehru expressed serious doubts that the British colonial government would approve visas for travel to China, but he supported the idea in principle.

---

[13] From 1912 to 1933, the US occupied Nicaragua in order to prevent the construction of a canal linking the Pacific Ocean to the Gulf of Mexico.

[14] Minutes of the Executive Council Meeting of the League against Imperialism, March 29–30, 1927, 542/1/12/3–6, RGASPI.

[15] Ibid.   [16] Ibid.

As fate would have it, the Hankou conference would never come to fruition, since drastic shifts in Chinese politics were imminent in April of 1927. Only two weeks after the executive meeting, the alliance between the nationalist forces of the KMT under Chiang on the one hand, and the Chinese Communist Party (CCP) and trade unionists on the other, disintegrated into open hostility and conflict. On April 12, Chiang marched his military into Shanghai, where strikes and communist activities against foreign imperialists had paralyzed the city for nearly a year. Rather than honor the KMT and communist alliance, Chiang defected from the united front and massacred thousands of suspected communists and trade unionists. He combined his forces with another faction of the KMT based in Wuhan under the leadership of Wang Jingwei, and together the two forces brutally suppressed communists and eliminated their presence from major cities in China by December 1927. Chiang's coup had embarrassed Stalin and the Comintern, whose policies were to support the united front in China under the umbrella of the KMT as late as 1928. But it also proved problematic for the LAI, which had focused so intensely on the united front against imperialism in China. Indeed, the March executive meeting would be the last time that a strong consensus on anti-imperialist policy in China emerged.

The details of the LAI organization became the next and most dominant issue for the rest of the sessions, and Nehru provided a strong and instrumental voice for noncommunists in the debates. A chief concern was a resolution on membership rules. Because the League brought together activists from a wide spectrum of political affiliations, some sympathetic to anticolonial nationalist resistance but by no means active in the struggle, the institution had to be accommodative and flexible in its membership. Membership rules also dictated the fundamental question: Who was an anti-imperialist? In Amsterdam, few parameters were set to exclude those seeking membership as an anti-imperialist. Nehru had been a primary advocate for inclusive membership rules. In particular, he thought that the INC might welcome the League's anti-imperialist message; however, it would not accept the socialist- and communist-inspired agenda. To address the issue, Nehru advocated for a two-tiered structure for membership based on *affiliation* or *association*. Affiliated organizations or individuals were bound by all of the League programs and policies, including both the socialist and anticolonial nationalist creed, while associated members were linked to the League to a lesser extent and could profess cooperation without toeing the official League line. As Nehru explained in a report to the INC: "I pressed for this rule chiefly in the interests of the Indian Congress and I feel that the Congress can take advantage of it without in any way committing itself to anything it does not approve of."[17]

Beyond the complexities of bringing together nationalists and working-class leaders, this more accommodative membership structure allowed flexibility for socialists and communists to work together. The mistrust between the two camps was deep and historical. The roots of such tensions can be found in the fundamental antagonisms between the Labor Socialist International (LSI), or Second International, and the Comintern, or Third International. Both the LSI and the Comintern professed to be descendants of the First International (1864–1876), founded by Karl Marx and Friedrich Engels to unite workers internationally for a worldwide struggle against capitalism. The Second International (1889–1914) established a loose federation of socialist organizations from across Europe, although its largest section was the German Social Democratic Party. Key points of contention emerged between members of the Second International, espe-cially over the means of attaining socialist change. One camp (often labeled revisionists) sought gradual or evolutionary socialist reforms within exist-ing capitalist states, while the other considered revolution and the over-throw of the existing state a necessary prerequisite for change. When World War I broke out, the divisions between these camps reached fever pitch. Reformist sections from France, Germany, and Britain backed their respec-tive nations' capitalist classes in the war, while revolutionaries called for international solidarity in opposition to the war. The split led the revolu-tionary forces to gravitate toward the Third International or Comintern, founded by Lenin in 1920 after the Bolshevik Revolution. The reformists regrouped after the war and formed the LSI. Deep animosities and distrust between the LSI and the Comintern persisted throughout the interwar years.

The specter of these tensions loomed over all of the meetings of the LAI in 1927. Already, the LSI saw the LAI as nothing more than a communist front organization. Even more alarming for the LSI, the Comintern, through the vehicle of the LAI, had taken up the colonial question on a grandiose scale and reached out to the colonized in a way that the LSI had not yet done. On the other hand, Münzenberg intended to use socialists within the LAI as a means to demonstrate its non-political and non-partisan composition. In letters to Moscow, he also expressed anxiety about his inability to control the LAI and his fear that socialists might

<hr>

[17] Nehru, "Note for the Working Committee," April 4, 1927, *SWJN*, vol. 2, 322.

usurp power and turn nationalists from the colonies away from commun-ism. Nehru was specifically mentioned in Münzenberg's March letter to the Comintern as a nationalist susceptible to the influence of British socialists from the LP.[18] Nehru had already noted these tensions immedi-ately after the Brussels Congress, and feared that "British Labour as well as some other important trade unions would keep away."[19]

The executive committee worked in earnest to preserve equilibrium between socialists and communists by several means. The financial back-ing of key noncommunists was one way of ensuring leadership for the LAI that was not dictated entirely by the Comintern. Of course, the member-ship rules also provided that neither camp would be asked to follow the other's party doctrine as an associate of the LAI. Thirdly, the selection of LAI executive officers acted as a way to maintain equity. Two noncom-munists, George Lansbury and Edo Fimmen, served as chairman and vice-chairman respectively. They shared leadership with the secretaries, two Comintern agents named Liau Hansin and Louis Gibarti. Thus, a semblance of balance between communists and noncommunists existed in even the highest echelons of the LAI.

The League also had to connect anti-imperialists across the globe, which posed a geographical challenge on an unprecedented scale. By the end of 1927, self-funded national sections of the League had already begun work in Argentina, Brazil, China, Cuba, Ecuador, France, Germany, Great Britain, Holland, Ireland, Japan, Mexico, Nicaragua, Palestine, Philippines, Puerto Rico, San Salvador, South Africa, the United States, and Uruguay.[20] Connecting these sections, through propaganda and correspondence, pre-sented an issue. Colonial censorship was one ongoing problem – although in the case of India, LAI publications arrived in the subcontinent after the British authorities intercepted, copied, and forwarded them to their desig-nated recipients. Another challenge was the linguistic diversity of members. This was addressed in a number of ways. First, the central secretariat initially planned to produce documents in three European languages: English, French, and German. Moreover, the executive committee resolved to establish linguistic departments within the secretariat dedicated to printing ephemera in several non-European languages: Spanish for Latin

---

[18] Münzenberg to Secretary of the Comintern, March 11, 1927, 542/1/7/159–160, RGASPI (German).
[19] Nehru, Brussels Report, *SWJN*, vol. 2, 287.
[20] For a comprehensive list of League against Imperialism members and national branches, see File 2, LAI, IISH.

America, Arabic for Northern Africa and Western Asia, and Chinese and Hindustani for the "Eastern countries."[21] Notably, the non-Western language departments were never actually formed, likely because the treasury never budgeted for printing costs in more than three languages or the personnel for specialized departments. Hence, European languages became the printed standard for the LAI, despite its aspirations to use languages native to the colonial world.

Selecting a location for the secretariat was another pre-eminent concern. The provisional center was located in Berlin, where the organizers of the Brussels Congress resided, but the executive committee intended to relocate the main office to Paris. Paris had been an epicenter for anti-imperialist activities before the Brussels Congress, and French communists, socialists, trade unionists, and revolutionaries from the colonies had worked in close alliance before 1927.[22] At the March meeting, however, relocation was deemed impossible after Senghor's arrest for his Brussels Congress speeches. This atmosphere forced the executives to produce a shortlist of alternatives: London, Brussels, Amsterdam, and Berlin respectively. The resolution at the first executive meeting was that a smaller subcommittee would work on a relocation plan. Nehru recognized the paramount importance of the secretariat and volunteered to lead this subcommittee. Other volunteers included Lansbury and Fimmen. Although not a part of the group, Roger Baldwin also became a close confidant of Nehru's, and the two were perhaps the most instrumental in shaping the progress of the LAI center in the months following the Amsterdam meeting.

In April, Nehru and Baldwin met privately in Switzerland on several occasions to discuss the state of the Berlin office and formulate a comprehensive plan for improving the secretariat. From his talks with Baldwin, Nehru produced a scathing 22-point critique of the Berlin headquarters on behalf of the executive committee. On May 3, it was sent to both League secretaries and Edo Fimmen in Amsterdam. Baldwin had endorsed the letter wholeheartedly, and wrote to Nehru that it was a "more patient and thorough job than I would have done," but "between us I think we have said all there is to say."[23] The Nehru–Baldwin critique ranged from criticism of the secretariat's reports on the Brussels Congress and the Amsterdam meeting to the larger issues of the general focus and direction

---

[21] Nehru, Note to the Working Committee, April 4, 1927, *SWJN*, vol. 2, 316–323.
[22] Goebel, *Anti-Imperialist Metropolis*.
[23] Baldwin to Nehru, May 7, 1927, Box 8, Folder 2, Baldwin Papers.

of League work. The letter opened by stating that "all is not well with the League and we ought to wake up to this fact and take speedy action to put matters right."[24] However, Nehru wrote: "I feel strongly that the League supplies a real want and it can develop into a powerful organization ... [Nevertheless] no number of pious resolutions, fervent appeals and exaggerated statements will do us much good or bring helpers and associates if the substance behind them is lacking."[25]

Nehru's criticism covered a gamut of issues. He characterized the secretariat reports as inaccurate, poorly translated, and slow to be distributed, all pointing to what he perceived as the "confusion that must exist" in the Berlin office. He lamented that the LAI propaganda was "exaggerated," and that no news from China, the critical site of the anti-imperialist struggle, had been circulated. Among the most revealing and problematic issues was his accusation that the secretaries had kept the executive committee "in the dark" by failing to produce financial statements after the Amsterdam meeting. He argued that it was "impossible for any [executive] committee to work or exercise any control if it is treated in this way."[26]

The letter spoke directly to the crux of the matter: Who had the authority to "exercise control" over the LAI? The governing body was the executive committee, a well-balanced group of communists, socialists, and nationalists. Yet, the secretaries in Berlin had the most substantial duties of carrying out LAI work on a daily basis. The archival record affirms that their agenda differed widely from that of the other executive committee members. The Berlin office staff – Münzenberg, Gibarti, and Liau – operated under the directives and party line of the Comintern rather than the executives. There was little doubt in anyone's mind that the three in the secretariat were communists, but the extent to which they involved the Comintern in administrative and policy decisions for the LAI was concealed until much later. At the time, the provisional secretariat in Berlin shared office space with Münzenberg's other organization, the WIR, an institution with strong ties to the Comintern.

The power to construct the meaning of anti-imperialism often rested in the hands of those in the secretariat producing LAI literature and managing networks. Much was at stake in the location and personnel decisions. A great responsibility fell on the secretariat to collect and translate information coming in from League members across the world, and also to recast such localized pieces as part of a cohesive, anti-imperialist discourse. Once

---

[24] Nehru to Gibarti, May 3, 1927, Box 8, Folder 2, Baldwin Papers.   [25] Ibid.   [26] Ibid.

functioning properly, the League press service would reach some of the most influential movements of the interwar period, notably the INC, but also Perhimpunan Indonesia (Indonesian National Independence Party), the Kuomintang Party in China, the Wafd Party in Egypt, the Egyptian Nationalist Party, the Sinn Fein Irish Republican movement, the ACLU, the NAACPs and labor organizations such as the Confederation Generale du Travail Unitaire (CGTU) in France, South African Trade Union Congress, and the AITUC.

The Nehru–Baldwin letter addressed concerns about the Berlin personnel. Both Liau and Gibarti were known communists who received income from Moscow to fund their activities in Berlin. Liau primarily worked on Chinese propaganda for the LAI, while Gibarti ran the day-to-day operations. Gibarti's command of five European languages made him an obvious choice for the secretary position, although most LAI members were skeptical of his organizational skills and trustworthiness. Much later, Baldwin remembered Gibarti as "slippery," a character who operated with "carelessness and manipulation."[27] He also recalled that Nehru distrusted Gibarti even more and thought he was a man of "deliberate deception."[28] Even his closest ally, Münzenberg, thought Gibarti should be "strictly controlled" by the party to prevent him from instigating political intrigue wherever he worked.[29] Despite his concerns, Münzenberg left LAI functions primarily to Gibarti.

The Nehru–Baldwin letter also critiqued the focus of the LAI since Brussels. Gibarti and Münzenberg concentrated on preliminary plans to sponsor the anti-imperialist conference in Hankou, the assurance that the British section of the LAI would be established, and the development of new national sections across the colonized world. Aside from these plans, the secretariat focused on propaganda work, a specialty of Münzenberg's. These projects were radically different from the pragmatic aims of Baldwin and Nehru, who sought to build a strong international center, plan conferences, and develop strong national sections rather than produce and disseminate propaganda. Nehru caustically remarked on this divergence in his letter: "I almost suspect that some people imagine that if a sufficient quantity of printed and type-written matter is let loose on the world it will automatically result in strong organization." He professed to

---

[27] Roger Baldwin, "Reflections of Jawaharlal Nehru," undated 1967, Box 7, Folder 30, 4, Baldwin Papers.
[28] Ibid.   [29] Petersson, *Willi Münzenberg*, 306. Evidence is in file 542/1/7/170, RGASPI.

hold no such illusions, and that it was essential the headquarters be put "in order immediately."[30]

The letter revisited the idea of shifting the secretariat to Paris. By May, it seemed possible to resume anti-imperialist activities in France after the release of Senghor. Nehru thought Paris was "the greatest international centre and [had] a tradition and atmosphere which no other city possesse[d]."[31] Most importantly, both Nehru and Baldwin were staying in Paris throughout the entire month of May, and they could steal some control of the secretariat from their Berlin communist counterparts. Indeed, the two intended to personally oversee the relocation and the implementation of executive orders within the secretariat. In response to Nehru's letter, Baldwin reiterated to his Indian colleague: "I only hope the office will be moved while you are there, to get some of the benefit of yours."[32]

The push from the Nehru–Baldwin critique proved significant enough for a compromise to emerge between the Berlin secretaries and the wishes of the executive committee. The Paris office opened later in May, only a few weeks after the Nehru–Baldwin letter. It shared status as an international center of the LAI with the existing Berlin office, which remained open and active as well. Gibarti retained his position as secretary throughout 1927, but he shifted to Paris to spearhead the opening of the second office. Liau stayed in Berlin, and Chatto began to take on a more active and supportive role in the LAI office. Chatto, like Gibarti, was a polyglot, but he had an unmatched ability to organize and administrate institutions. Chatto would become indispensable by the end of 1927, and he assumed the official title of the LAI secretary in January 1928. Despite the relocation efforts and Nehru's hard work, the Paris office ultimately had a short shelf life. French colonial authorities prevented any meaningful work from being carried out there, while a meager budget could not sustain two international centers. The departures of Nehru and Baldwin from Europe shortly thereafter had also enabled the Berlin office to reclaim control of the LAI secretariat. By 1928, Berlin was the only surviving international office of the LAI. Even so, Nehru and Baldwin's success in relocating the secretariat, even if temporarily, demonstrated the importance of noncommunist voices in the making of the LAI.

---

[30] Nehru to Gibarti, May 3, 1927, Box 8, Folder 2, Baldwin Papers.
[31] Nehru to Fimmen, May 3, 1927, with enclosed copy of letter to Gibarti cited above. Box 8, Folder 2, Baldwin Papers.
[32] Baldwin to Nehru, May 7, 1927, Box 8, Folder 2, Baldwin Papers.

The future of the LAI appeared to be promising by the summer months of 1927, but changes would soon upset the institution's balance between communists and noncommunists. In June 1927, the Comintern established an anti-imperialist commission in Moscow to oversee the work of the LAI more directly. This commission resolved to send directives to the Berlin secretaries for the policies and future plans of the LAI, as well as a monthly stipend to support the expenses of the secretariat.[33] The direction and funds were a striking reversal from Moscow's silence since the Brussels Congress. As a consequence, the anti-imperialist commission began to chart a new course for the LAI, one tied more closely to Moscow gold. The salaries for the secretaries and the operating budget would be secured through financial channels running from Moscow to Berlin. In addition, directives from Moscow called for the LAI to concentrate its efforts on releasing propaganda decrying the crisis in China and British aggression in the Far East and against the Soviet Union. Neither initiative spoke to the organizational work of the LAI or the concerns of the wider colonial world.

With this new turn of events, the Comintern's anti-imperialist commission and the executive committee emerged as dual masters of the LAI secretariat. The shift presented a complex dilemma that was never fully resolved. In principle, the LAI executive committee arbitrated the institution's fate and finances, but the Comintern secured the financial and directional control of the secretariat in June 1927. Initially, the Comintern's financial takeover did not pose a serious problem since the two entities were not entirely oppositional. The executives and the Comintern both sought to maintain a robust membership of communists, socialists, and nationalists, albeit for different reasons. Perhaps more importantly, the Comintern leaders had clear ambitions to use the LAI to foster greater contacts with anticolonial nationalists such as Nehru. Since Brussels, Nehru had become one of the most coveted prizes for Münzenberg and the Comintern. Communists in the LAI were to work with him to "establish connection with the prominent men in the Left Wing of the Indian National Congress."[34] That Nehru also sought to connect with anti-imperialists abroad regardless of their fidelities to communism only strengthened the potential for this collaborative relationship to flourish in 1927.

[33] Resolutions of the Anti-Imperialist Commission, Moscow, June 15, 1927, 495/3/18/136–139, RGASPI.
[34] This resolution was passed by a small committee of the executive committee of the Comintern based on Katayama's reports from Brussels, February 28, 1927, 495/60/115/5, RGASPI.

The significance of the compromise over the secretariat location and the power of the noncommunists within the executive committee to shape the LAI in its formative stages should not be overlooked. It provided evidence that the League was not communist-dominated, and its location, discourse, and trajectory remained up for grabs in 1927. Even with additional funds flowing into the LAI treasury from Moscow, the secretariat and executive committee continued to work across party lines for the anti-imperialist cause. Moreover, Nehru emerged as a principal figure in the LAI as it weathered turbulent months of financial crisis and organizational uncertainty. In doing so, Nehru became a high-profile leader within the League in 1927, and his personal work on the secretariat paved the way for a more professional and organized center for anti-imperialist collaboration.

NEHRU AND HIS COMRADES AGAINST IMPERIALISM

As the League blossomed in the summer months of 1927, Nehru grew convinced that the time was ripe to make a stronger case for INC association to the LAI. Over the course of the summer, Nehru wrote more persuasive notes to the INC working committee that marginalized the organizational uncertainties within the LAI and emphasized the possibilities of anti-imperialist internationalism. No doubt he had reservations about the capability of the LAI staff and the intentions of communists within the institution, but he reserved these. In April, he wrote: "I am clearly of opinion that the Congress should take any risk, if risk there is, and associate itself with the League."[35] He underscored the importance of the INC to engage with the wider world, especially in the context of the growing war danger. Reciting a now-familiar warning that Britain would instigate a war in China and the Soviet Union to protect imperialist interests, Nehru then stressed that India could not, "without peril to [itself] permit events to march to their tragic conclusion without trying [its] best to shape them." He concluded that "These events will not wait, nor will the world remain in a state of suspended animation, in order to give us time to settle our differences and create an 'atmosphere' for action."[36] Consequently, the INC working committee resolved in May 1927 to associate with the LAI and remit funds to support the institution.

---

[35] Nehru, Note to the Working Committee, April 4, 1927, *SWJN*, vol. 2, 316–323.
[36] Ibid., 322–323.

His letter to India emblemized a deeper and richer commitment to anti-imperialism that was emerging as Nehru traveled Europe in the service of the LAI. While the Brussels Congress had introduced Nehru to many ideas about the relationship between anticolonial resistance and internationalism, the LAI strengthened his dedication to the anti-imperialist cause. In particular, the LAI executive work provided fruitful opportunities for Nehru to continue meeting and collaborating with like-minded comrades. Beyond these meetings, however, the LAI also began producing a steady stream of propaganda and literature that constructed an imagined community of anti-imperialism. Through his encounters, Nehru came to be integrated into this community, as well as a network of comrades with a shared worldview.

The LAI literature was one avenue in which Nehru came to be integrated into anti-imperialism. In reading these circulars, Nehru strengthened his knowledge about imperialism in other parts of the world, while also recognizing his work at the national and international levels as interdependent. The League circulars aimed to recast the local struggles of workers and anticolonial activists as an interconnected part of a worldwide campaign. The common issues of oppression, resistance, and emancipation were at stake for Leaguers across the twentieth-century world, and the LAI publications began to provide materials reminding Nehru and his comrades that they were not alone in their struggles for national and social justice.

By June 1927, the LAI secretariat began to produce a steady flow of anti-imperialist circulars for its members. These earliest texts were not periodicals with essays and polemic propaganda, but updates from around the anti-imperialist world and from the secretariat. Of course, the development of the international office was one of the headlines in the first circular dated June 15, 1927. In it was the announcement that the LAI office in Paris had opened. The second headline congratulated Nehru for his fine work in encouraging the INC working committee to consider association with the League and his dedication to sending favorable publicity on the Brussels Congress to India.[37] Other news underscored the activities of the LAI members across the world in places such as Dutch Java and Sumatra, France, Britain, Egypt, Indonesia, and Latin America.[38] Collectively, these

---

[37] There is no central archive for LAI publications. For this particular piece, see League against Imperialism Circular Letter (from Berlin office), June 15, 1927, Copy intercepted and archived by the British intelligence, L/P&J/12/265, IPI.

[38] League against Imperialism Circular Letter (from Paris Office), July 20, 1927, 542/1/10/15, RGASPI.

brief reports on anti-imperialism highlighted the links between such diverse places where members contributed to global anti-imperialism.

China became a central focus of the literature. The press service dated July 15, 1927, for example, ran a story on the British government's refusal of passports to Indian medical volunteers seeking to provide humanitarian aid in China.[39] In July, Liau Hansin released a special report from the LAI secretariat drafted by Chan Kuen, the Brussels delegate representing the All-Chinese Trade Union Federation, who had returned to China in May 1927. Chan provided a firsthand account of the Northern Expedition of Chiang: "The Chinese bourgeoisie with General Chiang Kai-shek at its head allied itself with the imperialists in order to crush its onetime ally the working class."[40] Chan appealed to LAI members to extend moral support and solidarity to the workers of China, who were repressed by the double yoke of the Chinese bourgeoisie and foreign imperialists. The cover letter from Liau and the report from Chan both urged Leaguers across the world to protest "upon humanitarian grounds or upon revolutionary grounds" the behavior of Chiang, his military, and the KMT.[41]

The League was especially appealing to Nehru because it offered information and perspectives on China that were not available in mainstream media outlets in Europe or India, both filtered through imperial lenses. Nehru wrote an article for an Indian publication on the Chinese situation and reminded readers that "The news that India receives about the Chinese struggle comes almost entirely from prejudiced sources." He added, "We should be on guard against this and not be misled by the exaggerated and misleading reports."[42] This is not to say that the League's press service was not exaggerated or polemical, but it offered Nehru a new reference point for information and ideas outside the metropolitan and imperial spheres. The Chinese circular also illustrated the ways in which the League was more than just a tool for learning; it was also an outlet for Nehru to express his grievances and protests to the wider community of anti-imperialists. He could send his words of sympathy and solidarity to the Berlin office, where they would be redistributed to China and across the anti-imperialist world.

---

[39] Press Service of the League against Imperialism and for National Independence, July 15, 1927, published jointly by Paris and Berlin office, 542/1/5/65–68, RGASPI.

[40] League against Imperialism Circular on China, July [undated], 1927, 542/1/18/38, RGASPI.

[41] LAI, Circular on China, July 1927, 542/1/18/38–39, RGASPI.

[42] Nehru, "The Situation in China and India's Duty," originally published in *The Volunteer*, April 1927, repr. in *SWJN*, vol. 2, 328.

In addition to LAI literature, Nehru's encounters and meetings with LAI comrades around this time were another important avenue for his burgeoning sense of international community. After meetings about the secretariat, Baldwin became his most trustworthy comrade. The American came to Europe in 1927 to study the political situation on the continent and in the Soviet Union. His travel itinerary included several months in Geneva, followed by a month in Paris, before embarking on an extended trip to the Soviet Union later in the summer of 1927. Indeed, his primary aim in Europe was the study of political prisoners abroad on behalf of the ICPP. In addition, he secured a book contract and journalist visa to publish a short piece on civil liberties in the Soviet Union. The inauguration of the LAI in Brussels, however, provided another agenda for Baldwin, which brought him into frequent contact with Nehru.

The Baldwin–Nehru relationship blossomed in this period. Many years later, Baldwin fondly recalled his time spent with Nehru's wife, daughter, sister, and father as a "treasured experience."[43] Baldwin attended "casual" social functions at the Nehru residence and characterized the family as "cultivated, charming," and "vivacious."[44] Of Nehru, Baldwin recalled that "his mind was agile, his language polished, his wit quick."[45] The admiration was mutual, and when Nehru considered his time in Europe in 1927, Baldwin stood out as his "Anglo-American" colleague who shared "a certain similarity in outlook."[46] Yet, more than the personal engagements, it was their "common interests" in the LAI's development that brought Baldwin and Nehru closer, and, as Baldwin recalled, the two "attended committee meetings faithfully."[47]

In addition to Baldwin, Chatto became a significant comrade in Nehru's inner circle during this period. Nehru traveled frequently to Berlin in the aftermath of the Brussels Congress and for his work on the LAI executive committee. He visited Chatto on these occasions. In his autobiography, Nehru described Chatto as one of the few Indians in Europe who "impressed [him] intellectually."[48] Their meetings in Europe have not been well documented in the archives, although others in Berlin, like Chatto's partner, Agnes Smedley, remarked on the close and personal relationship the two Indian leaders developed.[49] These meetings paved the way for a robust and frequent correspondence once Nehru left Europe for India.

[43] Baldwin, "Recollections of Jawaharlal Nehru," 3.   [44] Ibid., 3–4.   [45] Ibid., 5.
[46] Nehru, *Autobiography*, 172.   [47] Baldwin, "Recollections," 4.
[48] Nehru, *Autobiography*, 161.
[49] Ruth Price, *The Lives of Agnes Smedley* (Oxford: Oxford University Press, 2005), 159.

Fresh encounters with comrades at the second executive meeting in Cologne during August 1927 were also instrumental to developing Nehru's networks and anti-imperialist worldview. Once again, US imperialism was the target of attack in Cologne. This time, the LAI executives discussed the American Red Scare and the fear of communist expansion into the United States exemplified by the Sacco-Vanzetti trial (1927), a controversial US trial against two men suspected of being communists and anarchists. There was unanimous approval to send a telegram to the US government calling for the Supreme Court to overturn the conviction of Sacco and Vanzetti. Immediately following the executive meeting, Nehru and Baldwin traveled together to Dusseldorf for a political rally in support of the American accused.

The Cologne meeting also markedly expanded Nehru's contacts and understanding of the Dutch East Indies. One of the principal discussions at the second executive meeting in Cologne had concerned a possible commission to Java for three months to observe Dutch colonialism on the ground.[50] A series of uprisings in Java and Sumatra from 1926 to 1927 provoked a crackdown on anticolonial activity in Indonesia and Holland. In a statement on the situation, a Dutch LAI member, P. J. Schmidt, wrote: "The [Dutch] rulers may provoke and suppress, they may kill and murder to fill their prisons, but they will never succeed in killing the spirit of revolt of the Indonesian workers and intellectuals."[51] Nehru was moved by the plight of the Indonesian nationalists and workers, and he would later write a foreword for Schmidt's book on imperialism.[52] Nehru also had more opportunities to discuss the shared experience of colonialism and anticolonial resistance with Mohamed Hatta, fellow executive member, who also attended the Cologne meeting.[53] These experiences shaped

---

[50] The LAI commission to Indonesia turned out to be a debacle. There were no funds to send the commission. Even so, Mardy Jones, a British member, departed for Indonesia via India without LAI permission. When he returned, Jones attempted to collect reimbursement for his travels, which were not available.

[51] P. J. Schmidt, "Statement on Dutch Java and Sumatra," November 1927, 542/1/5/ 138–139, RGASPI.

[52] This article was originally written for P. J. Schmidt's *The Imperialist Danger* in May 1928, but also published in the Indian National Congress publication, *The Tribune*, on July 24, 1929, repr. in *SWJN*, vol. 3, 151–158.

[53] Mohamed Hatta befriended Nehru at the Brussels Congress. The two kept in touch during the interwar years and worked together after 1947, most notably on the 1955 Bandung Conference. See Mohammed Hatta, interviewed by B. R. Nanda, September 1972, interview transcript 121, Nehru Memorial Museum and Library Oral History Collection, NMML, New Delhi, India.

a more nuanced appraisal of Indonesia than the one Nehru offered in his Brussels Congress report.

By the time of the Cologne meeting, Nehru had emerged as a vital member of the LAI, and other committee members saw the colonial conditions in India as pivotal to the anti-imperialist struggle. In Cologne, Nehru's comrades celebrated his meager successes with the INC and the LAI secretariat, but also called upon him to do more. Nehru's impending return to India at the end of year would provide the LAI with a strong and direct contact with the anticolonial movement on the ground. Shapurji Saklatvala spoke on this issue extensively in Cologne. Although not yet an official member of the executive committee, he had been invited to speak about his recent tour of India. Saklatvala was an Indian-born expatriate living in England and a member of the Communist Party of Great Britain (CPGB).[54] Saklatvala knew Münzenberg and his Berlin networks well. Upon his return from India, Saklatvala took on a more active role in the LAI from Britain, and he began regularly attending executive committee meetings of the international LAI in August 1927. Foremost, Saklatvala argued that the LAI should foster connections with the INC as the "most influential body in India."[55] He stressed that Nehru was the ideal candidate to persuade the INC to associate with the LAI. Secondly, in the spirit of the nationalist and working-class solidarity sprung from the LAI mission, Saklatvala underscored the importance of the INC in taking up the cause of Indian workers and joining forces with the AITUC. To this end, Saklatvala believed that "Nehru [could] do a lot to achieve a convergence and united work of the trade union movement and the Congress."[56] The committee passed a unanimous decision in favor of Nehru's leadership in India, which reaffirmed his prominent role in the LAI and the executive's vote of confidence in the challenging task of persuading his INC colleagues to unite in support of Indian workers and the anti-imperialist world.

Through the LAI meetings, encounters, and discourse, Nehru became both an observer and a participant in the great anti-imperialist struggles of his times. By late 1927, Nehru's political vision and activities began to straddle two spheres: the discourse and circuits of an internationalist world of anti-imperialism, and the politics of anticolonial struggle against

---

[54] For a study of Saklatvala during this period, see chapter four in Susan Pennybacker, *Scottsboro to Munich*.

[55] Minutes of the Executive Council of the League against Imperialism on August 20–21, 1927, 542/1/12/8–13, RGASPI.

[56] Ibid.

the raj in India. The amalgam of nationalism and internationalism for Nehru strengthened as 1927 progressed and as the LAI secretariat began to function with a greater degree of regularity and professionalism. As a result, Nehru made stronger appeals to his Indian colleagues to join the ranks of the LAI. At the same time, LAI comrades around the world increasingly saw the Indian anticolonial struggle as essential to the toppling of imperialism and capitalism worldwide.

BRITAIN AND THE SOCIALIST RETREAT

While Cologne was a high point in Nehru's LAI service, the meeting also marked a turning point for the institution's tenuous solidarities between communists and socialists. The composition of attendees in Cologne signaled the shift. In addition to the executive committee members, who represented a balance of socialists, communists, and nationalists, the Berlin secretaries invited almost as many visitors and observers to attend and even speak in Cologne. Among them were Saklatvala, Chatto, and other Indian expatriates who were overwhelmingly communist in their political affiliations. Moreover, the conspicuous absence of high-profile British LP delegates such as Lansbury, who had been instrumental to the Brussels Congress and Amsterdam meeting, was most striking. The retreat of British socialists from the executive committee was a response to the LSI's clarion call for all members to abandon connections with the LAI. The ripples of the LSI's attack on the League would dramatically impact the LAI and especially its British national section. Much to Nehru's dismay, differences among British working-class leaders proved too powerful for socialist and communist comrades in the metropole to unite in support of anti-imperialism in the colonial world.

At nearly the same moment as the Cologne meeting, Fenner Brockway, chairman of the British ILP and one of Britain's LAI executive members, published a brief article on the Brussels Congress and the League against Imperialism. Of Brussels, he effusively remarked: "As one looked on the sea of black, brown, yellow, and white faces one felt that here at last was something approaching a Parliament of Mankind."[57] The League stood in strong contrast to the LSI, said Brockway, in which "there was no 'coloured' representative among the thousands of delegates."[58] Brockway

---

[57] Fenner Brockway, "The Coloured Peoples' International," *The New Leader*, August 26, 1927. Extract in L/P&J/ 12/267, IPI.
[58] Ibid. [quotations in the original].

was perplexed by the LSI's resistance to cooperating with such an epic and progressive institution, and he argued to his socialist audience that it would be "suicidal" not to join the LAI because it had "done what the Socialist International [had] failed to do – seriously begun the task of uniting the proletarian movements among the coloured races."[59] Brockway concluded with an appeal to the ILP to work with the LAI to unite the socialist movement with the workers in the colonies. The LAI, he said, "may easily prove to be one of the most significant movements for equality and freedom in human history."[60]

By the time of his publication, Brockway was deeply entrenched in a heated debate over the LAI between socialists within the LSI and those within the British left. Immediately following the Brussels Congress, the LSI launched an investigation of the LAI with the intent of proving it to be a communist organization. The reports based on the investigation led to outright accusations of exaggerated attendance. The most damning claim was that the League was a communist front organization controlled and funded by Moscow.[61] The LSI's attack spilled over into the internal politics of the British left. Still, in April 1927, Lansbury, Brockway, Bridgeman, and others met in the British House of Commons and resolved to create a national branch of the LAI in London. Brockway had been the driving force behind the decision, but he agreed with his comrades from both the LP and ILP that their activities within the League would need to be approved by the LSI. Brockway became the chairman of the British national section of the LAI, while Bridgeman and Lansbury also held offices. The British League decided that funds should come from British sources only, not from Berlin, and the members collected subscriptions from the LP, the ILP, and other leftist organizations.[62]

Nehru was present at the second meeting of the British League in June 1927. At this meeting, Lansbury buckled under the pressure from the LP and LSI and announced his resignation from the chairmanship of the international LAI and from his position as treasurer of the British League.[63] Since the Brussels Congress, Nehru had admired Lansbury's

---

[59] Ibid.   [60] Ibid.

[61] See Jean Jones, *The League against Imperialism*, Socialist History Occasional Pamphlet Series (Lancashire: The Socialist History Society and the Lancashire Community Press, 1996).

[62] Reginald Bridgeman, "Secretary's Report" in Report of the National Conference of the League against Imperialism (British Section), February 1931 (London: League against Imperialism, 1931), File DBN/25/1, Bridgeman Papers.

[63] Lansbury did promise to remain a member of the British League and attended a July meeting, although he left the organization shortly after.

speech, calling its "special blend" of nationalism and internationalism "eloquent and ... proof that the [Brussels] Congress was not so rabid after all, nor was it merely hitched on to the star of Communism."[64] The reversal of Lansbury's commitment to the League in June greatly disappointed Nehru, who was "hurt by this sudden change in a person whose speech I had admired only two or three months earlier."[65]

The British League survived the shake-up, however, and continued under the management of Brockway and Bridgeman. By the time Brockway published his defense of the League in August, the LSI was deciding the fate of those holding dual memberships of both the LAI and the LSI. On September 2, the LSI concluded that the League was a tool of the Comintern and therefore a proscribed organization. The LSI published its decision in October and called for all LSI members to withdraw from the LAI or risk losing their LSI affiliation. Brockway, in order to preserve his place on the LSI executive, resigned from his posts on both the international and national Leagues. It is important to note, however, that LP and ILP members without connections to the LSI executive continued to associate with the LAI until the Labour Party deemed it a proscribed organization much later in November 1929.[66]

Of the three primary organizers of the British LAI, only Reginald Bridgeman remained, but at the cost of eventually losing his membership in the LP for nearly a decade.[67] There was some discussion by communists in Moscow and the Communist Party of Great Britain about a complete takeover of the British section of the LAI, although it retained in 1927 an ILP–CPGB alliance of members. Saklatvala, whose voice was significant in the Cologne meeting, became in this context a strong and active voice in the British League. In the aftermath of the socialist retreat at the end of 1927, James Maxton, British Member of Parliament from Glasgow, took over the chairmanship of the British section, while Bridgeman remained the secretary. Maxton, a key figure of the ILP, was somewhat of a renegade of the British left. He openly criticized the LP and moderate socialists in the House of Commons and eventually led the ILP to break with the LP in 1931.[68] He was a suitable replacement because he secured permission from the ILP to chair both the national and international

---

[64] Nehru, *Autobiography*, 171.   [65] Ibid., 172.   [66] Bridgeman, "Secretary's Report."
[67] *Dictionary of Labour Biography*, vol. 7, ed. by Joyce M. Bellamy and John Saville (London: Macmillan Press, 1984), s.v. "Reginald Bridgeman," 40–49.
[68] Vidya Sagar Anand and Francis A. Ridley. *James Maxton and British Socialism* (London: Medusa Press, 1970).

Leagues. Even if Maxton presided, Bridgeman was the heart and soul of the British office. Although Nehru was disappointed by the retreat of many prominent Labour Party leaders, he admired the dedication of the small cadre of British anti-imperialists who remained in the League.

The British LP withdrawal was only the first of several successive withdrawals in 1927 and 1928. For example, the very active Dutch LAI collapsed when founders, including P. J. Schmidt and others, were forced to resign under pressure from the Dutch Social Democratic Party. At the same time, more communists came to the international and national sections to fill the void left by fleeing socialists. To be sure, the most pressing concern became whether the LAI could continue without socialists. This question would dominate discussions and negotiations between Nehru and his League colleagues in the months and years to come.

Nehru remained an avid supporter of the LAI despite the fallout of the British LAI and the tensions with communists in Berlin over the secretariat. The early months of institution-building exposed a contested and politicized terrain for comrades such as Nehru to navigate. Setbacks in London fractured socialists and communists and fomented distrust among the disparate activists represented in the executive committee and the secretariat. Nehru was undoubtedly frustrated with the secretaries in Berlin and the British LP representatives, but he reserved his critical commentary. Instead, he professed his support for the LAI in his publications and letters home. The story of Nehru and the LAI in 1927 was one of resilience, commitment, and compromise despite the obstacles presented by political partisanship and sectarian conflict. At the same moment the LSI concluded their deliberations on the LAI, and well after the fateful British LAI meeting in June, Nehru wrote his first public statement that defended anti-imperialist internationalism and summoned his Indian readers inside and outside of the INC to take up the worldwide resistance to imperialism.

INDIA AND THE ANTI-IMPERIALIST WORLD

Nehru's "A Foreign Policy for India," written in September 1927, echoed in great detail the message of anti-imperialist internationalism, rooted in Brussels and strengthened in the LAI experience. The article was a turning point for Nehru, whose ideas about India and anti-imperialism were expressed only privately in letters before this publication. Nehru's experiences between February and September offered him the relevant and necessary time to reflect and consider the arguments for anti-imperialism from the Indian perspective.

The text began by painting a picture of the interconnected world he came to encounter in Brussels and through the LAI:

A shooting in London is followed by a murder in Warsaw and many executions in Moscow, and has its reverberations on the North-West Frontier in India. ... The American marines take possession of Nicaragua because Messrs. Brown Brothers of New York have money invested there ... Meanwhile, China cannot be free because too much British and Japanese capital is locked up there.[69]

The nodal points captured here, of course, reflect the preoccupations of the LAI throughout 1927, including the LAI focus on China; the war danger pitting Britain against the Soviet Union; India as a pivotal place for armament; and American imperialism in Nicaragua. Nehru's introduction concluded with a warning that "India cannot keep apart from the tangled web, and her refusing to take heed of it may indeed lead her to disaster."[70] The premises outlined for India's foreign policy represented a now-familiar discourse about the necessity of "international joint action" against imperialism. Nehru reminded his readers that India was not unique in its experience of imperialist oppression: "Let us remember that there are many countries and many peoples who suffer as India does today. They have to face the same problems as ours and it must be to the advantage of both of us to know more of each other and to cooperate where possible."[71] He cited INC involvement in the Brussels Congress and the LAI as steps in the right direction.

Moreover, Nehru made a strong case for Indian anti-imperialist solidarities in the face of a growing war danger. Foremost, India had to establish solidarity and connections with its neighbors in the "East," specifically Nepal, China, Japan, Indonesia, Annam, Afghanistan, Persia, Turkey, and Egypt. Secondly, India needed to align itself with Soviet Russia as a "friend of all the oppressed nationalities" because the Soviets had "always been for the oppressed and the exploited."[72] To complete the anti-imperialist picture for Indian readers, Nehru's article concluded with a discussion of the war danger reminiscent of the Brussels discourse. He argued that in the near future, British imperialist aggression would lead to conflict with Russia. Inevitably, Britain would coerce India into fighting Russia, its anti-imperialist ally. In response, Nehru emphatically argued

---

[69] Nehru, "A Foreign Policy for India," September 13, 1927, *SWJN*, vol. 2, 348–364.
[70] Ibid., 353.   [71] Ibid., 353.   [72] Ibid., 362.

that the INC should resist and reject any war that benefited imperialism and undermined anti-imperialism in the Soviet Union or Asia.[73]

Nehru's arguments about the anti-imperialist world also informed his case for a greater commitment to anticolonialism at home. The fundamental aim of the Brussels Congress and the LAI was coordinating movements dedicated to the overthrow of European colonialism worldwide; consequently, Nehru recognized that the INC must demand complete independence from Britain. This was no easy task even in 1927. Since its establishment in 1885, the INC had been incapable of reaching a consensus on whether it sought constitutional reforms and dominion status within the British Empire or complete independence from Britain's rule The advent of Gandhi's leadership made this question even murkier. Under his guidance, the INC sought *swaraj*, a term with multiple meanings in the 1920s. It is roughly translated to mean "self-rule," yet Gandhi used the term to define a social reform agenda that rejected Western and colonial modes of production and epistemology.[74] Gandhi's *swaraj* was not, however, implicitly about political independence from British rule. To others within the INC, likely the vast majority in 1927, *swaraj* meant greater political autonomy for Indians within the colonial state and included the demand for more representation in legislatures and opportunities in colonial administration. A more radical minority, including Nehru, sought a *swaraj* that meant complete independence from the British.

Nehru's article was one of many sustained attempts between 1927 and 1929 to persuade the INC to contribute to the anti-imperialist cause worldwide by seeking independence rather than constitutional reforms at home. He outlined several reasons to reject dominion status. First, Nehru referenced well-known cases of British racism in South Africa to demonstrate that even greater reforms and dominion status within the empire would not bring about real equality. Second, remaining in the British Empire meant lending Indian support to the greatest "bully of Eastern Nations."[75] Drawing upon a familiar set of examples from Brussels, Nehru cited British imperialist aggression in China and Egypt as evidence. By accepting dominion status, India would allow the British to continue to deploy Indian manpower and resources to "bully" India's neighbors,

[73] Ibid., 362–363.
[74] See Mohandas K. Gandhi, *Hind Swaraj or Indian Home Rule* (Madras: S. Ganesan & Co., 1921). The tract was first written and printed as a pamphlet in South Africa.
[75] Nehru, "A Foreign Policy for India," 348–364.

which Nehru counted as an "immoral act and crime against the freedom of all who are oppressed."[76] Further, dominion status within the British Empire would change very little in terms of India's ability to control its own destiny and its contacts abroad. For these reasons, declared Nehru, "[t]he only possible goal we can have is one of full independence."[77]

For a rather moderate INC, Nehru's calls to break completely with imperialist ties were not always welcome. When he returned home to India in the late 1920s, he would emerge as a luminary of the leftwing of the congress and those seeking independence from the empire, but Nehru would also meet staunch resistance from Gandhi and many moderates seeking greater reforms within the colonial state structure. This ongoing contention would become an uphill battle for Nehru in the months and years to come. Privately, Nehru wrote to his father and Gandhi about the possibilities anti-imperialist internationalism held for India and the necessity of setting independence as the INC's goal. To his father, Nehru argued for a broader vision of *swaraj* as independence, the freedom to develop both "the external relations of our country and the internal organization."[78] India, thought Nehru, should be able to choose whether to maintain a relationship with Britain, and whether to establish cooperative relations with other countries, such as China. "Thus all the rights that an independent country enjoys in this respect should be those of our country also," wrote Nehru. "To say even now that we shall always be associated with England, as a Dominion or in some other form, seems to me inappropriate, for it lessens our freedom of choice in the future."[79] As early as 1927, Nehru envisioned a greater role for India in the world beyond political independence. He argued to his father, "I hope that after gaining freedom we shall use our energy for extending peace in the world."[80] Importantly, Nehru's father was a more willing recipient of his son's ideas, and he attended the LAI's third executive council meeting in December, a gathering held shortly after the younger Nehru had left for India.

Gandhi's more parochial views of the Indian colonial situation forced Nehru to tread more cautiously in approaching the elder INC leader. Much has been written about Gandhi's ideas and his tensions with Nehru, especially in relation to their visions for a postcolonial India.

[76] Ibid., 355.   [77] Ibid., 357.
[78] Jawaharlal Nehru, "On the Indian Situation," published in *Aaj*, March 2, 1927, repr. in *SWJN*, vol. 2, 297.
[79] Ibid., 297.   [80] Ibid., 297.

Yet, their worldviews also differed substantially. Interestingly, in Brussels, Nehru made a case for Indian internationalism by drawing upon the words of Gandhi, who was not especially well known for his interest in world affairs. In his speech, Nehru asserted, "the Indian National Congress is necessarily national and has nationalism as its basis, but as our great leader Gandhi has said, our nationalism is based on the most intense internationalism."[81] Here, Nehru referenced a 1925 statement by the Mahatma in which Gandhi advocated internationalism:

> It is impossible for one to be internationalist without being a nationalist ... [it] is not nationalism that is evil, it is the narrowness, selfishness, exclusiveness, which is the bane of modern nations, which is evil ... India has, I hope, struck a different path. It wants to organize itself or to find full self-expression for the benefit and service of humanity at large.[82]

For Gandhi, India's role in the world was to model exemplary action. In *Hind Swaraj*, a political tract written in South Africa in 1909, Gandhi envisaged *swaraj* as a program of social and national reform that would be a model for others to emulate. Living a life of truth (*ahisma*) through non-violence (*satyagraha*) would not only free India of British rule, but also pave the way for change worldwide.

On the other hand, Nehru's nationalism and internationalism sought concrete partnerships and a dynamic relationship of exchange between anti-imperialist forces worldwide. He thought India had much to contribute to the anti-imperialist struggle – indeed, was essential to it – but the INC also had much to learn from its anti-imperialist counterparts abroad. His position was clearly articulated in a letter to Gandhi about his experiences with the Brussels Congress and LAI: "I welcome all legitimate methods of getting into touch with other countries and peoples so that we may be able to understand their viewpoint and world politics generally. I do not think it desirable nor indeed is it possible for India to plough a lonely furrow now or in the future." He concluded: "It is solely with a view to self-education and self-improvement that I desire external contacts." Nehru went on to critique Gandhi's and the INC's vision for India's relationship with the world: "I am afraid we are terribly narrow in our outlook and the sooner we get rid of this narrowness the better. Our

---

[81] Nehru, Press Statement made in Brussels, February 9, 1927, *SWJN*, vol. 2, 270.
[82] Mohandas Gandhi, "Notes on Nationalism and Internationalism," published in *Young India*, June 18, 1925, repr. in *Collected Works of Mahatma Gandhi* (electronic book) (New Delhi: Publications Division of the Government of India, 1999), vol. 32, 12 (hereafter *CWMG*).

salvation can of course come only from the internal strength that we may evolve but one of the methods of evolving such strength should be the study of other people and their ideas."[83]

From his letters and writing from Europe, it is clear that Nehru's conceptualization of Indian nationalism became tempered by anti-imperialist internationalism in a way that interconnected both projects. In his assessment of the goals for the INC, Nehru articulated a stronger stance on independence than ever before. Brussels and the LAI taught Nehru that imperialist oppression was universal and worldwide, and that the Indian colonial situation was only one part of a broader problem. As Nehru came to envision Indian nationalism in relation to international anti-imperialism, he began to make more radical claims against the colonial state. On a personal level, Nehru argued that he had a right to join the international anti-imperialist community of the League. More broadly, he held that India ought to have the freedom to act internationally and along anti-imperialist lines, free from the constraints of the British Empire.

The contradictions and tensions within the LAI that Nehru witnessed in Europe never figured into his unwavering commitment to anti-imperialist internationalism in the late 1920s. Strikingly, this discord also had no effect on his public statements on socialism. Indeed, it was somewhat paradoxical that Nehru became a professed socialist during the same moment socialists turned their backs on the LAI. Given the failure of the British and international left to cooperate with the anti-imperialist resistance campaign of the League, it would seem logical that Nehru might cast a skeptical eye over the international socialist enterprise. Instead, from 1927 to 1929, he expressed more prominently his belief in socialism as the answer not only to India's problems with the raj, but also to poverty and social inequality within the subcontinent.[84] He first did so privately in the Brussels Congress report to the INC, then publicly in articles for the Indian press.[85] When he presided over the 1929 INC annual meeting, which accepted his *purna swaraj* declaration, he used the platform to state emphatically that he was a socialist.[86]

---

[83] Nehru to Gandhi, April 22, 1927, *SWJN*, vol. 2, 326.

[84] On the ambiguities of socialism in Indian nationalist thought, see Franziska Roy and Benjamin Zachariah, "Meerut and a Hanging: 'Young India' Popular Socialism and the Dynamics of Imperialism," *Comparative Studies of South Asia, Africa and the Middle East*, 33, no. 3 (December 2013): 360–377.

[85] Nehru, Report on the Brussels Congress, *SWJN*, vol. 2, 287; also, for example, "Swaraj and Socialism," August 11, 1928, *SWJN*, vol. 3, 369–371.

[86] Nehru, Presidential Address at the 1929 INC sessions in Lahore, repr. in *India and the World: Essays by Jawaharlal Nehru* (George Allen and Unwin: London, 1936).

To some extent, it was Nehru's encounter with communism that profoundly shaped his belief in the Marxist–Leninist critique of capitalism and
imperialism. But Nehru, as an advocate of non-violence, could not accept
the Leninist doctrine of violent revolution and dictatorship of the proletariat. Even so, his understanding of doctrine and the intricacies of socialism
and communism of the 1920s were only budding in the aftermath of the
Brussels Congress. His encounters in Brussels sparked Nehru's interest in
communism especially, but it was his trip to Moscow later
in November 1927 that nearly converted him. Once again, Nehru packed
his bags and he embarked on another journey to the heart of the revolution.
This trip was as transformative as the Brussels sojourn earlier that year.

THE FASCINATION OF SOVIET RUSSIA

In November 1927, Nehru's entire family – father, wife, sister, and daughter – trekked across Eastern Europe and the Russian frontier from Germany
to Moscow for a three-day tour of the Soviet capital during the festivities
marking the tenth anniversary of the Bolshevik Revolution. As it had with
many anticolonial travelers to Moscow in the 1920s, the Soviet capital
captivated Nehru's imagination in a way that usurped his admiration for
any other European city: "Paris is supposed to be the greatest international
centre of Europe. One comes across people from all countries there, but
they are all in the standard costume of the West ... But in Moscow Asia
peeps out from every corner ... its streets and squares full of strange peoples
from East and the West."[87] No doubt the welcoming committee for the
Nehrus – a crowd of Indian expatriates and travelers headed by his LAI
comrade Saklatvala – strengthened the notion that Soviet Russia was the
meeting ground for anti-imperialists of the "East and West."

Nehru's LAI connections made the trip possible. Like the invitation to
the Brussels Congress, the invitation to Moscow came from Chatto, who
worked with M. N. Roy to facilitate the travel arrangements. According
to Chatto in his letter to Roy, the arrival of the Nehru family meant that
the "big guns of the [Indian National] Congress" would be well represented in Moscow.[88] To secure a safe passage under the watchful eye of

[87] Nehru, "Impressions of Moscow," *SWJN*, vol. 2, 387–390.
[88] Chatto to M. N. Roy, August 26, 1927, 495/68/204, 13. Reprinted in *Indo-Russian
     Relations, 1917–1947: Select Documents from the Archives of the Russian Federation*,
     Part I. Purabi Roy, Sobhanlal Das Gupta, and Hari Vasudevan, eds. (Calcutta:
     The Asiatic Society, 1999).

colonial intelligence, Chatto ensured that the formal arrangements were made through a nominally non-political group called the Society for Cultural Relations with the Soviet Union. Behind the scenes, however, communists in Berlin and Moscow made the preparations for the Nehru family's journey.

Only a few months earlier, Nehru's LAI comrade Roger Baldwin had made a similar trip to study the conditions of prisoners and the status of civil liberties in Soviet Russia. Baldwin's assessment was favorable despite evidence of Soviet repression of political opposition and heavy surveillance and censorship of its citizens. Baldwin concluded in his 1927 book *Liberty under the Soviets* that "there [was] more liberty of essential sorts for more of the Russian people today than ever before in their history, and more of some sorts than elsewhere in the world."[89] Nehru's writings about Moscow echoed his American comrade's favorable observations: "The picture I carry away from Russia is one of admiration for the men who accomplished so much within a few years in spite of all the disadvantages that one can imagine."[90] Indeed, Nehru and Baldwin were not alone in pinning their hopes on the Soviet Union as an alternative blueprint for political and social equality worldwide. Liberals, leftists, writers, artists, and intellectuals flocked to the heart of the revolution and the "great experiment" underway in Soviet Russia during the late 1920s.

The year 1927 was a unique moment that engendered both hope and uncertainty about the future of the revolution and communism in Russia. Nehru arrived during the final throes of revolutionary Russia and on the eve of Stalinization. The November anniversary of Lenin's leadership marked a closure in many ways to a turbulent period of revolution and civil war. It was followed by a power struggle within the upper echelons of Soviet leadership in the wake of Lenin's death in 1924. Only a month before the anniversary celebration, one of the main contenders for power within the Soviet regime, Joseph Stalin, had successfully eliminated a key rival, Leon Trotsky. Stalin's rise to power and elimination of other political opponents was to follow on the heels of Nehru's departure from Moscow. These later developments ushered in a new era of Soviet history characterized by greater repression, violent purges, and consolidation of state power. Still, this eventual outcome was not altogether certain in November 1927.

---

[89] Roger Baldwin, *Liberty under the Soviets* (New York: Vanguard Press, 1928), 5. He also makes this case in his ICPP report, Baldwin (Paris) report to ICPP (New York), September 23, 1927, Box 11, Folder 9, Baldwin Papers.
[90] Nehru to his sister, Vijayalakshmi Pandit, November 12, 1927, *SWJN*, vol. 2, 371.

Much later, Baldwin recalled this period of ambivalence and transition: "The atmosphere in Moscow then in the summer of 1927 was evidently freer than it has ever been since. It was the last of the period before the Stalin-Trotsky conflict broke out, resulting in far tougher measures ... [T]he police state was then firmly and finally established. I had seen only the preliminaries and gauged them wrong."[91] As early as January 1930, events in Soviet Russia forced Baldwin to "add a word of caution" in a special preface to reprints of his 1927 book: "The readers should modify what I have set forth in this book in order to shift more emphasis upon the machinery and policies of repression, less upon the liberties." However, Baldwin's faith in the Soviet experiment was not completely lost as late as 1930: "With all this increased control and repression, the economic advances of the regime toward socialism leave unaffected the underlying sympathy and hope which this book voices."[92]

Nehru's observations in 1927 left a lasting and unwavering impression of the Soviet Union as a bastion of liberty, freedom and anti-imperialism. Unlike Baldwin's, Nehru's effusive appraisal did not change significantly after Stalin came to power. Nehru's views were captured in a series of articles he first published in the Indian press and later collated into a small volume on Soviet Russia. In it, his "fascination" with all things Russian was clear, as well as his regret that his sojourn was altogether too brief.[93] He professed that the Bolshevik Revolution "was undoubtedly one of the greatest events of world history."[94] After his brief stay, Nehru became an avid reader of any literature on Soviet Russia that he could find. By the time he returned to India, Nehru had read and recommended texts on communism by Marx, Engels, Lenin, and Trotsky. He also familiarized himself with the major debates within communism, in particular those between revisionists such as Eduard Bernstein and Karl Kautsky on the one hand, and revolutionaries such as Lenin on the other.[95] While never fully committing to communism or joining the party, Nehru admired communist theory from afar.

Not only did his LAI connections facilitate Nehru's journey, but the anti-imperialist discourse of the League also shaped his encounters and impressions of Soviet Russia. In his observations, Nehru described Soviet Russia as a haven for anti-imperialism and a stalwart against the British

---

[91] Baldwin, *Reminiscences*, 407.   [92] Baldwin, *Liberty under the Soviets*, xv–xvi.
[93] Nehru, "Impressions of Moscow," vol. 2 390.
[94] Nehru, "Lenin," *SWJN*, vol. 2 403–408.
[95] Nehru, "Some Books on Russia," vol. 2 402.

Empire in much the same way the Brussels Congress did. Nehru argued that Russia and India "should live as the best of neighbors," but British foreign policy prevented such an alliance. "The continual friction that we see today is between England and Russia, not between India and Russia. Is there any reason why we in India should inherit the age-long rivalry of England and Russia?" he asked. His further arguments embodied the anti-imperialist discourse based upon Brussels and the LAI that emphasized the war danger between Britain and Soviet Russia, as well as the pivotal place of India in such a conflict. The rivalry between the Soviets and Britain, according to Nehru, was "based on the greed and covetousness of British imperialism," while India's "interests surely [lay] in ending this imperialism and not supporting and strengthening it." Once again, and perhaps with a stronger confidence in his worldview after visiting Moscow, Nehru appealed to his Indian readers: "[W]e shall not permit ourselves to be used as pawns in England's imperial game to be moved hither and tither for her benefit."[96]

Beyond anti-imperialist solidarity, the Soviet Union also offered many important lessons for India. According to Nehru, the INC might have benefited from studying the admirable qualities of Lenin, who "realized … what we in India are dimly beginning to appreciate, that it is a difficult, if not an impossible task, for amateurs with little time to spare from their daily routine and no special training, to fight whole-timers who are experts at their business of defending the existing regime."[97] The Soviet model of development also provided hope for Nehru and India. He likened Russia's agrarian and poverty-stricken conditions under the Tsar to colonial India's state under the British raj. Of Russia and India, Nehru wrote, "Both are vast agricultural countries with only the beginnings of industrialization, and both have to face poverty and illiteracy. If Russia finds a satisfactory solution for these, our work in India is made easier."[98] Even Nehru's father, a more conservative moderate in the INC, admitted with some hesitation that there could be much to learn from the Soviet model. Motilal later said that *swaraj* must also mean "independence of the workers and peasants."[99] And, "What I saw in Russia I admired, but the conclusion I have come to is this – the Soviet

---

[96] Nehru "Russia and India," vol. 2 451.   [97] Ibid., 450–451.
[98] Nehru, "The Fascination of Russia," vol. 2
[99] Motilal Nehru, Statement at the League against Imperialism General Council meeting, December 9, 1927, 542/1/14/11, RGASPI.

Government is trying a gigantic experiment. It is not yet past the stage of experiment, even they admit."[100]

The "gigantic experiment" engendered profound optimism for many, although even the enthusiastic younger Nehru recognized that the Soviet project was still in the making. The Soviet Union promised social and economic equality for all; however, the state existed as a repressive dictatorship. Nehru dismissed much of the latter and even commented on his visit to a prison in Moscow as evidence. He saw Russian prisons as institutions seeking to change prisoners into "good citizens."[101] Although Nehru suspected that the particular prison they visited was a "show place specially meant for the edification of visitors," he still argued that the Russian prisoner had a "far preferable" life to a factory worker in colonial India. Only political opponents of the regime suffered from "red terror and Bolshevik tyranny," yet Nehru minimized this shortcoming by suggesting that these prisoners were merely 5 percent of the population, compared to the 95 percent of beneficiaries of the new regime. Nehru also acknowledged that Soviet Russia existed as a dictatorship in his observations, although, like Baldwin, Nehru gauged it as a temporary state of affairs: "We have the dictatorship of the proletariat today. But this, we are told, is a period of transition only, or a period of preparation for the great time to come when class conflicts will entirely cease as there will be only one class, and the State itself will sink into insignificance."[102]

In addition to strengthening his admiration for Soviet Russia, Nehru encountered in Moscow many comrades from Asia. The itinerary for the events in Moscow included a World Congress of the Friends of the USSR, and a delegation of "friends" from the "East" met as a smaller conference in advance of the larger one.[103] Both the elder and the younger Nehru attended the meeting as observers although refrained from making any statements during the proceedings. No doubt they intermingled with a variety of students, intellectuals, and communist party members from across India and Asia. Overall, the basic platforms of the conference reflected many of the key ideas in the Brussels Congress. Speakers and resolutions argued that the Soviet Union was an anti-imperialist friend to the East and especially China. In addition, the conference proceedings

---

[100] Ibid.   [101] Nehru, "A Prison," *SWJN*, vol. 2, 420.
[102] Nehru, "The Constitution of the USSR," *SWJN*, vol. 2, 398.
[103] Nehru makes no mention of this Congress in his articles on Soviet Russia, but the Indian Political Intelligence files place him here. See File L/P&J/12/292, IPI.

called on the Eastern delegates to support Soviet Russia against imperialist aggression in the context of the growing war danger.

The most significant encounter at the conference was Nehru's introduction to his most important and valued connection to China: Madame Sun Yat-Sen. Born as Soong Ch'ing-ling, Madame Sun Yat-Sen was the widow of the late Dr. Sun Yat-Sen (1866–1925), the pioneer of the nationalist movement in China.[104] Her sister, Soong Mei-ling, later married General Chiang Kai-shek. Madame Sun attended the events in Moscow and chaired the conference of the friends from the East. She arrived and stayed in Moscow at a precarious moment when the Chinese situation was uncertain. She had communist sympathies and served on the executive of the KMT, although by late 1927 most communists were purged by Chiang Kai-shek. She did not return to China permanently until 1931.

Nehru admitted that Madame Sun "fascinated" him.[105] He wrote of her in a letter about his trip that she was "delightful, look[ed] twenty five and [was] full of life and energy."[106] Nehru knew of Madame Sun from the Brussels Congress, which she had not attended but had sent messages of support and served as an honorary president. The personal encounter with Madame Sun crystallized Nehru's appreciation for China's anti-imperialist struggle and connections with India. In the preceding chapter, we saw that Nehru had not been particularly impressed with the Chinese delegates at Brussels, but the chance meeting in Moscow with Madame Sun changed his indifference. Nehru had also taken the opportunity of meeting Madame Sun to personally extend an invitation to her to go to India for the annual INC meeting in December. She accepted and applied for a visa through Berlin only to be denied by the British government.[107] Even so, Nehru and Madame Sun retained a steady correspondence as the turbulent situations in China and India unfolded over the interwar period.

The sights and people in Moscow captured Nehru's heart and mind in 1927. He returned to India a changed man, which had much to do with the LAI and his trip to Moscow. The Soviet sojourn had convinced him that Russia was indeed an alternative to imperialism. He wrote that Russia had "upset the old order of things and brought a new world into existence, where values have changed utterly and old standards have given place to

---

[104] Jung Chang and Jon Halliday, *Mme Sun Yat-sen* (Middlesex, England: Penguin Books, 1986).
[105] Nehru to Vijayalakshmi Pandit, November 12, 1927, *SWJN*, vol. 2, 371.
[106] Ibid., 371.   [107] "Refusal of a passport to Mme. Sun Yat Sen," L/P&J/12/268, IPI.

new."[108] It was the faith in the promises of the revolution that enabled Nehru, Baldwin, and others to overlook the evidence of inequality, state repression, and violence within the Soviet regime. For Nehru, who by then had bought into the Soviet experiment and its anti-imperialist rhetoric, the ability to look objectively at Stalin's Russia would become nearly impossible after 1927. Rather, Soviet Russia retained a stable and significant placeholder in Nehru's anti-imperialist worldview even throughout the purges of the 1930s and beyond. Nehru also had a new friend and colleague from China. Madame Sun would be an important person in both his imagined and tangible connections between India and China.

CONCLUSION

The months Nehru spent in Europe working in service of the LAI profoundly altered his political and intellectual understanding of India and the world. During his time in Europe, Nehru became deeply involved in the politics of the LAI, and his work on the executive committee firmly established him as a pivotal partner in the international struggle against empires. Nehru also left for India with an arsenal of partners against imperialism. In particular, Baldwin, Chatto, and Madame Sun were comrades whom Nehru could draw upon for moral, financial, and political support. As a consequence of his LAI activities, Nehru's political and intellectual horizons were no longer bounded by locality and nation, but were part of a wider international network of exchanges with people and ideas from countries as distant as the United States, the Soviet Union, China, Egypt, and Indonesia.

Nehru's anti-imperialist worldview, as sparked in Brussels, had been thoroughly strengthened by his LAI service. He had been convinced that imperialism and capitalism were two sides of the same coin, and both had to be combated with the forces of nationalism and socialism in the colonies. The struggle also had to be waged by "blending" nationalism and internationalism. In other words, the nationalist struggle was only a small part of a larger, internationalist project against imperialism worldwide. His anti-imperialist worldview also produced an imagined geography of anti-imperialism. Foremost, Nehru saw the Soviet Union and China as India's most coveted anti-imperialist allies. His encounters in Europe and the Soviet Union strengthened this. Even when confronted with evidence of Stalin's brutal repression or the failure of the united front

---

[108] Nehru, "The Fascination of Russia," *SWJN*, vol. 2, 382.

in China, Nehru could not break from his core belief in Soviet Russia's anti-imperialism and China's comradeship. Finally, according to Nehru, the United States was unquestionably imperialist and posed the greatest danger to India and the anti-imperialist world. These pillars of his world-view would be so transformative that he would never fully shake them off, not even when the global events of the later 1930s and World War II complicated any facile analysis of the world.

As 1927 came to a close and Nehru prepared to return to India, he departed with a cautious optimism about the future of the LAI despite the internal tensions and threat of a communist takeover. Much to his dismay, the League's numbers of international socialists and trade unionists dwindled in the fall of 1927. The shift toward a more communist compo-sition within the LAI would only increase as noncommunist leaders like Nehru and Baldwin left Europe for their respective homes in the months to come. Nehru departed first. As the Indian leader set sail, his American colleague wrote to him to express his deep concerns about the future of the LAI: "[T]here were too many communists present, who insisted on following lines of Communist propaganda – which is after all, entirely to my way of thinking, so far as the colonial issue is concerned. But we don't need an abundance of communists to push what we all agree on, and we certainly ought to steer clear of communist phraseology."[109] Baldwin concluded frankly in his letter to Nehru with this final assessment:

My judgment is that the League will continue to exist, but that its financial necessities are going to force it to seek support more and more from the left – which means the communist and Russian trade unions. The socialists are boycotting it, and the colonial peoples are too poor to keep it going, although they have come across handsomely so far.[110]

More than ever, the uncertainties laid out by Baldwin about the League's future required Nehru to redouble his efforts in India and build a strong coalition of noncommunists to balance the power of their com-munist counterparts. His most trenchant contribution to this dilemma, as he saw it, was the assurance that Indian nationalists and trade unionists would associate with the movement and offer a voice from the periphery. He knew the INC would not associate with the anti-imperialist League if it became a communist-dominated institution, and the movement itself could not function properly without an inclusive space for anti-imperialists of any political persuasion. Much was at stake as Nehru

[109] Baldwin to Nehru, December 12, 1927, Box 8, Folder 2, Baldwin Papers.   [110] Ibid.

contemplated his return to the often contentious and divisive terrain of Indian politics. But he remained committed to the anti-imperialist cause, and his new mission was the internationalization of the nationalist question in India. Fueled by this purpose, Nehru returned home to initiate some of the greatest political risks and struggles yet in his lengthy career as an anticolonial leader.

3

Internationalizing Nationalism in India, 1928–1929

On December 4, 1927, Nehru boarded the SS Angers in Marseilles, France, and bid farewell to the European continent that had been home for nearly two years. He sailed directly to Madras, far away from his home in Allahabad, to attend the annual sessions of the INC. Nehru's autobiography is particularly revealing about his intentions on the eve of his homecoming. He set out to "train and prepare" India for the "world events" that would bring "big eruptions and mighty changes" in the near future.[1] Nehru also foreshadowed a menacing imperialist war danger that could only be prevented by anti-imperialist action in India and worldwide. He sought to show his colleagues that "nationalism by itself" was "definitely a narrow and insufficient creed."[2] Instead, nationalism had to be blended with internationalism.

The political situation in India was ripe for change. In November 1927, the conservative government in Britain announced the creation of a Royal Commission to visit India and evaluate the colony's fitness for self-rule. The Simon Commission, named after its lead member Sir John Simon, neglected to invite a single Indian to participate on the committee. When the Simon Commission finally arrived in India in February 1928, the all-white committee encountered angry protesters wielding black flags and calling out "Go Back Simon!" Mobilization against the Simon Commission became a catalyst for resolving the political stalemate within the INC between Swarajists and Gandhian no-changers that had characterized the period since the end of the non-cooperation campaign in 1922. When Nehru arrived in Madras, discontent over the announcement of the Simon Commission was already widespread, and Nehru's mission to "train and prepare" his Indian colleagues appealed to a significant audience.

This chapter seeks to offer a more nuanced reading of the ways Nehru's nationalist and internationalist projects came together and found expression

---

[1] Nehru, *Autobiography*, 175. [2] Ibid.

in India. In most historical accounts, Nehru's political agenda for India after his return from Europe is treated as either completely distinct from or unconnected to his internationalism. Biographers such as Gopal even suggest that Nehru's experiences in Brussels and through the LAI encouraged him to abandon authentically indigenous ideas about India for foreign ones rooted not in Indian epistemology but in "European radical tradition."[3] This chapter contends with these claims by arguing that Nehru's anticolonial and anti-imperial projects were not mutually exclusive and cannot be understood without examining the national and the international dimensions together. Moreover, as the preceding chapters have demonstrated, Nehru's internationalism was not rooted in European tradition, but rather informed by an internationalist idiom that incorporated a broader world of anti-imperialism beyond Europe.

Nehru appropriated and reconfigured anti-imperialist internationalism to fit Indian conditions in 1928. This had three important registers that linked the international with the national. First, the basic premise of anti-imperialist struggle necessitated all comrades in the colonies to accept as an objective the goal of independence. Nehru sought foremost to persuade his fellow congressmen to demand complete independence from the British raj. The quest for independence as the ultimate demand of the Indian people was the essential prerequisite for anti-imperialist action in India and worldwide. Indeed, independence in India was the only means to amalgamate the nationalist movement and the anti-imperialist project. Not all nationalist leaders welcomed Nehru's calls for independence as the defining feature of the INC, however, and the first sections of this chapter recount Nehru's independence campaign alongside the story of resistance from his congress colleagues who sought to remain within the British Empire as a dominion state similar to Canada or Australia.

A second dimension "blended" nationalism and socialism in India. Nehru wrote in his autobiography about his ideas for India in this moment: "political freedom, independence, were no doubt essential, but they were steps only in the right direction; without social freedom and socialistic structure of society and the State, neither the country nor the individual could develop much."[4] The period between his homecoming to India in 1927 and his autobiography in 1935 was marked by a gradual and more polished stance on socialism, as defined by his experiences in the LAI and in particular his work on bringing together those seeking social justice with those seeking political independence. Nehru's commitment to socialism and

---

[3] Gopal, *Nehru*, 71.   [4] Nehru, *Autobiography*, 175.

trade unionism came to be a staple in his public writings and speeches after 1927, and he extended this mission further by participating in and even presiding over the AITUC.

The final element of Nehru's strategy was the integration of an anti-imperialist worldview into the nationalist movement in India. In two successive annual INC meetings, Nehru emerged as a vocal advocate of thinking beyond "narrow-minded nationalism" and situating the Indian congress within the world of anti-imperialism. The apex of this was the annual meeting of the INC in Calcutta in 1928. In his capacity as general secretary of the AICC, Nehru went to great lengths to stage the world in Calcutta by sponsoring fraternal delegates and soliciting an unprecedented number of messages of solidarity with India from anti-imperialist comrades worldwide. He made the case at the Calcutta Congress that the anti-imperialist comrades, whose messages were presented in the opening sessions, depended on the INC to take a stronger stand on independence from British imperialism not only for India, but also for the world.

Each of these registers tells the story of Nehru's efforts to internationalize nationalism. His political projects after his return from Europe marked a paradigmatic shift in his conceptualization of Indian nationalism and the world. He looked to "blend" the discourse and circuits of an internationalist world of anti-imperialism with the local politics of anticolonial struggle against the raj. For Nehru, the distinction between national and international, or India and the world, became inextricably linked.

THE QUEST FOR INDIAN INDEPENDENCE
IN AN ANTI-IMPERIALIST WORLD

Taking place within days of each other, two key events revealed the possibilities and limitations of the INC as an anti-imperialist force in the wider world. The first was the annual session of the INC in Madras in December 1927, where Nehru launched his campaign to "train and prepare" his colleagues by piloting no fewer than four resolutions inspired by anti-imperialist internationalism. The centerpiece was a simple but profound statement on independence: "This Congress declares the goal of the Indian people to be complete national independence."[5] Other resolutions expressed the INC's solidarity with the LAI and the Chinese. The meeting

---

[5] "Indian National Congress: Resolutions Passed by the Indian National Congress at its 42nd session held in Madras on December 26, 27 and 28, 1927." Published by the Under Secretary of the All India Congress Committee, March 1928, File 4–1927, AICC.

was an early triumph for Nehru's anti-imperialist project for India. At the same time, and paradoxically, Nehru's father made a compelling case before the LAI executive committee meeting in Brussels that the INC stood for dominion status within the British Empire rather than "complete national independence." The elder Motilal Nehru attended the executive meeting in the place of his son and undid many of his son's arguments within the LAI that the INC was a force for independence and therefore anti-imperialism.

The question of Indian independence was central to both meetings. Could the INC remain an anti-imperialist member, even leader, of the LAI if it had not come to the conclusion that independence meant the British had to quit India? The LAI sought the overthrow of imperialism worldwide, and members of individual movements had to share in this primary objective. Thus, the INC acceptance of independence over any form of self-government within the empire was the essential link between the nationalist and internationalist struggles. The divergent views on the goals of the INC, expressed by father and son, underscored the central dilemma inherent in the INC and LAI relationship, one that was never fully resolved in 1928. The story of these events in Brussels and then Madras reveals the contested nature of nationalist politics in India, as well as the central problem in Nehru's attempt to internationalize nationalism.

Motilal's participation in the LAI meeting in Brussels set the stage for a debate over India's commitment to anti-imperialism. The Brussels meeting brought together for the first time the general council, a group of associated and affiliated members larger than the executive council. Attendees included delegates from India, China, Egypt, Indonesia, Korea, Indo-China, Palestine, Persia, Syria, Mexico, Argentina, Uruguay, Holland, Belgium, France, Germany, Britain, Japan, the United States, and South Africa. Despite this impressive geographical spread, many members of the original executive committee, who had been influential in keeping the LAI afloat that year, had left for their respective homes or resigned from their posts. The attrition of socialists continued after the resignations of the British and Dutch LSI members in 1927. At the same time, colonial authorities detained and arrested key members of the LAI from the colonies. Mohammed Hatta, the Indonesian delegate, was incarcerated. Others, like Nehru, returned to their homes for prolonged anticolonial struggles.

The question of Indian independence was central to the executive committee meeting of the LAI, which took place immediately before the opening sessions of the general council. This smaller meeting was the one Motilal attended, and he spoke on behalf of India, although he did not have an official mandate from the INC. The elder Nehru presented a dramatically different picture of the INC than the one his son offered in the months he served the League in Europe. Motilal stressed that the INC was a platform for various viewpoints to meet, and that many worked for independence within the empire. He argued that Gandhi's *swaraj* meant "independence with the British Empire, if possible, and without the British Empire, if necessary."[6] He added that this view of *swaraj* as "independence within the British Empire" represented the "majority opinion."[7] Motilal never offered his personal position on the question, although he admitted that there might be a shift in India toward independence without empire following the Simon Commission announcement.

The elder Nehru's commentary on the Indian situation remained highly unsatisfying for other Indian members in the audience, such as Chatto and Saklatvala. Chatto found it "very strange" that only a minority in India sought a break from the British Empire, and argued that it was "unfair" to represent the entirety of India as a place where no organizations sought "absolute independence for India."[8] Both Chatto and Saklatvala also expressed deep concerns that the INC might betray the Indian workers and peasants as the KMT had in China. Accepting dominion status within the empire would exemplify this betrayal and show clearly that the INC was not representative of Indian workers and especially those sympathetic to communism. In a second speech, Motilal addressed his colleagues' fears by assuring them that the INC represented a diverse variety of peoples in India, peasants and workers included. However, the INC was not communist or even socialist, asserted Motilal. He added that he attended the meeting on the assumption that the LAI was an organization "in which one need[ed] not be a communist to join [and] all the members were not communists."[9] Motilal concluded defensively by arguing the INC reserved the right to determine its goals regardless of what anti-imperialists abroad thought.

At nearly the same time, Motilal's son piloted the INC's first resolution accepting independence. His sweeping success in Madras led observers such as Indulal Yagnik, editor of the Bombay-based *Hindustan*, to recall the Madras INC meeting in 1927 as "historic" because Nehru, "having new

---

[6] The minutes to the General Council meeting are found in the Comintern Papers (English, German and French). For an English transcript of Motilal's speeches, see 542/1/14/6–7 and 542/1/14/15–20, RGASPI. This reference is from 542/1/14/15.
[7] Ibid.   [8] Chatto's statement at General Council Meeting, 542/1/14/11, RGASPI.
[9] Minutes, 542/1/14/7, RGASPI.

idealism and ideals … became eager to lead the country on the path of revolution after his return to the country."[10] In Madras, Nehru set in motion several key resolutions within the INC to further align the anticolonial nationalist movement and the anti-imperialist League. Among the most relevant was the formal resolution declaring the INC's association with the LAI, a decision already approved by the AICC. The second resolution was specific to Nehru's experiences in Brussels and his aim to forge greater anti-imperialist ties with China. This resolution sent India's "warmest greetings" to China and recognized the Chinese people as "comrades of the Indian people in their joint struggle against Imperialism." Another resolution, "The War Danger," read like a recitation of the LAI's discourse, stating that the INC recognized the "extensive war preparations" undertaken by the British and predicted that "an attempt [would] be made to make India again a tool in the hands of foreign imperialists." It concluded that it was the "duty" of Indian people to refuse to cooperate in any way with these war preparations.[11]

The final and most significant contribution – the independence resolution – was the first to move away from the ambiguities of *swaraj* and toward a clear and definite goal of "national independence." It also was the one resolution that required a rethinking of INC policy, as the others were simply informed by expressions of solidarity. The departure in INC policy on the question of independence was discussed extensively in the working committee of the INC, which approved it before the open sessions and after three hours of debate.[12] Nehru moved the resolution on the first day of the open sessions with a special statement that sought to focus on the ambiguities of the INC goals. He argued that acceptance of this resolution meant control of "defense forces," "financial and economic policy," and "relations with foreign countries."[13] In doing so, his statement underscored the importance of this resolution in outlining a specific set of criteria for independence that countered dominion status in anti-imperialist terms.

The Madras sessions were a preliminary but important step for Nehru. They marked his first attempt to shape the future trajectory of the INC in

---

[10] Indulal Yagnik, *The Autobiography of Indulal Yagnik*, ed. and trans. from Gujarati to English by Devavrat N. Pathak, Howard Spodek, and John R. Wood. New Delhi: Manohar Publishers & Distributors, 2011. See vol. 2, part II, 358.

[11] "Resolutions, 1927," File 4–1927, AICC.

[12] Nehru to Gandhi, January 11, 1928, *SWJN*, vol. 3, 11–14

[13] Nehru, Move to accept Independence Resolution, December 27, 1927, *SWJN*, vol. 3, 6.

ways that contended with leading luminaries who supported dominion status. Yet, the glaring omission, in his resolutions, of socialism and working-class mobilization, which had been central to the "special blend" of the LAI, demonstrated some restraint on Nehru's part in late 1927. He recognized independence as a potential fulcrum for a shift in INC priorities. At the same time, socialism and social equality for the peasants and workers would have to wait for a more confident and polished Nehru to articulate them at a later date. He was prudent to constrain some of his ideas, for several important INC leaders, notably Nehru's father and Gandhi, were not in Madras for the annual meeting.

Sadly for Nehru and the LAI, the high tide of the Madras Congress began to recede immediately after the final session closed and he returned home to Allahabad. No more than a week after the sessions wrapped up, Gandhi sent a personal letter to Nehru expressing his displeasure in the resolutions passed in the annual congress, which he thought were "careless."[14] Gandhi followed the letter with a public assault on the independence resolution in an article appropriately titled "Independence vs. Swaraj," which appeared in his publication *Young India*. In the article, Gandhi called the resolution a "tragedy," for it was hastily passed and without a thought for action.[15] Instead, he argued that *swaraj*, as an indigenous term, was more appropriate than independence, which used the language of the British to define the INC goals.[16] Beyond semantics, *swaraj*, according to Gandhi, was "greater than and include[d] independence" because it sought "freedom from the English yoke" and the

---

[14] Gandhi to Nehru, January 4, 1928, *CWMG*, vol. 41, 79–80.
[15] Mohandas Gandhi, "Independence v. Swaraj," *Young India*, January 12, 1928, in *CWMG*, vol. 41, 104–107.
[16] Nehru later changed his demand to *purna swaraj* rather than the English term "complete independence." This is largely because of Gandhi's linguistic criticism. Volumes of studies on the linguistic and ideological meaning of *swaraj* exists. For a recent study of the founding figures of India, including a chapter on Gandhi's *swaraj*, see Ananya Vajpeyi, *Righteous Republic: The Political Foundations of Modern India* (Cambridge, MA: Harvard University Press, 2012). This book is important in resituating nationalist discourse and ideas within an authentically Indian epistemology, but much of it reduces the complex ideas of founding figures such as Gandhi and Nehru to ancient Indian texts. For a more sophisticated examination of Gandhi and his ideas, see David Hardiman, *Gandhi in His Time and Ours: The Global Legacy of His Ideas* (New York: Columbia University Press, 2003); or the classic biographical texts on Gandhi: B. R. Nanda, *Gandhi and His Critics* (Delhi: Oxford University Press, 1985); Judith M. Brown. *Gandhi: Prisoner of Hope* (New Haven: Yale University Press, 1989); and Bhikhu C. Parekh, *Gandhi* (Oxford: Oxford University Press, 1997).

deliverance of the "so-called weaker races of the earth from the crushing heels of Western exploitation in which England is the greatest partner."[17]

The tensions between Nehru and Gandhi, often characterized as struggles over nationalist imperatives, grew from divergent ideas about India's role in the world as much as from those about all-Indian nationalist politics. From its earliest articulation, Gandhi's *swaraj* was globally informed, in particular by his conception of Western civilization as oppositional to an indigenous and authentic Indian civilization. This was laid out very early in his political career, when he wrote *Hind Swaraj* in 1909.[18] For Gandhi, the great social and cultural ills of the world rested at the feet of Western civilization and everything it represented. Western civilization was immoral and materialistic, while Indian civilization retained for the world a religious, moral, and ethical compass. However, Gandhi maintained that *swaraj* was a transformation within Indian society and that the British could stay as long as indigenous norms and culture were accepted and protected.[19]

Whereas Gandhi's *swaraj* reflected a worldview divided along the fault lines of East and West, Nehru saw a world split between imperialism and anti-imperialism. In both cases, industrialization divided the two binaries, but for Gandhi the fruits of industry were not desirable for India. On the other hand, Nehru attributed no fault to industrialization, but to the capitalist and imperialist exploitation driving the process. A reversal of capitalism, rather than industrialization, was the answer for anti-imperialists such as Nehru. Throughout 1928, Nehru increasingly worked to convince the INC that Indian independence was an absolute necessity. For him, the debate was not merely semantic, but the pivot on which all other projects for national, social, and international liberation rested. At stake in the debate was not only the future of the INC, but also that of India and the world.

In a letter to Gandhi, Nehru defended his position on independence by framing it in relation to the world. Nehru made it a point that he attached "more importance to it [independence] than to almost anything else," and that the resolution on independence was the result of hours of debate and many speeches.[20] It was hardly "careless," as Gandhi had accused. Nehru continued by arguing that he found his own vision of India's future to be "very different" to Gandhi's. He cited that Gandhi had no plan for the continuing work of the INC beyond constructive projects and *khadi*

---

[17] Gandhi, "Independence v. Swaraj," 106.   [18] Gandhi, *Hind Swaraj*, 1909.   [19] Ibid.
[20] Nehru to Gandhi, January 11, 1928, *SWJN*, vol. 3, 11.

(home-spun goods) production. Tongue in cheek, he added that *khadi* would do very little good for India if another war came. Instead, the INC had to train and prepare for world events. Moreover, he argued that Gandhi's constructive programs and rural uplift were "well and fine, but none of them [struck] at the core reasons" for Indian poverty.[21] Further, Nehru wrote that Gandhi's attempts to "belittle and ridicule" his resolutions and leadership in Madras had been a "painful experience."[22]

For Nehru, imperialism and capitalism were the "core reasons" for oppressive conditions in India and the world – ones which Gandhi inaccurately called Western civilization. Nehru wrote that the West possessed many excellent qualities, and that Gandhi's sweeping condemnation of Western civilization was troubling. More pointedly, he likened Gandhi's writings on the United States and France to Katherine Mayo's highly offensive writing on India, which Gandhi had called a "drain inspector's report."[23] For Nehru, Gandhi's worldview missed the mark. Global problems were not caused by inherent values and morals of the West or industrialization, but rather by capitalist – and, by extension, imperialist – expansion. Nehru also stressed that India had much to learn from the wider world and the West. From Egypt, it was clear that nominal independence within the empire did not bring greater freedom. From Soviet Russia, Nehru argued that India could learn new and alternative means to deal with poverty and inequality.

Nehru also went to the public to defend his position in the schism with Gandhi. He spoke directly to the title of Gandhi's earlier article, "Independence vs. *Swaraj*," by arguing that there was "no conflict" between the two terms.[24] "Swaraj can and does mean complete freedom," and the independence resolution passed in Madras had cemented this definition, argued Nehru. He claimed that ambiguities had "crept into" the INC's interpretation of *swaraj* over the years since the non-cooperation campaign; subsequently, many sought to substitute dominion status for *swaraj*. However, Nehru declared unequivocally, the independence resolution removed such ambiguities and proved beyond doubt that *swaraj* means

---

[21] Ibid., 12.   [22] Ibid.
[23] Nehru to Gandhi, *SWJN*, vol. 3, 14. Gandhi called Katherine Mayo's book on India a "drain inspectors report." In general, Indians were outraged by the one-sided perspective of Mayo, an American who argued for the benefits of British imperialism. See her *Mother India* (New York: Harcourt, Brace & Co., 1927). For a book on the Indian responses to this report, see Mrinalini Sinha, *Specters of Mother India*.
[24] Nehru, Statement on the Independence Resolution, *The Tribune*, January 27, 1928. Reprinted in *SWJN*, vol. 3, 20–23.

independence. He also argued that dominion status was no answer for India, as it supported British imperialist oppression around the world, especially in China, Egypt, Mesopotamia, and Persia.

The public conflict with Gandhi was the first in Nehru's prolonged struggle to convince his fellow nationalists that the question of independence was not only a local and all-India expression, but also a global anti-imperialist cause with implications beyond the subcontinent. Gandhi and Nehru somewhat resolved their differences in February 1927, when the two met in person. They came to a temporary détente over the issue of independence, although it would continue to divide the two congressmen until the passage of a second independence resolution in 1930. In the time between their meeting and the affirmation of independence in 1930, the INC would backslide on the question of independence on several occasions, forcing Nehru into compromising between his internationalist and nationalist allegiances and aspirations.

More was at stake for Nehru than the nuances of linguistics or national aspirations for India. Nehru criticized Gandhi's *swaraj* on the grounds that nothing short of independence would challenge British influence across the world, where Indian manpower, resources, and military had bolstered the empire. Moreover, independence was the only way for India to participate in a wider campaign against the dual forces of oppression worldwide: capitalism and imperialism. Nehru's critique of Gandhi was grounded in anti-imperialist discourse, which now became a primary set of ideas guiding Nehru's politics in India. Nehru's argument for independence would be tempered by anti-imperialist internationalism, which increasingly placed him at odds with his political mentor Gandhi and many of his fellow congressmen, including his father.

THE LAI AND THE INDEPENDENCE FOR INDIA LEAGUE

In July 1928, Chatto launched the LAI's first journal, the *Anti-Imperialist Review (AIR)*. The inaugural edition featured six essays voicing the LAI's fundamental ideas about anti-imperialism consistent with the Brussels Congress discourse in 1927. The essays underscored the special "blend" of anti-imperialism and the urgency for collective action in the face of the menacing war danger posed by imperialists. James Maxton, chairman of the LAI, had the honor of capturing the spirit and message in his opening remarks, in which he reminded readers that the working classes and the colonized shared a common oppression at the hands of capitalism: "Life under capitalism is bad enough for the Working Class in the highly developed industrial countries of Europe, but it is infinitely worse for the subject peoples, and particularly the coloured races, subjected as they are, to the double tyranny of foreign government and foreign capitalism." The LAI, Maxton argued, was the first organization to coordinate "every part of the world" in the pursuit of "the common task of emancipation."[25]

AIR was emblematic of the myriad of propaganda and letters pouring out of Berlin to anti-imperialists worldwide in 1928, which kept Nehru connected in solidarity with his many comrades from the LAI. The propaganda and letters offered a powerful medium that created for Nehru an imagined community of anti-imperialists, even when the distance between India and the wider world seemed vast and all-encompassing. Much has been written about print culture as a means to construct and reinforce nationalism as an imagined community.[26] The circulation of propaganda, alongside a rich and robust exchange of letters between Nehru and his comrades, constructed a supranational community that enabled anticolonial leaders, socialists, and communists across the world to simultaneously engage with a shared set of ideas about anti-imperialism and confront the capitalist-imperialist world collectively. Nehru continued to engage with anti-imperialism at the same time as he campaigned for independence within the nationalist movement. These activities, national and international, were not mutually exclusive for Nehru; rather, his interfaces with anti-imperialists abroad came to inform his nationalist project in India. This exchange is especially illustrative in the case of Nehru's decision to establish the Independence for India League in the later months of 1928. He created the Indian League as a bridgehead between the INC and the LAI.

For many of the months after Nehru's return from Europe, he depended on Chatto in Berlin for his connections to the world of anti-imperialism. In February 1928, Chatto assumed the primary duties of international secretary of the Berlin office.[27] With Chatto at the helm, the LAI entered a new era of anti-imperialist activism. Chatto had a supreme ability to organize the movement. He wielded an impressive number of contacts worldwide and deftly managed widespread propaganda networks. He had done so in other capacities in London, Stockholm, and Berlin, and he was a polyglot

---

[25] *Anti-Imperial Review* 1, no. 1 (July 1928), File 37, LAI Papers, P.C. Joshi Archives, Jawaharlal Nehru University (JNU), New Delhi (hereafter LAI Papers, JNU).

[26] See the seminal text by Benedict Anderson, *Imagined Communities*.

[27] Gibarti left for a mission to the USA, while Liau left Berlin because of personality conflicts with Münzenberg. For the latter point, see Petersson, *Willi Münzenberg*.

who commanded several languages, including English, French, German, Swedish, Russian, and Bengali. The LAI propaganda networks blossomed under Chatto's tutelage, and Nehru and executives such as Baldwin and Bridgeman noted in their letters that the secretariat was markedly more professional and active under the Berlin exile's leadership.

Nehru benefited substantially from this advantageous shift in LAI personnel. Chatto and he developed a strong professional and personal relationship in this period. While the archival record of their burgeoning relationship is thin for the time Nehru lived in Europe, the correspondence between the two comrades after 1927 is abundant and revealing. These exchanges were often personal and filled with rich anecdotes on the life and times of Indian activists in the 1920s. They shared not only political news but also updates on Chatto's health and financial stability, as well as Nehru's anxieties over Kamala's illness and chronic relapses. On one occasion, Nehru sent Chatto tea from India in order to relieve his homesickness.[28] At the same time, the political discussions between Nehru and Chatto on the issues of Indian politics and the INC demonstrated a frank and at times contentious dialogue. Their letters especially provided an opportunity for debate over the best means and goals for the Indian anticolonial movement. Chatto supported a more radical and immediate agenda for India's independence struggle, while Nehru argued for a gradual "training" of India's political elite. Even in the most hostile exchanges, however, the correspondence retained collegiality and respect for the opposing ideas shared in their letters.

Nehru primarily came to imagine and engage with the anti-imperialist world through the letters and propaganda produced by Chatto in the Berlin secretariat. Correspondence was difficult, if not impossible, between India and other colonies. Travel and postal routes flowed with greater consistency and frequency between India and Europe, especially the metropole. Of course, the Indian government intercepted a great deal of correspondence, and the colonial intelligence was especially suspicious of letters between India and countries like China, Indonesia, Egypt, and Soviet Russia.[29] Nevertheless, Nehru communicated solidarity and comradeship with other colonies through the League networks. He shared news about India with Chatto as a means to spread updates throughout the LAI. Whenever

---

[28] Nehru to Chatto, July (no date) 1928, *SWJN*, vol. 3, 133.
[29] There are files of confiscated LAI correspondence between Nehru and Chatto, for example. See File 11, LAI, JNU. Most letters eventually arrived at the specified destination after delay.

his correspondence and news could not reach anti-imperialist comrades abroad, Nehru wrote to Chatto to convey his messages. Of the imprisonment of Mohamed Hatta, the Indonesian member of the League, for instance, Nehru wrote Berlin: "I am anxiously awaiting the decision in Mohammed Hatta's case. Send my love to him if you are writing to him."[30]

Together with Nehru, Chatto imagined and celebrated the possibilities of an anti-imperialist world that connected India and all of Asia in solidarity against imperialism. Chatto wrote to share news of an LAI affiliation in Iraq in early 1929, and added to Nehru: "You personally enjoy a very considerable reputation in Irak, as you will have seen from the letter published in the 'Mahratt' from its Baghdad correspondent."[31] He similarly celebrated with Nehru the official support of the Wafd Party in early 1929.[32] He intoned that Egyptian nationalists had "come to realize that the more the nationalist movements mean business, the more they must cooperate with the world's anti-imperialist forces."[33] As he saw it, the LAI was successful in convincing the nationalists in Egypt that "imperialisms hang together and must be hanged together."[34] Chatto also reported that the Indonesian nationalist papers had given such praise to the League that its anti-imperial literature had been translated into Malay and distributed widely. According to an optimistic Chatto, the League would soon "have the satisfaction of recording the affiliation of all national movements from Morocco to Indonesia."[35]

Another important task to Chatto and Nehru had been the integration into the League of other noteworthy organizations in India, such as the AITUC; the Hindustani Seva Dal; the Sikh League; Kirti Kisan Sabha; and the Workers and Peasants Party (WPP) of Bombay, Bengal, and Madras. To Mangal Singh of the Sikh League, Nehru wrote: "I feel that it is very desirable for our organizations to associate themselves with international bodies like the League against Imperialism. This helps the anti-imperialist cause and at the same time broadens our own outlook."[36]

An additional scheme devised by Nehru and Chatto sought to revitalize the Berlin Indian Information Bureau. Chatto had developed this bureau in 1925 to disseminate propaganda for Indian independence throughout

---

[30] Nehru to Liau Hansin, April 18, 1928, *SWJN*, vol. 3, 128–129.
[31] Chatto to Nehru, April 3, 1929, File 6, LAI, JNU.
[32] The Wafd Party formed in 1920 to go to the League of Nations and lobby for Egyptian independence. See Noor Khan, *Egyptian-Indian Nationalist Collaboration*.
[33] Chatto to Nehru, April 3, 1929, File 6, LAI, JNU.
[34] Chatto to Nehru, April 9, 1929, File 1–1929, AICC.
[35] Chatto to Nehru, April 3, 1929.
[36] Nehru to Mangal Singh, July 10, 1928, *SWJN*, vol. 3, 136.

Continental Europe.[37] Nehru secured some INC funds for Chatto to reopen the bureau and develop additional programs designed to funnel Indian students to Berlin rather than London for their educational needs in 1928. In addition to Chatto, another Indian expatriate in Berlin, A. C. N. Nambiar, helped run the INC-funded information bureau.[38] The letters from Chatto in his personal capacity and as the secretary of the LAI or the Information Bureau expressed a strong desire to coordinate as much as possible Nehru's work in India with the international anti-imperialist community. Indeed, Chatto reminded Nehru: "If you think that there is any special action we can undertake please let us know by letter or by wire and we shall do our very best to carry it through."[39]

A consistent exchange of letters with Bridgeman in London and Baldwin in New York further enhanced Nehru's connections with anti-imperialism abroad. In his correspondence with both Bridgeman and Baldwin, Nehru continued to participate in a collaborative venture to strengthen the LAI institutionally and mobilize sympathizers to the Indian anti-imperialist cause in Britain and the USA respectively. Nehru and Baldwin continued their discussions about the LAI's organization and finances. Baldwin had already been in regular touch with the Berlin secretariat on these matters.[40] To Nehru, Baldwin confided his ongoing concerns that the LAI had little money and would increasingly turn to Moscow to finance itself.[41] The two, however, felt confident that Chatto would ensure a proper balance of communists and noncommunists. Moreover, Nehru continued to fundraise and remit donations to the LAI on behalf of the INC. Nehru's monthly letters to Bridgeman focused primarily on the policies of the metropole and the work of the British LAI.[42] These relationships with Baldwin and Bridgeman would be imperative to Nehru's internationalist activities throughout the late 1920s and 1930s as the Indian independence campaign developed apace.

The first edition of *AIR* was probably the most compelling and power-ful avenue for Nehru to stay connected. He received his first copy in

---

[37] Barooah, *Chatto*.
[38] A. C. N. Nambiar was another Indian expatriate in Berlin, and Nehru appointed him Indian ambassador to West Germany after independence.
[39] Chatto to Nehru, April 9, 1929, File 1–1929, AICC.
[40] Baldwin wrote Chatto several letters about the budget. He arranged for a loan of $500 to keep the LAI afloat in 1927 and worked with Chatto on a plan to repay it. Their exchanges at one time included a financial statement from the LAI, although this document is not in the archive. Box 8, File 3, Baldwin Papers.
[41] See Nehru–Baldwin correspondence *SWJN*, vol. 3.
[42] Nehru and Bridgeman correspondence (1928–1929), File FD-23, AICC.

October 1928, and he applauded it by writing to Chatto: "I liked it. I hope you will be able to continue and maintain a high standard."[43] *AIR* also arrived at the headquarters of some of the most influential movements of the interwar period, in places as far flung as Argentina, Brazil, China, Cuba, Ecuador, Egypt, France, Germany, Great Britain, Holland, Ireland, Japan, Mexico, Nicaragua, Palestine, Philippines, Puerto Rico, San Salvador, South Africa, the United States, and Uruguay. The League's information and propaganda also provided rich material for recirculation in Indian publications such as the *Forward,* the *Bombay Chronicle, The Hindu,* and the *Hindustan Times.* It often frequented the pages of INC bulletins as a constant reminder that India's struggle was part of broader anti-imperialist campaign.

The first *AIR* articulated a shared history and future for anti-imperialists and the LAI. It began with short greetings from not only James Maxton, but also from Madame Sun Yat-Sen and Srinivasa Iyengar, an ex-president of the INC from Madras who had traveled to London and officially represented the nationalist movement at a British LAI meeting. The rest of the articles followed and expanded upon familiar themes rooted in the Brussels Congress and early LAI discourse: the war danger and the necessity for anti-imperialist solidarities across socialist, communist, and nationalist divides. Many of these essays delivered strong criticism of the LSI for its attack on the LAI, as well as the KMT for turning on Chinese communists. Additionally, the articles represented an impressive breadth of geographic coverage and highlighted anti-imperialist struggles in Latin America, Africa, and Asia.

Chatto invited Nehru to write an essay for the first edition, but he did not finish a draft in time. Instead, Saklatvala, the Indian member of the CPGB, wrote the main article dedicated to India, "British Imperialism in India: A World Menace."[44] In it, Saklatvala recited a familiar argument about India and anti-imperialism. The history of the British in India was

---

[43] *Anti-Imperial Review,* July 1928, LAI, JNU.
[44] Sharpurji Saklatvala, "British Imperialism in India: A World Menace," *Anti-Imperialist Review,* July 1928, 25–31, LAI, JNU. On Saklatvala, see J. A. Zumoff, "'Is America Afraid of the Truth?': The Aborted North American Trip of Shapuriji Saklatvala, MP," *Indian Economic and Social History Review* 53, no. 3 (2016): 405–447. Only three biographies exist: Marc Wadsworth, *Comrade Sak: Shapurji Saklatvala MP, A Political Biography* (Leeds: Peepal Tree, 1998); Mike Squires, *Saklatvala: A Political Biography* (London: Lawrence & Wishart, 1990); and Panchanan Saha, *Shapurji Saklatvala: A Short Biography* (Delhi: Peoples' Pub. House, 1970). See also Nicholas Owen, *The British Left and India.*

one of imperialism as an outgrowth of capitalism and its desire to extract labor and goods from the colony. Secondly, imperial rivalry had led to armament worldwide and posed a serious war danger threat. He cited British arms development in India and the American occupation of Nicaragua. Saklatavala used this platform to argue that Indian nationalists needed to recognize India as a world problem because it supplied resources and manpower for British imperialism. He argued forcibly (and in bold print) that given the war danger, Indian leaders were "no longer at liberty" to "compromise with British imperialism" for their own personal gains and at the expense of the masses.[45]

The first issue of the *AIR* also welcomed the growing relationship between the INC and the LAI. In a report on the LAI's activities, no doubt written by Chatto, the section on India represented the nationalist movement as a powerful anti-imperialist force and praised Nehru's work on strengthening the LAI–INC connection. The LAI and its members worldwide, wrote Chatto, had "no hesitation" in stating that Nehru's participation in Brussels "had a definite effect upon [the] international and internal policy" of the INC. The resolution in Madras, the first to accept independence as the INC goal, was the clearest example of the importance of anti-imperialism and the LAI to the shaping of Indian nationalist politics. The report further cited the frequency with which LAI news appeared in the Indian press and the statements of other key Indian leaders, such as Dr. M. A. Ansari, Srinivasa Iyengar, and Motilal Nehru, who all endorsed closer ties between the INC and anti-imperialism abroad.[46] The most crucial aspect of the LAI in these early years was its ability to support the INC even when the nationalist movement had strong voices advocating for dominion status. The LAI circulars throughout 1928 celebrated the meager successes of Nehru and encouraged the INC to take up the gauntlet and join the worldwide struggle. In a resolution on India approved at the executive meeting of the LAI in April 1928, the LAI continued to praise the work of the INC and championed Nehru's independence resolution for recognizing that "all other formulas of so-called 'freedom within the Empire' are but camouflage forms of foreign domination."[47]

---

[45] Saklatvala, "British Imperialism in India."
[46] Report on the Development of the League against Imperialism, *Anti-Imperialist Review*, July 1928, 83–93, LAI, JNU.
[47] Resolutions of the League against Imperialism Executive Committee Meeting, April 28, 1929, File 11, LAI, JNU.

The centerpiece of the first edition of *AIR* was an article by founder Willi Münzenberg, which expounded the first history of the LAI since the Brussels Congress. In an essay entitled "From Demonstration to Organization," Münzenberg celebrated the Brussels Congress and the foundation of the LAI in 1927 as profound "demonstration[s]" of solidarity against imperialism. Proof was found in three places: first, the LAI was a menace to imperialism and immediately provoked colonial authorities to act against it in places like the Netherlands, France, and India. Second, its importance to the colonial world forced the LSI to proscribe it. According to Münzenberg, this renunciation was a sign that only the LAI was truly anti-imperialist and representative of those struggling for national sovereignty and social equality in the colonies. Third, Münzenberg focused on India and argued that the INC's association and Nehru's role on the executive committee demonstrated that the Brussels Congress and LAI had "taken a definite place in the Indian struggle for national liberty."[48] Additionally, Münzenberg appealed to members to maintain the LAI's solidarity across ideological, geographic, and party lines even in the face of resistance from socialists and the LSI.

The future trajectory of the anti-imperialist movement, and the relationship between bourgeois nationalists and socialists or communists, presented a dilemma that Münzenberg skirted around in his piece for *AIR*. In spirit, his essay stressed solidarity and the active overlooking of differences among working-class mobilizations and anticolonial nationalism. But when considering the tasks that lay ahead, Münzenberg considered the mobilization of workers and peasants as essential, and this led him to some difficult conclusions in thinking about India: "Although the class differentiation that is fast growing among the Indian people must some day inevitably lead to a struggle, the common interest of otherwise socially different groups against imperialist oppressors is so strong that they are able to unite in a common movement for the overthrow of foreign imperialism."[49] This passage is revealed "inevitably" of struggle between those seeking working-class mobilization worldwide and those elites engaged in anticolonial struggle. In retrospect, these may appear impossible to reconcile; however, in 1928, it was not only possible but also desirable to seek common cause even when contradiction and conflict were foreseen in some imagined future. In other words, this

---

[48] Ibid.
[49] Willi Münzenberg, "From Demonstration to Organization," *Anti-Imperialist Review*, July 1928, 4–10, LAI, JNU.

ability to actively overlook contradiction and difference was reflective of the internationalist moment of the late 1920s in which the LAI was rooted. In addition to praising the growing relationship between the INC and the LAI, Münzenberg called for the LAI to transition from being a "demonstration" in Brussels to a solid "organization." For Münzenberg, the LAI's solidification meant the establishment of national sections worldwide devoted to working across party lines for the greater causes of anti-capitalism and anti-imperialism. He found inspiration from the Mexican anti-imperialist league and their monthly publication, *Liberator*. He called upon the United States, India, and South Africa specifically to do the same. Münzenberg's final message was a clarion call to all anti-imperialists. The suffering "hundreds of millions" needed the urgent help of the LAI and its members. Only "strong, active and efficient organizations" of the LAI could help the suffering masses. "Therefore: ALL HANDS ON BOARD! HELP US TO DEVELOP FROM THE DEMONSTRATION INTO THE ORGANIZATION!" charged Münzenberg to his readers.[50]

Nehru took up the call for India to "organize" a national league for anti-imperialism in 1928, when he piloted the first Independence for India League. The India League was the product of two forces. The "organization" of an Indian national branch was of central importance to the LAI, and it was underscored repeatedly in *AIR* articles and other circulars and letters from Berlin. Nehru moved cautiously on this idea after the Madras Congress and fallout with Gandhi. But when the INC appeared to backslide on the Madras independence resolution and toward dominion status within the empire as its goal in August 1928, Nehru prepared for more dramatic measures. He launched a distinct anti-imperialist "organization" to unite Indians within the subcontinent for the cause of independence.

The major event that overturned the independence resolution was the All-Parties Conference, which had the task of proposing constitutional reforms for India. The All-Parties committee, on which Motilal Nehru chaired and Jawaharlal Nehru served as secretary, had several broad aims. It brought together a wider group of Indian leaders beyond the INC and included other political and social organizations to propose a constitution that would counter the one submitted by the Simon Commission. The draft constitution, known as the Nehru Report, was the crowning achievement of its primary architect, Motilal Nehru, who introduced it at an all-parties session in Lucknow in August 1928. The document tackled many domestic

[50] Ibid.

concerns, such as religious and communal tensions. Most controversially, it rejected separate electorates and instead proposed a plan to have reserved seats for Muslim minorities in the central government only for those provinces in which Hindus formed a majority.[51] This contentious decision led to Mohammed Ali Jinnah's withdrawal from the INC, setting the stage for his later leadership of the Muslim League and its demand for Pakistan.

Equally contentious and relevant to the younger Nehru was the report's acceptance of dominion status within the British Empire. The unveiling of this document prompted a crisis within the Nehru household and the INC. The younger Nehru took to the podium and voiced his objection to any constitution that backpedaled on the independence resolution passed in Madras. He implored his fellow congressmen to think beyond India and consider the implications of dominion status for the worldwide struggle against imperialism. He asked his colleagues rhetorically: "When we obtain Dominion Status ... Are we going to assist England and the other Dominions in exploiting Egypt and Africa?"[52] He argued that dominion status could only mean India and Britain sharing in a "joint imperial foreign policy."[53] He also chastised the drafters of the Nehru Report for ignoring the concerns and rights of Indian workers and peasants, who continued to be abused by British capitalists. Nehru reminded his audience members that they represented at most the wealthiest 5 percent of India. How could they speak for the nation without recognizing the exploitative and oppressive nature of the British raj on the vast majority of Indians?

Nehru completely withdrew his support from the Nehru Report and announced the establishment of the Independence for India League, which convened its first meeting on the same grounds as the All-Parties Conference. Nehru read a statement to the all-parties delegation, signed by a number of high-profile congressmen, who alongside Nehru collectively disavowed the report and its rejection of Indian independence. In it, he stated firmly that a constitution for India "should only be based on full independence."[54] More than twenty attendees met under the auspices of the new Independence League, which set out to ensure that the INC

---

[51] Nehru Report, reprinted in *Selected Works of Motilal Nehru*, ed. by Ravinder Kumar, D. N. Panigrahi, and H. D. Sharma, vol. 6 (Vikas: New Delhi: 1982).

[52] Nehru, Speech at All-Parties Conference in Lucknow, August 29, 1928, reprinted in *SWJN*, vol. 3, 57.

[53] Ibid., 57.   [54] Ibid., 61.

upheld the Madras resolution on independence. To be clear, the all-parties report was not a mandate for the INC, but rather a set of recommendations for the full congress delegation to consider at its annual meeting later that year. The Independence League aimed to ensure that the full delegation of the INC would not support the Nehru Report. However, the endorsement of Motilal Nehru and later Gandhi meant that the younger Nehru's newly minted Independence League had an uphill battle to fight.

This was a critical moment for Nehru to take a firm stance on the issue of Indian nationalism and its relationship to anti-imperialist internationalism. Independence came to mean more to Nehru than peacekeeping with his father or Gandhi, although this decision was not easy for him. He recounted in his autobiography a rather painful memory of the conflict with his father over the report: "We did not argue about the matter much, but there was a definite feeling of mental conflict between us, an attempt to pull different ways . . . [B]oth of us were unhappy about it."[55] Still, the younger Nehru pressed on with his resistance to dominion status.

A second meeting of the Independence League took place in Delhi on November 4–5, 1928. This charted a mission and program of action.[56] A constitution, drawn up primarily by Nehru, met the approval of its constituent members. The overall aim of the Independence League was the promotion of independence within the INC, so members of the new organization also had to be members of the congress. The rest of the constitution represented important elements of Nehru's anti-imperialism. Written into the first documents recorded on the Independence League was its association with the LAI. More than association, however, the Independence League aimed to replicate the LAI's solidarity between nationalists and representatives of workers' and peasants' organizations by specifically making workers' rights and social equality a central issue for the League.[57] In a press interview about the Independence League, Nehru went further than ever in declaring his belief that independence could only be achieved with a socialist plan when he stressed that the newly created organization sought the "reconstruction of Indian society on a basis of social and economic equality."[58]

---

[55] Nehru, *Autobiography*, 198.
[56] Minutes of the Independence for India League Meeting, November 4–5, 1928 (Delhi), File 7–1928, AICC.
[57] Ibid.
[58] Nehru, Interview to the Press for *The Searchlight*, November 21, 1928, reprinted in SWJN, vol. 3, 76–77.

Among his fellow India Leaguers were a handful of prominent congress-men who pushed for independence and social equality, including Subhas Chandra Bose and Srinivasa Iyengar. The latter was a leading nationalist from Madras who served as the INC president in 1926. Among the most notable co-signatories was Bose, a Bengali with similar inclinations toward independence, socialism, and anti-imperialist internationalism.[59] In the late 1920s and early 1930s, Nehru and Bose emerged as leading advocates for complete independence within the INC and also among youth movements, workers' and peasants' parties, and trade unions. Both traveled the Indian countryside and cities in 1928 and 1929 to rally support for complete independence and socialist reform within and outside the framework of the newly created Independence League.

Another notable officer, Shiva Prasad Gupta, deserves some attention. He was a very active member of the INC, serving as treasurer since 1924, and he enlisted his financial services for the Independence League in 1928. No historical scholarship on Gupta exists, although Gandhi ordained him Rashtra Ratna (Jewel of the Nation). In 1988, the government of India issued a stamp bearing his image. He is celebrated in India as a nationalist, as well as a philanthropist for building temples, hospitals and universities in his native city, Varanasi. Gupta came from a wealthy family of indus-trialists, and his fortunes enabled him to serve the INC in the 1920s. He founded *Aaj*, one of the longest running Hindi language publications that promoted the INC struggle in the colonial period. For Nehru, Gupta would become a critical ally in the independence and anti-imperialist struggle not only because of his brief stint in the Independence League, but also because Gupta would represent the INC at the next LAI world congress in 1929, a story taken up in the next chapter.

Nehru was given great leverage as the chief secretary and organizer to oversee the activities and discourse of the Independence League. The program of action agreed upon in the November meeting was threefold: to seek formal association with the LAI, to create a weekly newspaper with a focus on independence, and to prepare for the next meeting, set to take place immediately before the annual sessions of the INC scheduled for December in Calcutta. These goals and plans were made in consultation

---

[59] On Subhas Chandra Bose, see Sugata Bose, *His Majesty's Opponent Subhas Chandra Bose and India's Struggle against Empire* (Cambridge, Mass: Belknap Press of Harvard University Press, 2011). A classic text on Subhas and his brother is Leonard A. Gordon, *Brothers against the Raj: A Biography of Indian Nationalists Sarat and Subhas Chandra Bose* (New York: Columbia University Press, 1990).

with Chatto. In October, Nehru wrote to Chatto with cautious optimism that the Independence League could be the "meeting ground for anti-imperialist activities" in India.[60] Still, Nehru was rightly cautious in his optimism. The Independence League had benefited from the great momentum after the All-Parties Conference, but much remained uncertain in the run-up to Calcutta. Gandhi, a strong opponent of independence as conceptualized by Nehru, would lead the congress, and he had a tremendous ability to shape the course of events and policies in Calcutta. In a letter to Chatto in October, Nehru noted the INC's tendency to "backslide" on the independence resolution and that this position was "gaining ground." He added that while it is easy to pass resolutions, such as the Madras independence resolution, "it is extraordinarily difficult to induce people to act."[61]

Although Chatto had more ambitious plans for the Independence League – such as creating an international office dedicated to LAI work, and having the India League host the first Indian conference of the LAI – the realities on the ground were not amendable to Chatto's grand scheme or even Nehru's modest attempt to organize anti-imperialism in India. The financial resources for the Independence League were meager, and most members did not pay their minimal dues. Nehru advanced the initial money for postage and stationary, which he never recovered. Much to his dismay, the initial momentum of the movement faded after the November meeting in Delhi. The fellow Independence Leaguers returned to their respective homes and did little on behalf of building the organization. Most did not respond to Nehru's letters and appeals, and he admitted that the League existed only on paper by the time of the annual meeting of the Calcutta Congress.

The momentum for the Independence League was further usurped by the energy expended in the INC negotiations over the acceptance of the Nehru Report in Calcutta. Nehru recalled that although there was interest in meeting, the League sessions were conducted "hurriedly" in order to concentrate on the Calcutta Congress. Afterward, Nehru wrote to his Independence League comrades that the group "came away from Calcutta with no definite directions."[62] The India League was moribund thereafter, and by early 1929 Nehru had circulated his final call for Leaguers to participate in the movement by paying dues, responding to his letters, or organizing provincial and local meetings. No responses were

[60] Nehru to Chatto, October 3, 1928, *SWJN*, vol. 3, 143.   [61] Ibid.
[62] Nehru to Independence League members, January 31, 1929, File 7–1928, AICC.

forthcoming, and Nehru gave up the initiative after a final plea to members in April 1929.[63]

Even if the Independence League failed to launch in 1928, it demonstrated several significant points worth mentioning again. Nehru's commitment to Indian independence was deeply ensconced in his ideas about the world and anti-imperialism. He said as much in his letters, and worked with Chatto more than his colleagues in India to launch the Independence League. Secondly, independence was central to Nehru's conceptualization of international and national politics, so much so that he would consider breaking with his father and Gandhi over it. He contemplated leaving his role as secretary of the INC, only to be persuaded to stay on by his fellow congressman and his LAI colleague, Chatto. Even so, both Nehru and the LAI in 1928 saw the INC as the only vehicle in India capable of leading an anticolonial struggle that could connect with the international anti-imperialist movement. Nehru also gained valuable partners within the INC by developing the Independence League with a small cohort of like-minded leftist internationalists. These Indian comrades would help Nehru continue the work of "training" the INC. Meanwhile, Nehru and Chatto continued to collaborate on the best means of persuading congressmen to accept the call to join the anti-imperialist cause and fight for independence from the empire.

The Independence League was the natural fruition of Nehru's goal to internationalize nationalism by bringing the INC in line with the LAI. There has been a great deal of misunderstanding about the Independence League in historical scholarship, likely because of its short existence, from August 1928 to April 1929, and its unimpressive record of activity.[64] The Independence League's failure should not diminish the fact that its creation marked a critical juncture in Nehru's anti-imperialist project. Although discontentment over the Nehru Report informed the immediate context in which it was created, the Independence League also was a product of Münzenberg's clarion call to members of the LAI to develop affiliated organizations locally.

In all, Nehru's correspondence with LAI comrades and engagement with propaganda in the *AIR* informed his strategies in relation to the INC and in maintaining his anti-imperialist solidarities abroad. Nehru benefited from a robust correspondence with a small inner circle of comrades, namely Chatto, Bridgeman, and Baldwin, who contributed a steady

---

[63] Nehru to Independence League members, April 16, 1929, File 7–1928, AICC.
[64] Historians have linked its founding to many different INC leaders. For a short treatment of the League, see Bipan Chandra, *India's Struggle for Independence*, 298–299.

supply of news and moral support as Nehru worked for Indian independence. These letters, and publications like *AIR*, further strengthened Nehru's imagined community of anti-imperialism, which was critical to the continued momentum of the LAI after members of nationalist movements like Nehru returned to their respective colonies to continue their struggles against European colonialism.

SOCIALISM, TRADE UNIONISM, AND THE ANTI-CAPITALIST STRUGGLE IN INDIA

Nehru's socialist impulses and desire to replicate the special "blend" of nationalism, socialism, and communism in India led him to take a more active role in the AITUC. He began attending meetings of the executive committee as an observer in March 1928, and later as a participant in the much larger annual session that December. In both cases, he sought to foster stronger relations between the AITUC and the INC, as well as between Indian trade unionists and the LAI. In the Indian context, the connections between anticolonial nationalism and trade unionism, which included both communists and socialists, replicated the "blend" of anti-imperialism and anti-capitalism worldwide. It was also consistent with Nehru's and Chatto's aim to secure LAI affiliation from every major trade unionist movement across India and Asia. The political terrain of the AITUC was as complicated as that of the INC, and Nehru's navigation of this arena presented equally formidable challenges. Nevertheless, it was this project that served as Nehru's crowning success in 1928, thanks to unforeseen events that unfolded when the LAI sent a fraternal delegate to the AITUC annual session in December of that year.

Nehru joined AITUC discussions at a turning point in the history of the trade union movement in India.[65] The mobilization of the working class and the intensification of strikes reached an apex in 1928. According to AITUC reports, more than 500,000 workers participated in more than 200 strikes in 1928 alone.[66] Striking textile workers in Bombay had

---

[65] Indian labor historiography is voluminous. A good starting point is Rajnarayan Chandavarkar, *Imperial Power and Popular Politics: Class, Resistance and the State in India, c. 1850–1950* (Cambridge: Cambridge University Press, 1998), and also his *The Origins of Industrial Capitalism in India: Business Strategies and the Working Classes in Bombay, 1900–1940* (Cambridge: Cambridge University Press, 1994).

[66] AITUC annual reports have been published in P. S. Gupta, *A Short History of the All-Indian Trade Union, 1920–1947* (New Delhi, AITUC, 1980). For this reference, see the Report on Ninth Session of AITUC, Jharia, December 18–20, 1928, 118.

paralyzed the city and delivered a crushing blow to the colonial economy. At the same time, a growing sectarian divide between moderate and radical trade unionists had accompanied these strikes. The more moderate leaders hoped to work for reforms within the existing colonial state and looked toward the LSI and the International Labor Organization (ILO) in Geneva for support and guidance. On the other hand, more radical leaders pushed for a proletarian revolution, which would overthrow the colonial state and challenge the Indian bourgeoisie. This latter group looked to the Comintern and Moscow for inspiration and directives.

The question of international affiliation was at the crux of AITUC debates in 1928. As Carolien Stolte has argued the divisions within the Indian trade unionist movement often took place over their international affinities and associations rather than local and all-Indian imperatives.[67] To be sure, the AITUC was a coveted prize for international labor organizations worldwide, primarily because it was one of the largest trade union federations of the time. Main contenders like the Comintern and the ILO made bids for the AITUC's loyalty with formal gestures and financial support. However, these attempts failed to sway a majority in either direction until 1928.

The other, equally divisive issue dominating the all-India trade unionist movement was whether the AITUC should support the All-Parties Conference and constitution proposed by the Nehru Report. Should trade unionists participate in a bourgeois-led conference set to determine future constitutional reforms for India? In March, the AITUC executive decided to send observers to the All-Parties Conference set for August. In his capacity as general secretary of the All-Parties Committee, Nehru worked to bring trade unionists into the conversation and in support of a stronger stance on independence. More moderate leaders favored this participation, while other, more radical leaders held that workers struggled against the Indian bourgeoisie as much as against the British colonial ruling class.

Throughout 1928, Nehru and Chatto explored the best strategies for the LAI to gain AITUC and individual trade union affiliations. In Berlin, the international secretariat had made trade union affiliations the primary concentration for the LAI by early 1928.[68] Chatto requested that Nehru "strain every nerve" in bringing this about. By April, Chatto and Nehru worked together to secure association from major labor unions, such as

---

[67] See, Carolien Stolte, "Trade Unions on Trial," *Studies of South Asia, Africa and the Middle East.*
[68] Chatto to Nehru, October 3, 1928. File 11, LAI, JNU.

the Bombay Mill Workers Union, the Bombay Engineering Workers Union, and the Bombay Port Trust Railwaymen's Union.[69] Chatto had already established some important contacts with individual trade unions and the newly established WPP. This latter group was established in 1926, first in Bengal and later in the UP, Bombay, and Punjab. It had stronger ideological affiliations with and connections to the Comintern and communist parties worldwide. The WPP officially joined the ranks of the LAI by 1928.

Still, the AITUC remained the elusive prize that the LAI sought to capture, and Nehru began attending meetings in March and December in an attempt to draw the trade unionist movement closer to the League. Immediately at his first AITUC meeting in March, he recognized the complexities of international affiliation for the AITUC when no consensus emerged on the central question: Should it affiliate with the International Federation of Trade Unions (IFTU) in Amsterdam, an organization associated with the ILO? Nehru, even in his capacity as an observer, spoke out against this affiliation since it would make a formal relationship between the AITUC and the LAI difficult if not impossible. Nehru's second AITUC meeting in December took place in Jharia, when the federation met for its annual session. In a surprising turn of events, Nehru found himself elected president of the AITUC for the upcoming year (1929) by a narrow margin, replacing the outgoing president, C. F. Andrews. His candidacy was supported by trade unionists in the hopes that an outsider to the AITUC might work to bridge the growing divide between radical and moderate members.[70] Nehru intended to make use of this position to promote the LAI within the AITUC.

The AITUC meeting in December 1928 was remarkable for another reason. The LAI managed to send a fraternal delegate, J. W. Johnstone, to Jharia for the session.[71] Johnstone's itinerary included both annual sessions of the AITUC and the INC, although colonial authorities detained him before he arrived in Calcutta for the latter. Johnstone was an American

---

[69] Jhabvala to Chatto, April 19, 1928, File 11, LAI, JNU.

[70] D. B. Kulkarny (Vice-President of AITUC) explains this in a letter to Nehru (President of AITUC), September 6, 1929, File 16–1929, AICC.

[71] For a lengthier discussion of Johnstone's India sojourn and the anticommunist efforts of the British in this story, see Michele Louro, "The Johnstone Affair and Anti-Communism in India," *Journal of Contemporary History*, forthcoming, DOI: 10.1177/0022009416688257. The other essays in this forthcoming issue of the *Journal of Contemporary History* offer a much-need global and transnational reading of anti-communism in the interwar and early postwar years.

citizen and active communist based in Chicago. The historiography on Johnstone is scarce, and he makes only brief and marginal appearances in the major works on American communism. No definitive biography of Johnstone exists.[72] In the United States, Johnstone had been one of the main ringleaders of a deeply divided factionalism that had run rampant in the American communist movement. By 1928, the Comintern identified Johnstone as a chief instigator of division in the US communist movement, and the leadership in Moscow decided to send him on a voyage to India in the hope that his absence would improve solidarity in the American movement. When Johnstone traveled to Moscow in 1928, the Comintern directed him to travel to Berlin to secure proper paperwork for his trip to India.[73]

Johnstone knew very little about India and the anti-imperialist movement before his arrival in Berlin. In fact, he relied on talking points about India and the LAI drafted by Clemens Palme Dutt, an Indian expatriate and CPGB member in London who also belonged to the British national section of the League.[74] Johnstone also carried a copy of the League's first edition of the *AIR* for reference as he prepared to meet with the leading figures of Indian labor and the INC. Johnstone's limited knowledge of India outside of the League literature was further complicated by a departure from Berlin that was so hasty that the LAI headquarters had no time to notify Nehru of his impending arrival. By the time Nehru received a formal introduction to Johnstone by telegram from Berlin, the American had already found his way to Jharia and met Nehru in person.[75] In a rather belated letter, Chatto wrote to Nehru that Johnstone was "not perhaps the very best representative" for the LAI at the AITUC and the INC conferences since he had no time to prepare for his task and the Berlin office had offered only a "bare outline of the history, constitution and work of the League."[76]

Nevertheless, on the first day, Johnstone made a polemic appeal for the AITUC to internationalize its struggle. He argued that India's struggle was "not an isolated one; it is linked up with that of all the oppressed peoples

---

[72] See Theodore Draper, *American Communism and Soviet Russia* (New York: Viking Press, 1960); and Jacob Zumoff, *The Communist International and US Communism, 1919–1929* (Leiden: Brill Publishing, 2014). Even histories of communism in Chicago make little mention of Johnstone. See Randi Storch, *Red Chicago: American Communism at Its Grassroots, 1928–1935* (Champaign: University of Illinois Press, 2009).

[73] Instructions for Johnstone's work in India can be found in the Comintern files, 542/1/26/65–67, RGASPI.

[74] Ibid.   [75] Telegram, LAI to Nehru, no date, File O17-1928, AICC.

[76] Chatto to Nehru, December 5, 1928, File 7, LAI, JNU.

and classes of the world."[77] He reminded his audience that the conditions of Indian workers and those of the "negro" workers in the Jim Crow United States were similar. Both were victims of capitalist and imperialist exploitation at the hands of British and American elites. At the same time, according to Johnstone, India's struggles were not unlike those fought against French imperialism in Syria and Morocco; Dutch imperialism in Java, Sumatra, and Indonesia; and European interventions in China.

Echoing a concern previously voiced by Nehru, Johnstone also inserted a strong argument for AITUC's affiliation to the LAI and the Comintern by claiming that the ILO and LSI supported workers in imperialist countries and neglected the conditions and demands of the colonized. He argued that the two internationals, the Second and Third, continued to talk "different languages" that were "diametrically opposed to each other." He framed these differences in a way that had the Second International supporting imperialism and the Third International representing anti-imperialism: "One speaks the language of imperialist domination and the other speaks the language of the oppressed people. One demands freedom, the other demands a little bright spot in the imperialist crown."[78]

Johnstone's appeal was entirely in line with the positions of Nehru and the LAI, yet it countered the general trend of speeches by AITUC leaders in the 1928 sessions. Most delegates sought to avoid entanglements with international groups abroad. Indeed, nearly 200 delegates attended, all of which were divided in their views on international affiliation. On the table were several resolutions on whether to affiliate with the LAI, IFTU, and the Pan-Pacific Trade Union (connected to the Comintern), as well as on the decisions to participate in an Asiatic Labour Conference (connected to the ILO in Geneva) or the ILO meeting in May 1929. In fact, Jack Ryan, an Australian communist, also attended the sessions and advocated for the AITUC's affiliation to the Pan-Pacific Trade Union. The president of the AITUC, C. F. Andrews, attached great importance to the question of international affiliations in his opening remarks.[79] Andrews was not in

---

[77] For another account of the proceedings, see AITUC Bulletin, Report on Ninth Session of AITUC, Jharia 18–20 December, 1928 (microfilm, NMML) roll 3384.

[78] Gupta, Report on the Ninth Session, 13.

[79] Charles Freer Andrews (1871–1940) was an ordained priest born in England who later became involved with Gandhi's movement in South Africa and India. He was not known for his involvement in Indian trade unionism, although AITUC often elected high-profile and symbolic figures rather than trade unionists. Andrews did not attend AITUC in 1928, but the general secretary read his comments on the first day. Gupta, Report on Ninth Session, 192–130.

attendance in 1928, and his comments were read to the delegation. He argued for the AITUC to "avoid entangling engagements" with either side of the "terrific struggle" that was "amounting to really a Civil War between the two Labour Internationals."[80]

Johnstone was an unlikely candidate to effect change in this environment. Even his meeting with Nehru, a fellow LAI colleague, was not memorable for either anti-imperialist. Nehru made no mention of Johnstone's speech in his letters to Berlin. Johnstone's report to the Comintern later in February 1929 painted Nehru in a rather unfavorable light. He remarked, "Nehru, in fact, is a good anti-imperialist in Europe, but in India he forgets he is a member of the League against Imperialism." He added that Nehru "said nothing at all about the League and made no attempt to support [Johnstone's] speech."[81]

In an abrupt turn of events, however, Johnstone's story took a decisive turn after his arrest on the first day of proceedings in Jharia. In the weeks Johnstone had been in India, the colonial state launched an extensive and worldwide investigation into his identity and potential ties to communism. When authorities confirmed his ties to the Comintern, they issued a warrant for Johnstone's arrest. Johnstone managed to reach Jharia, but colonial authorities were hot on his trail. Immediately following the proceedings on the first day of the congress, British colonial authorities whisked him away in an unmarked car and detained him for two weeks before deporting him on January 2, 1929.[82] His sudden arrest in Jharia – on the opening day of AITUC meetings, no less – ignited an immediate and strong anticolonial protest that shaped the tone and resolutions for the rest of the annual meeting. Johnstone's arrest resonated with moderate and radical leaders alike, who interpreted it as a sign that the colonial state sought to restrict Indian connections to the wider world even if there was no consensus on which international connections trade unionists sought most.

In response, the AITUC delegation took unprecedented steps to affiliate with the LAI in protest of Johnstone's arrest with a series of three resolutions. In the first resolution, the AITUC expressed great "indignation" and "condemnation" over Johnstone's arrest because the colonial state actively prevented "fraternal delegates from overseas from cooperating with the Congress." Further, the AITUC called Johnstone's arrest "a deliberate attack

---

[80] Gupta, Report on Ninth Session, 129–130.
[81] Report by Johnstone to Comintern, 542/1/26/65, RGASPI.
[82] Nehru recalled the event in a letter to Chatto, January 23, 1929, *SWJN*, vol. 3, 296–297.

not only on the rights of workers' organizations from cooperating with each other, but also on the building up of strong labour organization in this country."[83] The second resolution "record[ed] its emphatic protest" against the arrest by declaring AITUC's affiliation with the LAI for a term of one year. The third resolution promised to send two AITUC delegates to the LAI's world congress, planned for mid-1929. Although the resolution to affiliate with the LAI stood for only a year and was more of a symbolic gesture than a substantive one, it was the only decision about international affiliation that all AITUC members could agree upon in 1928.

The atmosphere of "indignation" and "emphatic protest" in AITUC over Johnstone's arrest also spilled over into the annual meeting of the INC in Calcutta a few days later. Nehru was a primary agent in carrying this momentum. In Calcutta, he piloted a resolution demanding Johnstone's immediate release. The formal resolution condemned his deportation as a "deliberate attempt on the part of the Government to prevent the Congress from developing international contacts."[84] The "Johnstone affair," as Nehru called it, was a globally relevant phenomenon to take place on the eve of the INC Calcutta Congress. It demonstrated the salience of India's connections to the world, and the threat these bonds posed to colonial control over India.

In a relatively short period of time, Nehru's political involvement in the Indian trade union movement was marked with success. He transitioned from observer to president, and his primary goal to affiliate the AITUC to the LAI carried the day in Jharia. This was an unlikely and unexpected outcome, and one that Nehru had little to do with. At the same time, these events indicated for Nehru that anti-imperialism, as a special blend of nationalism, socialism, and communism, was possible and perhaps desirable for a wider audience than the INC. In fact, his first forays into trade unionism proved more successful than his attempts to push forward a more anti-imperialist trajectory for the INC in the Calcutta proceedings.

STAGING THE WORLD AT THE CALCUTTA CONGRESS

The *Congress Bulletin*, a weekly circular for local and provincial congress committees, released an entire volume dedicated to the "unique feature" of the 43rd annual session of the INC in Calcutta in December 1928,

---

[83] AITUC Bulletin, Report on Ninth Session (microfilm, NMML), roll 3384.
[84] *Congress Bulletin:* Issued by the Office of the All India Congress Committee, January 15, 1929, File 41–1929, AICC.

a much-anticipated and historic congress set to debate the acceptance of the Nehru Report and the further demands of the INC for constitutional reforms.[85] Yet, the "unique feature" was not this momentous debate, but rather the unprecedented volume of messages expressing solidarity and support for the INC that poured into India from all over the world. These messages showed "how the Indian struggle for freedom was being closely followed in other countries and especially those countries which are themselves suffering under alien domination."[86] Unsurprisingly, Nehru, as general secretary of the INC, wrote this volume of the *Congress Bulletin*, and he went to great lengths to underscore the significance of the Calcutta Congress in crystallizing the anti-imperialist relationship between India and the world.

The *Congress Bulletin* represented one of Nehru's overarching aims to make the Calcutta Congress "unique" by staging the anti-imperialist world in India.[87] This was a carefully developed plot led by Nehru in collaboration with Chatto. In the most ambitious of plans, Nehru and Chatto attempted to facilitate the safe passage and attendance of high-profile members of the LAI, including delegates from Egypt, South Africa, Indonesia, Syria, and China. Such travelers faced rigorous inspection by colonial authorities and needed substantial funds to make the journey. Attendance was not possible for most invitees, and so Nehru and Chatto ensured that all associated and affiliated organizations of the LAI sent messages of solidarity to the INC during the annual meeting. In doing so, the voices of the anti-imperialists came to be heard in Calcutta. This also served to support Nehru's stance that independence, if conceived in reference to the wider world, was instrumental not only to the nation, but also to the many abroad who reached out to the INC in their messages.

The most significant delegate who agreed to attend the congress was Madame Sun, who was keen to make the trip to India and join Nehru and his colleagues. Already denied a visa to India for the Madras Congress in 1927, Madame Sun applied again from Moscow through the Berlin passport office in 1928. British colonial intelligence immediately intercepted her application and considered the best means to deny her entry. She, like so many anti-imperialists, presented a serious problem for colonial authorities. Madame Sun was not a communist party member, although she lived in exile in Moscow after Chiang Kai-shek's bloody repression of communists and communist sympathizers. Thus, she could not be denied

---

[85] *Congress Bulletin*, January 27, 1929, File 41–1929, AICC.   [86] Ibid.
[87] I borrow here from Rebecca E. Karl's work on China. See her *Staging the World*.

a visa on the grounds of being an official communist party member. The second objection was that Madame Sun was a member of the LAI, an organization that was not illegal in Britain and had prominent Members of Parliament attached to it. As the intelligence report suggested, British MPs could raise red flags in parliament if Madame Sun was denied entry for being an LAI member. Nevertheless, the intelligence community collected names of LAI associates and generated a blacklist of all related organizations and individuals. Madame Sun topped the list and was officially denied her visa by the Passport Control Office in June 1928.[88]

The LAI managed to facilitate safe passage to India for an Indo-Chinese delegate named Duong Van Giau. There is little documentation in the LAI or INC archives that offers more information about the identity of Giau and his travels to India. Nehru mentioned his participation in the Calcutta Congress in a letter to Chatto in January 1929. Nehru wrote, "We were glad to have Duong Van Giau and another person from Indo China [*sic*] as fraternal delegates to the Congress here." He added: "they were troubled en route at Singapore and were delayed there but they managed to reach Calcutta just before the Congress ended."[89] It does not appear that Nehru knew Giau or spent any length of time with him; however, the delegate's mere appearance presented the INC with a clear indication of the importance of India to the anti-imperialist world.

Alongside Giau, the messages of support from LAI associates worldwide were presented in Calcutta in the open sessions. There is no doubt that the LAI master list of contacts was the same list of organizations that sent greetings to the Calcutta Congress. Nehru recognized as much and wrote to Chatto that the world messages were "thanks to your [Chatto's] efforts."[90] Nehru celebrated the presence of world support in his publication of the January *Congress Bulletin*, where he specifically commented on and cited messages of support from Romain Rolland and Henri Barbusse, two founding figures of the LAI, whom he knew from his time abroad. Nehru also included a rather long passage on Mohammed Hatta, the Indonesian member of the executive committee, who wrote a message of support only for it to be intercepted by British and Dutch authorities. Nehru went to great lengths to tell the history of Indonesian resistance to Dutch imperialism and liken it to the Indian struggle against the British. The rejection of Madame Sun's visa also generated a fair amount of

---

[88] Report, Madame Sun Yat-Sen (Refusal of Visa for India), L/P&J/12/276, IPI.
[89] Nehru to Chatto, January 16, 1929, File 1–1929, AICC.
[90] Nehru to Chatto, undated but likely early January, 1929, *SWJN*, vol. 3, 295.

discussion in the bulletin. In place of her attendance, Madame Sun sent two messages: one conveying solidarity between India and China, and another specifically expressing solidarity between Indian and Chinese women. When Nehru wrote to Madame Sun to express his thanks, he remarked on how "humiliating" it was that a "foreign power should prevent one whom India honours from visiting our country."[91]

On the table at the Calcutta meeting was a resolution for the INC to endorse the Nehru Report and dominion status. In his presentation of the report, Motilal Nehru stated, "What matters to me is that dominion status involves a very considerable measure of freedom bordering on complete independence and is any day preferable to complete dependence."[92] However, he diplomatically straddled the issue: "I am for complete independence – as complete as it can be – but I am not against full dominion status – as full as any dominion possesses it today – provided I get it before it loses all attraction. I am for severance of British connection as it subsists with us today but am not against it as it exists with the Dominions."[93] Gandhi supported the elder Nehru and advocated for the INC to back the report and dominion status.

Once again, Nehru found himself at odds with his father and Gandhi. In response to his father's argument, he made a passionate plea for his fellow congressmen to recognize that anything less than independence had implications beyond the borders of India and across the world. The staging of the world in Calcutta had a specific role to play in Nehru's defense of independence. In two statements, he called upon his colleagues to recognize the global weight of their decision, and he used the worldwide outpouring of messages as evidence. His first statement is worth citing at length:

Today you have received messages of sympathy from Java, Sumatra, and other down-trodden countries wishing you success because they feel that you are one of them and because they feel that by declaring independence you have joined in their struggle against imperialism all over the world. If you pull down the flag of independence and talk of dominion status ... you give up the cause of suffering nations who look forward to you for the success in their movement, not because you are going to Java to help them but because it is well-known in world history for the last hundred years that the greatest obstacle to freedom is the British Empire and the British possession of India ... Therefore to the extent you get rid

---

[91] Nehru to Madame Sun, File 7, LAI, JNU.
[92] Motilal Nehru, "Presidential Address, Calcutta Congress," December 29, 1928, *Selected Works of Motilal Nehru*, 449.
[93] Motilal Nehru, "Presidential Address," 449.

of this imperialism, to that extent you help these down-trodden countries; and if to gain some internal freedom you adopt the psychology of imperialism and of Dominion Status, you may gain a little certainly but you break the links with these people who are looking to you and are prepared to join with you in the struggle.[94]

By impelling his Indian colleagues to lead the "suffering nations" who sought their guidance, Nehru solidified the direct link between independence and anti-imperialist internationalism. He warned that a decision to "give up" independence would "break the links" with anti-imperialists worldwide. It was the world that spoke in Calcutta, and it called upon India to "join in their struggle against imperialism all over the world." Ultimately, Nehru argued that the messages from abroad, arriving with the assistance of the LAI and read before the delegation in Calcutta, were proof that India had a greater responsibility beyond its own borders, one that necessitated independence over dominion status.

Ultimately, Nehru's internationalist arguments produced mixed results. He introduced an amendment to a resolution on the Nehru Report, insisting the congress "[adhere] to the decision of the Madras Congress declaring independence to be the goal of the Indian people and ... [remain] of the opinion that there can be no true freedom till British connection is severed."[95] The INC did not attach this amendment to the approved resolution that ultimately accepted the Nehru Report and dominion status for India. At the same time, however, Nehru succeeded in securing several compromises on the final resolution. The first was an ultimatum: if the colonial state did not acquiesce to all demands in the Nehru Report within a year, the INC promised to up the ante and call for complete independence from the British Empire and commence a civil disobedience campaign. Nehru won a small concession in this decision by convincing the INC to limit the grace period to one year. He also advocated for the final clause: "[N]othing in this resolution shall interfere with the carrying on, in the name of the Congress, of propaganda for complete independence."[96] Nehru took this final clause seriously, and although defeated on the question of independence for the time being, he retained his role as general secretary as a means to continue his quest for independence "in the name of

---

[94] Nehru's speech at the Subjects Committee meeting of the Calcutta Congress on December 27, 1928. and reprinted by *Searchlight* on December 30, 1928. Reprinted in *SWJN*, vol. 3, 274.

[95] Report on the Subjects Committee of the Calcutta Congress, December 27, 1928, *SWJN*, vol. 3, 271.

[96] *Congress Bulletin*, January 15, 1929, File 41–1929, AICC.

the Congress." Chatto wholeheartedly supported his decision, and the two commenced their strategizing on behalf of the LAI.

The staging of the anti-imperialist world, and Indian nationalist relevance to it, were essential to the passage of other resolutions that forged sturdier connections between the INC and the LAI. The Calcutta Congress welcomed the LAI's second world congress, planned for 1929, and authorized the working committee to appoint a representative of the INC to attend. Another resolution "reiterate[d] the War Danger resolution of the Madras sessions of the Congress," which operated on the fundamental assumption that India was a pawn in British imperialist warmongering and reaffirmed that the "people of India [had] no quarrel with the neighboring states or the other nations of the world and they [would] not permit themselves to be exploited by England to further her imperialist aims."[97] These resolutions were cardinal to Nehru's agenda.

Two more resolutions placing India in the world, not introduced by Nehru, called for India to lead in the construction of a "Pan-Asiatic Federation," and another extended "hearty congratulations" to China for achieving independence. Though Nehru was eager to connect India to the wider world, he knew the Asiatic and Chinese resolutions were ill-informed and not entirely accurate. In a letter to Chatto, he mocked the Pan-Asiatic resolution because "nobody quite [understands] what this [resolution] means, including the mover of the resolution." On the Chinese resolution, Nehru recognized it was "entirely wrong" and opposed it. China was by no means independent or at peace in 1928.[98]

A bolder choice for Nehru was the idea of establishing a foreign department within the INC to institutionalize the connections he was building personally and through his role as congress secretary. Nehru's resolution established a foreign department because the "Congress, being of opinion that the struggle of the Indian people for freedom [was] a part of the general world struggle against imperialism and its manifestations, consider[ed] it desirable that India should develop contacts with other countries and peoples who also suffer under imperialism and desire to combat it."[99] The first working committee meeting of the INC in 1929 nominated Nehru to oversee the foreign department.[100] Because of his

---

[97] Ibid.
[98] On Nehru's opposition to the resolutions on China and the Pan-Asiatic Congress, see his letter to Chatto, undated but likely in January 1929, *SWJN*, vol. 3, 295.
[99] *Congress Bulletin*, January 15, 1929, AICC.
[100] *Congress Bulletin*, January 20, 1929, AICC.

political programs and experiences in Brussels, Nehru quickly became the default choice for the INC on international issues and initiatives. Of course, Nehru turned to Chatto and the League to supply the contacts for the INC Foreign Department. In this capacity, Nehru began circulating the *Congress Bulletin* to the LAI in Berlin and directly to Leaguers across the anti-imperialist world on behalf of the foreign department.

At the end of the day, Nehru's staging of the world in Calcutta may have failed to ensure that independence carried the day in 1928, but the nationalist discourse began to integrate and recognize the relevance of the world to the anticolonial struggle in India. This new development was thanks in no small part to the countless hours of coordination between Nehru and Chatto in eliciting the messages of support that poured into Calcutta from around the world. The Calcutta Congress was a calculated attempt to flood the meeting with voices from the anti-imperialist world. These voices were heard and resonated in the passages of key resolutions building solidarity with the LAI, China, and Asia. They also prompted the INC to establish a foreign department. Nehru and Chatto sought to recast the INC as a spokesperson not only for India, but also for the anti-imperialist world. The question of independence was deferred for another year, but Nehru remained optimistic.

CONCLUSION

The events of 1928 marked a shift in Nehru's conceptualization of anticolonial resistance. He sought to interweave nationalism and internationalism into the political articulations of the anticolonial and trade unionist movements in India. Far too often, the historical narratives of all-Indian politics have failed to engage with the wider world and rethink the possibilities for individuals such as Nehru to conceptualize a "special blend" of anti-imperialist internationalism and Indian nationalism. This gap has much to do with the prevailing assumptions about internationalism and nationalism as oppositional binaries. For Nehru, nationalism and internationalism were not mutually exclusive, but overlapped and informed one another. This "special blend" inspired by the League retained a consistent and enduring place in Nehru's view of India and the world well beyond his months in Europe, as evidenced in this chapter.

In various capacities, and within both the INC and the AITUC, Nehru sought to yoke the Indian nationalist movement to anti-imperialism as a broadly defined "blend" of movements for national sovereignty and social equality. India's acceptance of complete independence was at the crux of this quest. In his leadership of the INC, Nehru fought a tireless and often frustrating campaign for independence in 1928, one in which he framed Indian national sovereignty in relation to the wider world. He also sought to embed himself in the AITUC as a proponent of solidarity between trade unionists and nationalists in India, and the association of both to the LAI. His anti-imperialist campaign in India to internationalize nationalism was an ambitious plan with many opponents, including fellow moderates, as well as the colonial state. Even so, he worked with the LAI to stage the world and provide a compelling case to his INC colleagues to think internationally and consider the implications of dominion status on the world.

After the annual sessions of the INC and the AITUC, Nehru's optimism reached a new apex. In January 1929, Nehru wrote to Chatto about the upcoming year: "The year is likely to be a heavy one both from the labour and political point of view."[101] He was certain that the government of India would not convert India into a dominion state by the year's end, and he prepared for an inevitable civil disobedience campaign and the restoration of independence as the INC's goal. He retained his position as general secretary of the INC to ensure that an anti-imperialist inflection found its proper place in the nationalist literature and propaganda, and he became more involved with the AITUC as its president for the year. Events and forces in India seemed to be moving toward an alliance of anti-imperialist forces, both nationally and internationally. There was little indication of the major eruptions ahead in 1929 that would challenge the fundamental core of his internationalist project and bring his relationship with the LAI to crisis point.

---

[101] Nehru to Chatto, undated January 1929, *SWJN*, vol. 3, 295.

4

Anti-Imperialism in Crisis, 1929–1930

The year 1929 was a transformative one for Nehru and the INC. The government of India failed to meet the demands of the Nehru Report, and the INC was headed toward another clash with the colonial state by the year's end. With no concessions from the raj, the INC converted its demand from dominion status to complete independence, or *purna swaraj*. Nehru was the obvious choice for the presidency of the Lahore Congress in December 1929, which officially declared independence as the INC's goal and announced the launch of a civil disobedience campaign to achieve it. In his presidential remarks, Nehru spoke of a new Indian nationalism ensconced in the anti-imperialist idiom of the LAI. He proclaimed unequivocally his faith in socialism, and stated that he was "no believer in kings and princes, or in the order which produced the modern kings of industry, who have greater power over the lives and fortunes of men than even the kings of old, and whose methods are as predatory as those of the old feudal aristocracy."[1] Nehru argued that the solution to Indian poverty was not simply political sovereignty from the British, but the overthrow of the capitalist and imperialist system worldwide. He concluded by celebrating the Lahore Congress as a historic moment in which the INC was no longer a movement informed by "narrow nationalism," but had become "part of the world movement" sweeping across the globe in places such as China, Turkey, Persia, Egypt, and Russia. He added pointedly: "[I]f we ignore the world, we do so at our peril."[2]

The Lahore Congress should have been the highpoint of Nehru's amalgamation of nationalist and internationalist projects, but paradoxically his relationship with the LAI ended at this very moment. As Nehru prepared for his remarks in Lahore, the LAI secretariat in Berlin sent out appeals across India for "true" anti-imperialist organizations to

[1] Nehru, Presidential Address at the 1929 INC sessions in Lahore, in *India and the World*.
[2] Ibid.

break ranks with the INC and establish a "real" Indian independence league that would stand in opposition to the nationalist movement. Immediately after the Lahore Congress in January 1930, Nehru fired off a lengthy criticism of the LAI's circular to India and demanded an explanation for its hostility toward the INC. Without a forthcoming explanation from Berlin, Nehru resigned from the executive committee and instructed the INC to stop all communication with the LAI in April 1930.

Nehru's resignation in 1930 stood in sharp contrast to his aims to build a strong LAI and internationalize India's anticolonial struggle during the late 1920s. Most scholarship has attributed Nehru's split with the LAI to the incompatibility between Indian nationalism and internationalism – especially communist-inspired internationalism.[3] Such narratives link the fallout within the LAI to Moscow's introduction of the class warfare tactics of the third period (1928–1932), when communists were directed to abandon united-front alliances in favor of ties strictly to orthodox communist organizations worldwide.[4] By 1929, the LAI secretariat was under intense pressure from the Comintern to conform to the third-period policies and purge noncommunists. The aims of the Comintern ran counter to the League's basic platforms articulated in Brussels which had celebrated a "special blend" of nationalists, socialists, and communists in a global struggle against capitalism, imperialism, and war. Even when leaders of the LAI recognized tension between the political projects housed beneath the anti-imperialist umbrella, they overlooked these differences.

The confrontation between these antithetical views reached a crisis point at the Second World Congress of the LAI, held in Frankfurt, Germany, in July 1929. The Frankfurt Congress, as it came to be known, was another impressive gathering of LAI members from across the globe and included many familiar faces, such as Roger Baldwin, Edo Fimmen, Reginald Bridgeman, Mohammed Hatta, and Chatto. Nehru could not attend the Frankfurt Congress, and instead the INC sent Shiva Prasad Gupta, a nationalist who shared Nehru's commitment to Indian independence and who incidentally had been in Europe at the time of the LAI congress. Much like the Brussels Congress, India and China took center stage, but in Frankfurt the struggles in Africa and Latin America also gained important roles in the proceedings, and special panels on women and youth leagues

---

[3] Gopal, *Nehru*, 71.
[4] On the Comintern, see McDermott and Agnew, *The Comintern*, 81–119; and Sobhanlal Datta Gupta, *The Comintern and the Destiny of Communism in India*.

added more dimensions.[5] The most significant difference between Brussels and Frankfurt, however, was the large presence of Comintern agents who carried with them directives from Moscow to stage the LAI's congress as a platform to attack socialists and anticolonial nationalists.

There is no doubt that the Comintern's interventions in Frankfurt dramatically impacted the solidarities within the LAI, but this is only a partial explanation for the break between Nehru and the League. Instead, this chapter tells the story of the Frankfurt Congress and argues that the event and its aftermath were far more complex than historians have suggested.[6] Not all communists within the LAI subscribed to the dictates imparted by Moscow in 1929, and international communism was not a monolithic bloc at the Frankfurt Congress. Instead, many communists, like Münzenberg, Saklatvala, and Chatto, continued to work collaboratively with noncommunists, like Nehru, Gupta, Fimmen, Baldwin, and Bridgeman, to chart a future for the LAI beyond the sectarianism introduced by Moscow's third period. Their story of camaraderie across party lines was remarkable in that it demonstrated the power of anti-imperialist solidarity despite calls to divide it.

Nehru's split with the LAI was informed more by the Indian context, and especially the question of independence for the INC. Several months after the Frankfurt Congress, the INC once again backpedaled on their commitment to independence when Gandhi met with the Viceroy of India to discuss a compromise in which the colonial state would grant dominion status in exchange for the INC's commitment to call off the civil disobedience campaign planned for 1930. On principle, Nehru refused to back the plan because it accepted dominion status, but he was persuaded to support it because he rightly saw Gandhi's talks with the viceroy as doomed to fail. Nevertheless, Nehru's signature on the INC's formal agreement to enter negotiations with the colonial state for dominion status proved to be the breaking point for his ties to the LAI. The question of Indian independence had complicated Nehru's relationship with the LAI since Brussels. Yet whereas the early years of flexibility and compromise within the LAI had left space for Nehru to "train and prepare" his Indian colleagues over time

---

[5] For a more specific discussion of youth leagues and anti-imperialist internationalism, see Franziska Roy, "International Utopia and National Discipline" Youth and Volunteer Movements in Interwar South Asia," in Raza, et al., *The Internationalist Moment.*

[6] There is a dearth of studies on the Second World Congress in Frankfurt even though this event produced substantially more documentation than the Brussels Congress. The few treatments characterize it as a platform for communist takeover of the LAI. See Petersson, *Willi Münzenberg*; and Prashad, *The Darker Nations.*

and with some caution, the new environment of mistrust fostered by the Comintern strained the League's ability to defend even temporary backslides from their nationalist comrades. The ambivalence of the INC on the independence question became the impenetrable divide between Indian nationalism and anti-imperialist internationalism in this contentious moment.

This chapter offers a fresh reading of the Frankfurt Congress and Nehru's break with the LAI at a moment when the flexibility of anti-imperialism in the late 1920s was challenged. The story of Frankfurt demonstrates the significance of communists and noncommunists who collectively resisted the Comintern's bid for power over the meaning and trajectory of the LAI. Such anti-imperialist solidarity between Nehru and his comrades during this turbulent moment points to a history in which the dichotomies of nationalism and communism did not hold up. Instead, Nehru worked across party lines to maintain solidarity, and only reluctantly succumbed to pressures from outside the LAI that stigmatized the categories of anti-imperialism and anti-capitalism. The collapse of the Nehru–LAI relationship depended on decisions made by the INC in 1929, which undermined India's relationship to anti-imperialism abroad. Nevertheless, as this chapter concludes, Nehru and his comrades never fully closed the door on reconciliation and future collaboration for the greater cause of anti-imperialism – although such cooperation would never take place under the more rigid institutional framework of the LAI, but rather in other projects inspired by the ideas of the organization.

THE ROOTS OF ANTI-IMPERIALIST CRISIS

On the eve of the Frankfurt Congress, Nehru sent the INC's delegate, Shiva Prashad Gupta, a letter of introduction to the LAI, and urged him to meet three comrades: "our friend" Chatto; Baldwin, with whom he expressed "great regard"; and Bridgeman, "one of the very few Englishmen who can view the Indian question minus the English prejudices."[7] Nehru also hoped Gupta would see "firsthand" in Frankfurt that the LAI was not an "out and out creature of the Communist International," as some suggest, but rather he would find that the LAI was an organization with communists and an "even stronger non-communist element." It was the cooperation between both elements that formed the basis of the LAI, without which the "whole thing would collapse," or at least lose all of its "vitality."[8]

---

[7] Nehru to Gupta, June 27, 1929, *SWJN*, vol. 3, 308–309.   [8] Ibid.

Nehru's message about the "vitality" of the LAI articulated a vision of anti-imperialism dating back to the Brussels Congress, one that contrasted sharply with the views of many communists in Frankfurt. Instead, the Comintern leadership argued that much had changed since the Brussels Congress. The "transition of the colonial national bourgeoisie to the camp of imperialism and counter-revolution" and the emergence of workers and peasants as the "driving force of colonial revolution" were vital shifts that had emerged *after* the establishment of the LAI in 1927.[9] At the same time, European socialists – especially the ILP, with Maxton at its helm – had betrayed the anti-imperialist struggle and had become "agents of imperialism" by cooperating with their respective governments and capitalist classes.[10] The Comintern's dramatically different narrative of the recent past made anti-imperialist solidarity with noncommunists untenable at best, and dangerous at worst.

The disparity of these anti-imperialist views informed the preparations and proceedings of the Frankfurt Congress, pitting many communist party members against their former comrades from socialist and nationalist organizations. However, the divide was never as simplistic as a binary between communist and noncommunist members of the LAI. Rather, the communists articulating class warfare tactics in Frankfurt were newcomers to the LAI without any appreciation for or prior engagement with the foundation of the movement in the late 1920s. These new arrivals may have been the loudest in Frankfurt; however, their more rigid vision of anti-imperialism did not go uncontested. The LAI's leadership from the Brussels days – familiar actors, including Nehru, Baldwin, Bridgeman, Fimmen, Chatto, and Münzenberg – resisted the upheavals introduced by Comintern agents and fought to retain the LAI's inclusiveness.

This struggle began much earlier, when the LAI secretariat in Berlin and the Comintern clashed over the planning of the Frankfurt Congress. In late 1928, the Berlin secretariat put forward a provisional agenda for Frankfurt that was historically consistent with the spirit of the Brussels Congress. The core theme of the panels and speeches, as Chatto and Münzenberg envisioned it, was the "unification of all anti-imperialist groups and organizations," and the schedule included a familiar cast of anti-imperialist veterans such as Jawaharlal Nehru, Henri Barbusse, James Maxton,

---

[9] Draft Resolution on the Lessons of the Second World Congress of the League against Imperialism and Its Immediate Tasks, unsigned and likely drafted by Alexandar Bittleman, 542/1/79/118–121, RGASPI.
[10] Ibid.

FIGURE 4.1 The Honorary Presidium and Executive Committee of the League against Imperialism. The Berlin secretariat published this document as a flyer announcing the Second World Congress of the LAI. It featured the founding members of the LAI from the Brussels Congress. Courtesy of Universal History Archive/Getty Images

Madame Sun Yat-Sen, William Pickens, Roger Baldwin, Diego Riveria, and Willi Münzenberg.[11] The greatest emphasis was placed on the participation of India and China, represented by the INC and KMT respectively. Chatto took the additional step of writing to Nehru in late 1928 and requesting that he serve as the primary organizer of a large and representative delegation for the Frankfurt Congress from India, Burma, and Ceylon. On October 20, Nehru circulated the provisional agenda of the congress along with his solicitation for delegates from affiliated and sympathetic organizations beyond India and across South Asia.[12]

In Moscow, the Berlin agenda became a source of hostile criticism for the LAI and reprimand for the secretaries. According to reports from the

[11] Invitation to the Second Anti-Imperialist World Congress of the League against Imperialism, File 5, LAI, JNU.
[12] Nehru, Circular on Second World Congress of the League against Imperialism, October 20, 1928, *SWJN*, vol. 3, 146–147.

Eastern Secretariat of the Comintern, the League's Berlin leadership "did not understand sufficiently the new situation in the colonial countries which the Comintern ha[d] on several occasions analyzed and stated, and did still less to adjust itself to this new situation."[13] Instead, the report argued that Berlin's provisional agenda "open[ed] up considerable political dangers" by its "overweighting of the non-Communist or even anti-Communist reporters, by its incorrect and even opportunistic formulations of the subjects to be discussed, and above all by its selection of persons."[14] The report concluded by criticizing Münzenberg in particular, and warning that "any repetition of such acts of indiscipline in the future would be extremely seriously considered."[15]

The Comintern's criticism of the LAI was informed by broader and more global transformations introduced by Moscow's disavowal of the united front and implementation of the class warfare tactics of the third period beginning in 1928. This tactical shift had much to do with the internal politics within the Soviet Union. The rise of Joseph Stalin in 1928, after a contentious power struggle in the wake of Lenin's death, opened this new era of rigid conformity to party lines within and outside the Soviet Union. The shift also had to do with the failed united front in China, which ended poorly for Soviet-trained Chinese communists and their Russian advisors. Although Stalin and the Comintern clung to the united-front policy throughout 1927 – even after the news that Chiang and the KMT had turned on communists – Moscow decreed by 1928 that nationalist forces could not be trusted, and the Comintern needed to build stronger ties exclusively to communist parties in Asia. A call to attack former communist allies on the left, anticolonial nationalist movements, and socialists began shortly after the introduction of the third period at the Sixth World Congress of the Comintern in mid-1928.

The Berlin agenda for the Frankfurt Congress stood in contradistinction to the aims of the Comintern in the third period. In response to Berlin's failure to implement new Comintern policies, the Political Secretariat and Eastern Secretariat created two special oversight commissions to direct the work of the LAI and its preparations for Frankfurt. The most active in revising the plans was the Eastern Secretariat's commission, led by its

---

[13] Alexandar Bittleman, Report on the Results and Lessons of the Second World Congress of the League against Imperialism, signed and submitted to the Comintern on August 15, 1929, 542/1/96/68–93, RGASPI. This report outlines in detail the main critiques of the Frankfurt Congress by Comintern members. It also recounts the story of preparations and the errors by Münzenberg according to the Comintern leadership.
[14] Ibid.   [15] Ibid.

chairman, Alexander Bittleman, who was a prominent American communist party member. At the first meeting of his commission in March 1929, communist leaders resolved that all future work of the LAI, both the "materials and resolutions," would be planned in Moscow and "in constant accord with the CI [Comintern]"[16] Further directives from Bittleman's commission to the Berlin office made clear that all speeches and statements in Frankfurt should "go beyond the resolutions, stating the full communist position on the role of the proletariat and the Communist Parties in the colonial revolutionary movement," while also "criticizing the wavering attitude of the so-called Left national reformists, as well as the attitude of the Baldwin-Maxton elements in the League."[17]

Bittleman's oversight commission in Moscow sought to stage the Frankfurt Congress as a public platform for international communists to articulate class warfare tactics and distance the LAI from organizations such as the INC, ILP, and KMT. The commission in Moscow redrafted the agenda, wrote all of the resolutions, and handpicked speakers to articulate the Comintern's new line in Frankfurt. More pointed, however, were the instructions for the Comintern delegates dispatched to Frankfurt, who carried specific orders from Moscow and met secretly during the congress. Moscow directed these agents to wage a "merciless struggle against those sections of the nationalist colonial bourgeoisie that have surrendered to imperialism and become its agents" and to commence a "sharp and systematic struggle against social reformism as agents of imperialism and systematic exposure of their collaborators – the colonial social reformists."[18]

The timing of the Comintern's call for communists to turn against the INC, and Nehru in particular, could not have been more fatal for the League's connections to India. On paper, the LAI boasted a far-reaching and widespread network linking it to many organizations in India. However, Nehru had been the primary facilitator in forging these connections. Abandoning him at this moment would come at a great cost to the LAI's Indian networks. Even more problematic was the lacuna of possible replacements for Nehru, especially ones who had the resources and capability to create and sustain the League's anti-imperialist work. It wasn't simply that Nehru was a committed anti-imperialist and had the time and

---

[16] Minutes of the Eastern Secretariat Commission on League against Imperialism, March 30, 1929, 542/1/79/26–27, RGASPI.

[17] Minutes of the Commission for the Preparation of the Anti-Imperialist League Congress, June 18, 1929, 542/1/79/64, RGASPI.

[18] Instructions to the Comintern representative at the Second World Congress, Endorsed by the Political Secretariat of the CI, June 25, 1929, 542/1/79/71, RGASPI.

funds to serve the LAI. The problem was that most of the leaders of the trade unionist movement and Workers and Peasants Leagues, who might have been sympathetic to the LAI, were imprisoned in a series of conspiracy cases launched by the colonial state in the 1920s. The most significant was the Meerut Conspiracy Case (1929–1934), which specifically named the LAI as an entity conspiring to overthrow the raj in India.[19] Possession of a letter from the LAI or any organization connected to communism was proof enough for the colonial state to detain and indict trade unionists in India. By March 1929, the likeliest Indian candidates for anti-imperialist collaboration with the LAI had been arrested or forced to carry out underground political work. None could have acquired proper paperwork or funds to travel abroad and attend the Frankfurt Congress.

Both Berlin and the Comintern hoped for a strong AITUC delegation for Frankfurt. Before the Meerut arrests, Nehru secured the appointment of a single AITUC delegate, although the trial made travel abroad for trade unionists nearly impossible. Of the Indian trade unionists in Europe at the time, none were willing to attend the LAI congress. Most were moderates attending the ILO conference in Geneva. Chatto hatched a plan to travel to Geneva and convince such delegates to reconsider. But these more moderate trade unionists, who were sympathetic to the LSI, declined to participate in Frankfurt. As a result, the INC's lone delegate and some representatives among the expatriate community in London comprised the only Indian delegation present.

Beyond India, the Comintern's attempt to reorient the League had a profound impact on the institution as a whole. Most importantly, it placed the two masters of the LAI, the Comintern and the executive committee, squarely at odds with one another, forcing to the foreground the question that had been unresolved since Brussels: Who had the power to define and control the anti-imperialist movement? In its earliest days, the executive committee worked with the secretariat on institution-building and fundraising. Nehru and Baldwin had been instrumental in this process, and they spent nearly a year in Europe working in the service of the LAI during 1927. Always in the background and in communication with Münzenberg and Chatto, however, was the Comintern. Although the Comintern offered little guidance in the formative years, its strong interest in the LAI's work

---

[19] For a fuller discussion of the Meerut Conspiracy Case and the LAI, see Michele Louro, "'Where National Revolutionary Ends and Communist Begins': The League against Imperialism and the Meerut Conspiracy Case," *Comparative Studies of South Asia, Africa and the Middle East* 33, no. 3 (2013): 331–44.

in the run-up to Frankfurt complicated the work of the anti-imperialist movement. Moscow now demanded that the secretaries subordinate to its authority and "wage merciless struggle" against the noncommunists who served prominently in the LAI's executive committee.[20]

The Berlin secretaries had to navigate this new environment carefully, and under the increasingly watchful eye of Moscow. As early as January 1928, Moscow dispatched several trusted agents to an executive committee meeting of the LAI in Cologne, where Grigorij Melnitschansky, Fritz Heckert, and James Ford made LAI history as the first delegation from the Soviet Union to join the organization. The trio officially represented the Central Council of the All-Russian Trade Union Federation, while another Comintern agent, R. Page Arnot, attended the executive meeting as an observer. These four comrades were no ordinary trade unionists, however; they were Moscow insiders who sought to impose Comintern policy on the LAI. Even the addition of a new co-secretary, a British communist party member named Emile Burns, to work alongside Chatto was an extra precaution taken by the Comintern to ensure greater power for communists in the League.

For both Chatto and Münzenberg, conforming to the Comintern's agenda for the LAI meant destroying the very solidarities they had worked so hard to forge since Brussels. In various ways, both resisted Moscow's pressure to reorient the LAI, although direct evidence of their views in the archives is scarce. In the months before and after Frankfurt, Chatto continued to write Nehru as the chief representative of the Indian anti-imperialist movement. His letters show no signs of tension. Instead, he continued to push Nehru to take a stronger stance on independence, draw the AITUC closer to the LAI, and organize anti-imperialist forces in India. Münzenberg left even less documentation of his own about the LAI during the crucial months of preparations for the Frankfurt Congress, but the Comintern records provide evidence of his resistance, too. He attempted unsuccessfully to recuse himself from speaking at the Frankfurt Congress, no doubt a gesture of his disapproval of the new direction the Comintern sought to impose on the LAI. His request to be removed from the agenda, however, was denied in June 1929. Instead, the planning commission in Moscow chose Münzenberg as the most important orator of the Frankfurt Congress by appointing him to speak in the concluding

---

[20] Instructions to the Comintern representative at the Second World Congress, Endorsed by the Political Secretariat of the CI, June 25, 1929, 542/1/79/71, RGASPI.

session, with instructions to deliver a summary of the proceedings that would include a final attack on any socialists and nationalists present.[21] Münzenberg reluctantly took up the role, but it remained uncertain whether he would fall in line with the new Comintern agenda.

Moscow's plans for the LAI set the stage in Frankfurt for a hostile coup d'état and prompted a crisis in the meaning of anti-imperialism for those who did not conform to the narrow and more rigid visions espoused by the Comintern. The directives placed many communists at odds with non-communists and charted a new direction for the LAI that would inevitably lead to conflict and crisis in Frankfurt. During the preparation for the congress, however, the Comintern's call to cleanse the ranks of the LAI created tensions between Berlin and Moscow. On the eve of the Frankfurt Congress, it was unclear whether the Berlin secretaries would go along with the new directives. It also remained uncertain whether the noncommunists, who had been so instrumental to the establishment of the LAI, would go gently into the night in Frankfurt.

THE FRANKFURT CONGRESS

The Frankfurt Congress prompted a crisis in anti-imperialism, one that was never fully resolved in 1927 and difficult to move beyond in 1929. The LAI Chairman, James Maxton of the ILP, best articulated the crisis during a speech in which he defended his place as an anti-imperialist in the face of mounting criticism from Comintern delegates. He began with the historic importance of the League's mission since the Brussels Congress. The League was the only organization of its time that sought to create a "world of men and women living in economic and political freedom, in free communities freed from the terror and menace of war."[22] As he saw it, the League was unique in bringing together "several diverse elements" of anti-imperialists that included nationalists, intellectuals, trade unionists, social democrats, pacifists, and communists. Two years after its inception, however, the League faced two questions: "have all these sections a place in the [anti-imperialist] struggle and secondly can they work together for a common end?"[23]

---

[21] Münzenberg proposed that he not be chosen to make the "political referat" to the Commission of the League against Imperialism, which was denied by the Commission on May 3, 1929, 542/1/79/44, RGASPI.
[22] James Maxton's speech, Frankfurt Congress, Copy, in 542/1/91/115–121, RGASPI.
[23] Ibid.

FIGURE 4.2 Chatto and James Maxton just before the Frankfurt Congress in Cologne, Germany, in January 1929. Horst Krueger Scholar Estate Archive, Leibniz-Zentrum Moderner Orient, Berlin, Germany. Photo credit: Ali Raza

The answers to these central questions were at the core of the debates taking place in Frankfurt. Maxton argued that there was a place for socialists and nationalists in the League, and that both could and should work across party lines with communists for the anti-imperialist cause. His position was representative of many like Nehru who continued the trend of the League's early years, encouraging nationalists and internationalists to bind together in the fight against capitalist and imperialist oppression. On the other hand, a faction of Comintern members selected and dispatched from Moscow had come to Frankfurt to challenge this inclusive and flexible formula. Their role in the congress was to demonstrate that noncommunists did not have "a place in the struggle" and that all elements of the movement could not "work together for a common end."

India was paramount in these debates. The INC posed the biggest threat to the Comintern's vision because it represented one of the most significant and high-profile nationalist movements within the LAI. Already at the Sixth World Congress of the Comintern in 1928, the resolution on the third period's colonial policy made special mention of "Gandhism in India" as traitorous to anti-imperialism.[24] In Frankfurt, the Indian nationalist movement became the primary target of communist vitriol. In the open and closed sessions, the India question also inspired a strong resistance to the Comintern agenda by those delegates, communists and noncommunists, who fought to protect the League's accommodative and inclusive environment. Nehru's inner circle of comrades – people such as Maxton, Hatta, Fimmen, Baldwin, and Gupta, as Nehru's proxy and representative of the INC – remained vigilant and argued that the INC had to retain a proper place in the League if the inclusiveness of the movement was to prevail.

The Frankfurt Congress opened with the first agenda item, the "Political Situation and War Danger," which became the launching pad for communist attacks against nationalists and socialists. Harry Pollitt, a League member since Brussels and the General Secretary of the CPGB, was the headliner for this session, which set the atmosphere for the entire congress. Pollitt was handpicked by Moscow to deliver the opening address, in which he made a clarion call to League comrades to "clean its ranks of those vacillating and confused elements" who professed to be anti-imperialists while at the same supported and compromised with imperialist powers. Pollitt argued that these "confused elements" included the "native bourgeoisie in the colonial countries" who "joined hands with foreign imperialists against the native workers and peasants." The social democrats were the other "element" guilty of "expressing sentiments of friendship toward the colonial peoples" with "ambiguous and empty phrases" that only confused workers and peasants. Simultaneously, claimed Pollitt, socialists and trade unionists defended capitalist and imperialist policy and, "if necessary, themselves [carried out] capitalism's colonial policy."[25] According to the précis of Pollitt's speech printed in the daily press service of the Frankfurt Congress, the audience on several occasions erupted into "protracted applause" and cheers of "Hear! Hear!"[26]

His speech accompanied the presentation of a draft resolution on the political situation and war danger. Like all of the resolutions in Frankfurt,

---

[24] "Theses on the Revolutionary Movement in Colonial and Semi-colonial Countries, Adopted by the Sixth Congress," September 1, 1928, reprinted in McDermott and Agnew, *The Comintern*, 236.
[25] Second Anti-Imperialist World Congress, Press Service No. 5, July 22, 1929, "The Danger of War and the Tasks of the League against Imperialism," excerpt of Pollitt's Speech, 542/1/87/18, RGASPI.
[26] Ibid., 542/1/87/19, RGASPI.

this document had been drafted, revised, and polished in Moscow under the auspices of the planning commissions of the Comintern. It was a call to resist imperialism and prepare for the imperialist war danger, although the battlegrounds had shifted dramatically since Brussels. Rather than a war danger articulated in Brussels in which imperialist and capitalist powers threatened the Soviet Union and the colonial world, the most urgent battle in Frankfurt necessitated anti-imperialists to wage an internal struggle against comrades within the League's ranks. In a complete turnaround, the anticolonial nationalists and European socialists, bulwarks of the anti-imperialist movement in 1927, were represented as agents of imperialism working hand-in-hand with the great powers and capitalist classes across the world. Their betrayal became the basis for a new war danger, which called upon "true" anti-imperialists to mobilize against imperialist war and protect the Soviet Union, while at the same time "expos[ing] the criminal activities of international Social Democracy and its reformist representatives in the colonies."[27] Prominent in his text was the Indian example: "the Right Wing of the national movement are attempting to substitute Dominion Status for independence [and] are taking a long step in the direction of complete capitulation to British imperialism."[28]

The "Political Situation and War Danger" also revised the geopolitical concerns and worldview of anti-imperialism. The earlier Brussels Congress discourse foreshadowed American and European imperialist aggression in China and later against the Soviet Union, all while the success of imperialist aggression depended on the use of Indian manpower and military bases. In this Brussels-inspired worldview, it was essential for anticolonial nationalists worldwide, and especially in India, to resist Britain's war effort. But the new line in Frankfurt predicted a different set of circumstances bringing about war. While imperialist powers continued to menace the world and threaten attacks against the Soviet Union, it argued that these Western powers, alongside China's Nanking government run by Chiang Kai-shek, were the primary aggressors bringing an inevitable world war. Indian nationalists, rather than the leaders of anti-imperialist resistance, were portrayed as collaborators, like the KMT, in aiding and assisting Britain's imperialist war designs. In this new vision of the impending fate of the world, the only hope for humanity was the resistance of workers and peasants in colonies such as India against their imperial and native bourgeois oppressors, as well as their support for the Soviet Union.

---

[27] "Resolution: The Political Situation and War Danger," File 90, LAI, IISH.
[28] Manifesto of the Second Anti-Imperialist World Congress, File 78, LAI, IISH.

Gupta had the unenviable position of defending the INC immediately after Pollitt's assault on nationalists. In a speech befitting his predecessor, Nehru, Gupta defended India as a pivotal ally in the anti-imperialist world. He professed not only the INC's commitment to the LAI, but also that "the people of India, have no quarrel with the peoples of neighboring states nor with other nations of the world."[29] In an attempt to connect with the emphasis on class struggle so prominent in the League, Gupta embellished the socialist trends within the INC: "We do not want only political freedom, but we want to enjoy true freedom in every department of life." In perhaps his most grandiose and exaggerated statement, Gupta added that India "does not tolerate class and caste."[30] He also addressed the war danger by echoing Nehru's calls for India to resist British attempts to use India as a pawn in imperialist wars. He argued that the INC had "expressed [its] will to the effect that we shall not permit ourselves to be exploited by the British Government to further their imperialist aims."[31] Like Nehru, Gupta also argued that India could not achieve independence alone and had to both "join hands with anti-imperialist forces of the world" and extend "the hand of friendship and comradeship to other struggling nations of the world."[32]

Gupta took many liberties in representing the INC as a revolutionary force seeking complete independence from the British even when the Indian nationalist movement had not yet ratified any resolution with this goal in mind. Instead, he argued that the INC, "under the leadership of [its] greatest man, Mohandas Gandhi," intended to launch a truly "revolutionary mass movement" in which "we trust will achieve independence for our country." He underscored the importance of "peaceful means" in India's epic struggle against the raj and assured the Frankfurt audience that the INC "shall avoid the shedding of blood of others, but shall be ever ready to make every sacrifice and shed our own blood to the last man if that be necessary."[33]

The independence quandary had been at the crux of the growing chasm between the INC and the LAI from the start. It was a specter that had haunted Nehru's relations with Chatto and the Berlin office since Brussels. Yet, from the perspective of both Nehru and Gupta, the INC was on the verge of realizing complete independence as its objective. The upcoming congress in Lahore that December, they thought, was likely to champion independence backed by the force of a mass civil disobedience campaign.

[29] Gupta, Speech at the Frankfurt Congress, File 1–1929, AICC.   [30] Ibid.   [31] Ibid.
[32] Ibid.   [33] Ibid.

Despite Nehru's and Gupta's optimism, the inevitability of this assumption, however, was not a given in July 1929. In fact, before the end of the year Gandhi indeed returned to round table negotiations and willingly placed independence on the table as a bargaining chip. Navigating the realities on the ground in India and the criticism from the LAI abroad remained as much a challenge for Gupta in Frankfurt as it was for Nehru in Brussels.

Moscow's handpicked delegate – Rajini Palme Dutt, a prominent expatriate living in London – also spoke on behalf of India, and his speech served as a counterpoint to Gupta's. Dutt officially represented the Workers' Welfare League of India, and he was an active communist party member in Britain. Although of Indian descent, Dutt was born and raised in England. His connections to the peasantry and workers in India were limited at best. In his speech, he took on some of the questions raised by Gupta about the INC. He found Gupta's appraisal of the Indian situation in relation to independence "encouraging," but reminded the audience that, "unfortunately ... not all the members of the INC were of this opinion."[34] He reserved his more pointed criticism, however, for the British ILP and their policies on India. Dutt argued that while the working masses in India had been "arrested, subjected to a farce of a trial and sentenced to periods of ... hard labour," the "big parties" in Britain during the general election had "entered into a conspiracy of silence concerning the Indian question."[35] Dutt directly faced off against James Maxton by asking pointedly for him to declare publicly that the ILP was "in favour of and works for the withdrawal of the British troops in India."[36] Maxton declined to comment.

The ILP's India policy was another avenue in which the Comintern sought to expose noncommunists as traitors to anti-imperialism. Indeed, the Comintern delegation was more critical of Maxton than Gupta. This agenda in many ways conformed to the history of the LAI in the earliest days as communists and socialists waged their most venomous attacks against one another. It also echoed similar attacks by the LSI that led to the socialist retreat in 1927, including key resignations by George Lansbury and Fenner Brockway. This time, however, communist delegates were on the offensive and sought "to weaken and destroy Maxton's prestige in the League, and to isolate him from the other delegates."[37] As Bittleman saw

---

[34] Excerpt from speech delivered July 24, reprinted in the LAI Press Service, No. 8, 542/1/87/27, RGASPI.
[35] Ibid.   [36] Ibid.   [37] Bittleman, Report on Lessons of Frankfurt Congress.

it, no concession should be made that might offer Maxton and the ILP a "certificate of being real fighters against imperialism."[38]

While the proceedings involved polemic speeches and intense inquisitions of noncommunists such as Maxton and Gupta, the greatest debate took place behind closed doors over the Comintern-drafted resolutions, especially the representation of the INC within them. In the executive committee meeting, Gupta threatened to walk out of the Frankfurt Congress if the executives did not revise the political resolution, which represented the INC most unfavorably. The document pre-drafted in Moscow characterized the INC as a puppet of imperialism:

The Swaraj Party and the Rightwing Sections of the Indian National Congress, together with the vacillating elements who have succumbed to their influence have betrayed the demand for independence, the basic demand of the Brussels Congress of the League – and by substituting the claim with Dominion Status have taken a large step in the direction of complete capitulation to British imperialism.[39]

Gupta argued that this was a gross and erroneous representation of the INC, one which denied the strong support for independence led by Nehru and others. In response, Gupta proposed a revision offering a different reading of the INC. In many ways, he also exaggerated the INC's position on independence by suggesting that it was the clear aim of India to break completely from the British Empire:

We welcome and appreciate the clear and unequivocal expression of opinion of the Indian National Congress in favour of complete independence for India, and hope and trust that the reactionary attempt which still exists in some quarter [*sic*] in Indian against independence will soon melt away, and we assure our full support to those national elements which are fighting against the biggest imperialist power, namely, British imperialism.[40]

In principle, the executive committee should have determined whether or not to accept the recommendations from Gupta. However, the committee was strongly influenced by a much larger number of communists, including longtime LAI leaders such as Münzenberg, Chatto, and Saklatvala, as well as newcomers like Melnichansky. These executives met in secret with the Comintern-appointed delegation to determine a course for responding to Gupta. Two essential questions were on the table. The first was whether the Comintern instructions allowed for flexibility in amending the

---

[38] Ibid.
[39] An explanation of the negotiations including the different drafts of the resolution is found in Gupta's report on the Frankfurt Congress to the INC, File 4, LAI, JNU.
[40] Ibid.

pre-drafted resolutions prepared for the Frankfurt Congress. The second was whether it was advisable to amend the resolution or let Gupta walk. Newcomers led by Alexandar Bittleman, the head of the Comintern preparations committee and author of the political resolution, argued that the Comintern instructions were to push forward the pre-drafted resolutions without revision regardless of Gupta's threat to withdraw. On the other hand, Münzenberg and Saklatvala saw a split in Frankfurt as fatal to the anti-imperialist movement and sought compromise in order to retain Gupta's participation.

The first secret meeting produced a wholesale rejection of Gupta's revisions, although a consensus emerged that the Comintern had left room in the instructions for some "editorial changes" to the resolution drafts.[41] Rather than withdraw the INC from the Frankfurt Congress, Gupta made another attempt to improve the resolution's representation of the INC. His second draft softened his statement that the INC was wholly supportive of independence and recognized that a "minority" of members had supported dominion status. Of course, it neglected the fact that the INC, as an institution, had not formally made "an unequivocal declaration" of independence. It read:

> We welcome and appreciate the views of those elements in the Indian National Congress who made an unequivocal declaration in favour of independence, but emphatically condemn the minority in the Congress who have attempted to substitute Dominion Status for complete independence, and we promise our full support to those national elements which are struggling for their emancipation from the biggest imperialist power, namely, British imperialism.[42]

Gupta's second submission sent the communist faction into another round of secret meetings, but this time its discussion of the INC engendered a more intense and divisive debate. It brought about a significant rift over the delegates' interpretation of the Comintern's instructions in regard to the India question. While the primary objective of the Comintern in Frankfurt was to criticize and expose nationalists and socialists as supporters of imperialism, the instructions were more ambiguous about whether the communist delegates should pursue a policy of purging them from the League altogether if they failed to conform to the new line. Once again, prominent founding members of the LAI like Münzenberg, Chatto, and Saklatvala, as well as Melnichansky, thought it vital to retain the INC within the LAI. Though they criticized nationalists and their moderate

---

[41] For details of the communist faction meeting, see 542/1/96/73, RGASPI.
[42] Gupta's report on the Frankfurt Congress to the AICC, File 4, LAI, JNU.

policies, they sought to avoid a complete split along the fault lines of communism and noncommunism at all costs, and preserving unity meant accepting some form of Gupta's suggested revisions. Conversely, Bittleman and others were prepared to force the noncommunists out of the League in Frankfurt rather than accept a single revision to the resolution. For Bittleman, Gupta and the INC were welcome to leave.

After intense debate, the communist faction agreed to accept some modification to the resolution to ensure that the INC remained within the LAI and the Frankfurt Congress. The final draft of the resolution showed a strange hybrid of both Gupta's revisions and much of the communist phraseology and critique of the INC:

We welcome and appreciate the views of those elements in the Indian National Congress who made an unequivocal declaration in favour of independence but emphatically condemn all those in the Indian National Congress and outside the Congress who are attempting to substitute Dominion Status for complete independence, and are taking a long step in the direction of complete capitulation to British imperialism. *The bourgeoisie in India, as everywhere else, is cooperating with the British exploiters in their ruthless suppression of the peasant and labour movements in India. We welcome particularly the heroic revolutionary struggle of the Indian workers and peasants for the betterment of their economic conditions and against British imperialism.* We pledge all support to the Indian nationalist revolutionary movement, and to all elements, which are fighting uncompromisingly for the overthrow of the biggest imperialist power – British imperialism.[43]

The compromise with Gupta produced a patchwork of contradictory viewpoints and positions on the leadership of the INC and hardly represented a clear or coherent statement on the League's policy on India. The opening and closing clauses integrated Gupta's sentiment that at least some INC members, like Nehru and himself, represented the fight for Indian independence, while other elements of the national congress conceded to dominion status. At the same time, the middle clauses (italicized here for emphasis) attacked the bourgeois leadership entirely and pitted them against the workers and peasants. The communist-inspired clauses echoed the class warfare rhetoric of the Comintern and criticized the bourgeoisie, of which most of the INC was comprised, for their class character regardless of their position on the independence question.

There is no doubt that many of the Comintern agents in Frankfurt were furious with the overall decision to revise the resolution, and it became

---

[43] Reprinted in Press service of the League against Imperialism, 542/1/87/98, RGASPI [author's emphasis].

a source of friction for months to come as the fallout of the Frankfurt Congress revealed a deep divide between those who subscribed to the solidarities of the past and those who sought to incite class warfare within the League. In his report on the Frankfurt Congress, Bittleman expressed deep regret over the concessions made to Gupta. He argued that the Comintern faction was forced to compromise with Gupta because there was not a single communist or representative of the workers from India present in Frankfurt. He criticized Gupta personally as "a large landowner and spokesman of Ghandi [*sic*]," and openly attacked Münzenberg and the League for failing to attract working-class leaders from India or making any effort to prevent Gupta's revisions from being implemented.[44] Bittleman added that in the future, cooperation with nationalists like Gupta and Nehru was "inadvisable," and that the League "must strive to free itself of such elements, [by] carrying on an energetic struggle against their influence in the colonial movements."[45]

The other fatal compromise, in the eyes of Bittleman and the newcomers from the Comintern, was the affordance lent to Maxton to defend his position on the final day of the Frankfurt Congress. Maxton took the opportunity to raise the central questions that had guided Frankfurt's executive meetings and official sessions: who was an anti-imperialist, and could communists and noncommunists "work together for a common end"? In a response to his critics in Frankfurt, Maxton emphatically stated, "I am a revolutionary socialist determined to wage an open fight for the overthrow of world capitalism and world imperialism."[46] He called upon his anti-imperialist comrades to forge a path for the continued collaboration within the LAI across the boundaries dividing communists and noncommunists. It was critical, in his view, to avoid "exaggerating differences of view point on minor matters."[47]

Maxton accentuated the precise question that would determine the future of the LAI: would differences between anti-imperialists be overlooked as they had in the past, or "exaggerated" as an outcome of new Comintern strategies? To address this central question in a climatic summary of the Frankfurt Congress, Münzenberg approached the podium. In a fashion consistent with his hopes and dreams for the LAI since 1927, Münzenberg celebrated the remarkable success of the League in bringing together a vast and diverse array of anti-imperialists. He argued

---

[44] Bittleman, Report on Lessons of Frankfurt Congress.   [45] Ibid.
[46] James Maxton's speech, Frankfurt Congress, 542/1/91/115–121, RGASPI.
[47] Extracts from Münzenberg's speech, LAI Press Service, 542/1/87/44, RGASPI.

that the League was the only organization to "unite streams of anti-imperialism" from places such as India, China, and Arabia. He added that Frankfurt, like Brussels, attracted not only individuals, but also representatives of mass organizations. The masses of exploited and oppressed were the "real basis" of the LAI. His final call to action appealed to delegates to return home and continue the anti-imperialist struggle and to protect the Soviet Union, the "great friend of the oppressed and exploited masses."[48] Nowhere in his speech did he attack his anti-imperialist comrades Nehru, Maxton, Gupta, Hatta, Fimmen, or Baldwin. His summation ultimately preserved the solidarities from the Brussels Congress moment. It was a testament to his commitment to his comrades and the fundamental basis of anti-imperialist solidarity, even if it placed him at odds with his party bosses and financiers in Moscow.

At the end of the day, the Frankfurt Congress retained the enduring and essential quality of embracing solidarity over differences in spite of the Comintern's efforts to stage the congress otherwise. Münzenberg would face serious consequences in the aftermath. Bittleman's report to Moscow lambasted the LAI secretariat for its failure to bring representatives of the workers and peasants from the colonies to Frankfurt. This oversight was not due to financial constraints or colonial police interventions, according to Bittleman, but rather because the League and its leadership had "lagged behind" in understanding the fundamental changes that had occurred since the Brussels Congress: namely, the emergence of the workers in the colonies as the only "truly" anti-imperialist force. He considered Münzenberg's role in ensuring that solidarity with noncommunists prevailed in Frankfurt a "gross distortion and infringement of the CI line."[49] In conclusion, he strongly urged the Comintern to reorganize the League and move the secretariat out of Berlin, at a safe distance from its founder, Münzenberg.

Later in 1929, Münzenberg was called to Moscow to explain his work with the LAI and answer Bittleman's accusations. Münzenberg made an appeal for the League to remain in Berlin by pointing out that Berlin, unlike any other city, allowed for easier communications with Moscow.[50] Security and surveillance in Berlin were minimal compared to London and Paris; hence, Münzenberg argued that the London and Paris branch offices should continue to function as auxiliaries to the international secretariat in Berlin, and that the Comintern's real focus should be on developing

---

[48] Ibid.   [49] Bittleman, Report on Lessons of Frankfurt Congress.
[50] "Alternative" proposal to Comintern from "W.M.," undated, 542/1/79/235–236, RGASPI.

Leagues worldwide, especially in the colonies. In a surprising turn, the Comintern leaders in Moscow continued to support the Berlin secretariat as the international center of the League, although it took extra measures to ensure the compliance of Münzenberg and Chatto by dispatching to Berlin more trustworthy communist party members to oversee the work of the secretariat. New secretaries meant stricter control and supervision direct from the Comintern, and these agents carried orders to send reports and act in accord with their Moscow bosses. The first to arrive in Berlin was Bohumíl Smeral, a Czechoslovakian member of the Comintern and a participant in Moscow's Frankfurt Congress planning commissions. The second, a Turkish Comintern agent named Bekar Ferdi, arrived later in 1930.

While solidarity prevailed in Frankfurt and the INC stayed on in the LAI for another day, Maxton and the ILP did not. The British section of the League against Imperialism handled the question of Maxton and the ILP in September 1929 by expelling him by unanimous resolution. Bridgeman explained the action in a letter to *The New Leader*.[51] He argued that Maxton and the ILP remained silent when the LP government dispatched British troops to Palestine to suppress unrest between Jews and Muslims. Simultaneously, the ILP did not protest the LP's ongoing execution of the Meerut Conspiracy Case. These ILP positions ran counter to the anti-imperialist mission according to Bridgeman. In addition, Bridgeman had asked Maxton to publish in *The New Leader* his speech supporting anti-imperialism in Frankfurt, but Maxton refused. When the executive committee of the British League met on September 17, Maxton did not attend. In his absence, the executive committee voted to remove him from the organization. At the same time, and as no coincidence, the CPGB became an official affiliate of the British LAI.

Nehru and other noncommunists were not entirely surprised by Maxton's expulsion. When Nehru first received word of it, he wrote to Gupta that he could "imagine some of the reasons why this conflict arose."[52] Bridgeman of the British League wrote to Nehru that the anti-imperialist movement would be more progressive "since Maxton [was] no longer connected with the LAI."[53] Chatto was pleased by Maxton's

---

[51] Letter from Bridgeman to the editor of *The New Leader*, September 30, 1929, copy in International Committee for Political Prisoners Records (microfilm), Box 3, Folder 19–21 (microform reel 5), New York Public Library (hereafter ICPP). Baldwin was the chairman of the ICPP.

[52] Nehru to Gupta, October 1, 1929, File FD1ii-1929, AICC.

[53] Bridgeman to Nehru, November 2, 1929, FD23-1929, AICC.

departure as well, and he wrote to Nehru that Maxton had deployed "radical phrases merely to deceive the subject peoples and gain time for imperialism." Chatto concluded that the INC should welcome the British League's move to expel him.[54]

Overall, this small slice of history from the Frankfurt Congress reveals several critical points. It was divisive, although the splits were not always between communists and noncommunists. The most heated debates took place in the secret meetings between communists who disagreed on the Comintern's intentions for the congress and the LAI. The League's communist founders, including Münzenberg and Saklatvala, were at odds with newcomers like Bittleman over the Comintern's fundamental position on nationalists within the anti-imperialist movement. This division was informed by distinct views of the history and future of the anti-imperialist movement and whether it was to remain an inclusive organization fostering solidarity or an exclusive one that encouraged difference. For the founding figures, who ran the Berlin secretariat and the British national section, the LAI could not exist without the flexibility embedded in its roots and mission. Nehru and later Gupta were in this camp as well. When both communists and noncommunists did tackle the questions of unity and the anti-imperialist authenticity of noncommunists within the League, they did so with some restraint and willingness to compromise. The political resolution's characterization of the INC was a case in point. While there remained loud and oppositional voices from the left of the communist faction, these voices were not necessarily representative of the congress as a whole, or even the communist delegation.

THE FALLOUT IN INDIA AND THE LAHORE CONGRESS

News from the Frankfurt Congress was slow to arrive in India. Nehru wrote a letter to Chatto on September 23 bemoaning the absence of any reports about the congress. He thought the heavy censorship of the colonial state was responsible for the silence.[55] When Nehru finally heard from Gupta, the news was troubling. Gupta wrote that he was "fed up" with the LAI and warned Nehru that an alliance between it and the INC was likely untenable.[56] At first, Nehru underestimated the seriousness of his letter, and instead thought Gupta was "not well acquainted with much that

[54] Chatto to Nehru, October 30, 1929, File 5, LAI, JNU.
[55] Nehru to Chatto, September 23, 1929, File 4, LAI, JNU.
[56] Gupta to Nehru, August 26, 1929, File 4, LAI, JNU (Hindi).

happens outside India."[57] In a letter asking Roger Baldwin about his impressions of Frankfurt, Nehru added that he could sympathize with Gupta "feeling hopelessly at sea in Frankfurt and not appreciating much that might have been said by the communist element in the Congress."[58]

Nehru had yet to appreciate the dramatically changed environment of the Frankfurt Congress. Although Gupta retained a place for the INC within the LAI, the contest over anti-imperialism continued in the months after Frankfurt, and particularly between Moscow and Berlin. At the end of the day, however, political events in India were pivotal to the undoing the INC–LAI relationship. Although Gandhi's trip to the roundtable to negotiate with the colonial state for acceptance of dominion status had little possibility of success, the mere potential for India to compromise on independence forced Berlin closer to Moscow. In an earlier and more flexible milieu, the LAI afforded Nehru ample space and time to convince his INC colleagues that independence was the only path forward. However, Moscow's intense pressure on Berlin forced the LAI to take a more critical stance on the INC's temporary truce with the raj in late 1929. This was not an inevitable outcome, however, and the split obscures the diligent attempts by LAI comrades on both sides of the communist divide to resist the forces cross-cutting the solidarities of anti-imperialism even as late as 1930.

Ironically, news of discord in Frankfurt arrived at a moment of tremendous support for the LAI in India. The support came as a response to the Meerut Conspiracy Case (1929–1934), a lengthy legal trial named after its location in a small Indian city within Nehru's home state of the United Provinces. The colonial state charged thirty-two suspects in India and sixty-three organizations and individuals abroad for conspiring with international communists to overthrow the British raj. The overarching objective of the trial was the eradication of communism in India, and it culminated with the banning of the communist party at the end of the trial in 1934. Of particular importance to the trial was the LAI, which came to be one of the conspirators in the case along with several of its key personnel, including Chatto, Münzenberg, Saklatvala, Pollitt, and J. W. Johnstone. Nehru narrowly escaped the docket despite his prominent role in the LAI, which was not an oversight on the part of colonial officials, but rather a deliberate attempt, in the words of Home Secretary H. G. Haig, to "convince in general as early as possible that Communism is not the kind of movement that should receive sympathy of

---

[57] Nehru to Baldwin, August 22, 1929, FD 1929–1931, AICC.   [58] Ibid.

Nationalists."[59] In the preliminary hearings, the prosecution mined volumes of confiscated evidence, including substantial volumes of Nehru's intercepted correspondence abroad, to build a case that the LAI was "anti-nationalist."[60]

Nehru launched a widespread campaign to counter the colonial imperatives in the Meerut trial. In June, Nehru and his father secured a mandate and funding from the INC to form a twelve-person defense committee for the accused. Gandhi even traveled to Meerut and visited the prisoners in a demonstration of solidarity between the INC and the defendants. Nehru also called upon his LAI comrades abroad to amplify and extend protests against the Meerut trial beyond India. Bridgeman became a strong ally on this front, and his propaganda work in London, from 1929 to 1933, consumed nearly all of the British LAI's resources. The focus on Meerut strengthened the British LAI and extended its appeal to a wider support base beyond London, to include local Leagues in Manchester, Birmingham, Edinburgh, Aberdeen, Liverpool, and Glasgow.[61] It also brought Nehru and Bridgeman closer together in their anti-imperialist work. Baldwin also proved to be an ambitious and able organizer on behalf of the Meerut accused, launching an intensive publicity campaign in the United States to raise awareness and collect funds for their defense. Nehru's letters to Baldwin once again offered some of his more candid reflections on the state of affairs in India. Tongue in cheek, Nehru remarked about the trial's attempt to label the LAI a communist organization: "If the Government had a better secret service than they actually possess, they might have known how hard you and others tried to prevent too great a communist influence in the inner councils of the League and how far you succeeded."[62]

The surge in INC support for the LAI weakened as the preliminary hearings proceeded, however. The prosecution delivered an arsenal of evidence that the defendants in India and abroad had harbored ill will and hostility toward the INC. The lead prosecutor struck a personal note

---

[59] Haig to James, April 29, 1929, in *Documents of the Communist Movement in India*, vol. II, Meerut Conspiracy Case (1929), edited by Jyoti Basu (Calcutta: National Book Agency, 1997).

[60] Langford James, "Opening Address of the Special Public prosecutor before R. Milner White in the Emperor vs. Phillip Spratt and Others," June 12, 1929 (Meerut: Saraswati Machine Printing Press, 1929).

[61] Reginald Bridgeman, "Secretary's Report," in Report of the National Conference of the League against Imperialism (British Section), February 1931 (London: League against Imperialism, 1931), DBN/25/1, Bridgeman Papers.

[62] Ibid.

for Nehru in his opening remarks when he argued that "Pandit Motilal Nehru is regarded by [the defendants] as a dangerous patriot. His son, Jawaharlal Nehru, is dubbed a tepid reformist. Mr. Subash Chunder Bose is a bourgeois and a somewhat ludicrous careerist. Mr. Gandhi they regard and dislike as a grotesque reactionary."[63] The colonial government even dispatched a public relations advisor to widely disseminate such evidence of ideological slippage between the accused and the INC, while the Indian press received government stipends to reprint the prosecution's opening remarks and any relevant evidence to support the state imperatives in Meerut. Nehru was aware of these colonial manipulations and described the trial to Chatto as a "pure propaganda effort and the obvious attempt . . . to prejudice the Meerut accused in the eyes of nationalists."[64]

INC support for the Meerut defendants ultimately became impossible after the communists on trial answered Moscow's call to refuse the assistance offered by Indian nationalists. As one Meerut defendant later recalled, a total of eighteen of the accused collectively decided to "transform the courtroom into a political forum for the dissemination of [their] ideology."[65] From this platform, they launched a caustic attack on the bourgeois nature of the INC and even the AITUC's more moderate members. Although few of the accused on trial had ties with the LAI, the organization was guilty by association. By late 1929, as Nehru learned more about the Frankfurt Congress tensions, the INC's defense committee for the Meerut prisoners disbanded and financial support evaporated. Even Nehru was shaken by the trial and expressed in a letter to Chatto his disbelief in the communists' "way of cursing nationalists in the most offensive languages."[66]

The news from the Frankfurt Congress presented Nehru with further evidence of discord between communists and noncommunists within the LAI. The most alarming picture came from Edo Fimmen, the trade unionist based in Amsterdam. Fimmen's letter to Nehru was a colorful one. He characterized the state of the League as "moribund" and called the Frankfurt Congress a "wild heresy hunt" led by the left wing of the Comintern. He added that the congress "was in no way a demonstration

---

[63] Langford James, "Opening Address."
[64] Nehru to Chatto, June 20, 1929, *SWJN*, vol. 4, 345.
[65] The collective statement of communist party members in Meerut is published in *Communists Challenge Imperialism from the Dock* with introduction by Muzaffar Ahmad (Calcutta: National Book Agency Private, 1967). For this quote, see introduction by Muzaffar Ahmad, ii.
[66] Nehru to Chatto, June 20, 1929, *SWJN*, vol. 3, 345.

of unity, but a kind of ecclesiastical court for the arraignment and execution of comrades showing any signs of not being strictly orthodox."[67] Fimmen added that he had had a long talk with Münzenberg, who agreed. Fimmen and Münzenberg met in person to discuss the League and the fallout over Frankfurt. Fimmen revealed to Nehru that Münzenberg was "very disturbed" by the League's turn, although "hopeful ... that he may be able, through his influence and activities, to bring the League back to its original policy."[68]

Meanwhile, Fimmen and Baldwin met in Amsterdam in an attempt to construct and unite a bloc of anti-imperialists within the League who supported the spirit of the Brussels Congress. In the letters from Baldwin and Fimmen to Nehru, both spoke about the troubles in the Berlin secretariat and the unenviable pressure placed on Münzenberg and Chatto by Moscow. Baldwin wrote that he knew "from an authoritative source that there [was] great tension existing between Moscow and Münzenberg." Baldwin added that Münzenberg knew very well it would be "stupid" to make the League a tool of the Comintern, but that the "eye of Moscow" had been in Frankfurt and reported on him in a "very unfavourable manner."[69] Both Baldwin and Fimmen proposed a pressure group within the LAI consisting of Nehru, Baldwin, Fimmen, Münzenberg, and others, who could counteract the Comintern and "ensure certain guarantees" that noncommunists were welcome in the League. If this plan failed, the alternative was for the bloc to collectively resign and reconstitute a new, more inclusive League for anti-imperialism that would be freed "from the imperialism of Moscow."[70]

By November, Nehru had pledged his support for the Baldwin–Fimmen proposed bloc.[71] This was not a bloc of noncommunists, although there were many in it, but an alliance of anti-imperialists working for the spirit and solidarity of the Brussels Congress rather than the Frankfurt Congress. Much was at stake for the bloc in ensuring the Berlin secretariat retained a strong commitment to solidarities between communists and noncommunists. Baldwin began to pressure Chatto: "You cannot build an antiimperial movement around the Communist Party" because "all you will get will be a purely stereotyped reflection of the policies (and politics) of the

---

[67] Fimmen to Nehru, November 12, 1929. File 8, LAI, JNU.   [68] Ibid.

[69] Baldwin to Nehru, October 24, 1929, File 11, LAI, JNU. Colonial authorities intercepted the letter, although Nehru recognized its receipt on November 25 in his response to Baldwin. His letter from Fimmen was intercepted as well, and Nehru did not receive it until March 1930.

[70] Ibid.   [71] Nehru to Baldwin, November 25, 1929, FD 16, 1929–1931, AICC.

dominant faction in the Party." Baldwin called the Frankfurt Congress a meeting of "political one-sidedness" that elected a general council "without much influence or particular interest in anti-imperialism."[72] Baldwin also wrote Nehru suggesting that he try to sway Chatto to ensure that noncommunists continue to have a role in the LAI. Nehru began to press Chatto on the matter by writing a "troubled" letter to him in November expressing his concerns about the LAI and noncommunists. He reminded Chatto that in the "early days" the League was not a purely communist organization, and noncommunists were both welcome and essential to it. However, Nehru wrote that now it appeared to be the "unfortunate policy" of the LAI to drive out the noncommunists, which was "bound to end in the complete collapse of the League."[73]

Behind the scenes, Chatto was already working against the grain of the Comintern. Both the secretariat and the Comintern agreed that India was the pre-eminent terrain for the anti-imperialist struggle. Both also agreed that the LAI should do whatever it could to organize and sponsor a meeting of anti-imperialists in India ahead of the INC annual sessions at the end of 1929. But their plans for this meeting were radically different. In August, Chatto and Burns, the co-secretaries in the international secretariat, formulated plans for a meeting in India to which all major Indian organizations would be invited, including the INC, AITUC, and WPP, among others. The manifestos and resolutions would be drafted in Berlin, and the League would pay for the conference. The final passage of the proposal listed potential organizers for the conference, including Nehru and another Bengali congressman, Kanailal Ganguli. Indeed, the document hailed them as "trusted workers" needed to rally "the discontented left wing elements" in India.[74]

In principle, the Comintern's response to the proposal was positive. Bittleman, who recently returned to Moscow from Frankfurt, offered the Comintern's response on behalf of the Eastern Secretariat, writing that his colleagues and he "attach[ed] great importance to the speedy organization of the League section in India." He also agreed that the League should fund the conference. However, he pushed Chatto for further clarification of the "trusted workers" on the ground in India. He wanted the specific names of those in India who would receive funds from the League. He

---

[72] Baldwin to Chatto, August 26, 1929, Box 8, Folder 3, Baldwin Papers.
[73] Nehru to Chatto, November 25, 1929. *SWJN*, vol. 3, 312–313.
[74] Proposal for All-India Anti-Imperialist Organization enclosed in letter from Emile Burns to ECCI of the Comintern, August 15, 1929, 542/1/30/100–103, RGASPI.

added that it would "not do at all" to send funds to Nehru or charge him with the task of organizing the League. Bittleman promised that once Chatto identified an alternative contact, the Comintern would take action to enable Chatto "to realize the plan."[75]

Chatto ignored Bittleman's orders and instead wrote to Nehru asking him to assume the leadership role of organizing an anti-imperialist federation in India. In a letter dated October 30, Chatto wrote that while he "thoroughly realiz[ed] the value of the National Congress as an All-India organization," it still remained "indispensable" to develop a "federation" of all anti-imperialist forces in India comprised of both members and non-members of the INC.[76] He concluded by asking once again that Nehru "think over the possibilities of organizing" such a federation. Chatto already knew that the Comintern wished the League to cease its work with Nehru and the INC by late October, but the letter demonstrated the Berlin office's resistance to Moscow's directives. It also demonstrated that Chatto still considered Nehru the LAI's ally in India despite the outcomes of the Frankfurt Congress and pressure from Moscow to abandon his connection to the INC.

By the end of October 1929, the LAI–INC relationship remained firmly intact. Moreover, a cross-party alliance of anti-imperialists had been forged between Chatto, Münzenberg, Fimmen, Baldwin, and Nehru, who collectively set out to rescue the anti-imperialist movement from the sectarian divide imposed by Moscow. In a show of his commitment to the League and his ongoing relationship with Chatto and the Berlin office, Nehru even supervised another remittance of INC funds in the amount of fifty pounds to support the LAI secretariat in October 1929.

Once again, the question of independence shook the alliance between Berlin and Nehru. The centrality of the independence question for India was best articulated by Emile Burns, who wrote a summary of the League activities and the Frankfurt Congress in *The Labour Monthly*. Burns stated that while Nehru's Indian resolutions and speeches in Brussels had clearly supported independence, the "Indian National Congress, by a majority under the influence of the Right Wing, has temporarily pushed the demand for full independence into the background and substituted the demand of Dominion Status." Burns concluded by voicing the question on

---

[75] Bittleman to Chatto, August 27, 1929, 542/1/33/10, RGASPI.
[76] Chatto to Nehru, October 30, 1929, File 5, LAI, JNU.

the minds of many within the LAI: Could "the League continue to work with the Indian National Congress in such circumstances?"[77] The answer to this question was determined in November 1929. In what famously became the Delhi Manifesto, named after the city where congress leaders met, the INC demanded immediate dominion status in exchange for preventing the civil disobedience movement. At first, Nehru resigned from the INC working committee because the Delhi Manifesto surrendered independence.[78] However, he was convinced to withdraw his resignation. In personal letters to Bridgeman and Chatto, Nehru explained that while the Delhi Manifesto offered to accept dominion status, it contained a list of demands the colonial state would not accept, and Nehru predicted that the colonial state's inevitable failure to meet such demands would strengthen the INC's resolve to push for independence and civil disobedience.[79]

The Delhi Manifesto was not that dissimilar to other compromises Nehru had already made to salvage the INC's solidarity while at the same time working from within the organization to rally it around independence. While both Nehru and Chatto recognized Gandhi's moderation and the INC's shortcomings, they had in the past collaborated and strategized on ways to pull the INC closer to that elusive goal of independence framed in the language of anti-imperialism. In fact, in his usual fashion, Chatto wrote Nehru a warning ahead of Nehru's final decision to sign the manifesto by reminding him that, "not very long ago [Nehru] declared somewhere, very correctly, that no negotiations [were] possible so long as the army of occupation was in the country." Chatto added that "the acceptance of Dominion Status in any form or under any conditions [could not] be regarded as an anti-imperialist attitude."[80] When Nehru finally signed the manifesto, however, it became increasingly unfeasible for Chatto to defend his colleague against the backdrop of the Comintern's pressure to cut ties with Indian nationalists.

That the compromise was fatal to Nehru's relationship with Chatto and ultimately the LAI was apparent immediately. On November 20, Chatto and Münzenberg signed and disseminated a letter to all affiliated and associated organizations based in India. The circular denounced the

---

[77] Emile Burns, "The World Congress of the League against Imperialism," *The Labour Monthly* 11, no. 9 (1929).
[78] For copies of resignation letters to the INC Working Committee from Bose, Iyengar, and Nehru, see File G117-1929, AICC.
[79] Nehru to Bridgeman, November 23, 1929, File 8, LAI, JNU.
[80] Chatto to Nehru, October 6, 1929, File 7, LAI, JNU.

INC and singled out Nehru as untrustworthy and hypocritical. Invoking the Nehru Report and the Delhi Manifesto for justification, the letter called for "real" anti-imperialists to abandon their faith in the INC as an anti-imperialist organization. According to the LAI, Nehru proclaimed to be a leader of independence and an executive member of the LAI, while at the same time accepting the terms of the Delhi Manifesto and dominion status. It concluded that the INC was no longer a "safe instrument" for the "uncompromising struggle" for independence, and it urged its readers to seek another vehicle for the anti-imperialist struggle in India.[81]

The great paradox at the end of 1929 was that Nehru presided over the signing of an all-India and Gandhi-supported independence resolution precisely when the League was imploring anti-imperialists to break ranks with the congress. As Nehru had predicted, the colonial state refused the demands of the Delhi Manifesto. Even more promising, the independence (or *purna swaraj*) declaration at the end of 1929 was accompanied by a call for a mass civil disobedience campaign to enforce its demand. The independence resolution was a crowning achievement of Nehru's attempts to bring together nationalism and internationalism, yet his triumph in the all-India arena came at the very moment his international-ist connections were strained to the breaking point. As Nehru prepared for the annual session of the INC in Lahore, he could not help but wonder whether the anti-imperialist institution he had helped create in 1927 would welcome the INC as it committed to complete independence from the British Empire and joined the anti-imperialist cause worldwide.

Even when the INC finally committed to pursuing full independence, the change failed to resolve the tensions between the LAI and the INC. Nehru's letters to Berlin after the Delhi Manifesto became more hostile. In response to the fateful circular in November attacking the INC, Nehru wrote to the LAI reminding his Berlin comrades that the INC was an associated body to the League and did not take directives from Berlin.[82] Another of Nehru's letters in January 1930 charged that the LAI's "earn-estness and good motives divorced from a real knowledge of the situation [in India] may well prove harmful for our [Congress] movement."[83] In this same letter, Nehru even offered an ultimatum: "If the League is

---

[81] LAI secretariat to All Indian Organizations affiliated to LAI, November 20, 1929, File 1–1929, AICC.
[82] Nehru to Chatto, November 26, 1929, *SWJN*, vol. 3, 312–313.
[83] Nehru to the League against Imperialism Secretariat, January 26, 1930, *SWJN*, vol. 3, 238.

going to function purely as a communist organization then clearly it is not the place for us."[84]

With independence removed as an obstacle, Berlin fell into line with the Comintern and emphasized conflicts over class and nation as the source of friction between the INC and the LAI. Beginning in January 1930, Münzenberg and Chatto launched an attack on the class character of Gandhi and the congress. They fired off a letter to Indian anti-imperialists that welcomed the congress' independence resolution in principle, but urged them also to remember that Gandhi protected the propertied classes, as the "chief support of the imperialist system, and ha[d] systematically acted against the interests of the workers and peasants by advocating cooperation with their oppressors."[85]

The secretariat's publication of excerpts from the Frankfurt Congress provided another avenue for the LAI to articulate the differences between the INC and anti-imperialists in terms similar to the Comintern's. Indeed, the LAI's publication of the political resolution contained none of Gupta's changes to the INC clauses agreed upon in Frankfurt, despite Gupta's letters of protest to Berlin.[86] Ironically, this document, not the one passed in Frankfurt, stands as the official record of the political resolution of the Second World Congress of the LAI. Rather than a compromise reached in Frankfurt, it reads as a communist-driven critique of the INC:

> The Swaraj Party, and other Rightwing sections of the Indian National Congress, together with the vacillating elements who have succumbed to their influence, have betrayed the demand for independence, the basic demand of the Brussels Congress of the League, and by substituting the claim for Dominion Status have taken a large step in the direction of complete capitulation to British imperialism; while the national bourgeoisie as a class are cooperating with the British exploiters in their ruthless suppression of the labour movement in India.[87]

Though the official exchanges between the LAI secretariat and Nehru as INC President took on more hostile overtones, the divide between them was not so deeply ingrained even as late as 1930. For his part, Nehru enclosed a separate and personal letter for Chatto in January 1930, expressing hope that the tensions between the congress and the League might still be repaired. He wrote to Chatto: "I can well understand

---

[84] Ibid.
[85] LAI Secretariat to all anti-imperialist organizations in India, November 20, 1929, FD 1–1929, AICC.
[86] See Gupta to LAI Secretariat, January 29, 1930, File 10, LAI, JNU.
[87] "Political Situation and the War Danger," Resolution from the Second Anti-Imperialist World Congress, File 90, page 2, LAI, IISH.

difference in outlook. If this difference is fundamental then cooperation is difficult. If there is a fair measure of agreement then it is desirable to work together."[88] In response, Chatto and Münzenberg requested that Nehru wait until the executive council met to discuss the "highly important and interesting questions of principle and of tactics concerning cooperation of non-communist national colonial organizations with communists."[89] The secretaries added that they had "no doubt" that the meeting would address Nehru's concerns, and "a basis [would] be found for successful cooperation of all anti-imperialist elements in the League."[90]

To what extent Chatto and Münzenberg felt the INC and its members were considered "anti-imperialist elements" was not clear in the official correspondence. However, Chatto added a personal note to Nehru along with the official reply from Berlin. In it, he wrote "privately" as an "Indian revolutionary" rather than the LAI secretary. He encouraged Nehru to rethink his position and "not allow political differences to embitter" him or "make [him] blind to mistakes simply because these happen to be pointed out by communists."[91] He promised a forthcoming letter with personal reflections on the INC and recent events, although such a letter never arrived. At nearly the same time, Chatto also wrote to Moscow and requested once again to stall Comintern impulses to purge Nehru, arguing that he clearly remained an anti-imperialist because he had piloted the INC's acceptance of *purna swaraj*.[92]

Nehru sent another letter to Berlin on April 9 inquiring about the executive council's response and the LAI's position on the INC. Clearly, Nehru had not given up completely; this letter was more pointed, however, because he asked that the secretaries offer their thoughts apart from whatever the executive committee decided. Since Brussels, the secretariat had served as the arbitrator of anti-imperialist policy, discourse, and activities. It had played into a position somewhere between the executive council and the Comintern, although the distinction between the two latter entities was quickly diminishing as more agents from Moscow filled vacancies left by Maxton and others. Nehru knew that the secretariat's position was critical to the future of the INC relationship with the LAI.

---

[88] Nehru to Chatto, January 26, 1930, File 10, LAI, JNU.
[89] LAI International Secretariat to President of the Indian National Congress, February 26, 1930, FD1-1929, AICC.
[90] Ibid.
[91] Letter from Chatto to Nehru accompanying the official correspondence on February 26, 1930, FD1-1929, AICC.
[92] Chatto to Comintern, undated, 542/1/44/55, RGASPI (German).

He wrote in his letter that "the main burden of carrying on the work lies on the Secretariat and if the Secretariat itself approves, as it probably does, recent circulars and activities of the League then it becomes difficult for the [Indian] National Congress to remain associated with the League."[93] In his final passage, Nehru added that he heard some newspapers in Berlin were reporting that he had been expelled from the executive council already. Most likely, Nehru's source was Gupta, who was still in Continental Europe at the time.[94] Nehru concluded that this news only "deepened [his] conviction that [his] outlook differ[ed] greatly from" the LAI's.[95] Nehru asked the secretariat to accept his resignation and remove his name from its committee, assuming it had not already expelled him. He sent copies of the letter to Fimmen, Baldwin, Bridgeman, and Gupta.

Nehru never received a response from Chatto or Berlin after that fateful day in April. He circulated an internal memo within the INC requesting that all correspondence with the LAI cease. Before Nehru had time to contemplate the split with the League, however, he found himself consumed with the Civil Disobedience Campaign of 1930. Gandhi opened the campaign in March 1930 with the legendary Salt March from his ashram in Ahmedabad to the coastline in Dandi to protest British taxation of salt. It was an unlikely commodity on which to hinge the national movement, but all Indians paid the salt tax, and the British held a monopoly over its production. Elites and masses alike joined in the initial phase of civil disobedience, which quickly became the most popularly based campaign against the British the subcontinent had ever witnessed. Nehru also piloted a no-rent and no-tax campaign in his home state to dovetail with the political protests of the civil disobedience movement. The campaigns sought to relieve the peasants in rural UP from both the falling agricultural prices in the context of the global depression and the heavy financial burdens levied by landlords and the government.

While Nehru returned to prison for his role in the Civil Disobedience Campaign, the LAI fell into a period of confusion, disorganization, and inactivity. By 1930, the LAI was a mere shadow of its former self. The state of the organization was best captured in a report from a Comintern agent to Moscow in February 1930. "York," a pseudonym for Hans

[93] Nehru to The Secretary of the League against Imperialism, April 9, 1930, File 10, LAI, JNU.
[94] Gupta wrote to Nehru to express concern about the LAI and the INC's relationship to it. Gupta to Nehru, March 4, 1930, File 10, LAI, JNU.
[95] Nehru to the Secretary of the League against Imperialism, April 9, 1930, File 10, LAI, JNU.

Thögersen, who eventually served as the LAI secretary for a newly created youth department in 1931, wrote to Moscow during a visit to the LAI. He observed that since Frankfurt, the League had lost all communication with affiliates in the colonies, and that the secretariat's "method of work [was] not a very energetic one." York concluded that "as far as a plan of work [was] concerned for the LIA [*sic*], there [was] none."[96] Münzenberg had withdrawn entirely from the League office, leaving Chatto as the only secretary working actively on the anti-imperialist movement. Equally troubling was the existence of several anti-imperialist Leagues in England, Australia, Indo-China, and India that operated independently and without communication with Berlin.

Even the British League and Bridgeman were at odds with the Berlin secretariat. The controversy over the League's circular to India and its split with the INC troubled anti-imperialists in London. When Bridgeman sent greetings to the INC in Lahore on behalf of the British LAI, a backlash in the Comintern emerged over its "tone and spirit." According to a Comintern agent named Ferguson, the use of pleasantries like "sir" and "yours truly" and comments such as "Foreign rule is degrading to both the conquered and the conquering race" in the British League letter were evidence of "undiluted liberal hypocrisy of the most nauseating type."[97] The response from London, drafted by the "communist fraction" of the British League, was revealing. The British League countered that only one difference existed between the letter it sent and the one sent by the international secretariat. The Berlin letter stated that the INC could not be "regarded as an instrument" for anti-imperialism. The British comrades argued that "the repudiation of the Congress as a whole has never before been put forward as the policy of the League, and at the Frankfurt Congress, the greatest efforts were made to keep the Indian National Congress as an affiliated body."[98]

The British LAI's letter cited egregious inconsistencies in League policy and asked for an explanation of the position toward the INC: Was it an associated body or not? If so, then the British letter asking for cooperation from the INC was not erroneous. If not, then the international secretariat had to clarify its position. A follow-up letter, dated the same as the above,

---

[96] York to Comintern, "Report on General Situation of AIL and Proposals," February 14, 1930, 542/1/39/26a-b, RGASPI.

[97] Ferguson to the LAI secretariat, December 17, 1929, 542/1/33/49, RGASPI.

[98] Letter from Communist Fraction of the British League against Imperialism (London) to the International Secretariat (Berlin), February 21, 1929, 542/1/44/61–63, RGASPI.

pointed out that while the British section of the LAI had expelled Maxton, the international secretariat still considered him a member of the international executive committee. The British League objected strongly to the "lack of meetings, directives, and communications," which had hampered progress within the League since Frankfurt.[99]

The LAI as an institution was in disarray, and Nehru's departure reflected this chaos as much as the split between communists and noncommunists. His fellow comrades, Baldwin and Fimmen, were ousted from the LAI in early 1930 as well. The secretariat's gradual subordination to the Comintern had set in motion events and forces that would destroy the LAI as an institution for noncommunists and communists to collectively challenge imperialism and capitalism. Without contacts in the colonies like Nehru, the LAI in Berlin became an organization for European communist party members. The secretariat in Berlin sputtered along for a few years after the splits in 1930, but it was never the grandiose organization capable of hosting world congresses and serving as the meeting ground for major leftist figures that it had been in the past. Its fate in Berlin was sealed when a police raid in December 1931 and a subsequent one by Nazis in 1933 made LAI work in Germany impossible.[100] Münzenberg was forced flee to Paris and Chatto to Moscow, while what little was left of the LAI was to be transferred to London for a second resurrection under Bridgeman's tutelage. It was under this new arrangement that Nehru would find opportunities to revisit his LAI relationships after the break with Berlin.

Ultimately, the concluding days of the Nehru–LAI relationship reveal the significant changes to the anti-imperialist game ushered in by 1929. A narrower vision of anti-imperialism emerged, one rooted in the Comintern's policies toward nationalists. These policies limited the possibilities of a flexible and inclusive blending of anti-imperialist elements. It was not that Nehru and his comrades abandoned the basic ideas of anti-imperialism as a special blend of nationalism and internationalism, but rather that external pressure forced the more flexible and inclusive internationalism of the League in its formative years to succumb to the fragmented and oppositional categories of communist and nationalist politics. The failure of the INC to wholeheartedly accept independence made the blending of anti-imperialist elements impossible to defend in this moment,

---

[99] Letter from British LAI, Colonial Department to the International Secretariat, February 21, 1930, 542/1/44/59, RGASPI.
[100] Brückenhaus, *Policing Transnational Protest*, 164–168 and 171–172.

and the split between Nehru and the LAI secretariat in Berlin became inevitable after the Delhi Manifesto.

CONCLUSION

The crisis in anti-imperialism prompted by the discursive shifts in Moscow had set the LAI on a destructive path. By forcing into the open questions about the relationship between Indian independence and anti-imperialism, as well as the solidarities between class and nation, a discourse of difference shook the fundamental ideas about the League's internationalism. In many ways, the split between Nehru and the LAI was emblematic of a broader and global transition happening during the interwar years. The Comintern's third period, the rise of fascism, and the onset of the global depression in 1929 made this particular year a catalyst in strengthening national boundaries and imaginaries at the expense of the internationalist cooperation that had been a hallmark of the earlier 1920s.

At the same time, this chapter argues for two interventions to this story. The first is a more nuanced reading of the split between Nehru and the LAI as one informed by contingencies in India and overlapping histories rather than grand historical narratives of either the Comintern or the INC. The LAI was never under the Comintern's complete and uncontested domination, while the Berlin secretariat resisted pressure from Moscow to sever ties with Nehru. It was only the INC's actions and the local contingencies in Indian anticolonial politics that finally provoked Chatto and Münzenberg to act against their Indian comrade. The resistance and pushback against Moscow was evident until the very end of the relationship between the INC and the LAI. Moreover, the history of the LAI split cannot be understood as a history dominated by the narrative and sources of international communism either. The debates within the anti-imperialist movement did not pit communists against noncommunists in the simplistic way we assume in our teleological readings of communism and nationalism as incompatible. The interwar movements for anti-imperialism saw squabbles over the doctrines and orthodoxies of the many political parties represented in the internationalist fronts, yet most activists continued to work across and through these divisions throughout the 1920s and even the 1930s, despite institutional policy shifts in Moscow, Berlin, or Delhi.

The ruptures in early 1930, however, were incomplete and temporary. As the next chapters show, Nehru's ideas about anti-imperialism remained despite the split, while his networks with comrades against imperialism expanded substantially in the 1930s. Nehru and many of his colleagues from Brussels came to reconceptualize the anti-imperialist movement as an integral part of a global struggle against fascism. Rather than a complete closure, the crisis in anti-imperialism prompted by the Comintern signaled the end of the beginning in Nehru's story of nationalism and internationalism. The next phase of this story demonstrates remarkable continuity despite the hostility and sectarianism of 1929 and 1930.

PART II

AFTERLIVES OF ANTI-IMPERIALISM

5

Nehru's Anti-Imperialism after 1930

When the Civil Disobedience Campaign began in April 1930, Nehru anticipated a heavy prison sentence. He wrote to his former LAI colleague, Edo Fimmen, that even though he may be arrested and unable to write, "that will not mean that we have forgotten you." He added, "Whatever happens I shall think of you and other friends in Europe and it will be a comfort to feel that we have your wholehearted sympathy."[1] Writing to Baldwin only days before his arrest, Nehru shared with him the excitement surrounding the Salt March. He mentioned nothing of the LAI breakup, but rather concentrated on the situation in India. Of his inevitable incarceration, he optimistically wrote that from prison we "shall think of our good friends abroad and this thought will cheer us up."[2] Only a few days later, colonial authorities arrested and detained Nehru for the first of four prison sentences that kept him incarcerated for nearly five years.[3]

Nehru's return to prison provided necessary time to evaluate the lessons he had learned from the LAI and reflect on the importance of his connections to his "good friends abroad." In the 1930s, Nehru's antiimperialist activism continued in spite of the ruptures and uncertainties at the close of the 1920s that fragmented the League as an institution and aligned the Berlin office more closely with Moscow. At the same time, the League breakup also encouraged spaces for more flexible connections and solidarities outside the institutional framework of the LAI and the Comintern. This is most clear in Nehru's continued commitment to antiimperialist internationalism as a political project and the maintenance of

---

[1] Nehru to Fimmen, March 4, 1930, File 10, LAI, JNU.
[2] Nehru to Baldwin, April 4, 1930, *SWJN*, vol. 4, 298–299.
[3] Nehru's prison terms during the Civil Disobedience Campaign: April 14, 1930–October 11, 1930; October 19, 1930–January 1931; December 26, 1931–August 30, 1933; and February 12, 1934–September 1935.

his connections with many of his former colleagues from the LAI throughout the 1930s. Ultimately, the institutional shifts within the Comintern
and the LAI had less impact than one might expect on the everyday politics
and practices of Nehru, who continued to participate in anti-imperialist
projects long after his formal association with the League ended.

Demonstrating these continuities requires a different conceptualization
of the changes taking place around the world in the 1930s. The
Comintern's third period, the global depression, and the rise of fascism
ushered in a rather different internationalist world. The global depression
gave rise to isolationist policies in the West. In Asia, Japan launched an
invasion of Mainland China in 1931–1932, annexing the northern province of Manchuria. By 1937, a full-scale war pitted the Japanese against
a united front of the Chinese KMT and communists. Hitler and the Nazi
Party came to power in 1933, and Italian fascist Benito Mussolini conquered Abyssinia (present-day Ethiopia) in 1936. German tanks rolled
into Poland in 1939, opening the European theater of World War II. Such
events bolstered national boundaries in economic, political, and intellectual spheres, and this has been the emphasis of histories of this moment.
Nevertheless, internationalism retained a powerful presence in this period
as anti-imperialists and antifascists joined in solidarity throughout the
1930s.

The story of continuities is one that also runs counter to most historical
treatments of Nehru in this period. Gopal argues that Nehru's departure
from the LAI was a favorable outcome since "the decks were clear," and
finally he "was free to act as he chose" and would not be "pushed off
course by his erstwhile friends on the left."[4] Ultimately, the split with the
LAI, according to Gopal, catalyzed Nehru's nationalist career, "freeing"
him from League pressures, as well as abruptly concluding his anti-
imperialist activities internationally. Few historical studies attempt to
trace the afterlife of the LAI in Nehru's internationalist activities and
worldview beyond 1930.

The archival record reveals a different story. Rather than simply breaking "free" from the chains of internationalism, Nehru instead doubled
down on his anti-imperialist commitments throughout the turbulent years
of the 1930s. There are four significant dimensions to his anti-imperialist
work in this period. First, his prison writings – notably his first book,
written between 1930 and 1934: *Glimpses of World History* – reveal the
ongoing significance of anti-imperialist internationalism to his personal

---

[4] Gopal, *Nehru*, 71.

and political conceptualization of India and the world. The second was his reunion with former comrades from the LAI when he returned to London in 1935 and 1936. Although Nehru never rejoined the LAI officially, he continued to work for the organization's causes, strengthening his connections with old comrades and expanding his network to include new anti-imperialist colleagues such as V. K. Krishna Menon, one of Nehru's closest advisors on Indian international relations during the run-up to independence and after. This chapter also demonstrates that as Nehru continued to articulate a commitment to anti-imperialist internationalism, he also expanded his views to include contemporary issues like antifascism and anticolonial struggles in Africa. This is most evident in his increasing awareness of Africa and his ties to Pan-Africanists in London, such as George Padmore. Finally, when Nehru returned home to India in 1936, after nearly five years of imprisonment and a trip abroad, he renewed his campaign to internationalize Indian nationalism. His speeches and writings in this moment present a familiar repertoire of anti-imperialism rooted in the special blend of nationalism and socialism, as well as his worldview based upon the solidarity of anticolonial struggles across Asia and Africa and anti-capitalist ones. Rather than a retreat, this period in Nehru's career marked a strengthening of his anti-imperialist resolve and an expansion of his contacts with comrades abroad.

AN ANTI-IMPERIALIST WORLD HISTORY

The clearest example of the importance of anti-imperialist internationalism to Nehru's ideas about India and the world can be found in his first book, *Glimpses of World History*, written immediately after the League split and while he sat in prison from 1930 to 1933. He chose to write a world history as his first substantial publication before his later work on the Indian nation, *Discovery of India* (1946), and his *Autobiography* (1936). Much later, in 1955, the aging Prime Minister Nehru recalled the time when he wrote *Glimpses* as a moment when "the whole picture of the world appeared before me. This attempt to write compelled me to think and helped me in my thought processes. I wanted to have a world perspective in which I could see India."[5] Through the act of writing about

---

[5] Nehru, speech at the youth congress of the AICC, New Delhi, September 27, 1955, reprinted in *SWJN*, second series, vol. 30, ed. by Ravinder Kumar, H. Y. Sharada, and S. Gopal (Oxford: Oxford University Press, 2001), 33.

the world, Nehru discovered India and articulated clearly the importance of the symbiotic relationship between nationalism and internationalism.

Glimpses of World History totaled nearly a thousand pages on world history in the form of letters to his daughter, beginning with ancient history and running up to its publication in 1934. The letters were never opened or read by Indira, but rather collected for publication purposes. A second edition of *Glimpses* brought the magnum opus up to 1939, and a third US edition enjoyed wide circulation in 1942. *Glimpses* became wildly popular in India in the early 1930s, so much so that it became difficult to locate copies within the subcontinent.[6] The construction of historical knowledge in *Glimpses* influenced an entire generation of the Indian literate classes who came to see India and its relation to the world through the eyes of Nehru.

Analyzing *Glimpses* within the context of his anti-imperialist experience sheds new light on Nehru's ideas about communism, socialism, and Marxism. His prison writings during the 1930s, as historian Sumit Sarkar has argued, "mark the height of Nehru's interest in and partial commitment to Marxian socialist ideas."[7] Even so, Gopal argues, Nehru's Marxism "was vague and confused, for his ideology was to a large extent based more on sympathy than on conviction."[8] Rather than "sympathy" or "partial commitment," Nehru selectively deployed Marxist and Leninist ideas within his broader arguments about international anti-imperialism that he developed in the late 1920s. Nehru's sampling of Marxist and Leninist interpretive frameworks were always tempered by his search in his own politics and writing for an understanding of the possibilities and problems inherent in interwar solidarities between anti-capitalist and anti-imperialist forces. In other words, his "vague and confused" sympathies or "partial commitment" to socialism and communism can best be understood by thinking about his commitment to anti-imperialism, which was an amalgam of ideas about class and nation that were "blended" together.

A reading of *Glimpses* as an anti-imperialist text also contends with more familiar arguments made by historians that cast Nehru's writing as a derivative of European epistemology. Scholars of South Asia have

---

[6] In his foreword to the second edition, Menon stated that the first edition was "sold out" in India. See Jawaharlal Nehru, *Glimpses of World History: Being Further Letters to His Daughter Written in Prison, and Containing a Rambling Account of History for Young People*, US edn. (New York: The John Day Company, 1942). (Citations from this edition).

[7] Sumit Sarkar, *Modern India, 1885–1947* (Macmillan: New Delhi, 1983), 331.

[8] Gopal, *Nehru*, 107.

questioned whether Nehru's texts, and elite nationalist discourse more generally, were derived from an authentically Indian knowledge. Postcolonial theorists such as Partha Chatterjee argue that Nehru's construction of Indian history, particularly in his later book, *Discovery of India* (1946), "produced a discourse in which, even as it challenged the colonial claims to political domination, it also accepted the very intellectual premises of 'modernity' on which colonial domination was based."[9] Of the few studies about his first book, *Glimpses*, David Kopf argues that Nehru's world history depends on the enlightenment notions of progress based upon a Eurocentric version of history.[10] There are some merits to these arguments, and Nehru's world history presented a narrative of progress closely associated with the basic events in Europe. Nehru recognized the influence of earlier European works, especially H. G. Wells' *Outline of World History*, in framing his story.[11] He also appeared to have been influenced by the Hegelian dialectics of history, in which history moved through periods of contradiction between thesis and antithesis only to be resolved by a synthesis of the former and latter.[12] Nehru often deployed the word "synthesis" to define progress. But "synthesis" for Nehru meant the outcome of encounters and exchanges between people from different geographic "civilizations" rather than the meeting of contradictory forces (thesis and antithesis), a distinction more reflective of his personal growth through interactions with anti-imperialists of the interwar period.

At the same time, the broader narrative of progress in *Glimpses* drew heavily upon the logic of anti-imperialist internationalism rather than an abstract conception of colonial knowledge or "modernity." Nehru framed his world history narrative around three historical moments reflective of this anti-imperialist worldview. First, he constructed a utopian past rich with instances of encounters and exchanges that benefited humanity. Pre-colonial India in particular emerged as a haven for cross-cultural encounters. Although a story of progress, Nehru's pre-colonial narrative emerged as a story of ebbs and flows based on the favorable conditions in India and worldwide for political and cultural interchange. Second, the

---

[9] Chatterjee, *Nationalist Thought and the Colonial World*, 30.
[10] David Kopf, "A Look at Nehru's World History from the Dark Side of Modernity," Journal of World History 2 (1991): 47–63.
[11] Nehru made special mention of Wells in his preface. See H. G. Wells, *Outline of World History: Being a Plain History of Life and Mankind* (New York: The Macmillan Company, 1921).
[12] For a discussion of Hegel, see *The Cambridge Companion to Hegel*, ed. by Frederick Beiser (Cambridge: Cambridge University Press, 1993).

narrative took a decisive turn with the advent of modern European imperialism – as the offshoot of capitalism – which ushered in a new era of conflict and competition rather than encounter and exchange. This shift reflected a Marxist-inspired teleology of a world moving from feudalism to capitalism. Drawing upon a familiar framework of anti-imperialism that he discovered through the League, this period of Nehru's history presented the broadly conceived Leninist interpretation of imperialism as the highest stage of capitalism. The capitalist-imperialist world created an atmosphere of "one country or people selfishly attacking or oppressing another, of one man exploiting another."[13] The third and final turn of Nehru's story ended with the uncertainties of the interwar world of the 1920s and early 1930s. He characterized this postwar world as one divided between forces of capitalism-imperialism on the one hand, and anti-capitalists and anti-imperialists on the other. In this world of ferment and transition, unsurprisingly, Nehru considered the key to future progress to be the collaboration between India and the anti-imperialist world, one that he personally tried to forge through his national and international activities in the League.

Nehru depended on a readily available geography of anti-imperialism to understand the issues impacting India and the world since the Great War. A quick glance at the table of contents for the postwar years provides ample evidence that Nehru based *Glimpses* on his global geography of anti-imperialism. It was primarily attentive to the story of India, set against the backdrop of events and forces at work in Europe, Russia, China, Egypt, and the United States. Other countries in Asia – Japan in particular – receive brief mention in cursory chapters when pertinent to Chinese history, while African countries – with the exception of Egypt – hardly appear at all. The absence of Africa from his anti-imperialist world history aligns with his experiences in Brussels, where he had been captivated by Asians rather than Africans and had little to say about Africa in his reports, speeches, and letters. This was to change in the later 1930s when Nehru returned to Europe and the LAI, but the silence on African anti-imperialism is striking in *Glimpses*.

The post-Great War years – the ones most formative to Nehru's personal formulations of nationalism and internationalism – are especially illustrative of the continuities in his anti-imperialist worldview. The detailed history of these years totaled a disproportionate one-third of the original 950-page manuscript. Writing this final third in the summer of 1933, Nehru was no longer drafting a distant history, but instead an

---

[13] Nehru, *Glimpses*, 6.

appraisal of current events as he saw them from his prison cell. According to Nehru, the Great War "shook the whole system of ideas on which we had grown up and made us begin to doubt the very basis of modern society and civilization ... It was an age of doubt and questioning which always come in a period of transition and rapid change."[14] European capitalists and imperialists were to blame for the war and remained the antagonists of his story, while the postwar rise of the United States – the "money lender to the world" – represented the most powerful capitalist-imperialist force after 1919.[15]

Nehru also considered new forces at work in the 1930s, such as fascism, but he did so within the familiar logic of anti-imperialism. He argued that fascism was only another manifestation of the symbiotic forces of capitalism-imperialism. In other words, the world struggle of the 1930s was one against capitalism-imperialism-fascism. The heroes of Nehru's postwar world in *Glimpses* mirrored the anti-imperialist elements from Brussels and the League – nationalists from the colonies, socialists, and communists. He especially underscored the significant roles of India, China, Egypt, and the Soviet Union in the international struggle against imperialism. Bringing his argument to its logical conclusion, Nehru hoped for a better future with the resurgence and cooperation of such anti-imperialist forces.

Hardly reflective of his tensions with communists in the League in 1930, Nehru cast the Soviet Union and international communism as the beacon of hope for anti-imperialism in the postwar struggle laid out in *Glimpses*. Nehru wrote, "While trade depression and slump and unemployment and repeated crises paralyse capitalism, and the old order gasps for breath, the Soviet Union is a land full of hope and energy and enthusiasm, feverishly building away and establishing the socialist order." It was "attracting thinking people all over the world."[16] Lenin was "the embodiment of an idea," and he lived on "in the mighty work he did, and in the hearts of hundreds of millions of workers today who find inspiration in his example, and the hope of a better day."[17] He also romanticized Stalin's leadership. Rather than recognize the great cost of human lives and suffering in the Five Year Plans under Stalin, Nehru argued that the people of the Soviet Union "tightened their belts" and "sacrificed the present for the great future that seemed to beckon to them and of which they were the proud and privileged builders."[18] For Nehru, the Soviet Union's transition from agricultural country to industrialized powerhouse was a lesson for India's and the world's future, one that enabled him to

[14] Ibid., 685.   [15] Ibid., 686.   [16] Ibid., 940.   [17] Ibid., 660.   [18] Ibid., 855.

overlook the crimes against humanity committed by Stalin, as well as the frigid relations the Soviet leadership developed with Nehru and the INC after 1930.

The reading of *Glimpses* as an international anti-imperialist narrative suggests two important points. First, despite Nehru's falling out with the League, his formulations for Indian nationalism in relation to an international anti-imperialist world continued after his institutional connection with Berlin ended. The formative moments in Brussels and the League helped Nehru construct a vision of Indian nationalism tempered by internationalism and the global geography of anti-imperialism. This persisted even when the institutional networks did not. Second, by widening the frames we use to examine Nehru, this reading offers a productive rethinking of his historical texts. Rather than a simplistic derivative of European epistemology or colonial discourse, Nehru's world history came to be a reflection of his experiences as an Indian nationalist on the international terrain of interwar anti-imperialist politics.

NEHRU'S ANTI-IMPERIALIST COMRADES AND THE LAI AFTER 1930

Shortly after his prison release in October 1935, Nehru returned to London for the first time since 1927. More than 120 supporters greeted him at Victoria Station, while more than 350 people attended his welcome reception held two days after his arrival. The attendees came from a diversity of backgrounds and included students and prominent members of the major political organizations in Britain, like the LP, ILP, and CPGB. The organizers of both events – at the train station and the formal reception – were none other than his comrades from the LAI days, Saklatvala and Bridgeman. At the end of the welcome reception, Saklatvala and Nehru met privately for nearly three hours. Over the course of his three-week stay, Nehru also held meetings with Bridgeman and Harry Pollitt, one of his fiercest critics at the Frankfurt Congress. Nehru also attended an LAI meeting and re-engaged with the anti-imperialist movement.[19] This was hardly evidence of a man "freed" from the chains of his anti-imperialist connections abroad.

Throughout the 1930s, Nehru and his comrades continued to collaborate on projects outside the institutional framework of the LAI but in the

---

[19] Nehru's movements were tracked by British intelligence. Extract from Scotland Yard Report No. 50, November 6, 1935, L/P&J/292, File 295/26, IPI.

spirit of anti-imperialism. Equally important, Nehru depended on his contacts with former comrades from the LAI to broaden his connections to new anti-imperialists colleagues. He met some of his most trusted allies, such as V. K. Krishna Menon, when he reconnected to the LAI in London in 1935. Nehru also encountered a robust and high-profile community of Pan-African activists through League circles in the metropole during his trip. In each case, we see a strengthening and expansion of Nehru's commitments to the League and anti-imperialist internationalism.

Even before 1935, Nehru managed to maintain his correspondence with former LAI comrades such as Roger Baldwin. Many of their exchanges demonstrate a growing friendship between the two colleagues. When Nehru's father died in February 1931, Baldwin sent a handwritten note expressing his deepest sympathies and his "endless admiration" for the many "high qualities" his father possessed.[20] On other occasions over the course of the Civil Disobedience Campaign, Baldwin encouraged Nehru to remain courageous in the face of British imperialist oppression. As Nehru headed to prison for a second term in 1932, Baldwin wrote: "From my own experience and connections, I can only wish you physical strength equal to your courage and determination to last out the term."[21]

Beyond moral encouragement, however, Nehru and Baldwin continued the collaborative task of strengthening anti-imperialist ties between India and the USA. Baldwin wrote a myriad of letters protesting British imperialism in India that were signed by hundreds of his American colleagues. Among the recipients were major leaders of all political parties in Britain, including the prime minister, the Secretary of State for India, and the British consulate in the United States. These letters were coupled with press releases in the USA that detailed the events underway in India. Whenever possible, Baldwin also sent money for the defense of Indian political prisoners throughout India. In fact, when Nehru was imprisoned, Baldwin worked through Bridgeman to secure the transfer of $100 to the London-based committee for the defense of the Meerut accused in 1930.[22] Baldwin also successfully sent funds to India, via friends in Berlin, to support the legal defense of M. N. Roy, who had been tried in India for allegations of sedition similar to those of the Meerut accused. During

---

[20] Baldwin to Nehru, February 13, 1931, vol. 6, JN Papers. Motilal Nehru died on February 6, 1931.
[21] Baldwin to Nehru, January 6, 1932, Box 3, Folder 24 (microform reel 5), ICPP.
[22] Correspondence between Baldwin and Bridgeman, Box 3, Folder 22–23 (microform reel 5), ICPP.

a brief release from prison, Nehru was at home in Allahabad in November 1931 to receive and acknowledge Baldwin's draft of $100 for Roy's defense.[23]

Once again, the question of Indian independence brought Nehru and Baldwin into close alignment in 1931. The two contemplated Gandhi's participation in the Second Round Table Conference, one of several conferences in London set to discuss constitutional reforms between 1930 and 1932. Gandhi had called for a temporary suspension of civil disobedience so that he could attend the roundtable as the sole representative of the INC. For much of 1931, Nehru and other INC colleagues were released from prison under this truce. Baldwin wrote to Nehru about his concerns that Gandhi would be "another Wilson at Paris" for he would be given "wide discretion" and at the same time had a strong "record for compromise."[24] Nehru assured Baldwin that Gandhi was "made of stern stuff" and that he would not compromise this time.[25] Still, in a separate cable to Baldwin, who was in Geneva at the time, Nehru urged his American comrade to travel to Paris and intercept Gandhi's London-bound train at the station.[26] In person, Baldwin could encourage Gandhi to remain steadfast on the question of independence. Nehru also suggested that Baldwin approach Gandhi about a plan to create a group within the USA that could be affiliated to the INC and agitate for Indian independence.[27] Baldwin followed Nehru's advice and with a little "good luck" he caught the attention of some Indian friends traveling with Gandhi and earned a coveted spot on the party's train. Baldwin rode with the Mahatma from Paris to Boulogne.

Baldwin's first and only meeting with Gandhi left a less than favorable impression. In a letter to Nehru, Baldwin characterized Gandhi and his entourage as "neither clear-cut, united, or enough determined," and "far too concentrated" on Gandhi's safety and dietary restrictions.[28] Nevertheless, Baldwin promised Nehru he would work in the USA on behalf of Gandhi and the INC on the assumption that the movement was

---

[23] Acknowledgment of receipt of $100 is found in a letter from Nehru to Baldwin, December 25, 1931, Box 3, Folder 24 (microform reel 5), ICPP.

[24] Baldwin to Nehru, April 29, 1931, vol. 6, JN Papers, 127.

[25] Nehru to Baldwin, September 17, 1931, vol. 6, JN Papers, 126.

[26] Baldwin thanked Nehru for the suggestion and traveled to Paris in the hopes of encountering Gandhi. The American was blacklisted from traveling to Britain. See his letter to Nehru, September 24, 1931, Box 7, Folder 30, Baldwin Papers.

[27] From 1931 to 1933, Baldwin wrote many letters that advocated this plan. See, for example, Baldwin to Nehru, August 27, 1931, vol. 6, JN Papers.

[28] Ibid.

based on complete independence, meaning Indian "control of army, finance, and foreign relations."[29] Baldwin also had the opportunity to pitch to Gandhi the idea for an INC-affiliated group in the USA. According to Baldwin, Gandhi showed some interest but did not commit. In his later recollections of this rare meeting with Gandhi, Baldwin admitted that he was embarrassed that he had "run out of questions and conversation," and retired early to another car.[30] In the same recollection, Baldwin candidly reflected on the central differences between Nehru and Gandhi: "Nehru the socialist, the internationalist, the practical man; Gandhi the orthodox religious Hindu, nationalist, pacifist. Both were politicians, one by the use of the rare power of love for the enemy, the other the more conventional tactician."[31] No doubt, the style and tactics of Nehru appealed more to Baldwin, as did his internationalist convictions.

Baldwin returned to the USA and created the American League for India's Freedom (ALIF), while Nehru and Gandhi returned to prison after the Second Round Table talks were unsuccessful. The mission of Baldwin's league was "to express American support of Indian independence through non-violence."[32] He wrote again to Nehru and Gandhi in 1933 about an INC affiliation to the group. Gandhi did not reply, but Nehru's response was not optimistic. Nehru wrote that "no arguments of yours are necessary to convince me," but there was little the INC could commit to the ALIF. The INC had become an illegal organization in colonial India and therefore meetings were not held regularly. Because of this, "there [we]re various groups pulling in different directions" and the INC had not been able to develop a unified and cohesive platform for some time. Nehru added that given these conditions, "it is not easy to say what exactly the Congress would stand for it if has the chance to express its opinion."[33] Nehru saw this time of uncertainty as one of growth, and he was "in no way perturbed" by the situation.[34] Although the INC affiliation to ALIF never came to fruition, it provided ongoing opportunities for Nehru and Baldwin to continue their anti-imperialist work beyond the institutional framework of the LAI and despite the limitations imposed by the colonial state during the Civil Disobedience Campaign.

Nehru's ultimate release from prison in 1935 provided more opportunities to renew his anti-imperialist projects and reconnect with comrades

---

[29] Ibid.   [30] Baldwin, *Reminiscences*, 422.   [31] Ibid., 423.
[32] The mission is printed on the American League for India's Freedom letterhead. For example, see Baldwin to Nehru, October 19, 1933, vol. 6, JN Papers, 132.
[33] Nehru to Baldwin, November 23, 1933, vol. 6, JN Papers, 134–136.   [34] Ibid.

from the LAI days. He returned to Europe because his wife's battle with chronic tuberculosis had taken a fatal turn. Doctors caring for Kamala in Badenweiler, Germany, cabled India to notify Nehru that her health was failing and to request that he come immediately. The colonial government allowed his early release from prison only if he promised to not to make public speeches or engage in political activities while in Europe. Nehru departed on a flight to Germany in September 1935. For most of the couple's years together, Nehru had been indifferent about marriage, and about Kamala herself, while his nationalist work and frequent trips to jail imposed long periods of separation. Over the years, however, Nehru slowly grew into his role as husband, and their relationship seemed to hit a high point during the Civil Disobedience Campaign when Kamala took an active role in protest and even served a prison term.[35] Nehru wrote of Kamala's role in the early days of civil disobedience affectionately in his autobiography, in that "She forgot her ill-health and rushed about the whole day in the sun, and showed remarkable powers of organization."[36]

Nehru traveled from Badenweiler to London twice, and visited the LAI secretaries on both occasions. The timing was ripe for a return to the League. By the time Nehru reached Europe, the international secretariat had shifted from Berlin to London after heavy Nazi persecution of communists and anticolonial activists. In a 1933 raid, the Nazis destroyed most of the documents and archival records of the Berlin office, while many of the personnel and associates of the League fled Germany for their lives. Chatto left Berlin for the Soviet Union in 1931, well before the fateful appointment of Hitler as Chancellor. It is likely that if Chatto had stayed in Europe rather than the Soviet Union, Nehru might have reconnected with him in 1935. The other founder of the LAI, Willi Münzenberg, fled Germany for Paris in 1933. There, he organized antifascist and anti-war campaigns, while also working to provide asylum and support for communists leaving Germany after Hitler took power. Nehru's collaborative work on peace, discussed in the next chapter, would bring him back into contact with Münzenberg's organizations.

Very little from the Berlin years survived the Nazi raid, and all Bridgeman received in the transfer to London was an outdated list of addresses.[37] In London, the early activities of the resurrected LAI focused on the colonial student population in the metropole. Bridgeman recognized

---

[35] On Kamala, see Nehru, *Autobiography*, 580–584.   [36] Ibid., 225.
[37] See Reginald Bridgeman, "League against Imperialism Report of the International Secretariat for 1934," DBN/25/1, Bridgeman Papers.

their importance as conduits of information to and from the colonial world. Within a year of the LAI relocation, Bridgeman embarked on some ambitious plans for the League. He traveled to Brussels, Amsterdam, Paris, and Dublin in the hopes of raising awareness for anti-imperialism and persuading comrades to reconstitute national branches of the LAI. He also worked closely with the London-based Scottsboro Defense Committee, which included fellow activists such as Johnstone Kenyatta.[38] By the end of 1934, Bridgeman also oversaw the publication of the first two editions of the League's *Colonial News*. According to his report on League activity, he sent out nearly 3,000 copies of the publication to individuals, organizations, and newspapers worldwide.[39]

The moment of Nehru's return to the LAI also coincided with the revival of cross-party alliances between communists and noncommunists in Europe. The collapse of the Comintern's third period in 1934 had given rise to the Popular Front, which called for communist alliances with antifascists, regardless of their leftwing or rightwing orientations.[40] As early as February 1933, the LSI reached out to the Comintern to develop a truce, while Moscow in 1934 shifted its tactics away from the sectarianism of the third period. In fact, most of Nehru's prison sentence coincided with the third period, while his return to Indian and world politics took place at a more collaborative time reflective of the Brussels days. Nehru saw the Popular Front solidarities as new evidence for his conclusions in *Glimpses* that the progressive forces of the world – anti-capitalist (socialists, communists, and especially Soviet Russia) and anti-imperialist (anticolonial nationalists) – must unite against fascism.

Without ties to Nehru, the LAI had limited connection to India. B. F. Bradley, one of two Europeans accused in the Meerut Conspiracy Case, worked with Bridgeman on renewing ties with the trade union movement in India. These efforts met with some success. Still, most Indians associated with the LAI were expatriates or students living in the metropole rather than India. One of the more significant newcomers to the LAI in the 1930s was V. K. Krishna Menon, an Indian expatriate who headed the India League (IL) in London, an anti-imperialist organization linked at first

---

[38] Pennybacker, *From Scottsboro to Munich*.
[39] Bridgeman, "League against Imperialism Report 1934."
[40] "Popular Front and Stalinist Terror, 1934–1939," in McDermott and Agnew, *The Comintern*.

to Annie Besant and the theosophists and later to the ILP and the CPGB.[41] The IL was one of several organizations of Indians in Britain competing to be the spokesman for all-Indian anticolonialism, although with limited success before 1935.

Bridgeman desired much closer ties with the INC and he appealed to Nehru to return to the anti-imperialist movement. He wrote to Nehru in November 1933 and again in February 1934 to stress to him "the need for India's participation in the world struggle against imperialism."[42] He added in a "personal" appeal: "I hope we may be able to think out a line of action for the closer cooperation of the Indian and British masses with the colonial masses in other lands for the overthrow of imperialism."[43] There is no evidence that either letter reached Nehru, especially given that the colonial regime in 1934 banned both the LAI and the INC in India.[44] In his 1934 report, Bridgeman admitted that Nehru might not have any interest in responding.[45] Others from the early League days, such as Edo Fimmen, became outright hostile toward the League after the Frankfurt fallout.[46]

Nehru's feelings about the League would be revealed in October 1935. In London, all of the hostilities were forgotten. As he recalled in his autobiography, completed while he was in Europe, the turbulent events leading to his break with the League were primarily his fault. Over his decision to support dominion status rather than complete independence from the British Empire, the League "grew exceedingly angry with me, and excommunicated me with bell, book, and candle – or to be more accurate, it expelled me by some kind of resolution."[47] He goes on to say, "I must confess that it had great provocation, but it might have given me some chance of explaining my position."[48] His visits with the LAI in London further confirmed that there were no longer hard feelings, although he never again sought formal association between the INC and the League. The connections would be personal rather than institutional.

There were critics of the League in London who sought to persuade Nehru to distance himself from Saklatvala and Bridgeman. Upon his arrival, a group of concerned Indians handed a letter to Nehru. It accused

---

[41] For overviews of the India League and Menon's relationship with the British left, see Stephen Howe, *Anticolonialism in British Politics*, 126–134; and Nicholas Owen, *The British Left and India*, 200–208.
[42] Bridgeman, "League against Imperialism Report."   [43] Ibid.
[44] By 1935, the LAI and the INC were proscribed organizations in India. Despite this, the LAI and CPGB were not deemed illegal in the metropole.
[45] Bridgeman, "League against Imperialism Report."   [46] Ibid.
[47] Nehru, *Autobiography*, 174.   [48] Ibid., 174–175.

his welcoming committee, composed of Saklatvala, Bridgeman, and Bradley, of being "anti-Indian propagandists" who had called the INC a "counter-revolutionary" organization.[49] Thirty-three members of the "London branch of the Indian National Congress" signed the document. Nehru regarded this rival group with suspicion, and he wrote to the INC secretary that the branch was up to "petty mischief" and was possibly exploiting the congress' name for their personal prestige.[50]

One of the most significant aspects of Nehru's trip to London and reunion with LAI comrades was his encounter with Menon and the IL. Nehru was "favourably impressed" by Menon and his organization.[51] In a remarkably short time, Menon earned Nehru's trust. After their meetings in 1935, Nehru employed Menon as his publishing agent and as an informal chaperone for his daughter, who had begun classes at Oxford University earlier that year. Their friendship and partnership blossomed after 1935. By the time Nehru assumed the responsibilities of Prime Minister of India in 1947, his relationship with Menon as his closest confident had catapulted the IL organizer into the highest offices of the new Indian State.[52] Menon was treated like family by Nehru, and his importance as a confidant shaped the policies of the Indian state during the Nehruvian era. The history of the Nehru–Menon relationship, however, has been confined to the Cold War in most scholarship, and only brief mentions of their first encounter in 1935 exist.[53] None connect Menon to the anti-imperialist circles of the LAI or the importance that their shared views of anti-imperialist internationalism played in the making of their close relationship.

---

[49] Letter addressed to Pandit Jawaharlal Nehru, copy in "Extract from Scotland Yard Report No. 50," November 6, 1935, L/P&J/292, File 295/26, IPI.

[50] Ibid.

[51] Nehru to INC secretary, Rajendra Prasad, November 20, 1935. *SWJN*, vol. 7, 42–43.

[52] Nehru later appointed Menon to several key foreign policymaking positions: High Commissioner to the United Kingdom (1947–1952), and Indian Delegate to the United Nations and Defense Minister of India (1952–1962). However, Menon resigned after India's military preparedness failed to prevent a Chinese invasion during the Sino-Indian War of 1962.

[53] Historiography on Menon is scarce because his personal papers are closed to scholars without special permission. The classic text based on interviews with Menon is Michael Brecher, *India and World Politics: Krishna Menon's View of the World* (New York: Fraeger, 1968). Other studies remain hagiographical in nature: Janaki Ram, *V. K. Krishna Menon: A Personal Memoir* (Delhi: Oxford University Press, 1997); and Suhash Chakravarty, *Crusader Extraordinary: Krishna Menon and the India League, 1932–1936*; K. C. Arora, *V. K. Krishna Menon: A Biography* (New Delhi: Sanchar Publishing House, 1998).

There is no doubt that Nehru's anti-imperialist contacts with the LAI and Bridgeman were critical to his meeting Menon for the first time. Since the early 1930s, Menon had participated in LAI meetings and collaborated with Bridgeman regularly. The British intelligence files place Bridgeman at most IL meetings, and Menon at most LAI meetings. As early as 1932, Menon and Bridgeman were working to fuse together the projects and goals of the LAI and IL.[54] Menon was among the 120 attendees at Victoria Station awaiting Nehru's arrival in London. He had crossed paths with Nehru briefly before 1935, but Menon's LAI connections afforded a more lengthy and meaningful encounter in this moment.

Menon, like so many of Nehru's comrades abroad from his LAI days, shared a vision of anti-imperialism and Indian nationalism, which no doubt facilitated their fraternity. Menon's ability to work for the anti-imperialist cause across party lines in the metropole was reflective of the spirit of internationalism from the early League days. He was an official member of the LP, and he served as a Labour Councillor from the North London borough of St. Pancras for several terms beginning in 1934. The ILP also had a strong relationship with Menon's India League. Several ILP members served on its executive council. At the same time, Menon worked closely with members of the CPGB, so much so that British intelligence files were convinced he was a communist party member. Those who attended his meetings and purchased the *India Review*, the IL's publication, included the same diversity of individuals who participated in the LAI – people such as Bridgeman, Saklatvala, Bradley, and R. P. Dutt. Indeed, Menon moved freely within the circles of the LP, ILP, and CPGB, enabling him to work with communists and noncommunists alike on propaganda and demonstrations for Indian independence.

In addition, Menon articulated a remarkably similar view of the world shared by Nehru and shaped by the anti-imperialist discourse of the day. In his publications, Menon wrote frequently about the need to internationalize the Indian struggle and to accept socialism as the necessary goal for the anticolonial nationalist movement. Even before 1935, Menon regularly cited and reprinted Nehru's speeches and writings in an effort to make his case for the importance of the worldwide anti-imperialist struggle. By the time he met Nehru in 1935, Menon had already been writing about the common struggle against fascism and imperialism.[55]

---

[54] For the records of Menon's India League, see L/PJ/12/448–453, IPI. For Menon's personal files, see L/PJ/12/323, IPI.
[55] Chakravarty, *Crusader Extraordinary*, 647–666.

Menon became Nehru's chosen confident, and the IL rapidly expanded in prestige and influence within a competitive field of organizations attempting to represent India in Britain. When Nehru returned to London for a second time in January 1936, he asked that Menon create his agenda. His suggestion was that the schedule be light on political meetings and heavy on meetings with "interesting" people and colleagues. He also hoped to see his LAI comrades Saklatvala, Bridgeman, and Dutt, who were specifically named in his request. Of Bridgeman, he intended to visit him "as a friend and active sympathizer of India's freedom."[56] Shortly after his letter to Menon and before his return to the metropole, however, the feisty veteran of communism in London, Saklatvala, died suddenly of a heart attack on January 16, 1936. Much of Nehru's time on the second trip included memorials and tributes to his former LAI comrade, one whose life he celebrated even after their fallout several years earlier.[57]

The reunion with anti-imperialists in London left a strong and lasting impression on Nehru. After his trip to London, Nehru drafted "India and the World" from Paris. In it, he argued that India is part of a world problem, which is "ultimately the one of imperialism." He stressed that the rise of fascism was a manifestation of imperialism. As a case study, he argued that "England, proudly laying stress on its democratic constitution at home, acts after the fascist fashion in India." He situated imperialism and its manifestation, fascism, as "fundamentally opposed" to the "new order" of the Soviet Union. Progress depended on the cooperation of the Soviet Union, India, and other anticolonial movements that struggle against imperialism.[58]

Nehru's return to the LAI and reconnection with comrades against imperialism were critical in strengthening his ongoing commitments to internationalism in the 1930s. In the case of Baldwin, Nehru's collaborative efforts persisted even when colonial repression during the Civil Disobedience Campaign made contact abroad difficult. Nehru's return to London demonstrated the significance he continued to attribute to the LAI and its many comrades, both communists and noncommunists. Nehru was drawn not only to the LAI, but also to its affiliated organizations, such as the IL under the stewardship of Menon. By the conclusion of

---

[56] These letters from Nehru to Menon in October and December are from the Menon Papers at the Nehru Memorial Museum and Library. Chakravarty cites them in *Crusader Extraordinary*, 686.

[57] For his itinerary and speeches, see L/PJ/12/294, IPI.

[58] Nehru, "India and the World," January 6, 1936, reprinted in *SWJN*, vol. 7, 52–58.

his trip, Nehru had solidified his partnerships with organizations closely linked to the former anti-imperialist comrades he met in the late 1920s through the LAI.

THE ROOTS OF AFRO-ASIAN SOLIDARITY FOR NEHRU

The renewal of connections to anti-imperialist comrades in London afforded Nehru new opportunities to engage more with the question of African anti-imperialism. This was a dramatic transformation for Nehru. While he had been captivated since Brussels by the anti-imperialist solidarities between India and China, Nehru had not written about or considered in any depth the struggle of Africans or the African diaspora, even as late as his writing of world history in *Glimpses*. His return to London would radically alter this limited worldview as Nehru came into greater contact with Pan-Africanists who closely identified with the LAI and Menon's IL.

London in the mid-1930s was a hotbed of anti-imperialist activities, and the opportunities for the intersection of African and Asian anticolonial politics were many.[59] The League was one of a variety of organizations bringing together the anti-imperialist agendas of Africa and Asia. Aside from India, the LAI's strongest contacts, both in the metropole and in the colonies, were with China and West Africa.[60] Bridgeman's connections with West African students, in particular, pushed Africa to the forefront of LAI work. Bridgeman oversaw the circulation of pamphlets and protests in the House of Commons over issues such as the Sedition Acts introduced in the Gold Coast in 1934.

It also was in London in the mid-1930s that the lives and networks of Nehru and prominent Pan-Africanist George Padmore intersected, even if the two activists never formally met. There is a myth that the two did in fact meet in London, but the archival record reveals that this was not so. A devoted anti-imperialist and frequenter of the LAI meetings, Cedric Dover, tried to arrange a meeting between Nehru and Padmore, but the latter was away from London at the time. Dover was an Anglo-Indian

---

[59] Pennybacker, *From Scottsboro to Munich*; Howe, *Anticolonialism in British Politics*, 82–104.

[60] Bridgeman was very active in British leftist campaigns to support China in the 1930s. He launched the Friends of the Chinese People in 1934 and was an active participant in the China Campaign Committee. See Buchanan, *East Wind*, 59–73.

from Calcutta living in London, and had strong interests in the links between African and Indian struggles against imperialism. He also had connections to a number of high-profile Pan-Africanists in Europe and the United States, such as Padmore, but also W. E. B. Du Bois and Jomo Kenyatta. In a later letter to the INC secretary of the foreign department, Padmore expressed his regrets over missing the opportunity to meet Nehru. He added that "Our enemy is a common foe, and it is therefore necessary for us to lay the basis of the establishment of a united front of the colonial peoples if progress is to be made."[61] Padmore also conveyed his warmest wishes to Nehru in particular: "It is hardly necessary for me to say in what high regard we hold your esteemed President, Comrade Nehru, and watch with great interest the lead which he is giving the Congress." Padmore concluded, "Again we salute you in the spirit of international anti-imperialist solidarity, and beg you convey our best regards to Comrade Nehru and his co-workers."[62]

The missed opportunity, however, remains significant nonetheless. Padmore's letter, which appeared on the surface to be nothing more than fan mail, represented the inception of a relationship between Asian and African anti-imperialism for Nehru.[63] It opened the lines of communication and possibilities for future collaboration between prominent Pan-Africanists and the INC. Indeed, Nehru's special affinity to Nkrumah and Ghanaian nationalism had its roots in this anti-imperialist encounter of the 1930s. The interwar propaganda networks created by Padmore were said to have extended to more than 4,000 recipients worldwide. In this instance, the INC and Nehru became a part of that network. At the same time, Nehru's encounters with Pan-Africanism within the greater framework of anti-imperialist internationalism provided impetus for a new engagement with Africa.

---

[61] Padmore to the INC Foreign Department (hereafter FD), August 5, 1936, File FD8-1936, AICC.

[62] Ibid.

[63] The connections between African Americans and Indian activists before the Cold War has been the subject of several recent works, including Nico Slate, *Colored Cosmopolitanism*; and Gerald Horne, *The End of Empires: African Americans and India* (Philadelphia: Temple University Press, 2008). Both works are significant in outlining the potential for solidarity, although often as a means of celebrating rather than thinking critically about them. More compelling analysis is in Pennybacker, *Scottsboro to Munich*. See also Robert Vitalis, *White World Order, Black Power Politics: The Birth of American International Relations* (Ithaca: Cornell University Press, 2015), 93–105. Although Vitalis seeks to historicize the contributions of African Americans to the field of international relations, his research on Pan-Africanists in the 1930s is useful.

Padmore and Nehru led political lives that intersected on a number of occasions in the years before 1935. Much like Nehru, Padmore was radically changed by his experiences in the LAI. Yet, it was the Frankfurt Congress rather than the Brussels Congress that launched Padmore's career as an anti-imperialist and communist. In the aftermath of Frankfurt, Padmore found himself appointed to several committees for "Negro" work within the Comintern. His most important appointments were as the head of the Comintern's International Trade Union Committee of Negro Workers (ITUC-NW) and as the editor of *Negro Worker*. Like Nehru, Padmore also fell out of favor with the Comintern, although this took place for the Pan-African leader in 1933. Later, he became a vocal critic of international communism and a leading advocate of Pan-Africanism as an alternative internationalism.[64]

Padmore also shared similar experiences with Berlin comrades such as Münzenberg in the context of Germany in the 1930s. Around nearly the same time as the League headquarters raid in Berlin, Padmore, who was living in Hamburg, was "dragged from his bed by Nazi police and imprisoned for about two weeks, during which time the Nazi[s] raided the offices of the Negro workers' Union and destroyed all their property."[65] Like most political refugees escaping Hitler's reign of terror, Padmore resettled in Paris and stayed with another prominent Pan-Africanist, Tiemoko Garan Kouyaté. Münzenberg followed a similar path in the early 1930s, from Comintern operative in Berlin to exile in Paris, where he was later excommunicated from the Comintern. For Padmore, more bad news came from Moscow in mid-1933 when the Comintern closed the ITUC-NW and shifted focus from the struggles in the colonies to European affairs. In 1934, Padmore was expelled from the party for his ties with noncommunists and even Kouyaté.

Nehru and Padmore reconnected with anti-imperialists in London in the 1930s, and circulated in similar spaces afforded by the LAI and the ILP. Although outside the boundaries of the communist party, and more so in London than Paris, these metropolitan circles of the LAI continued to be frequented by communists and noncommunists. Padmore reached London in the spring of 1935, where he began working with the prolific

---

[64] George Padmore, *Africa and World Peace* (London: M. Secker & Warburg, 1937). All citations are from the second edition: George Padmore, *Africa and World Peace*, with foreword by Sir Stafford Cripps and new introduction by W. M. Warren (London: Cass, 1972).

[65] "Fascist Terror against Negroes in Germany," *Negro Worker* 3, nos. 4–5 (April–May 1933): 2. Reprinted in Brent Hayes Edwards, *The Practice of Diaspora*, 265.

C. R. L. James and his organization, the International African Friends of Ethiopia. In 1937, Padmore and James organized the International African Service Bureau (IASB), which circulated print literature throughout the African diasporic world and did much to construct Pan-African internationalism. Padmore was on friendly terms with Indians in the metropole, including Menon. In fact, the IASB had been modeled after the Menon's IL.[66]

Padmore's activities were emblematic of the anti-imperialist internationalism of the interwar years in similar ways to Nehru's.[67] Even while he denounced the Comintern and communism in the 1930s, Padmore continued to work with a broad alliance of anti-imperialists and Pan-Africanists that had retained some connection to communist circles. As Brent Hayes Edwards eloquently stated in his recent book, Padmore's black internationalism was "at once inside communism, fiercely engaged with its ideological debates and funneled through its institutions, and at the same time aimed at a race-specific formation that rejects the Comintern's universalism, adamantly insisting that racial oppression involves factors and forces that cannot be summed up or submerged in a critique of class exploitation."[68] It was the remarkable fluidity of the interwar moment that gave rise to the collaborationism across fundamentally distinct and even contradictory ideas and institutions in the case of Padmore, who could overlook the differences between the "universalism" of communism and the aims of the "race-specific" agenda. In his study of Padmore, Edwards demonstrated that "black internationalism" during the interwar period "was not a supplement to revolutionary nationalism, the 'next level' of anti-colonial agitation." Rather, it "emerges through boundary crossing – black radicalism *is* an internationalism."[69] This border crossing and fluidity was equally important to Nehru, whose nationalism and internationalism were intimately connected, and his ties to the League and sympathies with the Soviet Union and international communism remained even after the visceral purges of the late 1920s.

In the early 1930s in the midst of the Comintern's third-period shakeup, both Padmore and Nehru looked to history, approaching it through

---

[66] Howe, *Anticolonialism in British Politics*, 87.
[67] The seminal text on Padmore is James R. Hooker, *Black Revolutionary: George Padmore's Path from Communism to Pan-Africanism* (New York: Frederick A. Praeger Publishing, 1967). See also, Edwards, *The Practice of Diaspora*, 241–305; and Pennybacker, *From Scottsboro to Munich*, 66–102. Another recent work based on Comintern records is Holger Weiss, *Framing a Radical African Atlantic*, 291–396.
[68] Edwards, *The Practice of Diaspora*, 245.   [69] Ibid., 243.

the lens of the anti-imperialist internationalism of the day, in order to understand the world and their struggles within it. Nehru's *Glimpses* hit the market only three years before Padmore's *Africa and World Peace*. Padmore's work sought to explain the growing threat of another world war and the Italian invasion of Abyssinia (present-day Ethiopia) in 1935. In doing so, he drew upon anti-imperialist internationalism to recount the recent history of Africa and the world. There is no evidence that Nehru read Padmore's book, although this is less important here. It is the shared framework and language of anti-imperialism despite their missed encounter in London that makes their comparison so significant.

Implicit in the histories by Nehru and Padmore were the main pillars of anti-imperialism inspired by Lenin, expounded in Brussels, and crystalized through the League. The first was that the world is menaced and endangered by the forces of capitalism and imperialism. According to Padmore, the world's problems were rooted in "capitalism in its imperialist stage."[70] The scramble for Africa, the focus of the book, revealed that wars were caused by the struggle between imperialist powers to dominate colonial territories, resources, and labor. These present conditions worldwide necessitated a collective anti-imperialist resistance that brought together, in Padmore's words, "the toiling masses and the subject peoples" against the dual forces of capitalism and imperialism. Even though he wrote this after his split with the Comintern, Padmore also favorably characterized the Soviet Union as the greatest hope for anti-imperialism as it "has removed one-sixth of the earth's surface from the imperialist system."[71] His later chapters articulated the rise of fascism as an offshoot of capitalism-imperialism. It was the "disintegration of capitalism-imperialism" which had forced the ruling classes to resort to fascism as a "terroristic dictatorship," especially in the case of Nazi Germany. For Nehru, British imperialism in India was another form of fascist repression.[72]

The anti-imperialist history of both books by Nehru and Padmore shared the basic assumptions of anti-imperialist internationalism even if the inflection was different. Padmore's focus is Africa, and his book was a story of the power politics and diplomacy underpinning European imperialist expansion in this region. While Nehru believed that India was the most pressing world problem because of its centrality to the British Empire, Padmore argued that "Africa holds the key to the peace of Europe."[73] He told a story of the scramble for Africa as it directly related

---

[70] Padmore, *Africa and World Peace*, 3.   [71] Ibid., 46.   [72] Ibid., 70.   [73] Ibid., 15.

to the contemporary crisis in Abyssinia in the 1930s. He stated that "the more Africa got inveigled into the vortex of these imperialist squabbles, the more hatred and bitterness, jealousies, and suspicions developed among the great Western Powers."[74] Even with its Afrocentric focus, Padmore's book demonstrated a shared framework of anti-imperialism. For both, it was a matter of making a case for their respective homes as the most urgent site in the overall mobilization against imperialist powers worldwide.

Both Nehru and Padmore also offered strikingly similar responses to a speech by Lloyd George in February 1936, in which he argued before the British Parliament that the key to world peace was the redistribution of colonial possessions between European "haves" and "have-nots." George was referencing the discontent of Germany and Italy as "have-nots." Nehru drafted a response to the argument in a British leftist weekly, *Time and Tide*. He argued that "so long as there are 'haves' and 'have-nots,' friction and conflict will continue." The only solution, according to Nehru, was the "ending of capitalist imperialism."[75] Compare this with a similar engagement by Padmore in his book: "World Imperialism can be divided into two main camps: 'The Haves,' those who possess colonies, and the 'Havenots,' those who seek to possess." The tensions between the "Haves" and "Havenots" were caused by the problem of the "unequal development of capitalism," and, according to Padmore, "can only be solved by a radical change in the present social order."[76] Later in his book, he added that the "Haves (England and France)" and the "Havenots (Germany and Italy)" directly "correspond to the political division of Europe into Fascist and non-Fascist."[77] The shared mode of writing about the anti-imperialist and antifascist struggles in the discourses of Padmore and Nehru was striking in this instance.

Equally important to Nehru's turn toward Africa was the Italian invasion of Abyssinia in 1935. A nominally independent kingdom, Abyssinia had appealed to the League of Nations for support against Italian aggression, but the Geneva-based institution failed to intervene. The fate of Abyssinia became a lightning rod for political activity among anti-imperialists worldwide.[78] The crisis prompted Padmore and his fellow

---

[74] Ibid., 23.
[75] Nehru, "The Way to Peace," February 24, 1936. First published in *Time and Tide* and later in *India and the World* (London, 1936), *SWJN*, vol. 7, 122.
[76] Padmore, *Africa and World Peace*, 8. [77] Ibid., 98.
[78] On the significance of the Italian invasion of Abyssinia to anti-imperialists, see Pennybacker, *Scottsboro to Munich*, 66–102; Von Eschen, *Race against Empire*,

Pan-Africanists in London, C. R. L. James and I. T. A Wallace, to create the International African Friends of Abyssinia, the forerunner to the IASB. By the time Nehru arrived in London, many British leftist organizations, including the IL and the LAI, had rallied behind the Abyssinians and openly criticized the refusal of the League of Nations and the British government to intervene. Menon, Bridgeman, Saklatvala, and Bradley collectively called upon Nehru to raise awareness in India of the Abyssinia crisis. Nehru would not disappoint his comrades.

Abyssinia became the central focus of Nehru's anti-imperialist campaign in the immediate aftermath of his trip to London and reconnection with the LAI. He argued publicly that Abyssinia had fallen to "fascist imperialism," and Indians must demonstrate solidarity and sympathy for their cause. Several days later, the Italian Consul-General in Calcutta issued a statement justifying their invasion of Abyssinia because Rome was the "teacher of civilization to the world" and offered the Abyssinian people an "era of disciplined development and of material and spiritual welfare."[79] In a lengthy response made in a press statement, Nehru rebuked the Italian claims to the civilizing mission by arguing that "I repudiate utterly the suggestion that imperialism has gone to Abyssinia, or come to India, for humanitarian motives or the spread of civilization." Instead, Italy invaded Abyssinia to exploit, much as the British exploit India, and the "messengers" of the Italian civilizing mission used "poison gas and liquid fire," which "reveal its nature more than any argument."[80]

Later in India, Nehru organized a protest against Italy and launched it with a fiery condemnation of fascism and imperialism in Abyssinia and India. He argued that Indians shared a "common bond" with Abyssinians as "victims of imperialist greed and exploitation."[81] He added that India was "the classic land where modern imperialism first established itself," while Abyssinia "is a new tale and the rape is still fresh and flagrant for the world to see."[82] The lessons he drew from Abyssinia were many. Fascism and imperialism were "fundamentally of the same nature" since

---

11–13; and Maria Framke, "The 1930s in India as a Formative Period," in *The Non-Aligned Movement and the Cold War: Delhi-Bandung-Belgrade*, ed. by Nataša Mišković, Harald Fischer-Tiné, and Nada Boškovska Leimgruber (London and New York: Routledge, 2014), 37–56.

[79] Nehru, Statement to the Press, Allahabad, May 8, 1936, reprinted in *SWJN*, vol. 7, 567–568.

[80] Ibid., 568.

[81] Speech on Abyssinia Day, Allahabad, May 9, 1936. Reprinted in *The Hindustan Times*, May 11, 1935, reprinted in *SWJN*, vol. 7, 569.

[82] Ibid.

both worked by the same means to exploit subject peoples. In a more pointed stance, Nehru stressed that Abyssinia is "not something distant and unrelated" to India, but Indians should "think of our own freedom struggle and see it in relation to the wider struggle against fascist imperialism the world over."[83] The other lessons were that Britain did very little to stymie the tide of imperialist fascism, while the crisis proved the "utter futility" of the League of Nations.

The case of Abyssinia prompted a stronger recognition of the connection between Indian and African struggles, while at the same time it strengthened Nehru's conceptualization of fascism as one and the same with imperialism. His views of India and the world in 1936 marked a high point in his anti-imperialist internationalism. In fact, his renewed connections with the LAI and its many comrades, the expansion of contacts with Africa, and the Abyssinian crisis prompted Nehru to take a stronger stance on the issues facing India and the world. He also articulated a more global conceptualization in comparison to his anti-imperialist worldview rooted in Brussels by the inclusion of African anticolonialism. His meetings with LAI comrades in London, who focused more on Africa in their activism, and his engagement with new and like-minded anti-imperialists had been significant to an expanding rather than contracting anti-imperialist worldview.

Nehru's political reawakening and renewed commitment to anti-imperialism was the silver lining in an otherwise tragic moment in his life. His journey to Europe ended with the passing of his wife on February 28 at the youthful age of thirty-seven. Having lost his father only a few years before, Nehru slipped into depression and loneliness with Kamala's death. In Germany, finishing revisions for his autobiography in February 1936, Nehru grievingly dedicated the book to his wife: "To Kamala who is no more."[84] As he departed Europe after her death, Italy's Benito Mussolini tried to meet Nehru when he stopped in Rome en route to India. Nehru politely declined the overture.[85] It was a testament to his belief that fascism and imperialism were part of the same project, as well as his solidarity with the Abyssinians. There would be no room for fascist collaborations with Mussolini or Hitler in Nehru's anti-imperialist view of the world.

From Rome, Nehru began a journey to India and the INC politics from which he had been separated by prison and travels for nearly six years. On the eve of his return, his old friend Roger Baldwin wrote a letter congratulating him on his election to become president of the INC in

---

[83] Ibid., 569–570.   [84] Nehru, *Autobiography*, v.   [85] Gopal, *Nehru*, 107.

1936.[86] Baldwin added that "it is the time for a man with your outlook to direct a movement that cannot live by nationalism alone."[87] As Nehru returned to India after fresh encounters with a reinvigorated anti-imperialist movement in London, he no doubt felt inspired to carry forward Baldwin's message that the INC "cannot live by nationalism alone" and rather must engage the world.

INC PRESIDENT AND THE CAMPAIGN TRAIL IN INDIA

Nehru crafted his presidential address for the annual session of the INC in 1936 as a statement piece on Indian nationalism within an anti-imperialist world. In the opening of his speech, Nehru appealed to his Indian colleagues to envision – as he did – the "organic bond" between India and the world.[88] The picture he painted of the anti-imperialist world now appeared more complete, spanning from Asia to Africa and the Soviet Union. He argued that India's "struggle was but part of a far wider struggle for freedom, and the forces that moved us were moving millions of people all over the world and driving them to action. All Asia was astir from the Mediterranean to the Far East, from the Islamic West to the Buddhist East; Africa responded to the new spirit." This new spirit, according to Nehru, moved India and the world toward a "new conception of human freedom and social equality."[89]

In his presidential address, Nehru also taught the INC a history lesson about the international struggle between imperialism and anti-imperialism in the postwar years, a lesson reminiscent of his own encounters and experiences with anti-imperialism abroad and the ideas he shared with comrades such as Menon and Padmore. He argued that "the world was divided up into two groups today – the imperialist and fascist on one side, the socialist and nationalist on the other." After the Great War, according to Nehru, an intensification of two forces – social freedom in Europe and nationalism in Asia – struggled against the existing capitalist and imperialist order. With the Great Depression, capitalism-imperialism took to fascism, and

---

[86] The INC elected Nehru while he was still in Europe in 1935. Once again, Gandhi had been the driving force behind his selection, although Nehru garnered much more support in his own right in 1936.

[87] Baldwin to Nehru, April 9, 1936. vol. 6, JN Papers, 137.

[88] Nehru, Presidential Address to the Indian National Congress session, reprinted in *SWJN*, vol. 8, 68.

[89] Ibid., 68.

Fascism and imperialism thus stood out as the two faces of the new decaying capitalism, and though they varied in different countries according to national characteristics and economic and political conditions, they represented the same forces of reaction and supported each other, and at the same time came into conflict with each other, for such conflict was inherent in their very nature.[90]

To counter this, and mirroring the solidarities forged in Brussels and the League, "socialism in the West, and the rising nationalisms of the East and other dependent countries, opposed this combination of Fascism and imperialism."[91] What did this bipolar world mean for India? According to Nehru, "Inevitably we take our stand with the progressive forces of the world which are ranged against Fascism and imperialism." For Nehru, this global struggle should begin by acting locally and nationally against the British Empire, the "oldest and the most far-reaching of the modern world, but powerful as it is, it is but one aspect of the world-imperialism."[92]

Nehru returned to Indian politics with a renewed rather than a diminished vision for anti-imperialist internationalism and India's role within it. He resumed his efforts to internationalize nationalism by advocating for complete independence and socialism. The political landscape in 1936 afforded new opportunities for his goals. The INC was running in the national elections established by the Government of India Act of 1935. This latest round of constitutional reforms enhanced the opportunity for Indian self-governance by introducing limited elections for complete control over provincial assemblies. The colonial state retained its power at the all-India center by securing power to veto resolutions or even suspend the provincial legislatures whenever the viceroy saw fit. Nevertheless, the INC, after much debate, resolved to stand for election, although it was not clear whether the congressmen would accept or boycott these coveted seats once elected. Nehru was among a minority that thought that taking up seats in the provincial assemblies under the control of a British-dominated all-India center was a betrayal to the calls for complete independence. Despite this stance, Nehru agreed to campaign on behalf of the INC in order to disseminate his own political ideas and internationalist agenda.

Much of Nehru's personal appeal and popularity in 1936 can be attributed to a significant support base from a burgeoning congress left that shared with him similar ideas about internationalism and socialism. Nehru had been somewhat of a maverick in the late 1920s as one of the few spokesmen for complete independence within the INC. The younger

[90] Ibid., 70.   [91] Ibid.   [92] Ibid.

Jawaharlal of the 1920s – although he turned forty in 1929 – rebelled against his father and his political mentor, Gandhi, in his attempts to persuade the INC to accept independence framed within a broader idiom of anti-imperialism. Only Subhas Chandra Bose rivaled his stature as a key figure on the left-leaning fringes of mainstream Indian politics in the late 1920s. By 1936, however, Nehru encountered a new environment within the INC. While he sat in prison for five years and traveled to Europe after his release, many left-leaning congressmen began building a mobilization within the INC that would formalize many of Nehru's goals for socialism and anti-imperialism. Founded in 1934, the Congress Socialist Party (CSP) provided an umbrella organization within the INC that articulated a Marxist–Leninist ideology. Members thought Gandhi pandered too much to Indian capitalist and landholding classes. The CSP also drew in Indian communists after the government of India banned the Communist Party of India in 1934.

While the CSP hoped that Nehru would join and lead the group once he returned to India in 1936, he remained aloof. Nehru's socialism was more flexible and malleable than the strict orthodoxy of his comrades in the CSP, and instead it was always tempered by and situated within a broader idiom of anti-imperialism. Because of his anti-imperialist experiences and commitments, Nehru no doubt considered the CSP too rigidly confined to socialist doctrine rather than his acceptance of a pragmatic and flexible socialism. In fact, his speeches on the campaign trail reveal his socialism to be informed by the "special blend" of nationalism and socialism for the greater cause of anti-imperialism. In a July article for the *Bombay Chronicle*, Nehru equated the dual programs of socialism and nationalism in India to anti-imperialism. In doing so, he argued that anti-imperialism was the basis of Indian struggle, and that this meant the "political aspect [independence] as seen from the socialistic viewpoint."[93]

Nehru was careful to state that the INC program was not socialist, no doubt a problematic point for the CSP as well. Rather, he personally sought to persuade – or "train" – his fellow congressmen and the wider public that socialism was the only means to eradicate poverty in India and inequality worldwide. He stressed in his talks that his role was not to impose socialism in India, but to offer "political education." He was also quick to distinguish himself from those within the CSP and other groups who saw socialism as more pressing and urgent than independence. He stressed that if India is not "politically free," then they "cannot carry out

---

[93] Nehru, *Bombay Chronicle*, July 15, 1936, reprinted in *SWJN*, vol. 7, 317.

a socialist programme."[94] From the late 1920s to 1936, national independence remained the prerequisite for socialism in India.

Nehru considered socialism the solution for India and the world,
although his explanation of socialism remained rather ambiguous.
Nehru never intended to use socialism in a purely Marxist sense; rather,
he formulated socialism within an anti-imperialist framework. His anti-
imperialist logic stressed that the key to progress remained cooperation
between anti-capitalists (socialists and communists) and anti-imperialists
(nationalists in the colonized world), and in India it meant welding
together the anti-imperialist forces of nationalism and socialism.
Socialism was a fluid and malleable doctrine that could adapt to the
local conditions of India, but its usefulness was that socialism challenged
the established capitalist-imperialist order. In his presidential address,
Nehru stressed that socialism in India meant a "new civilization radically
different from the present capitalist order."[95]

Nehru set off on an epic campaign tour of India to sell his brand of
socialism, however ambiguous it might be. When pressed to be more
precise in his definition of socialism and its application to India, Nehru
offered a remarkably important statement that retained the fundamental
premises of anti-imperialist discourse as a blend of nationalism, socialism,
and communism. He argued that nationalism and socialism in India must
be "combined." In his explanation of socialism, he stressed that he was
not interested in the "subtle theories and metaphysical questions, which
sometimes give rise to heated debates and splits among the socialists and
communists." Instead, he concerned himself with the ways a "socialist
outlook" might be appropriated for Indian people in order to understand
the "sufferings and tremendous tragedies of humanity."[96] In another
speech, Nehru presented socialism and communism as essentially the
same. When Nehru explained his selection of socialism rather than communism, he argued that the two words were interchangeable. He admitted
that he supported the "economic theory that underlies the social structure
of Russia," but he chose socialism as his goal because communism "has
come to signify Soviet Russia," and this had frightened many away.[97]

---

[94] Nehru, "World Struggle against Imperialism," speech (Delhi) May 28, 1936, reprinted in *SWJN*, vol. 7, 267.
[95] Nehru, Presidential Address, 83.
[96] Nehru, "Socialism and the India Struggle," speech (Madras), October 8, 1937, *SWJN*, vol. 7, 523.
[97] Nehru, Statement to the Press, June 5, 1936, reprinted in *SWJN*, vol. 7, 283.

Even Nehru knew the differences between socialism and communism, and especially the tensions between socialists and communists; however, these were obstacles in the way of a broader and more inclusive front against imperialism, one that his Indian colleagues had to be persuaded to accept. His seemingly ambiguous or even confused blending of political ideologies at a distance appeared to be dishonest or problematic at best. Given that nationalism, socialism, and communism were embedded in the anti-imperialist movement that had shaped his core ideas about India and the world, however, his position retained some consistency and authenticity to the roots of the special "blend."

Once again in 1936, Nehru met resistance within the Indian Congress on his worldview, election message, and programs. The congress rightwing – a mix of landholding elites, business owners and capitalists, as well as Hindu nationalists – had been alarmed by Nehru's demands for socialism and the redistribution of land and economic resources to the workers and peasants. Historians have considered INC politics in the mid-1930s as a battleground between the left and the right.[98] While the left had grown significantly in the 1930s and Nehru and Bose held the presidency of the INC for three consecutive years between 1936 and 1938, the rightwing dominated the working committee, and Gandhi, whose closest confidants included influential Indian capitalists such as G. D. Birla, backed the interests of traditional elites, landholders, and capitalists. Nehru had been more vocal in expressing the left-leaning critique of Gandhian polices in his autobiography, published in 1936. For example, Nehru openly and candidly criticized Gandhi's social reforms as a "glorification of poverty."[99] He added that "poverty seemed to me a hateful thing, to be fought and rooted out and not to be encouraged in any way." According to Nehru, Gandhi "would lay stress on the rich treating their riches as a trust for the people," a view that Nehru thought was of "considerable antiquity."[100] Seeing socialism as a solution to eradicate poverty, Nehru loathed Gandhi's ideas about trusteeship because they did not attack the root problem of social inequality.

In July 1936, seven members of the working committee resigned over their disagreement with Nehru on socialism. Gandhi had persuaded the working committee members to withdraw their resignations, but tensions were high. Even before Nehru accepted the presidency of the INC earlier

---

[98] Sumit Sarkar is particularly attentive to the tensions between the left and right. See his *Modern India*, 337–377.
[99] Nehru, *Autobiography*, 203.   [100] Ibid., 203.

in 1936, he made it a point that his ideas about socialism would not bring a congress endorsement of it, but at the same time he should be free to express his ideas on the issue.[101] When Nehru came into conflict with his INC colleagues, he described the situation to Gandhi as one in which he felt only "isolation." He stated that he had been purposely mild and vague in his pronouncements and speeches on socialism to ensure that he did not represent the INC as socialist, yet even this had made him the subject of attack by the working committee.[102] In his July letter to Gandhi, he even contemplated tendering his resignation from the INC.[103]

The general elections took place in January and February of 1937 and marked an important turning point for the INC, which won 716 out of 1,161 seats contested. Nehru had been instrumental to this victory, having campaigned heavily for the INC as a means to reconnect with the masses and deliver his own personal message of socialism and internationalism. But for Nehru the election was a means to deliver the message, while the provincial seats the INC won were to be boycotted. He successfully passed a resolution in his home state's provincial congress committee to abstain from taking office, and he headed to Delhi for the All-India Working Committee of the INC meeting in March to celebrate the popular success of the congress and to ensure that his colleagues would not participate in provincial ministries. He saw any INC participation as a betrayal of the resolution for complete independence in Calcutta (1929) and Madras (1927). In Delhi, the INC working committee elected Nehru as president for a second consecutive year. However, immediately after doing so, the committee promptly over-ruled his position on the boycott of provincial ministries and passed a fresh resolution in favor of forming ministries and transforming the INC into a governing body under the Government of India Act of 1935.

Nehru found himself locked into the position of INC president under a program that compromised on his key principle of independence and dismissed his ideas about socialism entirely. Nehru never resigned from the presidency, but he refrained from participating in the provincial governments, which were established in eight provinces: Madras, Bombay, Central Provinces, Orissa, Bihar, North-West Frontier Provinces, Assam, and even his home state, the UP. His silence on the issue drew criticism from the left, while the right recognized the power of INC consensus in placating Nehru's attempts to introduce socialism and a stronger stance on independence. The provincial ministries proved to be a rightwing-dominated and

---

[101] Nehru to Gandhi, July 5, 1936, *SWJN*, vol. 7, 311.   [102] Ibid.   [103] Ibid.

semi-loyalist affair that supported policies leading to a surge in British troops in India and China – policies Nehru had fiercely opposed since 1927. Nehru's efforts to internationalize nationalism in the 1930s met resistance similar to that of the late 1920s. Nehru had been emboldened to speak more forcefully about socialism and its connection to a wider crisis created by capitalism and imperialism. His fiery speeches and press statements presented a case for social freedom and equality that made many of his fellow congressmen uncomfortable. Moreover, the question of independence returned to the forefront of INC politics and remained in the balance throughout his campaign across India. Ultimately, his nationalist colleagues were willing to settle on partial autonomy rather than complete independence, and this served as a catalyst that split Nehru from the INC once again. Nehru's vision for complete independence, a prerequisite for India to emerge as an anti-imperialist actor on the world stage, remained unfulfilled in 1937.

Around this time, Nehru decided to escape India and travel abroad, a decision that would be important in the development of his worldview in the late 1930s. By the fall of 1937, Subhas Chandra Bose had been elected president of the INC for 1938 and Nehru was released from another painful year of compromising his internationalist and nationalist principles for the unity of the INC. Pushed by Gandhi and the working committee to serve another term as the general secretary of the INC, Nehru declined and opted to travel to Europe and visit his daughter at Oxford instead. What he thought would be a retreat from politics turned out to be a strong dose of political education about the changing world on the brink of war.

CONCLUSION

Anti-imperialist internationalism, as a set of ideas and practices, continued to inform Nehru's ideas about India and its relationship to the wider world of the 1930s. Despite Nehru's falling out with the LAI and the new context of the 1930s, his formulations for Indian nationalism in relation to anti-imperialist internationalism continued after his institutional connection with the League ended. Indeed, the internationalist solidarities against imperialism – across ideological and political boundaries – retained a remarkable continuity into the 1930s for many of his former LAI colleagues, although the platforms were changing. This is most evident in the emphasis on antifascism rather than anti-imperialism, and Africa rather than Asia.

The interwar years present a more complicated and layered milieu, one that is difficult for historians to study given the ebbs and flows of solidarities that emerged, fissured, and re-emerged at different moments. In the case of the LAI and its afterlives in the 1930s, the story cannot be explained fully by the history of the Comintern, nor can one adequately understand Nehru's allegiances to it without considering the overlapping and flexible nature of these interwar movements. The ideas and networks of anti-imperialism offer one way of rethinking this complex and neglected aspect of the interwar years, and especially the 1930s.

6

Peace and War, 1936–1939

Nehru's book, *China, Spain and the War*, hit the market just as the European theater of World War II opened.[1] The book focused on his travels to China and Spain in the late 1930s, where he visited battlefronts, witnessed aerial bombardments, and confronted the new realities of another global war. In June 1938, he arrived in Barcelona in the midst of the Spanish Civil War (1936–1939), where he stayed several days and witnessed firsthand the struggle between Republican Spain and Franco's forces. Nehru's visit to China also took place during wartime. The Japanese invasion of the mainland in July 1937 prompted a temporary truce between nationalists and communists and opened the Asian theater of World War II. Nehru traveled to Chungking, the wartime base of KMT General Chiang Kai-shek , in August 1939 as Chinese forces suffered nightly bombardment. In his book, Nehru concluded that the "frontiers" of India's independence struggle extended well beyond the subcontinent, and were "not only in our own country but in Spain and China as well."[2]

The "frontiers" of Nehru's politics were never bound by the nation, and by the late 1930s the struggle for Indian independence came to be part of a wider struggle against imperialism, capitalism, and fascism worldwide. His concerns about fascism in this period prompted Nehru to craft several foreign policy initiatives for India, all of which were approved by the INC in the annual proceedings between 1937 and 1939. The INC condemned fascism in Spain, expressed solidarity with the Republicans, and raised funds for food and medical assistance for the Spanish cause. A similar position was taken in relation to China. He planned public demonstrations for solidarity with the Chinese and organized boycotts of Japanese goods. In 1938, he even arranged for the INC to dispatch its own medical unit to China. Finally, he persuaded his Indian colleagues to approve INC

---

[1] Jawaharlal Nehru, *China, Spain and the War* (Allahabad and London: Kitabistan, 1940).
[2] Ibid., 58.

membership to the International Peace Campaign (IPC) in 1936, a Geneva-based institution to coordinate peace activism worldwide.

Nehru's commitment to peace and antifascism were hallmarks of his political activities in the run-up to the war, and ones grounded in his anti-imperialist ideas and associations dating back to the late 1920s. This argument necessitates a rethinking of historiography on both Nehru and anticolonial nationalism in India. In the case of anticolonial histories, there has been increased scholarly interest in India's engagement and appropriation of fascism and fascist ideas.[3] However, few consider the antifascist activism that afforded the INC opportunities to create a distinct foreign policy from Britain and provide humanitarian aid to places like Spain and China.[4] At the same time, the narrative of anticolonial nationalism in India has focused exclusively on Gandhian non-violence as the dominant ideology and practice informing INC leaders, while only recent histories have started to unpack the ideas of violence and terrorism embedded within mainstream nationalist politics.[5] It is especially difficult to untangle Nehru from this historical deduction of INC history to the Gandhian principles of non-violence, and this chapter is a major intervention in this regard. It seeks to situate Nehru's peace advocacy outside of Gandhian non-violence and in the internationalism of anti-imperialism and antifascism. In other words, Nehru's commitment to a struggle for global peace should be located in his anti-imperialist worldview rather than a simple projection of Gandhi's ideas onto world politics.

Equally significant, Nehru shared this new purpose and commitment to peace and antifascism with many of his former comrades from the League days. Each chapter of this book has considered in depth the important relationships Nehru forged with an inner circle of comrades against imperialism. In the 1930s, these same comrades followed a similar trajectory from

---

[3] Much of this scholarship concentrates on either early adherents and ideologues of *hindutva* who sought fascism as a model or Subhas Chandra Bose's turn toward fascist Germany, Japan, and Italy. New scholarship has explored the intersection between fascism and South Asian politics and cultures. See the essays and introduction of the themed-edition, "Völkisch and Fascist Movements in South Asia," in *South Asia: Journal of South Asian Studies*, 38:4 (2015), 608–612. See also Benjamin Zachariah, "Nazi-hunting and Intelligence-gathering in India on the Eve of the Second World War," in *An Imperial World at War*, edited by Ashley Jackson, Yasmin Khan, and Gajendra Singh (London: Ashgate, 2015). See also in German, Maria Framke, *Delhi-Rom-Berlin: die indische Wahrnehmung von Faschismus und Nationalsozialismus, 1922–1939* (Darmstadt: Wissenschaftliche Buchgesellschaft, 2013).

[4] One notable exception is Maria Framke, "Political Humanitarianism in the 1930s: Indian Aid for Republican Spain," *European Review of History*, 23:1–2 (2016), 63–81.

[5] See Kama Maclean, *A Revolutionary History of Interwar India*.

anti-imperialism to antifascism and world peace. This isn't surprising given the importance of the war danger to the earliest articulations of anti-imperialism in Brussels. All joined peace and antifascist leagues in their respective homes and organized protests against fascist interventions in Spain, China, and Abyssinia. Early on, these endeavors against fascism were often parallel to one another, but by 1936 the lives and politics of Nehru and his comrades intersected once more in the meeting halls of Geneva, Brussels, Paris, and London. Their parallel and intersecting journeys, from anti-imperialism to antifascism, remind us that despite the fallout over the LAI in 1930, their projects maintained a remarkable consistency and brought the same ensemble of characters together in solidarities against fascism and war.

While this chapter situates Nehru's commitment to peace and antifascism within the wider net of anti-imperialism, it also points to contradictions that emerged in the late 1930s as the geopolitical situation changed substantially. This chapter considers three specific cases in which Nehru amalgamated anti-imperialism with antifascism and peace in ways that reaffirmed his existing ideas about the world but also produced significant contradictions. First, it examines Nehru's involvement in the IPC and the ways in which the peace movement's primary objectives stood in contradiction to anti-imperialist internationalism. The IPC sought to bolster the power of the League of Nations as the premier institution to ensure peace and "collective security." This chapter argues that "collective security," a term that the IPC attributed to the League of Nations' mission, called for a strong interstate system. The interstate system of the interwar years emblemized by the League of Nations disempowered non-state actors and the colonized that were most central to the anti-imperialist movements. Moreover, the League of Nations and "collective security" promoted imperialism and welcomed staunch supporters of empire as the primary arbitrators of peace. In this final moment of interwar internationalism, Nehru confronted and appropriated the ultimate "blend" of political ideologies – ones that necessitated comradeship with imperialists and support for the interstate system he had sought to challenge through the LAI in the years before.

The second concern that engendered ambiguities in Nehru's thinking was the campaign for Republican Spain. A copious body of scholarship on the Spanish Civil War already exists.[6] It was a conflict deeply rooted in

---

[6] See Hugh Thomas, *The Spanish Civil War* (New York: Harper and Brothers, 1961); Gabriel Jackson, *The Spanish Republic and the Civil War* (Princeton: Princeton

Spain's historical transformation from a monarchy to a democratic republic (1931–1936), which ended in civil war and the establishment of an authoritarian dictatorship (1939). The war began in July 1936 when Franco's nationalist forces launched a military coup against the democratically elected leadership of Republican Spain. The war unleashed a variety of ideological conflicts that prompted a number of international actors to intervene, most notably Germany and Italy on the side of Franco and the Soviet Union on the side of the Republic.

Spain captivated Nehru's imagination, and he saw the Republican's struggle against Franco as similar to India's struggle against the British. This led Nehru to critique the British and French for their failure to intervene militarily on behalf of Republican Spain. In doing so, he confronted a similar dilemma that so many interwar antifascists and peace advocates faced. Antifascism and peace activism sought to prevent armament and militarization while at the same time aimed to challenge fascist aggression by advocating force. As David Cortright has argued, however, most peace advocates of the twentieth century were not absolutists who opposed military action in the face of aggression and genocide. Rather, peace advocates were "pragmatic" and recognized the necessity of "just war" to ensure peace and social justice worldwide, and especially against Hitler and Mussolini.[7] Nehru, like so many comrades of the late 1930s, accepted substantial incongruities within antifascist and peace activism in order to make sense of the world on the eve of war.

Finally, the chapter examines Nehru's travels to both Egypt (1938) and China (1939). Much has been written about Nehru and his engagement with China and Egypt after 1947, but there is a scarcity of scholarship on these connections before India's independence.[8] In Egypt and China, Nehru's encounters were filtered through an anti-imperialist lens in which

University Press, 1965); Paul Preston, *The Coming of the Spanish Civil War: Reform, Reaction and Revolution in the Second Republic* (London: Methuen, 1978), and his edited volume, *Revolution and War in Spain, 1931–1939* (London: 1984); and Guillermo Cabanellas, *La Guerra de los Mil Dias, Nacimiento, Vida y Muerte de la II Republica Española.* 2 vols. (Grijalbo: Buenos Aires, 1973). This list is hardly exhaustive.

[7] David Cortright, *Peace: A History of Movements and Ideas* (Cambridge: Cambridge University Press, 2008).

[8] For a history of India and Egypt between the wars, see Noor Khan, *Egyptian-Indian Nationalist Collaboration.* Khan focuses on Egyptian perspectives of Indian nationalism and has some discussion of Nehru and Egypt, although it is not the focus of the work. On Nehru and China, there is much in the period after 1947, but few consider the interwar years. One notable exception is Avinash Mohan Saktani, "Nehru, Chiang Kai-sheik and the Second World War," in Madhavi Thampi, ed., *India and China in the Colonial World* (New Delhi: Social Science Press, 2005), 167–184.

he saw both as comrades with a shared history of imperialist oppression and a common future as leaders of anti-imperialism in their respective homes and worldwide. Travels to China and Egypt provided rare opportunities for Nehru to witness the realities and conditions in places he once imagined as similar sites of anti-imperialist struggle. These interfaces for the most part reinforced his core belief in similarities and solidarities with China and Egypt, although he often had to overlook and ignore conflicting evidence and realities on the ground in order to fit these places into his existing anti-imperialist worldview. In other words, this moment of diplomatic travels for Nehru in the 1930s afforded him an opportunity to confirm his unwavering commitment to anti-imperialism, while it also revealed cleavages between his ideas and those of his comrades across the anti-imperialist and antifascist world.

FROM ANTI-IMPERIALISM TO WORLD PEACE

In September 1936, Nehru sent formal greetings to the Congress for World Peace held in Brussels. More than 4,000 delegates arrived in Brussels and worked for two days to develop a plan for a permanent peace organization, the IPC.[9] Delegates crammed into the Palais d'Egmont, the very same meeting hall that had hosted the LAI's inaugural congress nearly ten years earlier. This time, however, attendees hailed from radically diverse political backgrounds that spanned the left and the right. Although Nehru could not attend the congress, he sent formal greetings as the INC president and dispatched V. K. Krishna Menon from London to represent the Indian nationalist movement. In Nehru's message to the congress, he drew upon a familiar framework of anti-imperialism to argue that lasting peace necessitates the end of imperialism: "Peace in colonial countries can only be established with the removal of imperialist domination, for imperialism is itself the negation of peace."[10] Accordingly, the defeat of imperialism in India and worldwide was essential to building an "enduring foundation for peace and freedom and human progress."[11]

---

[9] There is surprisingly little scholarship on the International Peace Campaign (IPC), also known by its French equivalent, *Rassemblement universel pour la paix* (RUP). Its history has been told primarily from the standpoint of Europe or in relation to its connections with the League of Nations. See Zara Steiner, *The Triumph of the Dark: European International History, 1933–1939* (New York: Oxford University Press, 2011), 169–171.

[10] Jawaharlal Nehru, "Message to the World Peace Congress," August 6, 1936. Reprinted in *SWJN*, vol. 7, 576–577.

[11] Ibid., 577.

Nehru's message – that imperialism was the "negation of peace" – provided the basis for blending the older anti-imperialist discourse on the war danger with the newly constructed platform and solidarities of the IPC. Such blending in the IPC necessitated more flexibility than ever before. In the case of India and the IPC, Nehru began to form alliances with conservative activists and advocates of empire in order to protest fascist aggression and articulate support for world peace. Evidence of this remarkable flexibility within the IPC, and Nehru's commitment to it, runs counter to arguments made by historians that the 1930s witnessed an ideological hardening of political categories, party politics, and national boundaries. Histories of the 1930s focus on the proliferation of aggressive nationalism in the context of the global depression and the rise of fascism. But, equally powerful and equally neglected by historians were the movements and solidarities that aimed to break down aggressive nationalism and preserve peace. Moreover, the internationalism of the 1930s was more flexible and fluid in the case of the IPC, although it also was underpinned by more contradictions than even the 1920s blend of bourgeois nationalism and communism.

Scholarship on international movements for peace in the interwar period remains strikingly scarce. Perhaps the failure to prevent war by 1939 encourages this neglect. The few studies that address peace movements concentrate on the USA and Europe, and the establishment of norms and practices for interstate relations as well as international law.[12] The IPC was perhaps the strongest and most influential of the growing proliferation of peace movements of the 1930s.

Nehru and Menon sought to work within the IPC to promote antifascism and peace, while at the same time attempting to incorporate anti-imperialism into it. This also meant approaching India's relations with the world in a different manner by accepting the primacy of state actors and the interstate system of the League of Nations over the more amorphous blending of ideas and projects inherent in the internationalism of the anti-imperialist movement. The interstate approach recognized and negotiated difference, while internationalism overlooked such distinctions. Nehru never fully recognized this tension between anti-imperialist and

[12] See Cortright, *Peace*; Cecilia Lynch, *Beyond Appeasement: Interpreting Interwar Peace Movements in World Politics* (Ithaca: Cornell University Press, 1999); and Peter Brock and Thomas Paul Socknat, *Challenge to Mars: Essays on Pacifism from 1918 to 1945* (Toronto: University of Toronto Press, 1999). All of these focus on Europe and North America, and mainly the League of Nations or the British and US peace movements.

peace projects in the 1930s, even when colleagues pointed out the pitfalls and limitations of supporting the League of Nations and the interstate system that bolstered imperialism while at the same time promoting an anti-imperialist position within it.

Nehru was not alone in following a trajectory from anti-imperialism to peace. Nearly all of his former comrades from the LAI followed this path to the IPC and its ancillary organizations. In fact, most were involved in peace movements well before the inauguration of the IPC in 1936. As early as August 1932, Willi Münzenberg and Louis Gibarti, the original founding figures of the LAI, organized an international peace conference in Amsterdam. In total, nearly 2,200 delegates attended, even though the congress was deeply informed by the Comintern's class warfare strategy and retained an exclusionary and communist-dominated appeal. In one of the last editions of the *AIR*, Münzenberg described the anti-war congress as a clear outgrowth of anti-imperialist movement and the "centre" of LAI activities.[13] This anti-war campaign retained a strong consistency with the war danger platform of the LAI since the late 1920s by advocating for two things: active support for Chinese communists against Japan and the KMT, as well as the defense of the Soviet Union against imperialists threatening war against it.

Despite the pre-eminence of communist ideology, Münzenberg's Amsterdam conference was well attended by noncommunists and sparked a number of peace organizations that explicitly brought together communists and noncommunists well before the Soviet Union's official directives to party members to seek popular fronts against fascism in 1934. Other former LAI advocates also found their way to Amsterdam in 1932. Bridgeman attended as part of a large British delegation, which included the LP, ILP, and CPGB. Afterward, British delegates established a national section of the movement, the British Anti-War Council (BAWC), and Bridgeman became the international secretary.[14] The BAWC sought to work against armament, war preparations, jingoistic nationalism,

---

[13] Willi Münzenberg, "Five Years of Anti-Imperialist Struggle," *The Anti-Imperialist Review: Special Anti-War Number* 1, no. 3 (January–February, 1932), IISH. This was one of the final numbers of *AIR*, which ran only three more editions in 1932. The last was July–August 1932 at which point the LAI was under close surveillance by the Nazi party and ultimately the first raid of the headquarters took place that December.

[14] On the British peace movements, see Michael C. Pugh, *Liberal Internationalism: The Interwar Movement for Peace in Britain* (New York: Palgrave Macmillan, 2012). For the intersection of peace and anti-imperialism in Britain, see chapter 8 in Nicholas Owen, *The British Left and India*; and Tom Buchanan, *East Wind*, 48–80.

imperialism, and fascism. The platforms, under Bridgeman's leadership, were remarkably similar to the LAI of years past. BAWC publications argued that peace could be achieved only with an end to the "slander" aimed at the Soviet Union, the "dismemberment" of China by imperialist powers, and the "oppression and massacre of colonial peoples."[15] Moreover, it supported "national minorities and peoples fighting for their national and social independence," as well as Japanese workers struggling against "their own imperialist government."[16]

Bridgeman's writings on peace and antifascism, much like Nehru's, continued to draw upon the problem of imperialism as the root cause of war in the 1930s. In an undated and handwritten note on the Spanish Civil War, likely prepared for a speech he made to the Uxbridge Trade Council and Labour Party in early 1936, Bridgeman argued that antifascism was interconnected with anti-imperialism.[17] He explained that the failure of the Spanish Republic to take an anti-imperialist stance in relation to Morocco had led Moroccan soldiers to support Franco's military. Only if the republic offered Moroccan independence, and thus the overturning of imperialism, would there be peace in Spain. Bridgeman argued that this was a lesson for the British and used India as his example. Without Indian independence, world peace would remain elusive. Only the end of imperialism, he argued, could "open a new epoch in which equality between nations will become a reality."[18]

Baldwin also joined anti-war movements early on and at the prompting of Münzenberg's Amsterdam conference. He was a member of the US-based League against War and Fascism (LAWF), which sought to unite communists and noncommunists once again under the umbrella of peace.[19] LAWF was the creation of Louis Gibarti, who left Berlin for New York in 1929 under the direction of the Comintern. LAWF held national congresses and brought about local chapters in a great number of cities across the USA.[20] Although the organization nearly folded in 1934 after a clash between socialists and communists in New York, the ACLU chairman, Harry F. Ward, mended the tensions and the LAWF survived

[15] "British Anti-War Movement," Pamphlet, File DBN/12/1, Bridgeman Papers.
[16] Ibid.   [17] Bridgeman, speech undated, File DBN/15/1, Bridgeman Papers.   [18] Ibid.
[19] For American antifascism and peace, see Cecilia Lynch, *Beyond Appeasement*. For America aid for the Spanish Republic, see Eric C. Smith, *American Relief Aid and the Spanish Civil War* (Columbia: University of Missouri Press, 2013).
[20] The files on the LAWF are located in the American League for Peace and Democracy collection, Collection CDG-A, Swarthmore College Peace Collection in Philadelphia, PA. The LAWF changed its name to the League for Peace and Democracy in November 1937.

until 1939. Within LAWF, Baldwin worked closely with his ACLU comrades, Ward in particular, on strengthening the anti-war movement and ensuring solidarity between communists and noncommunists against fascism and for peace.

Much like Bridgeman's BAWC, LAWF's platforms echoed those of the LAI in the late 1920s. LAWF demanded protection of the Soviet Union, because as Baldwin recalled, many still looked with "greater hope to Russia as the antithesis of fascism."[21] At the same time, LAWF was flexible enough for those who had "reservations" about Stalin and his political purges. Shortly after the Amsterdam anti-war congress in 1932, Münzenberg visited the United States, and he accompanied Gibarti on a tour and fundraising campaign for the anti-war movement. Here again, former comrades such as Baldwin, Gibarti, and Münzenberg reconnected and intermingled in an effort to build a new internationalism of the 1930s.

The Amsterdam peace conference took place shortly before the Nazi regime forced Münzenberg to flee Germany and seek asylum in France. Communists and socialists were the first targets of the Nazi party, and Münzenberg narrowly escaped imprisonment and probably death in February 1933 when he left a political rally in Frankfurt minutes before a Nazi officer arrived to arrest him.[22] Forced into hiding and far from his home base in Berlin, Münzenberg heard about the Reichstag fire from Frankfurt and began plotting his escape. Thanks to some communist friends, he and his partner, Babette Gross, acquired falsified papers and traveled secretly to Paris, where both were able to secure asylum. His Parisian friends, mainly fellow travelers and communists, successfully managed to convince French authorities to grant him domicile, although Münzenberg had to promise to refrain from any communist propaganda activities.

Antifascism and anti-Nazi campaigns were not restricted in the agreement, and Münzenberg joined noncommunists and communists alike in organizing against Hitler and Mussolini.[23] Among his first projects was a book series criticizing Nazi Germany. The series was disseminated widely in several languages, and copies were smuggled into Germany. Connected to this, Münzenberg also established an organization that aided with the resettlement of German political refugees in Paris. His interests in anti-war and antifascism were not limited to Germany, however, and he established the *Comité contre la Guerre et le Fascisme*

---

[21] Baldwin, *Reminiscences*, 359.   [22] Gross, *Willi Münzenberg*, 221–227.
[23] Ibid., 241.

(CAGF) in order to continue the work laid out at the Amsterdam anti-war congress.

By 1936, the IPC emerged as the primary institution coordinating the efforts of smaller peace organizations like BAWC, LAWF, and CAGF, and most of the former membership of the LAI also attended the inaugural meeting. Bridgeman and Bradley attended as the LAI delegation, based in London since 1933. Münzenberg and Gibarti represented their respective peace movements in Paris and New York. Baldwin did not attend, but he followed the IPC proceedings and worked for the LAWF on its behalf. Menon's attendance brought Nehru and the INC into the movement as well.

The desire for peace was so substantial by 1936 that the organizers were unprepared for the overwhelming support of their first congress in Brussels, when nearly 1,500 delegates were left standing outside the meeting hall when the first session commenced.[24] Inside, slogans in both French and English adorned the walls: "Organize your forces – Stand together and you will save the peace of the world."[25] A world map also figured prominently in the meeting hall, and electric lights illuminated to indicate the country of each speaker as they took to the podium. The headliners were the founders of the organization, MPs from Britain and France, who called upon attendees to recognize that the "movement for peace is the supreme task of our generation."[26]

The genealogy and primary objectives of the IPC were quite distinct from earlier anti-war and anti-imperialist projects in that they were strongly grounded in the hegemony of great powers and interstate diplomacy reflective of the League of Nations. The idea for the IPC began as a conversation between Lord Robert Cecil and a French MP and former Minister of Air, M. Pierre Cot. Lord Cecil was a conservative Tory who spent much of his career building and serving the League of Nations and strengthening the existing interstate system of great powers. Cot began his career as a conservative but moved further to the left in the 1930s. Both were deeply invested in resurrecting the League of Nations as the primary arbitrator of peace, stability, and order in the 1930s. By March 1936, they agreed to plan a world congress with four central principles. These

---

[24] A description of the proceedings by Henrietta Roelofs, an American delegate, is useful for recreating the event. See her "Report on the Rassemblement Universel pour la Paix [International Peace Campaign], Brussels Belgium, September 3–8, 1936." Collection CDG-B Switzerland, Box 1, Swarthmore Peace Collection (hereafter Swarthmore).
[25] Ibid.   [26] Ibid.

included the recognition of treaty obligations, the reduction of arms, the strengthening of the League of Nations, and the establishment of "effective machinery" within the League for the prevention of war.[27]

The diverse membership of the IPC led to many conflicts within the movement. Even within European circles, the IPC suffered from similar tensions between communists and noncommunists who attempted to work for peace and antifascism collectively. In addition, the IPC experienced further division between those advocating absolute pacifism and those advocating military force to stymie fascist aggression in Spain and elsewhere.[28] Nehru fell into the latter camp by arguing for military intervention against fascism and imperialism in Spain, Abyssinia, and China. This argument, peace by means of war, distinguished him from more orthodox pacifists and even Gandhi, who had advocated consistently for the means, in this case non-violence, as more important to the goals of the INC movement.

India earned a coveted place in the impressive list of speakers slated for the opening day of the IPC's congress. Menon carried with him Nehru's greetings, which argued that peace cannot be attained without an end to imperialism. Echoing Nehru, Menon linked anti-imperialism and world peace by arguing that only "free peoples, liberated from domination" could be the "best guarantor of peace." This enabled him to present the case that India's struggle for national liberation was part of a wider struggle for international peace. Both sought to strengthen peace around the world. Menon also paid homage to Nehru by adding that the "great masses of people" in India have been "stirred" by the INC leader to recognize that "India has no destiny apart from the world."[29]

Over the course of the two-day congress, the delegates unanimously created the bilingual (English and French) IPC. During the sessions, smaller committees were established to plan the work of the institution. These included: Arts, Letters and Science; Aviators; Economic Affairs; International Agrarian Conference, Co-operatives, Ex-Soldiers; Education; Women's' Organizations; Parliamentary Organizations;

---

[27] The official report of the congress is published. See *World Peace Congress: Brussels, 3–6 September 1936*. Brussels: International Secretariat of the IPC, 1936.
[28] See Cortright, *Peace*; Steiner, *The Triumph of the Dark*: 169–171.
[29] Speech by V. K. Krishna Menon, Representative of the Indian National Congress to the World Peace Congress at Brussels, Delivered September 3, 1936 (the document states August 3, but this is an error given the dates of the congress and the program, which states that he delivered his address on the first day). File 60, *Rassemblement universel pour la paix* papers, International Institution of Social History (hereafter RUP, IISH).

Youth Organizations; and Trade Unions. Tellingly, no commission dealt directly with the question of imperialism, although neither Menon nor Nehru expressed trepidation about this fact and missed an opportune moment to question the difference in the agendas of the IPC and the INC.

The IPC existed in Geneva from 1936 to 1940. While Europeans staffed the secretariat, a more diverse general council included two delegates from each national committee for peace and one delegate from each international organization represented in the movement. China and India were represented in this latter group. Operating funds were derived from nominal dues paid by members of the general council, while donations were solicited for special projects. Among its greatest accomplishments was a peace pavilion created as part of the Paris World Exposition in 1937. It was substantially smaller and less prominent compared to the more famous buildings that represented Nazi Germany and the Soviet Union. The IPC also organized a speaking tour in which leading figures of the organization traveled Europe and even parts of Asia in an effort to educate audiences on the dangers of war and the importance of the League of Nations and disarmament. A bilingual newsletter in French and English from the IPC also enjoyed circulation across the world.[30]

Nehru and Menon committed India to the IPC campaign immediately upon its creation. Their objectives were two-fold. Within India, Nehru and Menon aimed to educate the Indian public as much as possible on the war danger. This was not all that different from Nehru's internationalist projects of previous years, but the emphasis on the threat of world war and antifascism above anti-imperialism offered new material and a different inflection. The INC officially supported the IPC in December 1936. Internationally, Menon worked closely with Nehru to promote the anti-imperialist agenda within the IPC. Menon served on the general council in 1936 and joined the executive council in 1937.[31]

Nehru managed many peace and antifascist activities on behalf of the INC through its newly reconstituted foreign department. Originally established in 1928 at the behest of Nehru, the development of the foreign department stagnated in the late 1920s and early 1930s during the Civil

---

[30] Collections of the IPC/RUP newsletters can be found in the RUP collections in Swarthmore and the IISH.
[31] IPC 6th General Council Meeting, September 13–14, 1937, Geneva (SM), Rassemblement Universel pour la Paix [International Peace Campaign], 1936–1942, Collection CDG-B Switzerland, Box 1, Swarthmore.

Disobedience Campaign. It was reconstituted in May 1936, nearly a decade later, when an INC resolution mandated its revitalization. Nehru was the logical candidate for revamping the foreign department, which was to be located in his hometown, Allahabad. While on the campaign trail during much of 1936, Nehru hired a full-time general secretary for the foreign department, Rammanohar Lohia, a much younger leftist congressman from the UP and one time Indian expatriate in Germany.[32]

Nehru and Lohia produced two sets of literature: one was prepared for an international audience to disseminate news about India to the world; the other informed the Indian literate classes of events unfolding around the world. In a short six months, the foreign department boasted a staggering network of exchange with over 400 anti-imperialist and peace partners worldwide, including the IPC and the LAI in London.[33] This development also prompted colonial authorities to raid the foreign department office in October 1936 and confiscate all "unauthorized news sheets."[34] Nevertheless, the office was up and running again by November and continued its work until the war.

The foreign department project afforded Nehru a more formal and structured platform to propagate his ideas about India and the world for a wider Indian public. Although Lohia issued the foreign department statements to the Indian press, Nehru informed much of its content. Nehru marked up and edited all of the department's releases to the Indian press, leaving little doubt that he had the final say in its presentation and message.[35] Further evidence is in the statements produced by the foreign department, which served as a mirror reflection of his priorities by emphasizing India's role in anti-imperialism, antifascism, and peace, with a focus on strengthening associations with the IPC, as well as solidarity with Abyssinia, Republican Spain, and China.

---

[32] Rammanohar Lohia (1910–1967) was a member of the Congress Socialist Party and the INC. He went to Berlin University in 1929 at the time Nehru and Chatto collaborated on the Indian Information Bureau that supported Indian students in Germany. Nehru appointed him FD secretary in 1936, where he worked until a series of critical articles on the British government landed him in jail in 1939 until and through the Quit India movement, 1942–1945. For works on Lohia, see Karuna Kaushik, *The Russian Revolution and Indian Nationalism: Studies of Lajpat Rai, Subhas Chandra Bose, and Rammanohar Lohia* (Delhi: Chanayaka Publications, 1984); and Indumati Kelkar, *Dr. Rammanohar Lohia: His Life and Philosophy* (Delhi: Anamika, 2009). More recently, see the essays in the themed-edition, "Politics and Ideas of Rammanohar Lohia," in *Economic and Political Weekly*, 45:40 (October 2, 2010).

[33] Report of the Foreign Department of the AICC by Rammanohar Lohia (general secretary), December 1936, File 40–1936, AICC.

[34] Ibid.   [35] See, for example, the papers in File 30–1936 and File 40–1936, AICC.

In the first months of its existence, the "primary duty" of the foreign department was to strengthen INC ties to the IPC.[36] The foreign department publicized widely the proceedings of the congress in the Indian press, while the report for the annual INC meeting in December 1936 argued that Menon had "achieved remarkable success in impressing upon the [peace] Congress that a continuing cause of war was the system of imperialism that generated imperialist rivalries and colonial domination and, consequently, wars."[37] According to the report, India "stands to gain substantially" by its association with the peace movement for the IPC remains a bulwark of progress in an increasingly reactionary world. As the report suggests in a now-familiar idiom, "the entire world split into two camps ... imperialism and fascism on the one hand and that of colonial freedom and democracy and socialism on the other."[38] Of this divide on a global scale, the latter groups included the IPC and the INC.

In Europe, Menon was a stalwart for the anti-imperialist cause within the IPC. He represented India as a critically important partner in the peace movement and advocated for a stronger stance against imperialism within the IPC. In 1937, Menon joined the much smaller executive council, where he continued to advocate strongly for supporting Abyssinia, Spain, and China. His strong anti-imperialist stance placed him at odds with other IPC leaders. In March 1937, Menon objected to a resolution that specifically referenced a League of Nations article that empowered the institution to renegotiate treaties that "endanger the peace of the world."[39] Menon argued that all treaties signed by imperialist powers were threats to peace, and only an anti-imperialist position within the IPC would attack the root cause of war. His comments engendered a debate within the IPC, although the fundamental premise of the resolution remained despite his objection.[40] Ultimately, the IPC dismissed calls made by the Indian delegate for anti-imperialism. Further illustrative of this point, the IPC president, Lord Cecil, frequently described Menon as a representative from the British Empire rather than India.[41]

---

[36] Report of the Foreign Department, Lohia, December 1936.   [37] Ibid.   [38] Ibid.
[39] The Covenant of the League of Nations Including Amendments Adopted to December, 1924, available digitally via the Avalon Project: Documents in Law, History and Diplomacy, Yale Law School and Lillian Goldman Law Library, http://avalon.law.yale .edu/20th_century/leagcov.asp.
[40] Minutes of General Council Meeting of the RUP/IPC, March 15–16, 1937, File 114, RUP, IISH.
[41] Viscount Cecil, "The International Peace Campaign," *Headway* (April 1937). Copy in File 114, RUP, IISH.

The failure to address incongruence between imperialism and anti-imperialism within the IPC clearly demonstrated the limits and flawed nature of this final attempt at solidarity in the 1930s. Both Nehru and Menon desired peace and anti-imperialism, but sought refuge for their internationalist project within an interstate organization like the IPC, which incidentally also supported imperialism. The flexibility that enabled the INC and the IPC to collaborate was the hallmark of the internationalist moment of the interwar period in which Nehru came to anti-imperialism and developed his worldview. India's participation in the IPC was another example in which the incompatibility of anti-imperialism and the imperatives of the IPC were dismissed in an attempt to construct comradely solidarity across a wide and contradictory divide. But, unlike the LAI, the other IPC members were not as flexible and many worked to support the interstate system of the League of Nations, which disempowered colonies and workers.

PEACE AND ANTI-IMPERIALISM IN EUROPE

Nehru engaged with the IPC from a distance in India until he traveled to Europe in late 1938. Nehru's schedule took him to Britain, France, Spain, Germany, and Czechoslovakia. He also expressed a keen interest in extending his travels further to include the Soviet Union and the United States, although the former rejected his visa application and the latter was not possible given his timeframe for travel. Very little has been written about Nehru's engagements with internationalist platforms during his last trip before the war and independence. Biographers such as Gopal have described his journey as an escape, as Nehru had been frustrated with INC politics and especially the decision of the INC to take up seats on the provincial legislatures.[42] Once again, internationalism is treated as a sideshow from the nationalist narrative. This is a real gap given the importance of this moment in his re-engagement with world politics. Not only did he continue to work with the IPC and its British affiliates, Nehru also traveled the European continent in an effort to connect more concretely the projects for peace, antifascism, and anti-imperialism.

His experiences in Europe before the war provide an important glimpse of the ambiguities and limits of his internationalism in the 1930s. Nehru

---

[42] The details of Nehru's European trip in 1938 are buried in a chapter entitled "Out of Tune with the Congress," in which Gopal contributes a mere four pages to the topic. See his *Nehru*, 120–124.

had to consider the complicated nature of joining the IPC and British peace campaigns and the ambivalent place of anti-imperialism within each. Much to Nehru's disappointment, the importance of anti-imperialism hardly figured into the agenda and discourse of the peace campaign. Instead, the peace movements underscored the importance of "collective security," a term that came to be synonymous with the League of Nations and its attempts to disarm and demilitarize nations, as well as to provide neutral spaces for interstate negotiations. The power of imperialism was never challenged in the conceptualization of collective security, the League of Nations, or the IPC and its affiliates. Even so, Nehru continued to advocate for the peace movement as the premier vehicle for anti-imperialist action.

Nehru's journey from India to Europe was eventful from the start. His steamer was destined for Genoa, Italy, and carried many fascist leaders. He described an Italian diplomatic mission returning from a successful trip to Japan where industrial and business ties were strengthened.[43] The Italians were "full of praises for Japan" and the "virtues of the fascist regime."[44] Nehru also met the Italian Viceroy of Ethiopia, the Duke of Aosta, and he found him "very delightful."[45] The statement seemed like an anathema to his antifascist and pro-Abyssinia stance, although for Nehru, politics were never about personal animosities but rather about global forces and structures of power. Imperialism, capitalism, and fascism were to be defeated, even if individuals were not held personally accountable for the systems they were implicit in creating and maintaining.

Nehru attracted considerable attention during his trip to Europe. Many in Britain and France worried about what India might do in the event of another world war. Nehru had long discussions with LP leaders, and he reported back to the INC that talks revolved around specific conditions for the future withdrawal of the British from India. But British authorities were not the only ones interested in Nehru. Nazi authorities contacted Nehru and invited him to Germany. Nehru remarked in his report to the INC that, "I was told that some high German officials were so keen on seeing me and discussing various matters with me, that they were prepared to travel to any part of Germany to do so."[46] While Nehru traveled to Munich for several days en route to Czechoslovakia, he refused to meet Nazi officials. If he had ever wavered on this question, the stay in

[43] Jawaharlal Nehru, Letter to Kripalani (INC Secretary), June 11–13, 1938, *SWJN*, vol. 9, 9.
[44] Ibid.
[45] Jawaharlal Nehru to Kripalani (INC Secretary), June 12, 1938, *SWJN*, vol. 9, 8.
[46] Ibid., 92.

Czechoslovakia strengthened his condemnation of German fascism as a bullying and aggressive element in the world.[47]

Nehru's engagement with the peace movement in Britain also revealed the complexity of blending anti-imperialism and collective security. He chaired the Conference on Peace and Empire held in London in 1938. Nehru opened the event with a provocative observation: "Peace and Empire – a curious combination of words and ideas fundamentally opposed to each other, and yet I think it was a happy idea to put them together in this way." He added that peace is not possible without ending imperialism, "Therefore the essence of the problem of peace is the problem of empire."[48] Nehru called upon a familiar repertoire of imagery that linked India's struggle to similar movements for freedom and equality in African countries, China, and Spain. In all such cases, the desire for peace and freedom from imperialism and fascism were one and the same. Nehru was quick to argue that fascism is simply an "intensified form of the same system which is imperialism. Therefore, if you seek to combat fascism you inevitably combat imperialism."[49] Nehru called upon the audience to overlook their disagreements over "minor matters" because "only a joint front, not a national joint front, but a world joint front, can achieve our purpose."[50]

The "minor matters" dividing the audience were many. The conference hosted a diverse and contentious group. It was convened by the IL and it sought to coordinate the forces for peace in Europe, mainly Britain and France, with the anti-imperialists from the colonies. More than 1,500 leaders attended, including mainstream and lesser-known movements based in London, such as the LP, ILP, CPGB, Left Book Club, and National Council for Civil Liberties. A strong contingent of Pan-Africanists also participated and included the Paris-based *Ligue de Defence de la Race Negre*, the Negro Welfare Association, and the IASB, which Padmore, C. R. L. James, and Kenyatta ran. It was Kenyatta who attended, and so did Bridgeman and Bradley from the LAI.[51] Among the most famous was the British Labour MP

---

[47] Nehru, "India and the European Crisis," reprinted in *Amrita Bazar Patrika* on September 15, 1938. *SWJN*, vol. 9, 130–131.

[48] Jawaharlal Nehru, "Peace and Empire" Presidential address at the conference on Peace and Empire, London, July 15, 1938. Reprinted in *Amrita Bazar Patrika* on July 22, 1938. *SWJN*, vol. 9, 61–68.

[49] Ibid.   [50] Ibid.

[51] A detailed report on the meeting is located in the Indian Political Intelligence file: Jawaharlal Nehru, "Conference on Peace and Empire," July 27, 1938, See File L/P&J/ 12/293, IPI.

Stafford Cripps, who began cultivating a strong relationship with Nehru during his stay in Britain in 1938. Cripps would later have an important role in preliminary negotiations over the transfer of power from Britain to India in the 1940s.

The conference was divisive from the start. Early arguments focused on providing an equitable balance between communist and noncommunist speakers. By 1938, the fascist threat had produced in Britain and France some new opportunities for communists and noncommunists to fight together against a common enemy. This became central when the delegation began considering the establishment of a permanent working committee for the group. Noncommunists promptly rejected the first shortlist of London-based leaders because four communists were included. However, Nehru assured delegates that representation of a widespread variety of members would be considered and approved collectively.

The greatest conflict emerged over the primary resolution of the conference, which advocated for both peace and collective security. Nehru offered the INC's support for the resolution. One audience member protested that the resolution "gives people the impression that the Indians are fighting for collective security in the sense known to this country." Instead, the conference should fight for "the unqualified rights of all people throughout the world."[52] Collective security, "in the sense known to this country," meant to many in Britain the support of the status quo, recognition of interstate treaties and diplomacy, and the support of the League of Nations. Kenyatta raised objections on the grounds that the British delegates should "clean your doorstep first" by ending imperialism before fighting fascists abroad. He added, "Instead of you people going to the German Embassy, I would like to see you march to the India Office and protest against oppression of that people."[53]

The conflict prompted Nehru to speak again about the resolution. He argued that in India the differences between collective security and antiimperialism were not so oppositional. Nehru recognized that those protesting in the audience made valid points in that "any person subject [to colonial rule] will not be very much interested in assisting to maintain a status quo which involves subjugation."[54] At the same time, he stressed that the INC struggled for independence first, but that it also acted for the "common good of all" and this included "world collective security."

---

[52] Ibid.   [53] Ibid.
[54] Concluding speech at the conference on Peace and Empire (London), July 16, 1938, reprinted in *Amrita Bazar Patrika*, July 22, 1938, *SWJN*, vol. 9, 69–71.

Nehru added that the INC "must think in larger terms, must think of the greater perils that are overshadowing the world and try to avert these perils."[55] In making this case, about the links between national and international, anti-imperialism and peace, Nehru dismissed the nuances of the debates and the cleavages between the INC and the peace campaigns in Britain and worldwide.

A letter following the conference from Fenner Brockway, a longtime friend from the ILP and an original delegate to the Brussels Congress, urged Nehru to recognize the significant contradictions between "collective security" and anti-imperialism. In it, he first clarified the ILP position: "we cannot possibly support a line of policy which would mean that in a war between the imperialist dictator and fascist dictator nations, we should be involved in supporting the imperialist dictator nations under the illusion that they are 'democracies.'"[56] He conceded to Nehru that collective security was "ideal in principle" but in the present geopolitical context this would mean the "defense of the existing distribution of territories in the world and the existing empires."[57] Instead, Brockway argued that socialists and nationalists must "advocate a new international order of independent nations" and only this would bring about a "collective security" worth supporting.[58] In many respects, Nehru agreed with Brockway entirely, but he had begun his work for peace within a framework of the IPC and its support of "collective security," and rather than recognize the incongruence with the peace movement and anti-imperialism, Nehru ignored it.

Nehru also traveled Continental Europe with his message of anti-imperialism and world peace. In Paris, he reconnected with Münzenberg. Although the archival record of the encounter is thin, Münzenberg's partner, Babette Gross, recalled that the two met and agreed that the world was coming to another war and that the crisis would be difficult to manage if Britain and France appeased Germany on the question of Czechoslovakia.[59] Nehru also delivered two speeches in Paris organized by the IPC. The first was a broadcast on French radio. In it, Nehru took the opportunity to punctuate the point that "till India is free from imperialist domination and has gained her independence, there will be no enduring peace in the world."[60] He argued that the INC supported the IPC because

---

[55] Ibid.   [56] Fenner Brockway to Nehru, August 6, 1938, vol. 10, JN Papers.   [57] Ibid.
[58] Ibid.   [59] Gross, *Münzenberg*, 314–315.
[60] Jawaharlal Nehru, broadcast over Paris radio, June 20, 1938, and reprinted in *Amrita Bazar Patrika* on June 30, 1938. *SWJN*, vol. 9, 19.

its primary task is "ensuring world peace based on freedom." The world must face "reactionary forces which dream in terms of war and imperialism and fascism. We cannot do this effectively or successfully unless the forces of peace and progress are also united and pulled together."[61] The following day, Nehru made another speech before the French section of the IPC in which he reiterated that "peace can come only when India is free."[62]

Nehru's debut in the IPC movement revealed the power of anti-imperialism in framing his views of peace, although it also demonstrated some ambivalence on the situation in Europe. When an audience member asked what India thought about the German annexation of Austria, Nehru dismissed it almost entirely. He stated that while there had been demonstrations against German aggression, "our people do not have any effective means of helping Austria." He added that in India, "we have to oppose British imperialism."[63] This response revealed that Nehru was comfortable working within an anti-imperialist framework and speaking of places beyond "British imperialism" such as China and Spain, but backpedaled on places that didn't fit so easily into the anti-imperialist discourse and worldview he had engaged since the late 1920s, particularly on imperialism within Europe.

In July 1938, Nehru officially represented India's delegation in Paris for the IPC-organized "World Conference for the Action on the Bombardment of Open Towns and the Restoration of Peace." The event hosted more than 1,000 delegates from over 30 countries.[64] The purpose of the meeting was a collective protest against the bombardment of towns in China and Spain especially. The chairman opened the three-day event by offering a graphic picture of "thousands of women and children massacred and the mutilated children who will grow up maimed and deformed as a result."[65] The IPC plan for the active mobilization of peace and the protection of civilians in warzones fit a general pattern underway since the mid-1930s. It called for delegates to assist the IPC in sending food and medical supplies to sites of conflict and bombardment. It also called for the establishment of a "peace hospital" in China. Finally, it encouraged delegates to work from their

---

[61] Ibid.
[62] Jawaharlal Nehru, speech and interview at the Hall of Nations, Paris, June 21, 1938. Reprinted in *Amrita Bazar Patrika* on June 30, 1938. *SWJN*, vol. 9, 20–21.
[63] Ibid.
[64] Report on World Conference for the Action on the Bombardment of Open Towns and the Restoration of Peace, July 23–24, 1938, File 189, RUP, IISH.
[65] Ibid.

respective homes to raise awareness of the atrocities in Spain and China and fundraise for medical and food assistance by taking part in an international solidarity week.

Nehru spoke on the third and final day of the conference, and he took the opportunity to inject an anti-imperialist agenda into a discourse primarily about peace and disarmament in the specific context of Spain and China. Nehru agreed with other delegates that the IPC should seek to "abolish war," but this task necessitated the removal of the "roots of war."[66] He argued that the immediate crisis was against fascist aggression, but that "we have long known it [fascism] under a different name – imperialism." He drove home the point: "There can be no world security founded on the subjection of colonial countries or on the continuance of imperialism ... If the aggressors of today have to be checked, the aggressors of yesterday have also to be called to account."[67] While Nehru expressed warm greetings and the solidarity of the INC with Spain and China, he also pointed out that Britain continues to bomb villages in India's North-West Frontier province, and this was no different than other tragedies that had become the focus of the IPC at the proceedings. For a truly authentic movement against aerial bombardment, Nehru argued, the IPC must call on Britain to cease its operations and relinquish its empire.

By the end of his sojourn, Nehru retained his commitment to the dual efforts of peace and anti-imperialism. Somewhere on a ship in the Arabian Sea returning to India, Nehru drafted a postscript for the new 1939 edition of *Glimpses of World History*. He wrote: "The growth of fascism during the last five years and its attack on every democratic principle and conception of freedom and civilization have made the defense of democracy the vital question today."[68] Fascism "seeks to crush democracy and freedom and dominate the world," while a "fascist international has grown up which not only carries on open, though undeclared wars, but is always intriguing in various countries and fomenting trouble so as to give it an opportunity to intervene."[69] Nehru added: "The present world conflict is not between communism and socialism on one hand and fascism on the other. It is between democracy and fascism, and all the

---

[66] Nehru, "The Bombing of Open Towns," Speech before IPC, Paris, on July 24, 1938 and reprinted for the Indian public in *Amrita Bazar Patrika* on August 3, 1938. *SWJN*, vol. 9, 85–89.

[67] Ibid.   [68] Nehru, *Glimpses*, 956.   [69] Ibid., 968.

real forces of democracy line up and become anti-fascists."[70] Despite this shift in emphasis from anti-imperialism to antifascism, the worldwide protagonists and logic remained consistent with the 1920s: socialists, communists, and nationalists from the colonized world were the forces "lining up" to become "anti-fascists." Moreover, Germany, Italy, and Japan represented international fascism, but they extended their power only with the help of imperialist "friends" such as Britain and France who "encourage fascist terrorism and the destruction of civilization and decency."[71] However, the United States stood out in the postscript as an exception to Nehru's now-familiar alignments. For the first time, Nehru began to see the USA as a possible ally and protector of political freedoms. He thought it might indeed stand for democracy and freedom during these turbulent times, but only time would tell.

Nehru added to this worldview the growing concern about Czechoslovakia. He was in Europe when news arrived that Britain and France had once again buckled and appeased Hitler rather than defend democracy against fascism in Czechoslovakia. This was simply another piece of evidence that fascism and imperialism were one and the same. He also traveled to Prague in a rare moment just before Germany engulfed Czechoslovakia within its empire. There, he employed Chatto's former colleague in the LAI and the Indian Information Bureau from the Berlin days, A. C. N. Nambiar, to be a correspondent in central Europe for his newly launched newspaper, *The National Herald*.

Nehru's European sojourn and engagement with the IPC and its British affiliated members had demonstrated the power of anti-imperialist ideas in his worldview even in the face of new conflicts in 1938. He remained clear in his view that vested interests, capitalists, imperialists, and fascists were the ultimate threat to world peace and equality. At the same time, he began to join fronts with imperialists and sympathizers to such vested interests. This cognitive dissonance was neither recognized nor deeply problematic for Nehru in this moment. Had he acknowledged the internal contradictions of his antifascist position, he might have foreseen the inevitable conflicts coming ahead as the world descended into a war that would pit fascism against imperialism. Nowhere was his inability to see contradiction and dissonance more clear than in the Spanish Civil War, a significant site for internationalist intervention and anti-imperialist imagination.

[70] Ibid., 956.   [71] Ibid., 970.

SPAIN

There were few events that warranted as much attention and anxiety among observers around the world as the Spanish Civil War, and Nehru made this event a focus of his political activism beginning in 1936. Nehru frankly admitted, "I am obsessed with the Spanish affair." The importance of the Spanish Civil War was simple for Nehru: "wrapped up with the fate of Spain is the fate of Europe, and wrapped up with the fate of Europe is the fate of the world."[72] Baldwin recalled a similar "obsessed" state over Spain. In hindsight, Baldwin argued that he knew already that if Franco, Mussolini, and Hitler were not stopped in Spain, then war would become inevitable. He concluded that: "Munich didn't trouble me nearly as much as Spain."[73] Even in his much later oral history, Baldwin recalled that Spain was a "cause close to my heart, and its tragedy is still poignant."[74]

The obsession with all things Spanish was not unique to Nehru or Baldwin, and the civil war quickly became a stage for foreign interventions on both sides of the fascist divide. Most historians agree that the civil war remains a tremendously complex event that cannot be reduced to a single narrative. Of works on the ramifications of the Spanish Civil War on global geopolitics, recent histories have benefited substantially from newly accessible archives in the former Soviet Union and the intelligence files of European powers that became involved in the Spanish affair. Even those considered "international histories" of the civil war, however, tend to focus on the common narratives of fascist and communist interventions by Germany, Italy, and the Soviet Union or the non-intervention policies of Britain or France.[75] Few have captured the importance of antifascism to those, especially in the colonized world, who had connected the aspirations of Republican Spain with the anti-imperialist struggle.

The scholarship on Nehru's campaign to support Republican Spain is scarce. Recently, Maria Framke has argued that Nehru's humanitarian aid program for Spain was his attempt to chart a legitimate place for India within the international community.[76] This is a compelling argument, and the essay is one of the first to consider in any depth Nehru and the Spanish Civil War. At the same time, this argument neglects the fact that the

---

[72] Nehru, "The Congress and the World Crisis," speech in Calcutta, November 5, 1936 and printed in *Amrita Bazar Patrika* on November 6, 1936. *SWJN*, vol. 7, 535–539.
[73] Baldwin, *Reminiscences*, 366.   [74] Ibid.
[75] For example, see Michael Alpert, *A New International History of the Spanish Civil War* (New York: Palgrave, 1994).
[76] Framke, "Political Humanitarianism in the 1930s," 63–81.

INC, through its stunning success in the general election and their self-governance in the ministerial period (1937–1939), already had become the internationally recognized heir to the British raj, while Nehru's travels to Europe in 1938 were accompanied by the widespread eagerness of many European state leaders and British politicians to meet him and discuss his plans for a postcolonial India. Nehru and the INC needed no "entrance ticket" to the world stage by 1938.[77] Moreover, for Nehru, India always had a critical place in the international community because of its geographic, economic, and strategic importance to the British Empire. Indian legitimacy in the world certainly would not have been a primary concern for Nehru and especially in his policies on Spain and China.

Instead, antifascism and peace, as extensions of anti-imperialist internationalism, were the primary forces driving Nehru's support for Republican Spain. For Nehru, the rush to aid Republican Spain was informed by his assumptions about the world rooted in the earlier anti-imperialist movement. It fit within a basic worldview that represented capitalism, imperialism, and fascism as different manifestations of the same world system of exploitation of the working classes and oppressed nations. Fascism was simply the latest offshoot of capitalism-imperialism. For Nehru, the heroes of the war were the Soviet Union-backed Republican government as a stalwart of anti-capitalism-imperialism-fascism. At the same time, he also criticized Britain for failing to intervene militarily on behalf of Republican Spain and against fascism. In doing so, his hawkish argument in regard to Spain ran counter to his advocacy of peace and the IPC in both India and the world. This incongruence was not specific to Nehru, but rather the entire peace movement was divided over the use of force against fascist and ultra nationalist aggression. Spain was the pre-eminent battleground for such tensions.

India's campaign to aid Republican Spain was the first to provide material support rather than expressions of solidarity. Nehru and Menon built the architecture for two institutional committees working for the Spanish cause, one from India and one from Britain. The India committee sought to raise awareness for the Spanish Republic and collect funds from political elites for medical and food supplies. It functioned as an ancillary to the foreign department of the INC, and Nehru and Lohia developed much of the ephemera and mechanisms for fundraising within India. In Britain, Menon established and chaired the Indian Committee for

---

[77] Ibid.

Food For Spain, a group that disseminated propaganda to Indians abroad, while at the same time facilitating the transfer of donations from Nehru's committee in India to Spain.

Nehru regularly argued that antifascism in Spain was an extension of their anti-imperialist struggle in India. In a pamphlet produced in London, Nehru wrote the foreword and framed the Spanish struggle as one against the dual forces of fascism and imperialism: "imperialism comes to the aid of fascism and seeks to starve the people of Spain into submission."[78] Thus, the duty of Indian people is to "recognise that the trial of Spain is equally theirs."[79] In another message to Menon's committee, reprinted in the Indian press, Nehru argued that "imperialism and fascism march hand in hand; they are blood brothers."[80] But this time Nehru added that the INC must do more than express solidarity, and instead offer "tangible support" in the form of medical and food assistance.[81] Nehru stressed that, "mere sympathy is not enough."[82] He added rather pointedly that Indian support was "consecrated to an ideal, to democracy, to freedom, for which we ourselves have suffered so much and will have to suffer still. And all those who care for freedom in this wide world of ours recognize us as their comrades and stand shoulder to shoulder with us."[83] For those less inclined to see anti-imperialism and antifascism as the foundation of Indian nationalism, Nehru made another appeal to distinguish India's foreign policy from the British. He argued that India's "ambassadors" were not British colonial administrators, but those leading missions to distribute food and medical supplies, and in doing so they have begun establishing "friendship and comradely ties between our people and theirs."[84]

A steady stream of supplies and troops flowed into Spain not only from India but also from around the world. In Paris, Münzenberg formed the Committee for the War Relief of Republican Spain several months before

---

[78] Pamphlet, *Spain! Why?* Foreword by Jawaharlal Nehru, Indian Committee for Food for Spain, undated (The India Committee for Food for Spain: London), copy available at the International Institute of Social History, Amsterdam, Netherlands.

[79] Ibid., 2.

[80] Nehru, "Fascism and Empire," March 27, 1937, message to the Spain-India Committee in London and reprinted in *The Hindu* on April 10, 1937. Reprinted in *SWJN*, vol. 8, 706–707.

[81] Nehru, "Appeal for Aid to Spain," published in *The Bombay Chronicle*, April 5, 1937, and reprinted in *SWJN*, vol. 8, 708–709.

[82] Nehru, handwritten statement sent to Lohia for press release, December 24, 1937, File 30–1936, AICC.

[83] Ibid., 3.   [84] Ibid., 5–6.

the Comintern and the Soviet Union officially announced their support for Spain. In the USA, the North American Committee to Aid Spanish Democracy (NACASD), which was affiliated with the LAWF, drew into the fold communists and noncommunists alike in the support of Republican Spain and against fascism.[85] Baldwin, who eagerly joined both the LAWF and the NACASD, remembered the Spanish aid committee as one with "a stormy sectarian career from the start" and that communists and noncommunists were an "uneasy team."[86] However, he admitted, the group did a lot of good by sending relief in the form of food, organizing film screenings, and fundraising on behalf of the Spanish ambassador, Dr. Fernando de Los Rios. Later, when the republic was overthrown and refugees from Spain poured into France, the sectarianism worsened over the next steps. Communists wanted to send aid to refugees with party affiliations only, while noncommunists sought to assist refugees regardless of political affiliation. This created a split in the movement along communist party lines. Still, the group, like so many popular fronts against fascism, existed until 1939.

Nehru's commitments to Spain intensified when he visited Barcelona and its contiguous battlefronts during his tour of Europe in 1938. Nehru landed in Genoa and traveled immediately to Marseille, where he spent an entire day getting paperwork together before flying to Barcelona. He arrived in the "beautiful city" of Barcelona where he described his five-night stay as one spent with the "accompaniment of aerial bombardment."[87] He visited orphanages for Spanish children, and the frontlines, where he spoke with Commander Enrique Líster and met members of the international brigade. He admired the resistance and resilience of the Spanish people, and he especially praised the leadership of Líster. In his reflections, he even toyed with the idea of staying and serving in the great cause: "something in me wanted to stay on this inhospitable looking hill-side which sheltered so much human courage, so much of what was worthwhile in life."[88] His reflections appear to have little evidence of a non-violent peace activist, and instead represented a strong admiration for belligerents and militancy. Later, when Nehru learned that many of the "gallant men" he met on his brief trip had fallen in the Battle of Ebro shortly after, he seemed haunted by this memory.

---

[85] Surprisingly little has been written about American humanitarian aid to Spain, although the literature on the international brigades is extensive. See Eric R. Smith, *American Relief Aid and the Spanish Civil War.*

[86] Baldwin, *Reminiscences*, 362–363.   [87] Nehru, *China, Spain and the War*, 64.

[88] Ibid., 77.

His experiences in Spain were significant for Nehru in that they crystalized several of his assumptions about the relationship between fascism
and imperialism that he had been formulating before his trip. The trip
strengthened his criticism of Britain in the case of Spain. He already had
argued that Britain remained "friendly to the development of fascist
powers," and the evidence was in its "shameful betrayal of Abyssinia"
and the "farce of non-intervention" in Spain. For Nehru, Britain may have
been a proponent of democracy at home and in domestic affairs, but its
foreign policy was imperialist and fascist. Britain failed to intervene
against Germany and Italy because its imperialism-fascism was consistent
with its European counterparts. If this was not so, according to Nehru,
Britain would have intervened on behalf of democracy and thus Republican
Spain. This was the "lesson" that "Spain teaches in her agony and through
her blood and suffering." India must stand with Spain "equally for the
ending of fascism and empire and all that they signify."[89]

Nehru refused to consider the implications of a war between imperialist
Britain and fascist Germany. When asked India's position in the event of
a war between Germany and Britain in an interview, Nehru dodged the
question. Instead, he restated that the British were drawing nearer and
nearer to fascism even if some competition and conflict remained between
Britain and Germany. When pressed again, Nehru added: "obviously, our
sympathies are not with fascism. We are also opposed to imperialism.
We've repeatedly stated that we won't be dragged into another war."[90]
In this moment, Nehru failed to consider the possibility that the war
danger might erupt along fault lines beyond the imperialist-fascist and
anti-imperialist-fascist axis. It was a question that would come back to
haunt Nehru and his comrades who shared in the belief that anti-
imperialism and antifascism were part of a global progressive project for
peace and equality of classes, races, and nations.

In his writings before and after his visit to Barcelona, Nehru imagined
the Spanish as comrades in arms. He appealed to Indians at home and in
Britain to support the Spanish Republic in word and deed. He collaborated with Menon on the first Indian aid program to send food and
medical assistance to the Spanish front. In doing so, he established several
priorities that often ran counter to some of his other positions on the

[89] Nehru, "Appeal for Aid to Spain," published in *The Bombay Chronicle*, April 5, 1937,
and reprinted in *SWJN*, vol. 8, 708–709.
[90] Nehru, "India and Britain" speech and interview at the Left Book Club in London, July 6,
1938. Reprinted in *Amrita Bazar Patrika* on July 13, 1938. *SWJN*, vol. 9, 54.

world in the 1930s. In the first place, he criticized the British and French for failing to intervene militarily against fascism and in support of Republican Spain. This argument, which fit within his worldview that blended anti-imperialism and antifascism, contended with his broader commitments to peace and even non-violence in India. Secondly, his anti-imperialist assumptions made impossible his reading of the forces increasingly pitting British imperialism against German and Italian fascism. These were crucial omissions that demonstrated the power of his core beliefs in anti-imperialism as the dominant narrative and conceptualization of the world. It was one he shared with a cohort of anti-imperialists from the League days who also saw in Spain the makings of a critical conflict that would determine the fate of a world divided along the fault lines of anti-imperialism and antifascism.

TRAVELING THE ANTI-IMPERIALIST WORLD IN THE 1930S: EGYPT AND CHINA

Much like his experiences in Spain and with the IPC, Nehru's travels to Egypt (1938) and China (1939) were tempered by anti-imperialism. Since the LAI days, Nehru had come to imagine an anti-imperialist geography, which comprised mainly Asian countries, although it also spanned from Egypt, northward to the Soviet Union, before moving eastward to China. Alongside India, these sites – Egypt, China, and the Soviet Union – were epicenters of anti-imperialism in the world. Specific events in the 1930s, such as the Italian invasion of Abyssinia and his encounters with Pan-Africanists in London, had prompted Nehru to belatedly include African countries in his anti-imperialist world. By the late 1930s, Nehru had his first opportunities to meet his anti-imperialist counterparts from Egypt and China in their respective countries and far from the meeting halls of European capitals. These travels to the anti-imperialist centers of Nehru's worldview had made a profound and lasting impression on the Indian leader.

Nehru's trips to Egypt and China demonstrate the possibilities and problems of his early engagements with anti-imperialist allies in the inter-war period. In both cases, Nehru met with leaders who were beleaguered by external conflict and domestic turmoil. His trip to Egypt brought him into conversation with Mustafa al-Nahhas Pasha (1879–1965) and other leaders of the Wafd Party. This nationalist group had been responsible for challenging the British occupation of Egypt, but the Wafd Party's popularity and appeal had peaked in the early 1920s. By 1938, rival parties had emerged and popular discontent with the Wafd Party was widespread. On the other hand, China was embattled in a war with Japan. Nehru's China itinerary concentrated on meetings with various KMT officials and General Chiang Kai-shek. While he intended to visit the communist party headquarters after receiving a personal invitation from Mao Zedong, the journey north proved too unsafe.[91] As a result, Nehru's encounters privileged the KMT and led him to view Chiang as the legitimate heir to China after the defeat of Japan.

Nehru failed to appreciate the complex and heterogeneous nature of politics in either China or Egypt. Instead, his travel accounts underscore how Indian, Chinese, and Egyptian nationalisms were one and the same. In doing so, he represented China, Egypt, and India as cohesive anticolonial nationalisms entrenched in local struggles against imperialist and fascist threats. Accordingly, the Wafd Party was the sole spokesman for Egypt, and the KMT for China. In each case, diversity within the local milieu was rendered irrelevant to the larger cause of nationalism. At the same time, these homogenized anticolonial movements shared in a joint international struggle against imperialism. Thus, Egypt, China, and India shared an imagined anti-imperialist past, present, and future.

His first diplomatic voyage to Egypt on behalf of the INC was unplanned. The Wafd Party contacted Nehru while he was en route to Europe in 1938. Historian Noor Khan has argued that Indian nationalists served as "teachers as well as compatriots" for Egyptian leaders in their attempts to establish an anticolonial nationalism and an anti-imperialist internationalism in the early twentieth century and especially since World War I.[92] Already by 1931, the Wafd Party leadership invited Gandhi to disembark and meet in Egypt while he was en route to India from London. British authorities on the ground dissuaded Gandhi from this, and the Indian leader never accepted the invitation. The Wafd Party found a more receptive audience in Nehru, given his internationalist credentials and fascination with Egypt since the Brussels Congress. He accepted the Wafd's invitation and disembarked in Suez, although confirmation of travel arrangements from the Egyptian leaders did not reach him in time. Nehru took matters into his own hands and arranged for a car to go to Cairo, where he first fulfilled a lifelong desire to visit the pyramids and the Sphinx. He remarked that both were "very impressive in the

---

[91] Nehru to Mao Zedong, July 11, 1939, *SWJN*, vol. 10, 75. The letter thanks Mao Zedong for his invitation to Nehru on May 24, 1939. The exchange was brief.

[92] Noor Khan, *Egyptian-Indian Nationalist Collaboration*, 4.

moonlight."[93] Wafd Party officials tracked him down there and arranged his meeting with Mustafa al-Nahhas.

Nehru found an ideal comrade and partner against imperialism in al-Nahhas. Their meeting in Cairo was the first of three occasions on which Nehru met him and other Wafd leaders in an attempt to develop stronger connections and collectively forge an international mobilization against imperialism from the periphery of empire. Both shared a secularist vision of nationalism rooted in an anticolonial struggle against the British. They also agreed that their struggles did not end with local independence, but rather were part of a global movement against imperialism world-wide. In his reports and letters, Nehru frequently represented the Wafd Party's movement for Egypt as "part of the great world struggle for freedom."[94] Echoing these sentiments, al-Nahhas Pasha wrote to Nehru shortly after their first encounter to express "profound joy" in meeting Nehru. He hoped that their encounter would prompt stronger "coordina-tion" between Egyptians and Indians in their "common struggle for freedom."[95]

Nehru and al-Nahhas quickly developed some concrete strategies for closer cooperation in the international struggle. These included a regular exchange of official ephemera and newsletters in an attempt to stay informed of the other's movement. The more significant and ambitious project was the dispatch of formal delegates to their respective annual congresses.[96] The Wafd Party was successful in sending a delegation in March to the 1939 INC annual sessions, although the onset of war prevented the INC from sending its delegation to Egypt. The Wafd visit in March 1939 also prompted Nehru once again to stress the Indian and Egyptian "bond" in the past and their shared struggle against imperialism in the present.[97]

The world situation also retained a pre-eminent place in these discus-sions, and Nehru urged al-Nahhas to commit the Wafd Party to an internationalism based on peace, antifascism, and anti-imperialism.

---

[93] Nehru, letter to INC Secretary on board SS Biancamano en route to Europe, June 11–13, 1938, *SWJN*, vol. 9, 11.

[94] Ibid., 11.

[95] Nahhas Pasha to Nehru, August 2, 1938 (Translated from French), File G60-1938, AICC.

[96] Nehru sent his minutes of their meetings to al-Nahhas in a letter from London dated October 1, 1938. *SWJN*, vol. 9, 175–179.

[97] Nehru, Farewell message to Wafd delegation, Allahabad, March 27, 1939. The delegation was led by the Wafd's Mahmood Bey. Al-Nahhas did not visit. *SWJN*, vol. 9, 246–248.

He wrote to al-Nahhas that India "had taken sides" in the struggles in Abyssinia, Spain, China, and other countries where "nationalist struggles for independence were going on." He added that the INC "had gone further and opposed fascism and generally but vaguely allied ourselves with the non-fascist forces."[98] In particular, Nehru noted the IPC as the institution that brought Indians "nearer to the progressive and anti-fascist forces of the world."[99] When Nehru stopped in Egypt on his return trip to India from Europe, he once again appealed to al-Nahhas to consider channeling his internationalist efforts through the IPC. He argued that in the case of India, "we associate ourselves with this organization because we believe in world peace and freedom." He added in a now-familiar argument that India "made it clear that peace in our opinion can only be established on a basis of freedom and anti-imperialism, imperialism, like fascism, being itself a negation of peace or freedom."[100]

Not all of the content of their talks was without tension and potential conflict. In reading below the surface of Nehru's letters and minutes from their meetings, there were several points of contention underpinning Indo-Egyptian comradeship. The first issue concerned the question of Muslims in the Indian nationalist movement. By 1938, the Muslim League had made great politic gains, although M. A. Jinnah had yet to deliver his demands for a separate homeland for Muslim minorities in India. Mustafa al-Nahhas was keen to raise the issue in his meetings with Nehru. When Nehru later wrote to al-Nahhas about the issue, he was careful to reiterate his point that the INC "built up a powerful platform of unity in India and among our most noted leaders and colleagues there are many Moslems."[101] In a true anti-imperialist fashion, he added that the tensions between Muslims and the INC had been "accentuated by the efforts of British imperialism to create divisions," and that the end of colonialism in India would do much to unite Indians regardless of religion. He also encouraged al-Nahhas and the Wafd Party to reach out to influential Muslims in India and remind them that imperialism sought to divide them from their Hindu counterparts in India and that they should instead "favour unity."[102] Given the Wafd Party's commitment to a secular nationalism and anti-imperialism, Nehru's line of thinking was satisfactory and the Muslim question did little to impact Indian–Egyptian relations in this moment.

---

[98] Nehru to al-Nahhas, October 1, 1938 from London, *SWJN*, vol. 9, 175–179.
[99] Ibid. [100] Ibid. [101] Ibid. [102] Ibid.

In his private reports to the INC, Nehru revealed a second tension bubbling below the surface that offered a rare glimpse of recognition that Egyptian nationalism was not as homogenous and compatible with India as he had publicly stated. The report, marked "not for publication," discussed at length the recent defeat of the Wafd Party in the Egyptian general election in April 1938, only months before his first visit.[103] Historically, the Wafd Party had been responsible for opposition to British occupation since the Great War and had worked to create a constitutional monarchy for Egypt. By 1938, however, their influence was waning. Their loss in April of that year came with widespread speculation that the palace, led by a monarchy hostile to the Wafd Party, had worked with the British to fix the elections in order to disempower al-Nahhas and his party. Rather than agree with this speculative argument as further evidence of British imperialist oppression, Nehru argued in his private report that the Wafd Party had been responsible for their losses. He wrote that the "real reason" was that the party lacked "organized mass support" and "did little or nothing for the peasantry" during their years in power.[104]

This interpretation demonstrated Nehru's belief that an authentic nationalist movement, in India as well as in Egypt, had to be built around anti-imperialism as a special blend of nationalism and socialism. The indictment of the Wafd Party for neglecting the masses served as both a criticism of his Egyptian comrades and a cautionary tale for his INC colleagues. The Wafd Party, like the INC, consisted of an elite class of professionals and lawyers seeking constitutional reforms and greater self-determination. Overtime, the party came to represent resistance to the monarchy and British occupation. For Nehru, this trajectory was similar to the Indian narrative in which the INC progressed from demanding moderate constitutional reforms to calling for complete independence. At the same time, the Wafd Party failed to incorporate the masses into their movement, and this made it distinct from the INC since the advent of Gandhi's leadership.

For Nehru, socialism or a "socialistic outlook" was at the crux of the difference. He believed that independence meant freedom from British imperialism and from emergent indigenous capitalism. This necessitated a nationalist movement that sought political independence from the British, and at the same time sought social freedom for the masses of workers and peasants across the subcontinent. Nehru had frankly explained to his

[103] Nehru, letter to INC Secretary, June 11–13, 1938, *SWJN*, vol. 9, 12–13. [104] Ibid.

Egyptian hosts: "Without the masses we were helpless and even independence meant to us the removal of the poverty and distress of our people and raising them to higher levels."[105] This stood in stark distinction to the Wafd Party in which, according to Nehru, "there is no real agrarian movement, no labour movement at all (trade unions are not permitted by law), and the whole outlook of the Wafd has been moderate and somewhat primitive."[106]

Nehru's anti-imperialist critique of Egypt was not available to a wider public. Instead, Nehru publicly emphasized and even exaggerated the common bonds of Indians and Egyptians in their struggle against imperialism. Upon his return to India in October 1938, Nehru spoke at length on Egypt in an interview reprinted in *The Hindu*. His comments on the Wafd Party loss in the election were revealing. Rather than criticize his Egyptian nationalist counterparts for their failures to engage the masses as he had done in his confidential report, Nehru supported the rumor wherein some argued that the elections had been fraudulent because of British imperialist intrigue. In his public statement, Nehru concluded that the elections "were a manipulated affair." He further argued that Egypt's "so-called independence" was no different than colonialism in India: "Egypt is more or less like a big Indian state." On the Wafd Party, Nehru concluded that it was "as popular as the Indian National Congress."[107]

The difference in the public statement and the INC report reflected clearly the tensions between Nehru's recognition of the political realities in Egypt and his desire to see the Wafd Party as the INC's counterpart and comrade against imperialism. In Egypt, Nehru had in some ways encountered a mirror reflection of India. Both the Wafd Party and the INC were led by elites, although Gandhi had done much to make contact with the masses. Still, as Nehru's own struggles to define a social program in India suggested, the INC had not committed to the kind of socialist agenda he sought to implement either. The Wafd Party served as a cautionary tale for his INC comrades to consider, and he used it as such by sending a message that their failure to tackle the difficult questions of social equality would lead to their failure at the ballot box as well. On the world stage and before a wider audience, however, Egypt had come to represent a significant site in his anti-imperialist worldview, so much so that he could not publicly admit differences between the INC and Wafd.

---

[105] Ibid., 14.   [106] Ibid., 13.

[107] Nehru, Interview to the Press in Bombay, November 17, 1938 and reprinted in *The Hindu* on November 18, 1938. *SWJN*, vol. 9, 206.

Nehru's journey to China, taken several months later in August 1939, reveals even more clearly the significance of anti-imperialism in filtering the Indian leader's encounters and experiences. More so than Egypt, China was a country that came to occupy a critical place in the Brussels Congress and the LAI, and also in Nehru's geography of anti-imperialism. Since 1927, Nehru had imagined India and China as comrades with a shared cultural past, anti-imperialist present, and postcolonial future. By the 1930s, Nehru organized campaigns in India for China. Among these was a "China Day" on January 9, 1938, when mass demonstrations against the Japanese invasions took place and donations were collected in an effort to send medical assistance. Nehru also launched a boycott of Japanese goods, which was particularly challenging given the tremendous saturation of Japanese and British goods in the Indian market. Finally, in 1938, the INC fulfilled a longtime project to send a medical ambulance to China. They had attempted a similar project in 1927 in the context of the civil war, but the British prevented it. In 1938, the INC sponsored and facilitated the dispatch of an ambulance and Indian doctors to assist in the struggle against the Japanese.

His brief sojourn, lasting thirteen days, proved decisive in shaping Nehru's assumptions about China, ones that privileged nationalism over communism, specifically likened the struggles of the KMT to the INC, and articulated the importance of Indian and Chinese solidarity in the anti-imperialist struggle worldwide. This required a set of mental gymnastics in reducing the discord between Chinese communism and nationalism as a means to represent China as a homogenous and cohesive nation like the INC saw India. Nehru also engaged in creative interpretations of the KMT in order to fit it within an idiom of anti-imperialism and recast it as a mirror image of the INC. In both efforts, Nehru overlooked evidence to suggest otherwise. In other words, the China trip was formative in crystalizing assumptions Nehru had about India's neighbor to the East as an anti-imperialist comrade even when the realities on the ground proved contrary.

The visit to China was risky and brought Nehru into the depths of war and the underground bunkers of a country under heavy aerial bombardment by the Japanese. Many Indian colleagues expressed concern for Nehru's safety given that China was ground zero for military conflict in Asia. Nevertheless, Nehru coordinated his trip through two means: the Chinese consulate in Calcutta and the Chinese Embassy in London. For the latter, Nehru worked exclusively with Menon to facilitate his visa documentation, passage from India to China, and his agenda upon his arrival.[108] The trip was prompted entirely by Nehru's longtime dream to travel to China, and only after he expressed his desire to go did Chiang Kai-shek and Mao Zedong extend their invitation.

The actual journey was remarkable and demonstrated the truly global dimensions of the late 1930s world.[109] He traveled by air on French and German carriers and stopped along the way in Akyab, Bangkok, Hanoi, and Kunming before reaching Chungking. At each stop, Nehru encountered small crowds of Indians eager to catch a glimpse of the leader. His landing in Chungking was an occasion to remember as well. High-ranking KMT officials and a representative of the medical unit dispatched by the INC met Nehru at the aerodrome in a ceremony in which India's unofficial anthem, "Bande Mataram," filled the air. The staging of his arrival appealed to his strong sense that the KMT and the INC were comrades in their struggles against the oppression of both the Japanese and the British, respectively.

Nehru's reflections on his trip, published at first in newspapers and then as part of his book, China, Spain and the War, offered familiar platitudes that praised the historical and contemporary importance of China to Asia and the world. According to Nehru, this was a China at once "rooted in her culture" from ancient times and at the same time "shedding the lethargy and weaknesses of ages" to rise as a power "strong and united, modern and with a human outlook."[110] In another passage, Nehru admired China as a "race" that was "wise and profound, deep in the lore of its own great past, but also a vital people, full of life and energy, adapting themselves to modern conditions."[111] It was this latter condition of adaptation to modernity that "impressed" Nehru and made him certain that a "people with this vitality and determination, and the strength of the ages behind them, could never be crushed."[112]

Even before his arrival, Nehru wrote enthusiastically that he was going to witness a "new" and "rising" China.[113] Nehru characterized this "new" China as "strong and united" under the leadership of the KMT and Chiang Kai-shek, who "embodies in himself the unity of China and her determination to free herself."[114] After arriving, Nehru argued that the "West was important because it dominated world politics today ... but, the East and

---

[108] The details of the arrangements can be found in his correspondence with Menon in London and the Consul-General of China, SWJN, vol. 10, 73–79.
[109] For the journey to China, see Nehru, China, Spain and the War, 29–35.
[110] Nehru, China, Spain and the War, 11–15.   [111] Ibid.   [112] Ibid.   [113] Ibid.
[114] Ibid., 23.

especially China, was equally, if not more, important for us, as in some respects there was an amazing similarity of problems" shared by India and China.[115] In a candid turn in the text, Nehru cautioned not to "generalize too much and seek similarities where there are none." But, equally important, one must "look below the surface" for some similarities and learn from one another. The similarities were many. Both countries sought the development of national unity in the face of an external adversary. For China, it is the unity of the nation, both nationalist and communist, in an attempt to defeat Japanese imperialism. For India, nationalism, and in particular the unity of Hindus and Muslims, alone can overthrow British imperialism. Already, Nehru had been quite dismissive of communal tensions within India by arguing that these would disappear once the British quit India. He projected this same dismissiveness onto the Chinese context in 1939 and suggested that China would unite nationally after Japan's defeat. In hindsight, of course, Nehru's prediction for both nationalisms could not have been more inaccurate.

Beyond political struggle, Nehru saw the economic and social challenges of India and China as historically rooted and similar. He argued that both suffer from the remnants of feudalism and the failure to industrialize at the same time as the West. Thus, for Nehru, the present struggle, one that was often violent, was for India and China to both industrialize and reform the existing and ancient systems of land use, agricultural production, and social inequalities stemming from such prevailing conditions. At no point in his journals and publications did he consider in depth the gulf that separated communists from the KMT. Rather, he concluded that "China is the symbol today of magnificent courage in the struggle for freedom, of a determination which has survived untold misery and unparalleled disaster, of unity before a common foe."[116]

While most of his representations of the KMT were filled primarily with superfluous praises, Nehru offered a few moments in his travel diary (which he later published) in which he questioned the policies and practices of his Chinese comrades. Much like his impression of Egypt, Nehru expressed reservations about the KMT as a party representing political freedom for all. For example, his impressions after meeting with high-ranking officials such as Dr. Chu Chia Hwa, the Secretary-General of party, were that the KMT "was not a very democratic body, though it calls itself democratic."[117] The comment was made inconspicuously and buried in a lengthy text on his travels, but it stands as a stark contradiction to

---

[115] Ibid.   [116] Ibid., 18.   [117] Ibid., 50.

his construction of China as an anti-imperialist comrade destined to bring national and social freedom to its country and then the world. In another discreet remark, Nehru wondered what the conditions of underground bunkers for the masses of Chungking were like. He was uncomfortable in the bunkers, which he visited nightly, and likened the experience to being a "rat in a hole."[118] Even so, he recognized that he had a privileged place in the bunkers of the foreign minister and later Chiang Kai-shek himself. He contemplated the conditions of other bunkers in a revealing passage: "If this was the condition of the favoured few, I wonder what was happening to the tens of thousands who must be crowding into the public dug-outs."[119]

The passages were minor dimensions to a larger text that praised the KMT and China while overlooking any evidence that the nationalists were perhaps not as progressive and anti-imperialist as he imagined. These rare glimpses demonstrate Nehru's doubt and uncertainty in his parallels between the INC and its Chinese nationalist counterpart. Here again, his writings on China offer an important window into the ways in which a dominant set of ideas about the world filtered his experiences on the ground and encounters with anti-imperialist comrades outside of India. That he publically praised the KMT for its power to unify the Chinese people and embody a set of ideas about nationalism and anti-imperialism was central to this, while the KMT weaknesses were marginalized altogether.

In his discussions with Chiang, Nehru suggested in person, and later in writing, a seven-point program for further ties between China and India. These were similar to the ones Nehru suggested to al-Nahhas, although he added more specific points for Chiang. The program included exchanges of news services, experts to study agrarian problems, university professors and students, and specialists in the fields of trade unionism, cooperatives, and women's movements. Beyond this, the KMT and INC should maintain direct contact through their foreign offices and whenever possible send delegations to their respective annual congresses. Finally, and most ambitiously, Nehru proposed that the KMT and the INC adopt a common policy on Europe and the world. Once the war was settled, Nehru argued that India and China needed to be advocates for Asia. Any world order should be based on a "free China and a free India, and must be based on the liquidation of imperialism and the suppression of aggression." In addition, Nehru argued that any peace should provide assurances that an Anglo–Japanese agreement would not harm Chinese freedom and that the

[118] Ibid., 48.   [119] Ibid., 47.

British would quit India. Here again, Nehru suggested that the KMT also consider joining the IPC, and that perhaps India and China should create a regional branch of the organization in order to articulate an Asian position within the peace movement.[120]

Without much warning, Nehru was called back to India urgently after he received word on September 3, 1939, that the British Empire was at war with Nazi Germany. The INC requested his immediate return so that he could lead the debate over India's policy on the world situation. Nehru's hasty departure cut short a trip that may have included a meeting with Mao Zedong and the Indian medical unit sponsored by the INC, as well as a road trip from China to Burma. A disappointed Nehru left immediately from Chungking by air and reached India on September 5. Despite his desire to see the frontline and meet Mao, Nehru's greatest disappointment in leaving early was his inability to see Madame Sun Yat-Sen in Hong Kong.[121] Only in a belated interview in late September, well after his return, did Nehru express some remorse at not visiting Mao's base, although his disappointment was over his inability to see the work of the Indian medical unit in action and to explore a part of China very different than Chungking. While he added, as an afterthought, the desire "to meet some of the leaders of the 8th Route Army who had invited me especially," Nehru never mentioned Mao by name.[122] No doubt this laid important groundwork for future tensions between Mao's China and Nehru's India. One might even speculate that the later Sino–Indian split was rooted in this early rebuff on Nehru's part in 1939.

Once he returned home to India, Nehru confronted a number of critics of his positions on China and the international situation as it related to Asia. Some, such as Rabindranath Tagore, had written Nehru to ask that he also visit Japan. But it was his fallout with Subhas Chandra Bose on India's position in relation to China and Asia that figured prominently in Nehru's writing and thinking about the world in the late 1930s. In a statement for the *National Herald*, his paper based in Allahabad, Nehru defended his worldview. Although the statement did not mention Subhas Chandra Bose specifically, it began by describing a "friend" that had written a letter criticizing Nehru's attachment to "lost causes" such as

---

[120] Nehru, "A Note on the Development of Contacts between China and India," August 29, 1939, *SWJN*, vol. 10, 101–108.
[121] Letters between Nehru and Madame Sun expose the disappointment on both sides that the meeting did not take place. See Nehru to Madame Sun, October 13, 1939; and Madame Sun to Nehru, November 15, 1939, Correspondence Files, vol. 95, JN Papers.
[122] Nehru, Interview, *The Hindu*, September 24, 1939, *SWJN*, vol. 10, 114.

Manchuria, Abyssinia, Czechoslovakia, and Spain. His "friend" suggested that Nehru always "seemed to be on the wrong side."[123] The letter he referenced was from Bose, who wrote Nehru in March 1939 and argued that "foreign policy is a realistic affair to be determined largely from the point of view of a nation's self-interest." He added that Nehru's championing of "lost causes" such as antifascism did little for India.[124] Months later, Nehru made public his differences with Bose when he argued that India should take a "longer perspective" and recognize that shared values and solidarities against oppression and imperialism would prevail even if the rise of fascist power and war lurked on the horizon. Nehru concluded: "I am unrepentant of my past and present attachments" for Republican Spain, Czechoslovakia, and China, for each represent the "values for which we have labored in India."[125]

Most historians have considered the split between Bose and Nehru in early 1939 within the context of INC politics and rarely in terms of their conflicting worldviews. Within the INC, Subhas Chandra Bose announced that he planned to run for a second term as president of the INC in 1939.[126] His decision went against the wishes of Gandhi, who had already handpicked a candidate for the position. However, unlike Nehru, Bose was willing to challenge Gandhi and the rightwing within the INC, and he moved forward with his candidacy. To further aggravate the situation, Bose ran on a platform that openly called for the leftwing of the congress to mobilize against the rightwing of the INC. Ultimately, Bose won the presidential election, but Gandhi and his congress allies, among them Sardar Patel, Rajendra Prasad, and J. B. Kripalani, resigned from the working committee in a successful attempt to pressure Bose to withdraw.

Nehru had been caught in the middle, at first trying to broker a compromise between Gandhi and Bose, but ultimately forced to choose whether to support Gandhi in calling for Bose to resign or whether to support Bose and the left. At first, Nehru wavered on the issue and wrote to Bose: "I cannot stomach this kind of politics and I have kept absolutely aloof from them for these many years."[127] But with Gandhi threatening withdrawal from the congress, and national unity threatened with his

---

[123] Nehru, *China, Spain and the War*, 16.
[124] Bose to Nehru, March 28, 1939, reprinted in Jawaharlal Nehru, *A Bunch of Old Letters* (London: Asia Publishing House, 1960), 334–335.
[125] Nehru, *China, Spain and the War*, 17.
[126] On Bose's history see Bose, *His Majesty's Opponent.*
[127] Nehru to Bose, February 4, 1939, *SWJN*, vol. 9, 483.

departure, Nehru refused to support Bose. In the end, Bose resigned from the congress and formed a new front, the Forward Bloc, first working within the INC and later in opposition to it. Retaining his faith in congress unity, Nehru condemned the Forward Bloc in May 1939: "I consider it improper to weaken the great organization like the Congress by the formation of separate groups. Such a course would not be in the interests of the country."[128]

The split, however, had a significant and unexplored internationalist dimension, and by 1939, Nehru's antifascism could no longer be reconciled with Bose's interest in aligning India with fascist powers for the cause of independence. Although both were internationalists and leftists, Bose loathed Nehru's antifascist framework for understanding the world and India's place within it. For Nehru, Bose's alliance with Nazi Germany, Fascist Italy, and Imperialist Japan was anathema to the anti-imperialist and antifascist framework for India and the world that he had crafted since 1927.

Nehru's interwar connections with China and Egypt strengthened this position and remained significant for many reasons. Nehru's highly successful talks and meetings, which culminated with the Wafd Party dispatching a delegation to the INC annual session in early 1939, created early connections between India and Egypt. The encounters produced some ambivalence in Nehru's thinking about Egypt. On the one hand, his meetings produced strong evidence of the differences between the Wafd and the INC, especially on the issue of representing the masses and social equality within Egypt. On the other hand, the dialogue with al-Nahhas strengthened Nehru's conceptualization of Egypt as an important anti-imperialist ally internationally. There is no doubt that his earliest encounters with Egyptian leaders paved the way for strong postcolonial ties between Egypt and India long before Gamal Abdel Nassar emerged as a possible leader and created with Nehru the nonaligned project of the 1960s.

Nehru's connections with China in 1939 also proved ambivalent and its legacies more problematic. By the time of Nehru's visit, two contra-distinctive Chinas competed for hegemony of the country.[129] Since 1927,

---

[128] Nehru, Speech May 21, 1939, in Kanpur, *SWJN*, vol. 9, 547.
[129] Ramachandra Guha has considered in some depth the relationship between Nehru and China after 1947. His brief discussion of Nehru's interwar encounters with China does not take up the importance of the difference between his communist and nationalist engagements. See his *India after Gandhi: The History of the World's Largest Democracy* (New York: Ecco, 2007).

China remained central to LAI politics: first as the model for a united front in the more flexible and inclusive days of the anti-imperialist movement, and later as the most significant evidence for communists that nationalist leaders like Chiang would always betray the masses and the revolution. Nehru largely ignored the nuances of these turns in anti-imperialist positions primarily because China also fit into an Indianized worldview of anti-imperialism that privileged the Sino–Indian relationship in history and in contemporary events. Since the Brussels Congress, Nehru unquestionably accepted China as an anti-imperialist ally sharing with India the great struggle against European colonial dominance in Asia. The neglect that there were two very different Chinese leaders and regimes vying for power over the country and against foreign intervention was not because Nehru was naïve; rather, it didn't fit within a cohesive anti-imperialist worldview that shaped his ideas and policies since 1927. The active overlooking of such differences and privileging of solidarity with the Chinese, regardless of nationalist or communist persuasions, was an essential aspect of interwar internationalism. Nehru's short trip, abbreviated by British declaration of war against Germany in September 1939, hastened his departure and prevented him from meeting Mao. Thus, Nehru's interwar conceptualization was rooted entirely in his engagement with Chinese nationalists rather than communists.

CONCLUSION

Even in the late 1930s, Nehru continued to see the world through an anti-imperialist perspective. He even extended his worldview to include antifascists alongside the special blend of nationalists, socialists, and communists, and this led him to make expressions of solidarity and to organize material support for places such as Spain, China, and Abyssinia. Nehru joined the IPC as the premier vehicle in the global struggle against fascism. In his travels, Nehru strengthened his relationship with counterparts in Egypt and China and imagined them as anti-imperialist allies on a world stage. In all of these ventures, he worked either in conversation with or in parallel to many other anti-imperialists with whom he shared in a vision for a future world of political freedom and social justice for all.

At the same time, Nehru's projects in this period required greater flexibility than ever before. His peace activism led him to support interstate structures that enabled and empowered imperialism and inequality worldwide. The Spanish aid program prompted him to take a firm stance on antifascism, but it also necessitated him to cast aside peace and anti-war activism in favor of militarization against fascist aggression. Similar tensions existed in his engagement with Egypt and China, where his anti-imperialist ideas blinded Nehru to the nuanced differences between India and his comrades abroad. While anti-imperialist internationalism had served Nehru well in the late 1920s, it became more difficult to reconfigure and remake as the world of the 1930s presented new challenges. The onset of World War II, explored in the concluding chapter, brought this internationalist moment to a close.

7

The War and the Fate of Anti-Imperialist Internationalism

In October 1939, only a month after Britain declared war against Germany, Baldwin wrote Nehru with his praise for *Glimpses of World History*. He read it with "vivid interest" and agreed with it on all accounts. Baldwin characterized the new war as "the most devastating transformation in history – with all the risks of coming out not on the side of world federation, disarmament and free trade as the conditions of stable peace"; instead, it might lead to the "imposition of new autocracies."[1] On a lighter note, Baldwin reminded Nehru: "Perhaps you don't realize what a world figure you are, or how vital is the Indian struggle in American eyes."[2] Nehru's grim reply to Baldwin in January 1940 revealed his pessimism and anxieties about the future of India and the world: "It is very gratifying to learn that one is a world figure, but the world grows progressively less worth figuring in. Everything seems to go wrong and all our fine idealisms become tarnished. Still I suppose one must carry on."[3]

Nehru's comments about a world "less worth figuring in" emblemized the tremendous disillusionment for many anti-imperialists in 1939. Few were surprised by the commencement of war, but comrades such as Nehru imagined a different set of circumstances leading to it. By March, the Spanish Republic had collapsed and a widespread refugee crisis swept over much of Europe. Shortly after, the appeasement of Hitler and the handing over of Czechoslovakia became the final act before German troops launched a full-scale invasion of Europe and the world plunged into another global war. Rather than a struggle between the Soviet Union and imperialist powers, however, the war pitted fascists against imperialists. These realities challenged the dichotomous construction of the world

[1] Baldwin to Nehru, October 12, 1939, Box 7, Folder 30, Baldwin Papers.
[2] Baldwin to Nehru, December 11, 1939, Box 7, Folder 30, Baldwin Papers.
[3] Nehru to Baldwin, January 5, 1940, Box 7, Folder 30, Baldwin Papers.

that had informed Nehru's worldview, one in which fascism and imperialism were "blood brothers."

Equally significant, the nonaggression pact between Hitler and Stalin, signed even before Britain and France declared war against Germany, was the "bombshell" heard around the anti-imperialist world that ruptured solidarities between communists and noncommunists forever.[4] The Soviet's reversal on antifascism and subsequent invasion of Finland forced even the staunchest anti-imperialist supporters of the Soviet Union to reconsider. Most anti-imperialists had ignored the evidence of Stalin's purges, as Nehru had in *Glimpses*, and actively forged solidarities with communists well beyond the splits of the third period in 1929. But the pact and the war made impossible the "blend" of communism and noncommunism for internationalist causes after 1939.

World War II did as much to dismantle anti-imperialist internationalism as the Great War did to create the environment that gave rise to it. Since 1927, Nehru had accepted a fundamental set of ideas about the world, ones that amalgamated unlikely and often-conflicting ideas. These ideas called upon a blending of nationalism with socialism, a worldview in which anti-imperialists including the Soviet Union and the colonies had collectively sought to challenge imperialism, and an awareness that an imperialist war danger was an ever-present threat to peace. After 1939, however, the world witnessed the hardening of distinctions between communist and noncommunist, which made impossible the anti-imperialist blending so emblematic of the interwar years. The aftermath of the war, and especially the Cold War, would ensure that anti-imperialist solidarities remained an artifact of the past. Not until the collapse of the Soviet Union became a distant memory would it be possible to recover the significant history of these comrades against imperialism who courageously worked for peace and freedom across and through the categories of communism, socialism, and anticolonial nationalism.

The war also prompted a new geopolitical milieu that privileged the nation-state and the interstate system as the dominant structures of the postwar world. The United Nations was central in making this possible, while waves of decolonization first in Asia and then in Africa advanced the rise of nation-states as the successors to colonial regimes. India was among the first colonies to achieve independence in 1947. The primacy of nation-states after 1945 precluded the possibilities for leaders from the former colonial world to construct anti-imperialist solidarities in ways

---

[4] Baldwin, *Reminiscences*, 359–360.

that interwar activists had done in the past. Instead, their relationships after the war would be predicated on negotiating difference and establishing interstate relations rather than internationalist solidarity.

This concluding chapter accounts for the demise of anti-imperialist comradeship in two acts. First, it moves away from Nehru's story and considers the circumstances leading to World War II that irreversibly closed the possibilities for "blending" communism and noncommunism. In particular, it traces the closing of the LAI and IPC, as well as the last days of Münzenberg and Chatto, neither of whom lived to see the end of World War II. Their deaths were symbolic of the wider closures that upended interwar anti-imperialism by 1939. Second, I return to Nehru's history and consider how the achievement of India's independence served not as a step toward global anti-imperialism as he had imagined, but rather became the primary obstacle in creating internationalist solidarities with the wider world after 1947. In particular, it focuses on Nehru's participation in the Asian-African Conference in Bandung, Indonesia, in 1955, a conference widely considered to be the sequel of the Brussels Congress. Instead, I argue that the Bandung Conference marked the triumph of the nation-state and interstate relations in the arena of Afro-Asian politics, and it stood in contradistinction to the anti-imperialist internationalism of the interwar years. In Bandung, newly minted leaders of former colonies answered to nation-state imperatives and Cold War obligations rather than universal calls for anti-imperialism.

THE FATE OF ANTI-IMPERIALISM AND NEHRU'S COMRADES

In May 1937, Reginald Bridgeman announced the closure of the LAI in a letter underscoring the "paramount importance" of the "broadening out" of the League's work to include the struggle against fascism.[5] This was best done by working for the cause of anti-imperialism not as a separate League, but rather within broader movements that included trade unions, labor movements, and peace campaigns with a wider base of members and unity. The closure came as no surprise to members and former comrades. Already, the LAI was experiencing an alarming rate of attrition and inactivity, and

---

[5] League against Imperialism secretariat to members, May 7, 1937, File DBN 25/2, Bridgeman Papers. The letter also announced the opening of a new organization, the Colonial Information Bureau (CIB), which sought to continue publicizing anti-imperialist literature on a smaller scale. The CIB existed until 1944.

only five members served on the British LAI executive committee by 1935. At the same time, Nehru and most of his colleagues had joined peace movements and sought to incorporate anti-imperialism into their new internationalist projects of the late 1930s. Former LAI comrades no doubt welcomed Bridgeman's call to work with other movements to further the cause of "colonial peoples in their struggle against exploitation," as well as "democratic rights and freedom" for all.[6]

The closure in 1937, however, marked more than a transition from anti-imperialism to peace; instead, it foreshadowed the demise of a broader internationalist moment that had come to shape Nehru's ideas about India and the world for more than a decade. Nearly all of the institutions associated at various moments with the work of anti-imperialism, anti-capitalism, and peace had collapsed within a few years of the LAI closure. The IPC officially closed in 1941. Of course, the premise of the entire movement was the strengthening of the League of Nations, an organization that did not survive the onset of war either. Even the dissolution of the Comintern took place shortly after, in 1943.

For comrades such as Münzenberg and Chatto, the war uprooted and ultimately ended their lives. In the years before Hitler's ascension to power, both had led movements that were dependent on transnational and international spaces of sedition. They funneled people, propaganda, and funds throughout the world, even under the watchful eye of European colonial intelligence and the nation-states in which they operated. They were most effective because they worked across state boundaries and existed in a space that was anti-imperialist and anti-capitalist without circumscribing themselves to the antagonistic party politics of either side. Their in-between and dubious positions, without clear citizenship and working at the margins of Comintern orthodoxy, was what made the LAI possible in Berlin and antifascist activism possible in Paris. Yet, because they did not neatly fit into the orthodoxies and silos of nations, states, or party politics, they also became the most vulnerable when Hitler and Stalin unleashed the powers of their state military machinery on the world and those who did not subscribe to their narrow and rigid views. While Hitler's regime forced both Chatto and Münzenberg to flee Germany, it was Stalin and the Soviet Union that ultimately had a hand in the deaths of the LAI's founders.

Chatto vanished from the historical record in 1937. What little we know about his years in the Soviet Union is located in the P. C. Joshi

[6] Ibid., 2.

Archives on Contemporary History at Jawaharlal Nehru University in New Delhi. Joshi (1907–1980) was an influential and lifelong communist in India, and his archive is a recovery project that houses endangered collections of communist and leftist papers including the foundational documents of the Communist Party of India (CPI). The files on Chatto are significant to documenting the final years of his life in the Soviet Union from 1933 to 1937, and include Joshi's interviews with Chatto's romantic partner in Leningrad, Lidiya Eduardonvna Karunovskaya.

After leaving Berlin for the Soviet Union in 1932, Chatto settled into academic life as a faculty member of the Institute of Ethnography at the Academy of Sciences in Leningrad. He quickly rose through the ranks and became the Head of the Department of India, Indonesia, and the Far East. At the institute, Chatto met Karunovskaya, an Indonesian specialist who became his professional and romantic partner. Karunovskaya characterized Chatto as a prodigious student of Russian, a committed party member, and an excellent teacher dedicated to his students and the communist cause. Compared to his years in Berlin, his time in Leningrad seem remarkably stable and productive, both academically and personally.

Despite his complete conversion to communism and prestigious appointment to the Academy of Science, Chatto did not evade the watchful eye of Stalin. He met what was likely a brutal end after the secret police of the Soviet State, the People's Commissariat for Internal Affairs (NKVD), arrested him in his home. His arrest coincided with the height of Stalin's purges in 1937, and unsurprisingly Karunovskaya never heard from Chatto again after he was whisked away by the NKVD. Only after Stalin's death in 1953 did Karunovskaya attempt to recover information about her partner's fate. In a series of letters to the Soviet Union in 1955 and 1956, Karunovskaya issued formal inquiries into Chatto's disappearance and requested rehabilitation of his name on the grounds that he was loyal to the communist cause throughout his life.[7] Although a certificate of rehabilitation was issued by the Soviet Union, the particulars of his detention and death were not available.[8]

Münzenberg met a similarly brutal ending, and likewise the story has been revealed primarily through the writings and recollections of his

---

[7] See two letters from Karunovskaya to N. S. Krushev, dated August 29, 1955 and March 19, 1956. (Original in Russian and translated to English by P. C. Joshi staff.) Files 31–33, Chattopadhyaya, JNU.

[8] From the War Committee Collegium, Supreme Court, USSR. Certificate about the Rehabilitation of Chattopadhyaya, April 28, 1956. File 34, Chattopadhyaya, JNU.

FIGURE 7.1 Chatto in Leningrad. Photo undated (after 1932). Horst Krueger Scholar Estate Archive, Leibniz-Zentrum Moderner Orient, Berlin, Germany. Photo credit: Ali Raza

wife, Babette Gross. She recalled in her published biography that only months before Chatto's arrest in Leningrad, the Soviet high command summoned Münzenberg to Moscow from Paris in October 1936. He appeared before the International Control Commission (ICC), which was an inquisition committee tasked with investigating deviators from the party line. According to Babette Gross's memoir, Münzenberg feared for his life and contemplated a secret escape from Moscow. However, a timely turn of events spared him. At the very moment of his hearing, Stalin announced Soviet support for Republican Spain, and Münzenberg's Spanish aid program in Paris became an important vehicle for this policy shift. Münzenberg was dispatched to Paris again, although he remained under heavy surveillance by Soviet spies and informants in France after 1936. Münzenberg refused to return to the Soviet Union again, even when Moscow continuously summoned him in 1937 and 1938.

Münzenberg officially resigned from the communist party in 1938. He gave his reasons in a statement published in the German communist press in March 1939, stating that he was leaving an "organization which has little in common with that of the original party," and argued that the workers' revolution would "not be won with regimented and bullied dead souls."[9] He was careful not to reference Stalin specifically or criticize the Soviet Union, but instead expressed his solidarity with the founding principles of international communism and those comrades he had worked with in the past:

I am parting company with this leadership and its organization but I do not part company with the hundreds perhaps thousands who arbitrarily, without reason, without trial, without the possibility of defense were illegally dismissed, "sacked" and expelled by faceless authorities. I do not part from the thousands with whom I have fought since 1906, first in the Socialist and later in the Communist movement, and who today solider on illegally in Germany together with the young cadres that are born in the daily battle. I have not changed my attitude towards the Soviet Union, the first country to build socialism, the great guarantor of peace and the most important ally in the struggle for a new Germany and its reconstruction, the country to which I devoted my activities in 1921 and subsequent years.[10]

His statement provides evidence of the double-edged sword that communism became for many in the late 1930s. He continued to praise the Soviet Union as the "great guarantor of peace," but the Stalinization of the movement narrowed the possibilities for internationalist solidarities in the struggle against capitalism, fascism, and imperialism. Münzenberg's flexibility in toeing the communist line and also working across party boundaries for anti-imperialism and peace was his greatest asset in the 1920s and early 1930s, but this ultimately isolated him from the

---

[9] From reprint in Gross, *Willi Münzenberg*, 307–308.   [10] Ibid., 308.

Comintern, an organization he helped found and a movement he served for most of his life. In the months between his resignation and the war, Münzenberg continued in his struggle against fascism, although he did so for the first time as a noncommunist. Even so, he was careful to avoid public criticism of Stalin and the Soviet Union despite his departure from the party.

After the Nazi–Soviet pact, however, Münzenberg made public for the first time his disapproval of Stalin. He called the pact a "Russian stab in the back."[11] He argued in the press that the "old ideology" of socialism was "dead and buried in Stalin's Russia" and that any peace and freedom for Germany ultimately meant a struggle against Hitler and Stalin.[12] This bold statement likely sealed his fate. When World War II commenced, German exiles, regardless of their position on fascism, were interned in camps across France. Münzenberg had been sent to a camp at Chambaran near Lyons in May 1940. By June 20, the camp was evacuated as Germans advanced south toward Lyons, and refugees made their way to Marseilles. Münzenberg vanished en route to Marseille, and his decomposing body turned up months later. His death is shrouded in mystery. He had a noose around his neck, although evidence collected by Gross and historians such as Susan Pennybacker suggest that an agent of the NKVD, the same force responsible for Chatto's death, carried out his murder.[13] Even in the context of war and far away in France, Münzenberg's sins against Stalin were punished by death.

The death of the Berlin anti-imperialists symbolized the moribund state of interwar internationalism in 1939. Its epitaph can be found in the memoirs of Münzenberg's wife and the papers of Chatto's partner. The roots of this closure date back to the more well-known stories of Stalin's elimination of Trotsky and Bukharin, as well as the great purges that left thousands of political rivals and non-conformists dead or locked away in gulags. Neither Münzenberg nor Chatto fitted into the new and more rigidly constructed category of communism in the era of Stalinization, although they had managed to evade persecution until the late 1930s and 1940s. By 1939, international communism as an anti-imperialist force was no longer recognizable either. Unlike the turns and shifts throughout the 1920s and 1930s, the pact with Nazism and the reversal of anti-imperialist and antifascist ideology, alongside the Stalinization and eventual dissolution of the Comintern, had made the divisions between communists and

---

[11] Ibid., 319.   [12] Ibid.
[13] Pennybacker, *From Scottsboro to Munich*, 257; Epilogue in Gross, *Willi Münzenberg*.

noncommunists permanent. The Cold War only reinforced and strengthened such ideological and political boundaries.

While Münzenberg's position as an antifascist and anti-imperialist,
without the tutelage of the Soviet Union and communists, precluded
the possibility of his finding a safe haven during the war, the fates of
Bridgeman, Baldwin, and Nehru proved strikingly different. Baldwin
became a champion of international human rights within the United
Nations and he served as a liaison for the cause in the reconstruction of
Japan and Germany after the war. Bridgeman was rehabilitated briefly
within the British LP and he continued his work for the anti-imperialist
cause as two decades of decolonization unfolded across the British
Empire. Of course, Nehru became India's first prime minister after the
transfer of power in 1947. To be sure, none found their way back to
collaborating with communists, although their views of the Soviet Union
and the "great experiment" differed substantially after 1939.

Bridgeman remained a leading advocate for anti-imperialism, antifascism,
and peace throughout the Second World War. By 1940, he boasted membership of many leftist organizations, including the National Council for
Civil Liberties, Abyssinia Association, Coloured Film Artistes' Association,
Committee for West Indian Affairs, China Campaign Committee, Society for
the Cultural Relations of the USSR, Anti-Slavery and Aborigines Protection
Society, and Royal Institute of International Affairs. This diverse range
demonstrated the flexibility of his politics and associations throughout his
time within the LAI and beyond it. His associations also reflected the kind of
internationalism that he and others such as Nehru promoted in the interwar
years, ones that brought together communists and noncommunists alike.

Even so, Bridgeman's commitment to ideological flexibility prevented
him from participating in mainstream British politics. After the LAI
closed, Bridgeman was eligible to rejoin the LP, and he was officially re-
admitted in 1937. By early 1938, Bridgeman became an LP parliamentary
candidate for the Hendon district. This reunion with the party was brief,
however, because Bridgeman's activities and associations with British
communists and other proscribed groups had not ceased even when the
LAI closed. Much like his fellow comrades and the LAI itself, the hallmark
of his work was the ability to reach across entrenched political divides in
order to construct an inclusive solidarity for international causes. By late
1940, he was forced to resign again from the LP after the party tried to
restrict him from speaking at two events with communist ties.[14] Rather

[14] Baldwin, *Reminiscences*, 359–360.

than conform to the party consensus, Bridgeman left the LP, although with little enmity. Until his death in 1968, Bridgeman worked for the Campaign for Nuclear Disarmament, no doubt a tribute to his ongoing commitment to peace alongside a world free from imperialism.

For Baldwin in the United States, the demise of the antifascist front was an immediate and memorable one. When Stalin had thrown his weight on the side of fascism and war in 1939, Baldwin's faith in the Soviet Union was "irrevocably destroyed."[15] Of course, Baldwin's oral history was written in the 1950s, during the height of the Cold War in the USA, and his anticommunist conclusions were shaped as much by his memories as by the context in which he remembered them. Even so, they are emblematic of the sentiments held by many who shared with Nehru and Baldwin a set of ideas about the interwar world. Baldwin was right when he concluded that with the Nazi–Soviet Pact "no [united-front] organization could endure long."[16]

The news of the pact and Stalin's invasion of Finland prompted the LAWF to issue a statement condemning the Soviet Union, and most communists immediately withdrew from it. Baldwin recalled this moment of finality as one in which the resolution against the Soviet Union was reached "only through liberal sweat and communist tears."[17] With these troubling events in 1939, Baldwin bitterly recalled that "the enemies had joined hands," and since the pact in 1939 "no explanation of Russia's need for defense moved me."[18] Instead, Baldwin's work after 1939 focused on human rights and he served as a consultant for the creation of civil liberties unions in postwar Germany, Austria, and Japan. He also became active in the United Nations, where he met Nehru again on several occasions.

In India, Nehru and the INC faced off with the British raj for a final time in the Quit India Campaign in 1942. Gandhi launched the civil disobedience movement in order to demand independence from the British Empire. By 1942, the colonial state was in no mood for resistance from the Indian leadership, and within hours of the movement's launch most of the INC congressmen found themselves imprisoned without trial and for the duration of the war. When the war ended, however, Nehru emerged from several years of prison to lead the negotiations for the British withdrawal from India. At midnight on August 15, 1947, Nehru became the first prime minister of an independent Indian nation. However, with the dissolution of the British Empire in South Asia and

---

[15] Ibid.   [16] Ibid., 359–360.   [17] Ibid.   [18] Ibid., 411.

the partition of India and Pakistan in 1947, Nehru also witnessed the most traumatic and violent communal upheavals of the postcolonial world. The violence of partition and the continued tensions and border disputes between India and Pakistan would haunt the South Asian subcontinent for the rest of the twentieth and early twenty-first centuries.

Even so, Nehru ushered India into the postcolonial era by articulating a new voice for the nation, one ensconced in an internationalist ethos and a renewed commitment to comradeship with those who continued to struggle against imperialism worldwide. At one of the greatest moments of his career, at the "stroke of the midnight hour" as India became free from Britain, Nehru chose to prioritize in his message the significance of the world and India's place within it. He called upon his fellow Indian citizens to remember that independence is "but a step" in a wider process of ensuring world progress. He concluded by addressing the world: "To the nations and peoples of the world we send greetings and pledge ourselves to cooperate with them in furthering peace, freedom and democracy."[19] This message served as a reminder that Nehru's nationalism had been tempered by and was interdependent on internationalism, even if the world was changing radically in the context of the 1940s.

Rather optimistically, Nehru marched India into an era of decolonization with a renewed commitment to both India and the wider world. Unlike many of his European comrades, forced to reconcile their anti-imperialist causes in the context of the war, Nehru's internationalism came to be challenged more forcefully only after 1947. It was in this later era that interwar anti-imperialism came to be usurped by the inter-state dynamics of the third world project, and Nehru's conceptualization of India and the world were irrevocably altered by the realities of the new global order emerging after World War II.

THE LIMITS OF ANTI-IMPERIALIST SOLIDARITY IN THE BANDUNG ERA

After their separation, the long-lost Afro-Asian brothers threw themselves into each other's arms. This was inevitable and even necessary and desirable. Only a little later, after the emotional reunion, did they discover that during the separation they had grown apart ... At Bandung the Afro-Asians came together, quite simply, as members of the same continents against their

---

[19] Nehru, "A Tryst with Destiny," August 14–15, 1947. Reprint in *SWJN*, Second Series, edited by S. Gopal, vol. 3 (Delhi: Oxford University Press), 135–137.

present or former rulers from another continent; and at this meeting the wave of sentiment barely managed to wash over the rocks of reality ... Bandung showed that joint participation in the same anti-colonial struggle was not a very strong link.[20]

To many observers, the Asia-African Conference held in Bandung, Indonesia (1955), represented the fruition of a lengthy history of anti-imperialist solidarities across the formerly colonized world that dated back to the LAI in 1927. Organized by leaders of India, Indonesia, Pakistan, Ceylon (Sri Lanka), and Burma (Myanmar), the Bandung Conference, as it came to be known, hosted representatives from twenty-nine newly independent countries, mostly from Asia but also from Ethiopia, Liberia, Sudan, Egypt, and the Gold Coast.[21] Indonesian President Sukarno opened the conference by commemorating the earlier Brussels Congress in 1927 as a pioneering moment for Asian and African solidarity when "many distinguished delegates who are present here today met to discuss their fight for independence."[22] Although Sukarno was not in Brussels, his vice-president, Mohamed Hatta, was present and befriended Nehru there. Hatta recalled later, in an oral history taken by Indian scholars of the Nehru Memorial Museum and Library, that the Brussels Congress and LAI were the pre-eminent inspirations for the Bandung Conference.[23]

While Bandung's Afro-Asianism may have drawn upon the symbolic inspiration of the LAI, the reality is that the two movements had very little in common. Instead, as Indian journalist G. H. Jansen suggested, Bandung demonstrated clearly that "joint participation in the same anti-colonial struggle was not a very strong link." Rather than a harmonious celebration of anti-imperialist victories and a general consensus on the remaining battlegrounds against imperialism in Asia and Africa, the proceedings were mired in discord and hostility. Even a common understanding of

---

[20] G. H. Jansen, *Nonalignment and the Afro-Asian States* (New York: Frederick A. Praeger Publishers, 1966), 17–18.

[21] The Gold Coast, still a colony, was not formally represented, and Kwame Nkrumah did not attend. However, the colony sent observers to act on behalf of the Gold Coast.

[22] Opening Address of President Sukarno, African and Asian Conference (Bandung, Indonesia), April 18, 1955. *Selected Documents of the Bandung Conference* (New York: Distributed by the Institute of Pacific Relations, 1955). Although Sukarno draws upon the LAI as an import forerunner, he did not attend the inaugural meeting in 1927.

[23] See Mohammed Hatta, interviewed by B. R. Nanda, September 1972, interview transcript 121, Nehru Memorial Museum and Library Oral History Collection, NMML, New Delhi, India.

the fundamental meaning of colonialism prompted vociferous debate and strong disagreement among the delegates. In the aftermath of the proceedings, Nehru refused to support multiple proposals to organize a sequel to Bandung for many years to come.

The failure of Bandung to find common ground on anti-imperialism and unite African and Asian leaders revealed the limits and unfulfilled promises of interwar anti-imperialism in the age of decolonization and the Cold War. As this book has argued, Nehru came to develop his ideas about India and the world during a moment in the interwar years when it was possible for Asian and African leaders to build upon commonalities, metaphors, and solidarities that transcended geographical and political boundaries. The later Afro-Asian project of the postcolonial years, most clearly articulated at the Bandung Conference, was distinct if not anathema to interwar anti-imperialism.[24] The Cold War made impossible the "blending" of communist and non-communist activism, as well as the heterogeneous and flexible solidarities that were easily constructed before World War II. This was further complicated by the importance of the state in the Asian and African arena. Rather than internationalists inspired by a collective and global struggle against imperialism and even capitalism, Nehru and his postcolonial comrades were heads of states with obligations to negotiate national imperatives on the basis of difference rather than shared commonalities.[25] Ironically, the capture of the Indian nation-state, for Nehru, limited and ultimately foreclosed the possibilities for his anti-imperialist project.

Much of Nehru's personal history as an architect of third-world solidarity and nonalignment has not been adequately understood in relation to his earlier activities as an anti-imperial internationalist. Cold War histories, told primarily through the sources and perspectives of Washington or Moscow, often treat Nehru as a "nativist" or "Hindu particularist" rather than the internationalist and well-traveled Indian

---

[24] Carolien Stolte marks the incongruence of interwar and postcolonial Pan-Asianism even earlier, at the Asian Relations Conference in New Delhi in 1946. See her "'The Asiatic Hour': New Perspectives on the Asian Relations Conference, New Delhi, 1947," in Mišković, et al., eds., *The Non-Aligned Movement and the Cold War.*

[25] For similar arguments on the importance of state imperatives within Afro-Asian or third world solidarity, see Byrne, *Mecca of Revolution*; and Frank Gerits, "'When the Bull Elephants Fight': Kwame Nkrumah, Non-alignment, and Pan-Africanism as an Interventionist Ideology in the Global Cold War, 1957–66," *The International History Review* 37, 5 (2015), 951–969.

leader he became in the 1920s and 1930s.[26] Moreover, historians writing about Nehru's participation in Bandung depend on several assumptions about the Indian statesman that neglect the history of his views about Asia, Africa, and the world before the 1950s. The first characterizes Nehru as a "carrier of gentlemanly models of statesmanship" informed by his British education and mannerisms, and these Anglophile qualities contrasted with the "rough manner" of his African contemporaries such as Jomo Kenyatta.[27] The second and interrelated assumption is that Nehru envisioned India as a pedagogical model for decolonization and looked upon his African colleagues through a patronizing lens – one that leaders like Nkrumah saw as a threat to emerging nations such as Ghana.[28] Neither argument considers in any depth Nehru's historical engagement with Africa that dated back to the 1930s and well before the Bandung Conference.

The overall significance of the Bandung Conference has not been well understood either. It has been revered in the popular imagination as the celebratory moment of emancipation for former colonies and the origins of a mythical Afro-Asian fraternity in the postcolonial third world.[29] These myths of anticolonial redemption and camaraderie have been perpetuated in the absence of a robust scholarship on the proceedings, although this is changing. A much-need groundswell of essays and edited

---

[26] For example, see Odd Arne Westad, *The Global Cold War: Third World Interventions and the Making of Our Times* (Cambridge: Cambridge University Press, 2005); and Andrew Rotter, *Comrades at Odds: The United States and India, 1947–1964* (Ithaca: Cornell University Press, 2000). Post-independence histories of Nehru have been slow to develop because his archival papers after 1947 have been closed to the public until recently. For some promising research on Nehru after 1947, see Swapna Kona Nayudu, *The Nehru Years: Indian Non-Alignment As the Critique, Discourse and Practice of Security (1947–1964)*, (PhD Thesis, Kings College, London, 2015); and Paul McGarr, *The Cold War in South Asia: Britain, the United States and the Indian Subcontinent, 1945–1965* (Cambridge: Cambridge University Press, 2013). For a history of India and the UN and human rights after World War II, see Manu Bhagavan, *India and the Quest for One World: The Peace Makers* (New York: Palgrave Macmillan, 2013).

[27] Antoinette Burton, *Africa in the Indian Imagination: Race and the Politics of Postcolonial Citation* (Durham: Duke University Press: 2016), 9.

[28] On the pedagogical model, see Dipesh Chakrahbarty, "The Legacies of Bandung: Decolonization and the Politics of Culture," in Lee, ed., *Making a World after Empire*; on Nkrumah's perception of Nehru as patronizing, see Gerits, "'When the Bull Elephants Fight.'"

[29] The representation of the Bandung Conference as a mythical triumph of decolonization has been made popular by several observers writing about the proceedings in the 1950s, most notably Richard Wright, *The Color Curtain, A Report on the Bandung Conference* (Cleveland and New York: The World Publishing Company, 1956).

volumes around the 50th and 60th commemorations of Bandung have offered more critical and empirically rich appraisals.[30] Much of this scholarship writes against mythical narratives of Bandung and underscores the tensions and differences among the many delegates who were driven more by their own geopolitical concerns than by transnational affinities.[31] The proliferation of scholarship on the history of the third world primarily by Cold War and diplomatic historians remains another body of scholarship that interrogates the significance of the Bandung Conference alongside other international platforms for Asian and African leaders in this period, although their conclusions have been divided.[32] Some underscore the significance of Bandung as the birthplace of the third world and the inspiration for the Non-Aligned Movement inaugurated later in Belgrade in 1961.[33] Others stress the importance of Bandung's Afro-Asianism as a rival to the Non-Aligned Movement.[34]

The Bandung Conference, from Nehru's vantage point, takes on new meaning if one considers it in relation to the interwar years. In doing so, Bandung proved to be a moment of closure for Nehru, one in which his final efforts to forge internationalist solidarities based on anti-imperialism

---

[30] For commemorative volumes, see Lee, ed., *Making a World after Empire*; See Seng Tan and Amitav Acharya, eds., *Bandung Revisited: The Legacy of the 1955 Asian-African Conference for International Order* (Singapore: National University of Singapore Press, 2008); and Mišković, et al., *The Non-Aligned Movement and the Cold War*.

[31] Several recent scholarly works have challenged the idea that Bandung was a site for solidarity. See Burton, *Africa in the Indian Imagination*, 1–26; Itty Abraham, "From Bandung to Nam: Non-alignment and Indian Foreign Policy, 1947–65," *Commonwealth and Comparative Politics*, 46, 2 (April 2008), 195–219; and Robert Vitalis, "The Midnight Ride of Kwame Nkrumah and Other Fables of Bandung (Ban-doong)," *Humanity: An International Journal of Human Rights, Humanitarianism, and Development* 4, no. 2 (2013), 261–288.

[32] Diplomatic histories of the third world have proliferated since the publication of Odd Arne Westad's seminal text, *The Global Cold War*: For a sampling of scholarship in its wake, see Robert McMahon, ed., *The Cold War in the Third World* (New York: Oxford University Press, 2013). See also Ryan Irwin, *Gordian Knot: Apartheid and the Unmaking of the Liberal World Order* (New York: Oxford University Press, 2012); Robert Rakove, *Kennedy, Johnson, and the Nonaligned World* (Cambridge: Cambridge University Press, 2013); Jason C. Parker, *Hearts, Minds, Voices: US Cold War Public Diplomacy and the Formation of the Third World* (New York: Oxford University Press, 2016); and Byrne, *Mecca of Revolution*.

[33] This argument is advanced in works like Prashad, *The Darker Nations*, and Lee, ed., *Making a World after Empire*.

[34] Although this argument was first made by G. H. Jansen, it has been enriched by the research of Robert Vitalis and Itty Abraham. See, again, Jansen, *Nonalignment and the Afro-Asian States*; Itty Abraham, "From Bandung to Nam"; Vitalis, "The Midnight Ride of Kwame Nkrumah."

proved futile in the geopolitical context of the 1950s. Ultimately, the limits of anti-imperialist internationalism, which could be located earlier in the contradictions between the anti-imperialist and peace movements of the 1930s, were clearly and publicly exposed in Bandung. Although beyond the scope of this book, Nehru's participation in the Non-Aligned Movement after 1955 marked a departure in strategy from Bandung and earlier attempts to construct anti-imperialist international-ism in Asia and Africa. Nonalignment, in contradistinction to Bandung, was a bloc of nation-states and an interstate collective rather than an internationalist community. In other words, by the conclusion of Bandung, and especially in its wake, Nehru came to accept the ascendancy of nation-states and interstate relations as the primary determinants of Indian relations with the wider world.

Before Bandung, in the time between India's independence in 1947 and the conference, anti-imperialism remained the compass that guided Nehru's policies in the early postcolonial years, although this produced varied outcomes. As Minister of External Affairs, Nehru's foreign policy for India opposed European imperialist ambitions to reclaim colonial territories in Asia after World War II, and he emerged as a key partner for anticolonial struggles in Africa.[35] At the same time, Nehru experienced the challenges of managing Indian state imperatives in relation to his commitments to the wider world in places like the United Nations, where he witnessed firsthand strong tensions between his Asian and African comrades even as they tried to forge a collective front against the remnants of imperialism. Even the Asian Relations Conference, held in Delhi on the eve of independence in 1947, was a site of conflict rather than cooperation.

Despite such setbacks, Nehru's anti-imperialist worldview retained some continuity between the interwar and the early postcolonial years. Nehru continued to prioritize the same countries – Egypt, Indonesia, and China – as India's foremost allies. In the case of Egypt, the Wafd Party paved the way for a shared imaginary of Indo-Egyptian solidarity against imperialism in the interwar years; however, it was the party's adversary, General Gamal Abdul Nasser (1918–1970), who became one of Nehru's closest comrades in the third world. Such regime changes in Egypt did not impact Nehru's vision of Indo-Egyptian ties, while Nasser proved willing to carry on such camaraderie. Nehru's brief but impressionable

[35] Gerard McCann, "From Diaspora to Third Worldism and the United Nations: India and the Politics of Decolonizing Africa" *Past and Present*, May 2013 Supplement, p258–280.

encounters with Mohammed Hatta likewise served as important precursors to his strong ties with Sukarno's Indonesia. Yet, in the case of China (discussed in detail later in this chapter), Nehru's privileging of Chiang Kai-shek and the KMT as the rightful heirs to China certainly curtailed the probability of establishing fraternal relations with Mao Zedong (1893–1976) after World War II. Even so, Nehru fought for China's inclusion in the United Nations and recognition as a nation-state throughout the world.

The Bandung Conference provided another global platform for Nehru to reconsider the connections between India and the wider world. This was an opportunity he approached with some caution by 1955. The Cold War deeply divided Asia and Africa in the years between 1947 and 1955. By the run-up to Bandung, Nehru argued that the organizers should "avoid too many differences" among the delegates, and suggested that even preparing an agenda ahead of the conference might raise too many objections.[36] In a letter to his Indonesian counterparts, Nehru characterized the conference as one of "high importance" for the "mere fact of our meeting," but he admitted with some trepidation that the conference required "tactful management" since many delegates harbored "diametrically opposing views."[37] The political diversity within Bandung was nothing new to Nehru, who had met similar contentions in the anti-imperialist movement and had fought for a common cause across such divisions within the LAI, the IPC, and even the UN. As it approached, Nehru suggested that the conference could find a "broad common approach" on the question of peace. Historically, Nehru's conceptualization of peace also meant the negation of imperialism.

Ultimately, Bandung became a final site for Nehru to articulate an anti-imperialist position for India and the world. In the closed sessions, he spoke at length about a shared past that drew upon a familiar repertoire of ideas about anti-imperialism. He argued that the global tensions across the Cold War world were only the latest manifestation of a longer history of global inequalities between a powerful Europe and America on the one hand, and a weakened and oppressed Asia and Africa on the other:

We may criticize communism, the Soviet Union, America, whatever we like, but all these things are parts of great historical processes – if we go back 150 or 160 or

---

[36] Nehru, Note dated December 20, 1954, reprinted in *SWJN*, Second Series, vol. 27, 109–111.
[37] Nehru to Ali Sastroamidjojo, February 20, 1955, reprinted in *SWJN*, Second Series, vol. 28, 97.

170 years – they are the culmination of the Industrial Revolution . . . Now, Asia fell back in the race of life because of the Industrial Revolution, which came to Europe first and then to America. Asia became a power vacuum.[38]

Once again, although without overtly inserting his views about the USA, Nehru pitted his protagonists – here Asia and Africa – against the capitalist and imperialist powers of Europe and America.

The question of anti-imperialism, however, was at the crux of deep and fundamental differences between Nehru and many of his comrades in Bandung. In fact, this has been one of the greatest misconceptions about the conference – that while discord and tension characterized much of the proceedings, one common area emerged within the question of anti-imperialism. This was not the case, and the Bandung delegation found a common understanding of imperialism and anti-imperialism elusive. At the heart of this debate had been the definition of colonialism itself and whether it remained the "old" colonialism of European empires or whether it should include the expansion of the Soviet Union into Eastern Europe.

Nehru's strongest stance at Bandung had been the defense of the Soviet Union against accusations that international communism was imperialist. Most delegates split along the lines of their Cold War allegiances, with those supporting the United States advocating for a resolution that condemned the Soviet Union as imperialists. At the end of the day, delegates approved a vague and open-ended resolution against "colonialism and all its manifestations."[39] Those who considered the Soviets as imperialists celebrated the addition of "all its manifestations" as recognition of their stance, while Nehru and others found the ambiguous language of the resolution a necessary compromise to avoid specific wording targeted at Moscow or Cold War bipolarities more generally.

Based on his historical understanding of the Soviet Union, Nehru could not imagine the country as an imperialist power. The argument was a complete anathema to his conception of imperialism and anti-imperialism, born out of his interwar worldview and despite his own turbulent experiences with the post-1929 communist-run LAI. His defense of the Soviet Union at Bandung, spelled out in a report to the Indian Parliament, stated: "Whatever views might be held of the

---

[38] Nehru, speech at closed sessions of Asian-African Conference, Bandung, 23 April 1955, *SWJN*, Second Series, vol. 28, 114–124.

[39] Final Communiqué, *Selected Documents of the Bandung Conference* (New York: Distributed by the Institute of Pacific Relations, 1955).

relationships that might exist between the Soviet Union and them [Eastern European countries], they could in no way be called colonies nor could their alleged problems come under the classification of colonialism."[40] When Nehru reflected on the event only days afterward, he admitted with great disappointment that the conflicts at Bandung had been the "projection of the cold war affiliations into the arena of the Asian-African Conference."[41]

Beyond the question of the Soviet Union and the definition of colonialism, Bandung's interstate environment proved to be equally challenging to Nehru as well. Anti-imperialist internationalism had emerged as a discourse and set of practices for the oppressed and stateless, which allowed Nehru and his comrades to work across and through imperial, ideological, and state boundaries with relative ease. It encouraged the active repression of difference in order to create a cohesive and collective solidarity against imperialist power. However, Bandung reinforced the primacy of the nation-state as the key geopolitical unit and reified the interstate system as the defining feature of politics in Asia and Africa. The importance of states as the primary actors included in Bandung is clear in the initial debates over the invitation list for the event. At the plenary session in Bogor, the organizers of Bandung – leaders of India, Indonesia, Pakistan, Ceylon (Sri Lanka), and Burma (Myanmar) – decided to invite only sovereign nation-states to the conference even though much of the African continent remained under European colonial rule. Of the twenty-nine invitees, only seven were African – and only five of these actually attended.[42] India's Ministry of External Affairs received several requests for reconsideration of the requirements of nation-state status for participation from places such as Nigeria and Israel.[43] Other petitions simply requested Nehru present their case before the Asian-African Conference.[44]

---

[40] Nehru, Speech to Lok Sabha, New Delhi, April 30, 1955 (New Delhi: Publications Division, Government of India, 1955), 17.

[41] Ibid., 17.

[42] Egypt, Ethiopia, Liberia, Libya, Sudan, Central African Federation, and the Gold Coast made the list. Of these, the Central African Federation declined, and the Gold Coast sent observers rather than representatives. For Bogor minutes, see File 1(4), Ministry of External Affairs, Asian-African Conference Papers, National Archives of India, New Delhi (Hereafter AAC). For Nkrumah's reason for not attending, see his letter to Nehru dated March 17, 1955, File 1(14), AAC.

[43] See File 1(5), AAC.

[44] For example, see Messali Hadj (Algeria) to Nehru, February 7, 1955, File 1(5), AAC Papers.

Nehru was not consistent on the question of invitees and their nation-state status, offering a glimpse of his uncertainties with the embrace of the interstate system for Bandung. Indeed, he supported the decision at Bogor and defended it in his letters to petitioners. Yet, he also made special exception for Kwame Nkrumah, who made the list of invitees despite the Gold Coast's "borderline" colonial status in 1955.[45] Nehru had been the greatest advocate for inviting the Gold Coast and even recognized that he made a special exception for Nkrumah's participation.[46] Of course, the Gold Coast held a significant place in his anti-imperialist imaginary of the 1930s after he met Pan-Africanists during his return to the League in 1936. The League and Bridgeman concentrated much of its propaganda work in the 1930s on the case of the Gold Coast, while Nehru's new anti-imperialist contacts included George Padmore, then an activist in London, and later an advisor to Nkrumah.[47] For Nehru, the Gold Coast retained a special place in his worldview, which resonated in his personal appeal to Nkrumah to attend Bandung: "I need not tell you how deeply interested I am in the progress and development of the Gold Coast. To me that is symbolical of the future of Africa."[48]

Nevertheless, Nkrumah, although often rumored to have attended, opted not to go to Bandung. He admitted in a personal letter to Nehru that there were great difficulties in sending representatives of the Gold Coast: "As you know, the Gold Coast is not yet a Sovereign state and, although we control our own internal affairs, the Governor is still responsible for external affairs of the country, including all matters affecting relations with foreign states."[49] What is not clear in this well-known exchange with Nkrumah is that Nehru and his administration had been working behind the scenes to ensure that the Gold Coast would be represented as a full member despite its colonial status. He wrote to the Indonesian secretariat:

Regarding the Gold Coast, we should point out that the people coming from there are really delegates as far as the Gold Coast Government is concerned, but that British Government is coming in the way in regard to their description. While we should try to get a proper designation given to these representatives, it would be

---

[45] Bogor Minutes, AAC.   [46] See Nehru, Memo dated April 2, 1955, File 1(16), AAC.
[47] For Padmore and Nehru connections, see Padmore to Indian National Congress Foreign Department, August 5, 1936, File FD8-1936, AICC.
[48] Nehru to Nkrumah, March 31, 1955, 1(14), AAC.
[49] Nkrumah to Nehru, March 17, 1955, 1(14), AAC. Nkrumah did send advisors to Bandung, while he finally met Nehru later in 1957.

unfortunate if we excluded Gold Coast reps for no fault of their own and because the British Colonial Office creates difficulties.

Nehru never contemplated this exception to the nation-state rule, and instead only expressed regret that Nkrumah could not attend.[50] Such flexibility was important to his ideas about anti-imperialist solidarity, but already the nation-state and interstate structure of Bandung challenged that.

Interstate relations also limited Nehru's ability to connect with colleagues at Bandung in the way he had with anti-imperialist comrades earlier in the interwar years. I return once again to the statement made by George Lansbury at the Brussels Congress: "Nationalism is to be blended with internationalism" and only this "blend" will serve as the "foundation of *international comradeship*."[51] Nehru was profoundly shaped by this view. Rather than internationalist connections, however, Bandung focused on national sovereignty, territorial boundaries, and interstate relations. The final communiqué of the Bandung Conference provided a statement on the nation-state as paramount and the interstate system as normative. Of the ten resolutions rounding out Bandung's final communiqué, most spoke to the pre-eminence of the nation-state and regulations between states. It called for "respect" for "territorial integrity" and "abstention from intervention or interference in the internal affairs of another country." Only two ambiguous resolutions tacked onto the end of the document addressed common cause or solidarity. The first called for the "promotion of mutual interests and cooperation," and the second for "respect for justice and international obligations."[52] At the end of the day, the final communiqué enshrined interstate relations and a world of nation-states as the defining structures of the emerging third world.

The Bandung experience was not one that Nehru sought to repeat. He refused to entertain new proposals for another Asian-African conference even though schemes for a sequel were pitched throughout the 1950s and 1960s. As early as December 1955, Ceylon's prime minister, John Kotewala, wrote to the Colombo Powers, the organizers of the Bandung Conference, to discuss plans for a 1956 sequel to be held in Cairo. Nehru

---

[50] Nehru to Nkrumah, March 31, 1955, 1(14), AAC.
[51] George Lansbury, "Speech at the Brussels Congress," February 13, 1927, File G29-1927, AICC (emphasis added).
[52] Final Communique, Asian-African Conference at Bandung, April 24, 1955, reprinted in "China and the Asian-African Conference," Foreign Language Press, Peking, 1955.

stopped the proposal dead in its tracks. He fired off several letters to the other Colombo Powers arguing that another Asian-African meeting might undermine the work done by Bandung. As he explained specifically in a letter to Kotewala: "The Bandung Conference created a very good effect not only in Asia but all over the world." He added that,

> It would be a pity to take any step, which might impair that unanimity. The major problems in the world today are difficult and intricate and there is considerable difference of opinion in regard to them. The result might well be that if we meet in June next, our discussion might not be so smooth and might not result in general agreement.[53]

He rallied Hatta of Indonesia and U Nu of Burma to support his position, and the plans were effectively squashed before Nasser could respond to Kotewala's suggestion for Egypt to host.

Further illustrative of Bandung as a moment of closure was the failure of India to initiate a single agenda item promoted by the Asian-African Conference final communiqué. To be sure, the proposal recommended specific economic, cultural, and technological exchanges with other nations across Asia and Africa. However, Nehru shelved these suggestions after 1955. Over a year later, the secretary of the Ministry of External Affairs drafted a memo explaining why the plans never transpired: "Much has of course happened since December last and the Asian-African solidarity forged with much difficulty at Bandung, has proved even more tenacious than before. Many new factors have arisen e.g. the bitterness brought about by Pakistan's relentless and malicious pursuit of the Kashmir question, the Suez issue, the intensification of the Baghdad Pact, the Eisenhower doctrine, etc."[54] His statement reflected an overall recognition that the Cold War and conflicting state interests between Asia and Africa had effectively suppressed the "Bandung Spirit."

Although beyond the scope of this book, Nehru's participation in the Non-Aligned Movement after 1955 marked a clear departure in strategy in his dealings with Asian and African comrades. As Itty Abraham has argued, Bandung's Asian-African solidarity was distinct from the Non-Aligned Movement in both membership and discourse.[55] Abraham sees the distinction as a shift from a discourse in which the Afro-Asianism in Bandung was an imagined community of racial solidarity, while the Non-Aligned Movement inaugurated in Belgrade (1961) was racially diverse,

[53] Nehru to Kotewala, December 7, 1955, File 1(49), AAC.
[54] Note by Minister of External Affairs, April 20, 1957, File 1(47), AAC.
[55] Abraham, "From Bandung to Nam."

with leading members from Asia, Africa, Latin America, and Europe. While evidence of a shift from 1955 and 1961 is clear in the Indian archival papers, the transformation for Nehru had less to do with race and more to do with his growing recognition that the realities imposed by a world of nation-states and guided by an interstate system produced a limited, if not impossible, space for anti-imperialist solidarities.

The importance of 1955 as a turning point from internationalist solidarity to interstatist relations is clear if one examines Nehru's position on nonalignment at Bandung. In the course of the proceedings in 1955, Nehru argued vehemently against a bloc of nation-states among the Asian and African leaders:

I say that we should not involve ourselves into a common danger by forming a separate bloc of nations ... By all means, if you all think in terms of forming a bloc of small nations, you can do so, but there are grave dangers involved in it as I feel that we are in a stage where we cannot help each other effectively. I do not quite understand how we can reduce the tension which exists today by making military alliances.[56]

His commentary reflects his desire to work across state boundaries against a "common danger" and for peace – ideas deeply informed by his interwar experiences. Yet, only a few years later, in Belgrade, he joined the Non-Aligned Movement, which was a bloc of nation-states working within an interstate agreement, one Nehru initially opposed at Bandung. Ultimately, nonalignment became Nehru's new strategy for coping with the interstate order of the world in the late 1950s and 1960s.

A final question about the relationship between the interwar and postcolonial years remains. If Nehru had been so influenced by anti-imperialism and its relevant worldview, why didn't he join the Soviet Union's Cold War alliance? Although Nehru adhered to the neutral and later nonaligned position in the Cold War, he also continued to admire the Soviet Union from afar and defended it against critics who characterized international communism as a neo-imperialist force in the world. Nehru argued frequently and adamantly that the Soviet Union was not imperialist in Bandung, and even after. This was reflective of his core set of ideas about the world in which the Soviet Union remained an anti-imperialist partner to the colonized and formerly colonized world. This core set of ideas remained with Nehru throughout the 1930s even as news of Stalin's great purges became widespread, and in the 1940s and 1950s when

---

[56] Nehru, Speech in closed session of the Asian-African Conference, April 23, 1955, reprinted in *SWJN*, Second Series, vol. 28, 121.

the Soviet Union advanced across Eastern Europe and Central Asia. The chilled relations between Nehru and the Soviet Union after 1947 also stemmed from Stalin's antagonism toward India for its nonaligned position. In fact, Stalin refused to receive an Indian ambassador to the USSR for two years, and until his death in 1953 Indo-Soviet relations were contentious. As the Indian ambassador to the Soviet Union, K. P. S. Menon (position held 1952–1961), remarked, "All one could do was, to put it bluntly, to wait in patience for Stalin to pass."[57]

No doubt Nehru's equally contentious meetings with leaders from the United States were informed by his belief since 1927 that the Cold War power had always been a capitalist-imperialist antagonist in the world. Most historians have characterized his policy toward the USA as ambivalent.[58] Nehru's first trip to the USA in 1949 further strained foreign relations between the two countries when the personalities of the Indian prime minister and President Truman clashed. Indo-American relations would become more complicated when the US Cold War imperatives led to their alliance with Pakistan in 1954.[59] Nehru's recognition of the People's Republic of China in 1950, along with his arguments that the United Nations should welcome China as a member, inflamed American policymakers. Not until the Kennedy administration did relations improve, mainly through economic packages and aid during the Sino–India border dispute in 1962.[60]

China also remained a significant element in this interwar story, and since 1927 Nehru had imagined an affinity between India and its great neighbor to the East. Since the Brussels Congress, Nehru held a belief that India and China shared a historic bond and common anti-imperialist mission, to be carried out collaboratively. However, Nehru's ideas about China born out of the 1920s and 1930s proved to be a catastrophe for Indian diplomacy after independence. When the CCP emerged as the victors in the 1949 revolution, Nehru continued to labor

[57] K. P. S. Menon, "India and the Soviet Union," in *Indian Foreign Policy: The Nehru Years*, ed. B. R. Nanda (Honolulu: University Press of Hawaii, 1976), 136.

[58] See, for example, Rotter, *Comrades at Odds*.

[59] Robert J. McMahon, *The Cold War on the Periphery: The United States, India, and Pakistan* (New York: Columbia University Press, 1994). On the USA, India, and the nonaligned world, see Rakove, *Kennedy, Johnson, and the Nonaligned World*.

[60] On development, see Dennis Merrill, *Bread and the Ballot: The United States and India's Economic Development, 1947–1963* (Chapel Hill: University of North Carolina Press, 1990); and David Engerman, *Staging Growth: Modernization, Development, and the Global Cold War* (Amherst: University of Massachusetts Press, 2003).

under the same assumptions and logic that India and China were "sisters in history" (*Glimpses*) or later in the 1950s, "*Chini-Hindi bhai bhai.*"[61] While the Chiangs and the KMT shared Nehru's logic of anti-imperialist solidarity, the CCP and Mao Zedong did not. Moreover, Nehru's trip to China in 1939 and subsequent writings on his encounters had focused on Chiang Kai-shek and nationalist China at the expense of meeting Mao and appreciating the differences between the KMT and the communist party.

These experiences and assumptions about China in the interwar years led to one of Nehru's greatest foreign policy blunders in 1962. A disputed territorial border between India and China (in present-day Arunachal Pradesh) provided impetus for a military attack by the Chinese in September.[62] The aggression was met with little resistance from troops at the Indian border, and for twenty-four hours it appeared to Nehru and the world that China might swiftly conquer the northern region of India or perhaps worse. Nehru wrote Kennedy a distressed letter on November 9, 1962, requesting significant military support to stop China. But as quickly as the crisis erupted, the Chinese withdrew. For Nehru who had imagined – at times collectively with Chiang – an idealized bond between India and China for nearly three decades, the border conflict imploded the strongest element of his anti-imperialist worldview. Historians and biographers agree that the event haunted him until his death two years later, and some speculate that he died of a broken heart.[63] Viewed from a broader sweep of history, from the 1920s to the 1960s, Nehru's failure to recognize China as a threat rather than a comrade in the world might be seen as a serious flaw in the Indian leader's ultimate unwillingness or inability to adapt his worldview to the changing conditions of the postcolonial and Cold War world even after Bandung.

[61] Following a meeting between Nehru and Chinese leader Chou En Lai in 1954, crowds gathered in the streets of India and chanted this slogan, meaning Chinese and Indians are brothers.

[62] Much scholarly debate exists on the causes and implications of the border dispute between China and India. For an overview of the dispute, see Ramachandra Guha, "An Asian Clash of Civilizations: Revisiting the Sino-Indian Conflict of 1962," *Economic and Political Weekly* 46, no. 44–45 (November 2011). For a discussion of India and China relations from the 1940s onward, see Duara, *The Global and Regional in China's Nation-Formation*, 186–200.

[63] See, for example, "Foreign Policy: The Nehru Era," in Bipan Chandra, Mridula Mukherjee, and Aditya Mukherjee, *India since Independence* (New Delhi: Penguin Books, 2008).

A brief, although not exhaustive, reading of Nehru, the Bandung Conference, and its aftermath demonstrates that the conventional narrative of pre-independence and post-independence divided strictly at 1947 may not be useful if we expand our scope and frame for studying Nehru's engagement with the wider world and think beyond the narrative of the Indian nation-state. In fact, the most appropriate entry point for Indian nonalignment must begin after 1955, while Nehru's interwar ideas and associations linking India to the world extended well beyond 1947. Moreover, rather than asking if connections simply existed between 1927 and 1955, one must ask how interwar anti-imperialism created and curtailed the possibilities for third-world solidarity in Bandung and after. This book encourages historians of the early independence years to dig deeper into the archive and break the colonial–postcolonial divide in attempting to understand the histories of international and interstate connections between India and what eventually became the third world. In doing so, we can begin to rethink the making of solidarities, ruptures, and transitions in India and the third world on their own terms, rather than along the terms defined by the Cold War or the West.

The Bandung Conference was not the origin for nonalignment; rather, it marked a moment of closure for Nehru. It was a capstone on nearly three decades of networking and conferencing for the cause of anti-imperialism and peace. Nehru had established contacts, networks, and a dynamic worldview long before he became Prime Minister and Minister of External Affairs of a newly independent India in 1947. His anti-imperialism remained relatively consistent in his thinking despite the changing conditions and dissonant information he encountered as the world transitioned into World War II. While his anti-imperialist worldview had served him well as an anticolonial nationalist and internationalist of the interwar years, these experiences and core ideas did not prepare him for the different geopolitical milieu of the Cold War and the interstate system of nation-states created out of the ashes of World War II. The slippage between the internationalist moment of the interwar years and the dominant interstate system of the Cold War is critical to this story. It was not simply that the Cold War bifurcation had crosscut anti-imperialist solidarities in the Afro-Asian world. The possibilities for making global claims and creating solidarities across Asia and Africa had radically transformed after World War II, from internationalism to inter-statism led by newly created heads of states across the global south.

NEHRU AND THE END OF ANTI-IMPERIALIST INTERNATIONALISM

At the crux of this book has been the story of Nehru's engagement with the internationalist world of the interwar years. As a result of his encounters and leadership of the LAI, Nehru's accepted a core and fundamental set of ideas about the world, ones that amalgamated unlikely and often-conflicting ideas. His ideas called upon a blending of nationalism with socialism, a worldview in which anti-imperialists including the Soviet Union and the colonies had collectively sought to challenge imperialism, and an awareness that an imperialist war danger was an ever-present threat to the peace of the world. His incorporation of fascism, as an extension of capitalism-imperialism, into his existing worldview enabled Nehru to make sense of the rapidly changing geopolitical milieu of the late 1930s within a familiar logic and framework of anti-imperialism. In doing so, the Italian invasion of Abyssinia (1935), the Spanish Civil War (1936), and the Japanese invasion of Mainland China (1937) were simply different manifestations of the central problematic that India faced – the march of imperialism and fascism worldwide. Interwar anti-imperialism was so significant to Nehru that he failed to see its limitations or reconcile its internal contradictions. By the 1930s, he actively supported peace and antifascist movements that at the same time bolstered imperialism and the interstate structures he sought to overturn.

The conclusion of the interwar period marked a closure in terms of what was possible. The afterlives of anti-imperialism were resurrected in a variety of movements and meetings in the 1940s and 1950s, but none were fully capable of creating a "special blend" of ideas and solidarities that reflected the accommodative and fluid nature of the interwar period.[64] World War II, and the circumstances leading up to it, had closed the possibilities for cross-political collective action and especially the blending of communist and noncommunist forces. When the dust settled and world peace returned, the Cold War ensured that such boundaries between communists and non-communists were reinforced and stigmatized to a greater extent than ever before.

---

[64] This did not prevent some internationalists from attempting postwar solidarities, although within a limited scope and set of possibilities. For projects in Europe, see A. I. Richards, "The Limits of Solidarity: Europeanism, Anti-colonialism and Socialism at the Congress of the Peoples of Europe, Asia and Africa at Puteaux, 1948, *European Review of History* 21, no. 4 (2014): 519–537.

The scholarly imagination was curtailed in the throes of the Cold War as well. Not until the Cold War was a distant memory, in the late twentieth and early twenty-first centuries, would it be possible again to imagine a time when comrades such as Bridgeman, Baldwin, and Nehru, as men of their times, advocated a rich blending of ideas and associations as a means to remake the world as free from oppression of class, race, and nation. Their remarkable stories of global activism and internationalism continued to be invisible in the many archives and historiographical silos that locked them into categories that they actively, in their own times, sought to break down. This book has been an attempt to recover some of the many stories long forgotten and reshaped by the imperatives of the Cold War and its dichotomous vision of a world divided by communism and noncommunism. Such histories instead marginalized the anti-imperialist struggles that transcended those and other boundaries.

The compartmentalization and prioritization of national histories have further complicated the recovery of interwar internationalism. Nehru's history, situated at the intersection of several movements in which Indian nationalism was only one, has been a central focus of this book because he emblemizes the silences and gaps in thinking historically about a critical moment in world history. Indian nationalism remained one of the dominant themes in this book on Nehru, yet it was not the only relevant framework for his formulations and ideas about India and the wider world. Nehru's crowning achievement in historiography may have been his leadership in the Indian nationalist movement, and yet the nationalist project was only a small piece of a broader worldview informed by anti-imperialist internationalism. His story extends across the globe and political boundaries of the world, and it informs us of possibilities and opportunities that were closed by 1947. Instead, his story has been locked away in archives, biographies, and histories of an Indian nation, while his story of internationalism and his worldview, perhaps the most significant to him in his own times, have been silenced. This book asks that we begin to consider new directions for scholarship on colonial history, in India and beyond, that have come to be dominated by studies of locality, province, and nation.

Bibliography

UNPUBLISHED ARCHIVAL SOURCES

Hull University Archives, Hull, United Kingdom

Papers of Reginald Orlando Bridgeman

International Institute of Social History, Amsterdam, the Netherlands

Labour and Socialist International Archive
League against Imperialism Archive
Rassemblement Universel pour la Paix (RUP) Archive

Lamont Library, Harvard University, Cambridge, MA

Indian Political Intelligence (IPI) Files, 1912–1950, India Office Library and Records, IDC Publishers, 2000 (microfilm).

Labour History Archive and Study Center (People's History Museum), Manchester, United Kingdom

The Labour Party Archive
The Communist Party of Great Britain Archive

Library of Congress, European Reading Room, Washington, DC

The Communist International Papers (Digitized from collection at Russian State Archive of Socio-Political History (RGASPI)).

National Archives of India, New Delhi, India

Asian-African Conference Papers
Meerut Conspiracy Case Papers
Ministry of External Affairs

Nehru Memorial Museum and Library (NMML), New Delhi, India

All-India Congress Committee Papers (AICC)
Jawaharlal Nehru Papers
Oral History Manuscripts

New York Public Library, New York, NY

International Committee for Political Prisoners (ICPP) Papers (microfilm).

Oral History Research Office, Columbia University, New York, NY

Baldwin, Roger N., *Reminiscences of Roger Nash Baldwin*. Oral History taken by Harlan B. Phillips, December 1953–January 1954 (microfilm).

Seeley G. Mudd Manuscript Library, Princeton University, Princeton, NJ

Roger Nash Baldwin Papers

P.C. Joshi Archives on Contemporary History, Jawaharlal Nehru University, New Delhi, India.

League against Imperialism Papers
V. Chattopadhyaya Papers

Swarthmore College Peace Collection, Philadelphia, PA

American Civil Liberties Union
American League for Peace and Democracy
British Anti-War Movement
Rassemblement Universel pour la Paix (RUP) Archive

Zentrum Moderner Orient (ZMO), Berlin, Germany

Horst Krüger Files: Papers on V. Chattopadhyaya
Papers on Afro-Asian Solidarity and the Conference of Bandung 1955
Papers on the Foreign Policy of India
V. Chattopadhyaya Papers – League against Imperialism, Berlin

PUBLISHED WORKS BY JAWAHARLAL NEHRU

Nehru, Jawaharlal. *Glimpses of World History: Being Further Letters to His Daughter Written in Prison, and Containing a Rambling Account of History for Young People.* Allahabad: Kitabistan, 1934. Reprinted as *Glimpses of World History.* New York: The John Day Company, 1942.

An Autobiography with Musings on Recent Events in India. London: John Lane, 1936. Reprint, New Delhi: Penguin Books India, 2004.

India and the World: Essays by Jawaharlal Nehru. London: George Allen and Unwin Ltd., 1936.

Eighteen Months in India, 1936–1937; Being Further Essays and Writings. Allahabad/London: Kitabistan, 1938.

China, Spain, and the War: Essays and Writings. Allahabad: Kitabistan, 1940.

Towards Freedom. New York: John Day Co., 1941.

The Discovery of India. Calcutta: Signet Press, 1946.

The Discovery of India. London: Meridian Books, 1946. Reprinted.

COLLECTED WORKS BY JAWAHARLAL NEHRU

Nehru, Jawaharlal. *The Unity of India: Collected Writings, 1934–1940.* London: Lindsay Drummond, 1948.

Independence and After: A Collection of Speeches. 1st American edn. New York: Day, 1950.

Asian-African Conference, April 18–24, 1955. Prime Minister Jawaharlal Nehru's Speeches; The Final Communique. New Delhi: Publications Division, Ministry of Information and Broadcasting, 1955.

A Bunch of Old Letters: Written Mostly to Jawaharlal Nehru and Some Written by Him. Bombay: Asia Publishing House, 1958.

India's Foreign Policy: Selected Speeches, September 1946–April 1961. Delhi: Publications Division, Ministry of Information and Broadcasting, 1961.

Selected Works of Jawaharlal Nehru (First Series), volumes 1–15. S. Gopal, ed. New Delhi: Orient Longman and Nehru Memorial Museum and Library, 1972.

Selected Works of Jawaharlal Nehru (Second Series). M. Chalapathi Rau, H. Y. Sharada Prasad, and B. R. Nanda, eds. New Delhi: Nehru Memorial Museum and Library, 1984.

The Essential Writings of Jawaharlal Nehru. Sarvepalli Gopal and Uma Iyengar, eds. New Delhi: Oxford University Press, 2003.

Gandhi, Indira and Jawaharlal Nehru. *Freedom's Daughter: Letters between Indira Gandhi and Jawaharlal Nehru, 1922–39.* London: Hodder and Stoughton, 1989.
Mende, Tibor and Jawaharlal Nehru. *Conversations with Mr. Nehru.* London: Secker & Warburg, 1956.

OTHER PUBLISHED PRIMARY SOURCES

Ahmad, Muzaffar, ed. *Communists Challenge Imperialism from the Dock.* Calcutta: National Book Agency, 1967.
Baldwin, Roger Nash. *Liberty under the Soviets.* New York: Vanguard Press, 1928.
Das Flammenzeichen vom Palais Egmont. Offizielles Protokoll des Kongresses gegen koloniale Unterdrückung und Imperialismus Brüssel, 10.–15. February 1927: Hrsg. von der Liga gegen Imperialismus und für nationale Unabhängigkeit. Berlin: Neuer Deutscher Verlag, 1927.
Basu, Jyoti, ed. *Documents of the Communist Movement in India,* vol. II, Meerut Conspiracy Case (1929). Calcutta: National Book Agency, 1997.
Gandhi, Mohandas K. *Hind Swaraj or Indian Home Rule.* Madras: S. Ganesan & Co., 1921.
The Collected Works of Mahatma Gandhi (Electronic Book). New Delhi, Publications Division Government of India, 1999.
Gupta, P. S. *A Short History of the All-Indian Trade Union, 1920–1947.* New Delhi: All-India Trade Union Congress, 1980.
Josh, Sohan Singh. *The Great Attack: Meerut Conspiracy Case.* Reprint. New Delhi: People's Publishing House, 1979.
Lenin, V. I. *Imperialism: The Highest Stage of Capitalism.* New York: International Publishers, 1939.
The State and Revolution. Originally published in 1917. Reprint. Mansfield: Martino Fine Books, 2009.
Nehru, Motilal. *Selected Works of Motilal Nehru,* vol. 5, ed. by Ravinder Kumar and Hari Dev Sharma. Nehru Memorial Museum and Library: New Delhi, 1993.
Padmore, George. *Africa and World Peace.* London: M. Secker & Warburg, 1937.
Roy, Purabi, Sobhanlal Das Gupta, and Hari Vasudevan, eds. *Indo-Russian Relations, 1917–1947: Select Documents from the Archives of the Russian Federation,* Part I. Calcutta: The Asiatic Society, 1999.
Yagnik, Indulal. *The Autobiography of Indulal Yagnik,* ed. and trans. from Gujarati to English by Devavrat N. Pathak, Howard Spodek, and John R. Wood. New Delhi: Manohar Publishers & Distributors, 2011.

SECONDARY LITERATURE

Aiyar, Sana. *Indians in Kenya: The Politics of Diaspora.* Cambridge, MA: Harvard University Press, 2015.
Alavi, Seema. *Muslim Cosmopolitanism in the Age of Empire.* Cambridge, MA: Harvard University Press, 2015.

Alpert, Michael. *A New International History of the Spanish Civil War.* New York: Palgrave, 1994.

Anand, Vidya Sagar and Francis A. Ridley. *James Maxton and British Socialism.* London: Medusa Press, 1970.

Anderson, Benedict. *Imagined Communities: Reflections on the Origin and Spread of Nationalism.* London: Verso, 1983.

Ashton, S. R. *Jawaharlal Nehru.* Oxford: Oxford University Press, 1990.

Arora, K. C. *V. K. Krishna Menon: A Biography.* New Delhi: Sanchar Publishing House, 1998.

Aydin, Cemil. *The Politics of Anti-Westernism in Asia: Visions of World Order in Pan-Islamic and Pan-Asian Thought.* New York: Columbia University Press, 2007.

The Idea of the Muslim World: A Global Intellectual History. Cambridge, MA: Harvard University Press, 2017.

Ballantyne, Tony and Antoinette Burton. *Empires and the Reach of the Global,* published in A World Connecting, 1870–1945, edited by Emily S. Rosenberg. Cambridge, MA: Belknap Press of Harvard University Press, 2012.

Barooah, Nirode K. *Chatto: The Life and Times of an Anti-Imperialist in Europe.* New Delhi: Oxford University Press, 2004.

Bayly, C. A. *Indian Society and the Making of the British Empire.* The New Cambridge History of India, II, 1. Cambridge: Cambridge University Press, 1987.

Imperial Meridian: The British Empire and the World, 1780–1830. London: Longman, 1989.

Origins of Nationality in South Asia: Patriotism and Ethical Government in the Making of Modern India. Delhi: Oxford University Press, 1998.

Bellamy, Joyce M. and John Saville, eds. *Dictionary of Labour Biography,* vol. VII. London: Macmillan Press, 1984.

Bhagavan, M. *India and the Quest for One World: The Peace Makers.* New York: Palgrave Macmillan, 2013.

Bose, Sugata. *A Hundred Horizons: The Indian Ocean in the Age of Global Empire.* Cambridge, MA: Harvard University Press, 2006.

His Majesty's Opponent Subhas Chandra Bose and India's Struggle against Empire. Cambridge, MA: Belknap Press of Harvard University Press, 2011.

Bose, Sugata and Ayesha Jalal. *Modern South Asia History, Culture, Political Economy.* New York: Routledge, 1998.

Bose, Sugata and Kris Manjapra, eds. *Cosmopolitan Thought Zones: South Asia and the Global Circulation of Ideas.* New York: Palgrave Macmillan, 2010.

Brass, Paul R. and Francis Robinson. *The Indian National Congress and Indian Society, 1885–1985: Ideology, Social Structure, and Political Dominance.* Delhi: Chanakya Publications, 1987.

Braunthal, Julius. *History of the International.* 3 vols. Praeger: New York, 1967.

Brecher, Michael. *Nehru: A Political Biography.* London: Oxford University Press, 1959.

India and World Politics: Krishna Menon's View of the World. New York: Praeger, 1968.

Brock, Peter and Thomas Paul Socknat. *Challenge to Mars: Essays on Pacifism from 1918 to 1945.* Toronto: University of Toronto Press, 1999.

Brown, Judith M. *Gandhi's Rise to Power: Indian Politics 1915–1922.* Cambridge South Asian Studies. Cambridge: University Press, 1972.

Modern India: The Origins of an Asian Democracy. The Short Oxford History of the Modern World. Delhi: Oxford University Press, 1985.

Gandhi: Prisoner of Hope. New Haven: Yale University Press, 1989.

Nehru: A Political Life. New Haven: Yale University Press, 2003.

"Jawaharlal Nehru and the British Empire: The Making of an 'Outsider' in Indian Politics," *South Asia,* 29, no. 1 (April 2006): 69–81.

"'Life Histories' and the History of Modern South Asia," in the *AHR Roundtable on Historians and Biography, American Historical Review* 114, no. 3 (June 2009), 587–595.

Brown, Judith and Wm. Roger Louis. *The Oxford History of the British Empire,* vol.4: *The Twentieth Century.* Oxford: Oxford University Press, 2001.

Brückenhaus, Daniel. *Policing Transnational Protest: Liberal Imperialism and the Surveillance of Anticolonialists in Europe, 1905–1945.* New York: Oxford University Press, 2017.

Buchanan, Tom. *East Wind: China and British Left, 1925–1976.* New York: Oxford University Press, 2012.

Burton, Antoinette M. *After the Imperial Turn: Thinking with and through the Nation.* Durham: Duke University Press, 2003.

Africa in the Indian Imagination: Race and the Politics of Postcolonial Citation. Durham: Duke University Press, 2016.

Byrne, Jeffrey James. "Beyond Continents, Colours, and the Cold War: Yugoslavia, Algeria, and the Struggle for Non-alignment," *The International History Review* 37, no. 5 (2015): 912–932.

Mecca of Revolution: Algeria, Decolonization, and the Third World Order. New York: Oxford University Press, 2016.

Cabanellas, Guillermo. *La Guerra de los Mil Dias: Nacimiento, Vida y Muerte de la II Republica Española.* 2 vols. Grijalbo: Buenos Aires, 1973.

Casanova, Julián. *The Spanish Republic and Civil War,* translated by Martin Douch. New York: Cambridge University Press, 2010.

Carr, E. H. *International Relations between the Two World Wars, 1919– 1939.* London: Macmillan, 1947.

Chakravarty, Suhash. *Crusader Extraordinary: Krishna Menon and the India League, 1932–1936.* New Delhi: India Research Press, 2006.

Chandra, Bipan. *India's Struggle for Independence, 1857–1947.* New Delhi: Penguin Books, 1989.

Chandra, Bipan, Aditya Mukherjee, and Mridula Mukherjee. *India since Independence.* New Delhi: Penguin Books, 2008.

Chandavarkar, Rajnarayan. *The Origins of Industrial Capitalism in India: Business Strategies and the Working Classes in Bombay, 1900–1940.* Cambridge: Cambridge University Press, 1994.

Imperial Power and Popular Politics: Class, Resistance and the State in India, C. 1850–1950. Cambridge: Cambridge University Press, 1998.

Chang, Jung and Jon Halliday. *Mme Sun Yat-sen.* Lives of Modern Women Series. Penguin Books: Middlesex, England, 1986.

Chatterjee, Partha. *Nationalist Thought and the Colonial World: A Derivative Discourse?* Minneapolis: University of Minnesota Press, 1993.
The Nation and Its Fragments: Colonial and Postcolonial Histories. Princeton studies in culture/power/history. Princeton: Princeton University Press, 1993.

Chhibber, V. N. *Jawaharlal Nehru; a Man of Letters.* Delhi: Vikas Publications, 1970.

Cho, Joanne Miyang, Eric Kurlander, and Douglas T. McGetchin. *Transcultural Encounters between Germany and India: Kindred Spirits in the Nineteenth and Twentieth Centuries.* New York: Routledge, 2014.

Clymer, Kenton J. "Jawaharlal Nehru and the United States: The Preindependence Years," *Diplomatic History,* 14, no. 2 (April 1990): 143–161.

Cooper, Frederick. *Colonialism in Question: Theory, Knowledge, History.* Berkeley: University of California Press, 2005.

Cooper, Frederick. and Ann Laura Stoler. *Tensions of Empire: Colonial Cultures in a Bourgeois World.* Berkeley: University of California Press, 1997.

Copland, Ian. *Jawaharlal Nehru of India, 1889–1964.* St. Lucia: University of Queensland Press, 1980.

Cortright, David. *Peace: A History of Movements and Ideas.* Cambridge: Cambridge University Press, 2008.

Cottrell, Robert C. *Roger Nash Baldwin and the American Civil Liberties Union.* Columbia University Press: New York, 2000.

Dikshit, Sheila and Jawaharlal Nehru. *Jawaharlal Nehru: Centenary Volume.* Delhi: Oxford University Press, 1989.

Draper, Theodore. *American Communism and Soviet Russia.* New York: Viking Press, 1960.

Duara, Prasenjit. *The Global and Regional in China's Nation-Formation.* New York: Routledge, 2009.

Edwards, Brent Hayes. *The Practice of Diaspora: Literature, Translation, and the Rise of Black Internationalism.* Cambridge: Harvard University Press, 2003.

Engerman, David C. *Staging Growth: Modernization, Development, and the Global Cold War.* Amherst: University of Massachusetts Press, 2003.
"Histories of the Future and the Futures of History," *American Historical Review* 117, no. 5 (2012): 1402–1410.
"Learning from the East: Soviet Experts and India in the Era of Competitive Coexistence," *Comparative Studies in South Asia, Africa, and the Middle East* 33, no. 2 (2013): 227–238.

Fenby, Jonathon. *Chiang Kai-shek: China's Generalissimo and the Nation He Lost.* New York: Carroll & Graf Publishers, 2004.

Framke, Maria. *Delhi-Rom-Berlin: die indische Wahrnehmung von Faschismus und Nationalsozialismus, 1922–1939.* Darmstadt: Wissenschaftliche Buchgesellschaft, 2013.
"Political Humanitarianism in the 1930s: Indian Aid for Republican Spain," *European Review of History,* 23, no. 1–2 (2016): 63–81.

Frankel, Francine R. and Harry Harding, eds. *The India-China Relationship: Rivalry and Engagement.* New Delhi: Oxford University Press, 2004.

Fredericks, Pierce C. *The Sepoy and the Cossack: The Anglo-Russian Confrontation in British India.* New York: The World Publishing Company, 1971.

Gallagher, John, Gordon Johnson, and Anil Seal. *Locality, Province, and Nation: Essays on Indian Politics 1870 to 1940*. Reprinted from Modern Asian Studies 1973. Cambridge: Cambridge University Press, 1973.

Gilroy, Paul. *The Black Atlantic: Modernity and Double Consciousness*. Cambridge, MA: Harvard University Press, 1993.

Ghosh, Durba and Dane Keith Kennedy, eds. *De-centering Empire*. Hyderabad: Orient Longman, 2006.

Ghosh, Pramita. *The Meerut Conspiracy Case and the Left Wing in India*. Calcutta: Papyrus, 1978.

Ghose, Sankar. *Jawaharlal Nehru: A Biography*. New Delhi: Allied Publishers, 1993.

Godbole, Madhav. *The God Who Failed: An Assessment of Jawaharlal Nehru's Leadership*. Calcutta: Rupa Publications, 2014.

Goebel, Michael. *Anti-Imperial Metropolis: Interwar Paris and the Seeds of Third World Nationalism*. New York: Cambridge University Press, 2015.

Gopal, Sarvepalli. *Jawaharlal Nehru: A Biography*. Cambridge, MA: Harvard University Press, 1976.

Gordon, Leonard A. *Brothers against the Raj: A Biography of Indian Nationalists Sarat and Subhas Chandra Bose*. New York: Columbia University Press, 1990.

Gorev, A. and V. Zimianin. *Jawaharlal Nehru*. Moscow: Progress, 1982.

Goswami, Manu. "Colonial Internationalisms and Imaginary Futures," *American Historical Review*, 117, no. 5 (2012): 1461–1485.

Grant, Kevin, Philippa Levin and Frank Trentman, eds. *Beyond Sovereignty: Britain, Empire and Transnationalism, 1880–1950*. New York: Palgrave, 2007.

Gross, Babette. *Willi Münzenberg: A Political Biography*. East Lansing: Michigan State University Press, 1974.

Guha, Ramachandra. *India after Gandhi: The History of the World's Largest Democracy*. New York: Ecco, 2007.

"An Asian Clash of Civilizations: Revisiting the Sino-Indian Conflict of 1962," *Economic and Political Weekly* 46, no. 44–45 (November 2011).

Guha, Ranajit, and Gayatri Chakravorty Spivak. *Selected Subaltern Studies*. New York: Oxford University Press, 1988.

Gupta, D. N. *Communism and Nationalism in Colonial India, 1939–45*. Los Angeles: SAGE, 2008.

Gupta, Partha Sarathi. *Imperialism and the British Labour Movement, 1914–1964*. New York: Holmes and Meier Publishers, 1975.

Gupta, Sobhanlal Datta. *Comintern and the Destiny of Communism in India: 1919–1943: Dialectics of Real and a Possible History*. Bakhrahat: Seribaan, 2006.

Haithcox, John Patrick. *Communism and Nationalism in India: M. N. Roy and Comintern Policy, 1920–1939*. Princeton: Princeton University Press, 1971.

Hall, Catherine. *Civilising Subjects: Colony and Metropole in the English Imagination, 1830–1867*. Chicago: University of Chicago Press, 2002.

Hardiman, David. *Gandhi in His Time and Ours: The Global Legacy of His Ideas*. New York: Columbia University Press, 2003.

Hooker, James R. *Black Revolutionary: George Padmore's Path from Communism to Pan-Africanism.* New York: Frederick A. Praeger Publishing, 1967.

Horne, Gerald. *The End of Empires: African Americans and India.* Philadelphia, PA: Temple University Press, 2008.

Howe, Stephen. *Anticolonialism in British Politics: The Left and the End of Empire, 1918–1964.* Oxford historical monographs. Oxford: Clarendon Press, 1993.

Immerman, Richard. "Intelligence and Strategy: Historicizing Psychology, Policy and Politics," *Diplomatic History* 32, no. 1 (January 2008): 1–23.

Empire for Liberty: A History of American Imperialism from Benjamin Franklin to Paul Wolfowitz. Princeton: Princeton University Press, 2010.

Iriye, Akira. *Cultural Internationalism and World Order.* Baltimore: Johns Hopkins University Press, 1997.

Global Community: The Role of International Organizations in the Making of the Contemporary World. Berkley: University of California Press, 2004.

Israel, Milton. *Communications and Power: Propaganda and the Press in the Indian National Struggle, 1920–1947.* Cambridge: Cambridge University Press, 1994.

Iyengar, Uma. *The Oxford India Nehru.* New Delhi: Oxford University Press, 2007.

Jackson, Ashley, Yasmin Khan, and Gajendra Singh, eds. *An Imperial World at War.* London: Ashgate, 2015.

Jackson, Gabriel. *The Spanish Republic and the Civil War.* Princeton: Princeton University Press, 1965.

Jansen, G. H. *Nonalignment and the Afro-Asian States.* New York: Frederick A. Praeger Publishers, 1966.

Jones, Jean. *The League against Imperialism.* Lancashire: The Socialist History Society and Lancashire Community Press, 1996.

Judd, Denis. *Jawaharlal Nehru.* Cardiff: GPC, 1993.

Karl, Rebecca E. *Staging the World: Chinese Nationalism at the Turn of the Twentieth Century.* Durham: Duke University Press, 2002.

Kaushik, Karuna. *The Russian Revolution and Indian Nationalism: Studies of Lajpat Rai, Subhas Chandra Bose, and Rammanohar Lohia.* Delhi: Chanayaka Publications, 1984.

Kelkar, Indumati. *Dr. Rammanohar Lohia: His Life and Philosophy.* Delhi: Anamika, 2009.

Khan, Noor. *Egyptian-Indian Nationalist Collaboration and the British Empire.* New York: Palgrave Macmillan, 2011.

Khilnani, Sunil. *The Idea of India.* New York: Farrar Straus Giroux, 1998.

Koch, Stephen. *Double Lives: Stalin, Willi Münzenberg, and the Seduction of the Intellectuals.* New York: Enigma Books, 2004.

Kopf, David. "A Look at Nehru's World History from the Dark Side of Modernity," *Journal of World History* 2 (1991), 47–63.

Krishna, Gopal. "Rammanohar Lohia: An Appreciation," *Economic and Political Weekly* 3, no. 26 (July 1968), 1105–1114.

Laqua, Daniel. ed. *Internationalism Reconfigured: Transnational Ideas and Movements between the Wars.* London: IB Tauris, 2011.

The Age of Internationalism and Belgium, 1880–1930: Peace, Progress, and Prestige. Manchester: Manchester University Press, 2013.

Lee, Christopher, ed. *Making a World after Empire: The Bandung Moment and Its Political Afterlives.* Athens: Ohio University Press, 2010.

"The Rise of Third World Diplomacy: Success and Its Meanings at the 1955 Asian-African Conference in Bandung, Indonesia," in *Foreign Policy Breakthroughs: Cases in Successful Diplomacy.* New York: Oxford University Press, 2015.

Lees, Lynn Hollen. *Planting Empire: Cultivating Subjects, 1786-1941.* Cambridge: Cambridge University Press, 2017.

Legg, Stephen. *Prostitution and the Ends of Empire: Scale, Governmentalities, and Interwar India.* Durham: Duke University Press, 2014.

Louro, Michele. "Rethinking Nehru's Internationalism: The League against Imperialism and Anti-Imperial Networks, 1927–1936," *Third Frame: Literature, Culture and Society* 2, no. 3 (September 2009): 79–94.

"'Where National Revolutionary Ends and Communist Begins': The League against Imperialism and the Meerut Conspiracy Case," *Comparative Studies of South Asia, Africa and the Middle East* 33, no. 3 (2013): 331–344.

"A Special Blend of Nationalism and Internationalism: India and the League against Imperialism," in *The Internationalist Moment: South Asia, Worlds, and World Views, 1917–1939.* Ali Raza, Franziska Roy, and Benjamin Zachariah, eds. Los Angeles: SAGE Publications, 2014.

"The Johnstone Affair and Anti-Communism in India," *Journal of Contemporary History,* forthcoming, DOI: 10.1177/0022009416688257, available at: http://journals.sagepub.com/eprint/KtJyw2cjeqmAgnrYNAH N/full

Louro, Michele and C. M. Stolte. "Meerut Conspiracy Case in Comparative and International Perspective," Introduction to Special Issue on Meerut Conspiracy Case. *Comparative Studies of South Asia, Africa and the Middle East* 33, no. 3 (2013): 310–315.

Low, D. A. *Congress and the Raj: Facets of the Indian Struggle, 1917–47.* New Delhi: Oxford University Press, 2004.

Lynch, Cececila. *Beyond Appeasement: Interpreting Interwar Peace Movements in World Politics.* Ithaca: Cornell University Press, 1999.

MacKinnon, Janice and Stephen MacKinnon. *Agnes Smedley: The Life and Times of an American Radical.* Berkley: University of California Press, 1988.

Maclean, Kama. *A Revolutionary History of Interwar India: Violence, Image, Voice and Text.* New York: Oxford University Press, 2015.

Manela, Erez. *The Wilsonian Moment: Self-Determination and the International Origins of Anticolonial Nationalism.* Oxford: Oxford University Press, 2007.

Manjapra, Kris. *M. N. Roy: Marxism and Colonial Cosmopolitanism.* Delhi: Routledge, 2010.

Age of Entanglement: German and Indian Intellectuals across Empire. Cambridge, MA: Harvard University Press, 2014.

McCann, Gerard. "From Diaspora to Third Worldism and the United Nations: India and the Politics of Decolonizing Africa," *Past and Present*, May 2013 Supplement, 258–280.

Mcdermott, Kevin and Jeremy Agnew. *The Comintern: A History of International Communism from Lenin to Stalin*. New York: St. Martin's Press, 1997.

McGarr, Paul. *The Cold War in South Asia: Britain, the United States and the Indian Subcontinent, 1945–1965*. Cambridge: Cambridge University Press, 2013.

McMahon, Robert J., *The Cold War on the Periphery: The United States, India, and Pakistan*. New York: Columbia University Press, 1994.

ed. *The Cold War in the Third World*. New York: Oxford University Press, 2013.

McMeekin, Sean. *The Red Millionaire: A Political Biography of Willi Münzenberg, Moscow's Secret Propaganda Tsar in the West*. New Haven: Yale University Press, 2005.

Merrill, Dennis. *Bread and the Ballot: The United States and India's Economic Development, 1947–1963*. Chapel Hill: University of North Carolina Press, 1990.

Metcalf, Thomas R. *Imperial Connections: India in the Indian Ocean Arena, 1860–1920*. Berkeley: University of California Press, 2007.

Mišković, Nataša, Harold Fischer-Tiné, and Nada Boškovska Leimgruber, eds., *The Non-Aligned Movement and the Cold War: Delhi – Bandung – Belgrade*. London: Routledge, 2014.

Moraes, F. R. *Jawaharlal Nehru: A Biography*. New York: Macmillan, 1956.

Moyn, Samuel and Andrew Sartori, eds. *Global Intellectual History*. New York: Columbia University Press, 2013.

Mukhopadhyay, Ashok Kumar, ed. *India and Communism: Secret British Documents*. Calcutta: National Book Agency, 1997.

Nanda, B. R. *The Nehrus: Motilal and Jawaharlal*. London: Allen & Unwin, 1962.

India's Struggle for Independence, 1857–1947. New Delhi, India: Penguin Books, 1989.

Gandhi and His Critics. Delhi: Oxford University Press, 1985.

Jawaharlal Nehru: Rebel and Statesman. New Delhi: Oxford University Press, 1995.

Nayudu, Swapna Kona. *The Nehru Years: Indian Non-Alignment As the Critique, Discourse and Practice of Security (1947–1964)*. PhD thesis. Kings College, London. 2015.

Noorani, A. G. *Indian Political Trials. 1775–1947*. New Delhi: Oxford University Press, 2005.

O'Malley, Kate. *Ireland, India and Empire: Indo-Irish Radical Connections, 1919–64*. Manchester: Manchester University Press, 2008.

Overstreet, Gene D. and Marshall Windmiller. *Communism in India*. Berkeley: University of California Press, 1959.

Owen, Nicholas. *The British Left and India: Metropolitan Anti-Imperialism, 1885–1947*. Oxford historical monographs. Oxford: Oxford University Press, 2007.

Parekh, Bhikhu C. *Gandhi*. Oxford: Oxford University Press, 1997.
Patel, Kiran Klaus. *The New Deal: A Global History*. Princeton: Princeton University Press, 2017.
Pattabhi Sitaramayya, B. *The History of the Indian National Congress, 1885–1947*. Bombay: Padma Publications, 1946.
Pedersen, Susan. *The Guardians: The League of Nations and the Crisis of Empire*. New York: Oxford University Press, 2015.
Pennybacker, Susan. *From Scottsboro to Munich: Race and Political Culture in 1930s Britain*. Princeton: Princeton University Press, 2009.
Petersson, Fredrik. *Willi Münzenberg, the League against Imperialism, and the Comintern, 1925–1933*. Lewiston: Queenston Press, 2013.
Prashad, Vijay. *The Darker Nations: A People's History of the Third World*. New York: New Press, 2007.
Preston, Paul. *The Coming of the Spanish Civil War: Reform, Reaction and Revolution in the Second Republic*. London: Methuen, 1978.
Price, Ruth. *The Lives of Agnes Smedley*. New York: Oxford University Press, 2005.
Pugh, Michael C. *Liberal Internationalism: The Interwar Movement for Peace in Britain*. New York: Palgrave Macmillan, 2012.
Puri, Harish K. *Ghadar Movement: Ideology, Organisation and Strategy*. Amritsar: Guru Nanak Dev University Press, 1983.
Rai Chowdhuri, Satyabrata. *Leftism in India, 1917–1947*. Basingstoke: Palgrave, 2007.
Rakove, Robert B. *Kennedy, Johnson, and the Nonaligned World*. Cambridge: Cambridge University Press, 2013.
Ram, V. Shiva, and Brij Mohan Sharma. *India and the League of Nations*. Lucknow: The Upper India Publishing House, 1932.
Ramnath, Maia. *Haj to Utopia: How the Ghadar Movement Charted Global Radicalism and Attempted to Overthrow the British Empire*. Berkeley: University of California Press, 2011.
Raza, Ali, Franziska Roy, and Benjamin Zachariah, eds. *The Internationalist Moment: South Asia, Worlds, and World Views, 1917–1939*. Los Angeles: SAGE Publications, 2014.
Raza, Ali and Franziska Roy, "Paramilitary Organisations in Interwar India," *South Asia: Journal of South Asian Studies* 38, no. 4 (2015): 671–689.
Richard, A. I. "The Limits of Solidarity: Europeanism, Anti-colonialism, and Socialism at the Congress of the Peoples of Europe, Asia and Africa at Puteaux, 1948," *European Review of History* 21, no. 4 (2014):519–537.
Rosenberg, Emily S. *Financial Missionaries to the World: The Politics and Culture of Dollar Diplomacy, 1900–1930*. Cambridge, MA: Harvard University Press, 1999.
Roy, Franziska and Benjamin Zachariah. "Meerut and a Hanging: 'Young India' Popular Socialism and the Dynamics of Imperialism," *Comparative Studies of South Asia, Africa and the Middle East*, 33, no. 3 (December 2013): 360–377.
Roy, Franziska. *Youth, Paramilitary Organizations and National Discipline in South Asia, 1915–1950*. PhD thesis, Warwick University, UK, 2013.

Rotter, Andrew J. *Comrades at Odds: The United States and India, 1947–1964.* Ithaca: Cornell University Press, 2000.

Rudolph, Lloyd I. and Susanne Hoeber Rudolph, *In Pursuit of Lakshmi: The Political Economy of the India State.* Chicago: The University of Chicago Press, 1987.

Saha, Panchanan. *Shapurji Saklatvala: A Short Biography.* Delhi: Peoples' Pub. House, 1970.

Sareen, Tilak Raj. *Indian Revolutionary Movement Abroad, 1905–1921.* New Delhi: Sterling, 1979.

Sarkar, Sumit. *Modern India, 1885–1947.* New York: St. Martin's Press, 1989.

Seal, Anil. *The Emergence of Indian Nationalism: Competition and Collaboration in the Later Nineteenth Century.* London: Cambridge, 1968.

Singh, Devendra. *Meerut Conspiracy Case and the Communist Movement in India, 1929–35.* Meerut: Research India, 1990.

Sinha, Mrinalini. *Specters of Mother India: The Global Restructuring of an Empire.* Durham: Duke University Press, 2006.

Slate, Nico. *The Prism of Race: W. E. B. DuBois, Langston Hughes, Paul Robeson, and the Colored World of Cedric Dover.* New York: Palgrave Macmillan, 2014.

  Colored Cosmopolitanism: The Shared Struggle for Freedom in the United States and India. Cambridge, MA: Harvard University Press, 2012.

Sluga, Glenda. *Internationalism in the Age of Nationalism.* Philadelphia: University of Pennsylvania Press, 2015.

Smith, Eric C. *American Relief Aid and the Spanish Civil War.* Columbia: University of Missouri Press, 2013.

Spivak, Gayatri Chakravorty. *Can the Subaltern Speak?* Basingstoke: Macmillan, 1988.

Steiner, Zara. *The Triumph of the Dark: European International History, 1933–1939.* New York: Oxford University Press, 2011.

Stolte C. M., "Trade Unions on Trial: The Meerut Conspiracy Case and Trade Union Internationalism, 1929–32," *Comparative Studies of South Asia, Africa and the Middle East* 33, no. 3 (2013): 345–359.

  Orienting India: Interwar Internationalism in an Asian Inflection, 1917–1937, PhD thesis. Institute for History, Humanities, Leiden University, 2013.

  "'Enough of the Great Napoleons!' Raja Mahendra Pratap's Pan-Asian projects (1929–1939)," *Modern Asian Studies* 46, no. 2 (2012): 403–423.

  "Bringing Asia to the World: Indian Trade Unionism and the Long Road Towards the Asiatic Labour Congress, 1919–1937," *Journal of Global History* 7, no. 2 (2012): 257–278.

Stolte C. M. and H. Fischer-Tiné. "Imagining Asia in India: Nationalism and Internationalism, 1905–1940," *Comparative Studies in Society and History* 54, no. 1 (2012):65–92.

Streets-Salter, Heather. "The Noulens Affair in East and Southeast Asia: International Communism in the Interwar Period," *Journal of American East Asian Relations* 21, no. 4 (2014): 394–414.

  World War One in Southeast Asia: Colonialism and Anticolonialism in an Era of Global Conflict. Cambridge: Cambridge University Press, 2017.

Stutje, Klaas. *Behind the Banner of Unity: Nationalism and Anticolonialism among Indonesian Students in Europe, 1917–1931*. PhD thesis, University of Amsterdam, 2016.

"Indonesian Identities Abroad: International Engagement of Colonial Students in the Netherlands, 1908–1931," *Low Countries Historical Review* 128, 1 (2013): 151–172.

Suny, Ronald Grigor. *The Soviet Experiment: Russia, the USSR, and the Successor States*. New York: Oxford University Press, 1998.

Squires, Mike. *Saklatvala: A Political Biography*. London: Lawrence & Wishart, 1990.

Tan, See Sang and Amitav Acharya, eds. *Bandung Revisited: The Legacy of the 1955 Asian-African Conference for International Order*. Singapore: National University of Singapore Press, 2008.

Thampi, Madhavi, ed. *India and China in the Colonial World*. New Delhi: Social Science Press, 2005.

Tharoor, Shashi. *Nehru: The Invention of India*. New York: Arcade Pub, 2003.

Thomas, Hugh. *The Spanish Civil War*. New York: Harper and Brothers, 1961.

Tiné, Harald Fischer, "Indian Nationalism and the 'World Forces': Transnational and Diasporic Dimensions of the Indian Freedom Movement on the Eve of the First World War," *Journal of Global History*, 2, no. 3 (2007): 325–344.

Tomlinson, B. R. *The Indian National Congress and the Raj, 1929–1942: The Penultimate Phase*. London: Macmillan, 1976.

Vajpeyi, Ananya. *Righteous Republic: The Political Foundations of Modern India*. Cambridge, MA: Harvard University Press, 2012.

Verma, Dina Nath. *India and the League of Nations*. Patna: Bharati Bhawan, 1968.

Verma, Ganeshi Lal. *Shyamji Krishna Varma, the Unknown Patriot*. New Delhi: Publications Division, Ministry of Information and Broadcasting, Govt. of India, 1993.

Vickers, Adrian. *A History of Modern Indonesia*. Cambridge: Cambridge University Press, 2005.

Vitalis, Robert. *White World Order, Black Power Politics: The Birth of American International Relations*. Ithaca: Cornell University Press, 2015.

"The Midnight Ride of Kwame Nkrumah and Other Fables of Bandung (Ban-doong)," *Humanity: An International Journal of Human Rights, Humanitarianism, and Development* 4, no. 2 (2013): 261–288.

Von Eschen, Penny M. *Race against Empire: Black Americans and Anticolonialism, 1937–1957*. Ithaca: Cornell University Press, 1997.

Wadsworth, Marc. *Comrade Sak: Shapurji Saklatvala MP, A Political Biography*. Leeds: Peepal Tree, 1998.

Weiss, Holger, ed. *International Communism and Transnational Solidarity: Radical Networks, Mass Movements and Global Politics, 1919–1939*. Leiden: Brill, 2017.

Framing a Radical African Atlantic: African American Agency, West African Intellectuals and the International Trade Union Committee of Negro Workers. Leiden: Brill, 2014.

Westad, Odd Arne. *The Global Cold War: Third World Interventions and the Making of Our Times*. Cambridge: Cambridge University Press, 2005.

Wolpert, Stanley A. *Nehru: A Tryst with Destiny*. New York: Oxford University Press, 1996.

Young, Robert J. C. *Postcolonialism: An Historical Introduction*. Oxford: Blackwell Publishers, 2001.

Zachariah, Benjamin. *Playing the Nation Game: The Ambiguities of Nationalism in India*. New Delhi: Yoda Press, 2011.

Nehru. Routledge Historical Biographies. London: Routledge, 2004.

Developing India: An Intellectual and Social History, c. 1930–50. New Delhi: Oxford University Press, 2005.

Zumoff, J. A. "'Is America Afraid of the Truth?': The Aborted North American Trip of Shapuriji Saklatvala, MP," *Indian Economic and Social History Review* 53, no. 3 (2016): 405–447.

The Communist International and US Communism, 1919–1929. Leiden: Brill Publishing, 2014.

Index

"A Foreign Policy for India," 88–91
"From Demonstration to Organization"
    (Münzenberg), 119–120
Aaj, 123
Abraham, Itty, 277
Abyssinia
    invasion by Italy, 57, 182, 201, 203–204
    Nehru views on invasion, 1, 204–205
Africa and pan-Africanism, 198, 212
    Abyssinia, invasion by Italy, 203
    focus on Gold Coast, 275
    LAI association, 198
    Nehru views of Africans, 182, 188
    Nehru's views, 11
    Padmore's role, 200
Africa and World Peace (Padmore), 201–203
Afro-Asian solidarity, 14, 198–199, 271,
    281, See also Bandung Conference
    (1955)
    LAI association, 198
All India Trade Union Congress (AITUC),
    53, 75
    international entanglements, 130
    Jharia meeting, 128–131
    Johnstone's arrest and deportation, 131
    Nehru's role, 104, 115, 126–127, 128,
    132, 138
    split over Nehru Report, 127
    trade unionists affiliation split, 127
All-Chinese Trade Union Federation, 81
All-Parties Conference, 120, 127
    dominion status acceptance, 121
    Nehru Report (Motilal), 120–122

al-Nahhas, Mustapha, 241, 242–245, 253
    Muslim homeland in India question, 244
American Civil Liberties Union (ACLU), 61,
    68, 75, 221
American League for India's Freedom
    (ALIF), 191
Amritsar. See India
Amsterdam International Federation of
    Trade Unions (AIFTU), 68
Amsterdam peace conference, 220–221, 222
Andrews, Charles Freer, 128, 130
Ansari, M.A., 118
anti-imperialism, definition of, 2
anti-imperialist internationalism (Nehru), 2,
    15, 39, 93, 181–184
    and LAI, 79, 88
    Bandung Conference (1955) and, 16
    Brussels experience, 23–24, 48–49, 65
    Indian independence and, 112, 122
    interstate system and, 14
    limits of, 11–12
    post-Great War years, 104, 105, 186,
    241–242, 254
    World War II effect, 257
Anti-Imperialist Review (AIR), 112–113,
    116–120, 125, 129, 220
anti-imperialist worldview (Nehru)
    "Congress Manifesto," 47, 51
    Bandung Conference (1955), 271,
    272–273
    Brussels Congress, 66
    fascism and peace, 187, 206, 212–213,
    240, 243

Argentine nationalist movement, 68
Arnot, R. Page, 149
Asian Relations Conference, 271
Asian-African Conference (Bandung). *See*
Bandung Conference (1955)
Autobiography (Nehru), 183, 194, 205, 210

Baldwin, Roger Nash, 68, 116, 141–142,
143, 221, 256
attempt to counteract Comintern LAI
takeover, 166–167
British imperialism in India
protested, 189
expelled from LAI, 175
friendship with Nehru, 6–7, 61–63, 66,
74, 82, 283
LAI secretariat question, 74–75
meeting with Gandhi to discuss Indian
independence, 190–191
Nehru correspondence, 74, 76–77,
101–102, 116, 164, 181, 189, 205
post-World War II, 264, 265
Soviet Union trip, 95, 96, 99
support for Republican Spain, 238
Ballantyne, Tony, 2
Bandung Conference (1955), 14–15, 16, 55,
258, 266–267, 269
Colombo powers, organizers, 276
failure of, 267–268
Gold Coast colony, 267, 275–276
inconsistency of African invitees, 275
India's decline to act on agenda, 277
Nehru at, 268, 270, 272–273,
276–277, 281
non-alignment, 278
primacy of sovereign nation states, 274,
276, 277, 278
request for sequel by Kotewala, 276
Soviet Union question, 273–274
Barbusse, Henri, 35, 68, 134
Barooah, Nirode K., 59
Berlin Indian Information Bureau, 115
Berstein, Eduard, 96
Besant, Annie, 193
Bey, Hafiz Ramadan, 56
Birla, Ghanshyam Das "G.D.," 210
Bittleman, Alexander, 146–147, 155, 156,
162, 167–168
Frankfurt Congress, 146–147, 157,
158–159, 160–161
black internationalism, 10, 201

blending. *See also* nationalism and
internationalism; nationalism and
socialism
blending of communism and
non-communism, 258, 263
resurection of ideas post-Cold War, 283
Bombay Chronicle, 116, 208
Bombay Engineering Workers Union, 127
Bombay Mill Workers Union, 127
Bombay Port Trust Railwaymen's Union,
127
Bose, Subhas Chandra, 123, 164, 207, 212
alliance with Nazi Germany, 251–253
INC presidency, 210, 212
Bradley, Benjamin Francis, 193, 194, 196,
203, 223
Conference on Peace and Empire, 230
Bridgeman, Reginald, 193–194, 258,
See also League against Imperialism
(LAI), British national section
at Frankfurt Congress, 141–142, 143
Bridgeman resurrects LAI in London,
220–221
Conference on Peace and Empire, 230
dilemma of peace and anti-fascism, 221
London meeting with Nehru, 188, 197
Maxton expulsion opinion, 161
Meerut trial protest, 164
Nehru correspondence, 116
post-World War II, 264–265
British Anti-War Council (BAWC), 220
British Empire, 28, *See also* Simon
Commission
expectation of war with Soviet Union, 96
Imperial War Conference, 27
importance of India, 39, 236
Indian Political Intelligence (IPI) Bureau, 28
Nehru's view of, 23, 24, 135
British Labour Party and labour movement,
1, 35, 42, 60–61
China protest, 70
distance from Comintern, 66, 72
retreat from LAI, 85, 86–88
British Miners Association, 35
Brockway, Fenner
Brussels Congress, 35, 85–86
collective security and anti-imperialism,
232
ILP secretary, 60
LAI British branch, 86–87
LAI resignation, 155

Brussels Congress, 19, 20, *See also* League against Imperialism (LAI)
"Congress Manifesto," 43–46, 47–48
anti-colonial speakers, 33, 36, 40
anti-imperialist internationalism, 19, 22–24, 40, 47
Comintern role, 20, 35–36, 59
focus on China and India, 37–38
INC participation, 33
Lansbury speech, 41–43
Mexico focus, 39
Nehru views of Africans, 57–58
pacifism and warnings of war, 40, 44, 45
Pan-Africanism, 40
pan-Asian solidarity, 40, 54–57
resolutions of, 36, 40, 46–47
success of, 34–35, 43
Brussels Congress against Colonial Oppression and Imperialism and for National Independence. *See* Brussels Congress
Burns, Emile, 149, 167, 168
Burton, Antoinette, 2

Calcutta Congress, 105, 123–125, 132–133, 134–136, 138
Cecil, Robert, 223, 227
Chan Kuen, 68, 81
Chatterjee, Partha, 184
Chattopadhyay, Virendranath (Chatto), 30–32, 59, 82, 94, 112–115, 141–142, 143, 163
and trade unionists, 127, 148
at LAI executive committee, 107
attempt to counteract Comintern LAI takeover, 166–167, 168
Berlin Indian Information Bureau, 115
break with Nehru over Delhi Manifesto, 169–170
death of, 258, 260, 263
flees Berlin to Moscow, 175, 192, 259–260
Independence League to support LAI, 124
LAI organizing in India, 167
LAI secretary, 77, 173
LAI-INC friction, 171
Maxton expulsion opinion, 161
Nehru correspondence, 82, 114–115, 116, 123, 125, 137, 139, 149, 171–172
Chiang Kai-shek, 37, 70, 71, 81, 241, 250

China. *See also* Kuomintang Party (KMT)
"Nanjing incident," 70
at World Congress of the Friends of the U.S.S.R., 99
Hands Off China" campaigns, 31
KMT and CCP split, 71
Nehru's private reflections, 249
Nehru's seven point program for China-India ties, 250
Nehru's visit, 214, 217
Nehru's visit and anti-imperialism, 241–242, 247–251, 253–254
Nehru's visit and views, 279–280
Nehru's visit, critics of, 251–252
relationship after World War II, 271, 280
role at Brussels Congress, 37, 52–53
territorial dispute with India, 280
China, Spain, and the War (Nehru), 214, 248
Chinese Communist Party (CCP), 71, 279
Chinese Information Bureau, 60
Chinese National Revolutionary Army (CNRA), 70
Chinese Trade Union Association, 68
Chu Chia Hwa, 249
Civil Disobedience campaign, 170, 189, 191–192, 197, 225
INC congressmen imprisoned during World War II, 265
Nehru imprisoned, 173, 181
Salt March, 173–174, 181
Cold War, effect of, 268–269
interstate system of nation-states, 281
collective security. *See* League of Nations
Colonial News, 192
Comintern (Communist International), 20, *See also* League against Imperialism (LAI); Münzenberg, Willi
anti-imperialist commission and LAI, 78
Chatto address to Third Congress, 30
cross-party alliances revived, 193
goals for Brussels Congress, 42–43
India trade unionists and, 126
Münzenberg expelled, 200
origins of, 72
Padmore's role in "Negro" work, 200
Sixth World Congress resolution on India, 151
united front alliance, 8
Comité contra la Guerre et le Fascisme (CAGF), 222

Committee for the War Relief of Republican
　　Spain, 238
communism. *See also* Meerut Conspiracy
　　Case (1929–1934)
　　anti-colonial revolution, 8, 22–23
　　Nehru's admiration after trip to Soviet
　　　Union, 96
　　Nehru's admiration for, 187
　　red scare in United States, 83
　　rejection of term, 210
Communist Party of Great Britain (CPGB),
　　84, 117, 129, 152, 155, 196
communists and non-communists, 9, 73,
　　165, 231, 257, 263, 264, 283, *See also*
　　Frankfurt Congress (Second World
　　Congress); League against Imperialism
　　(LAI)
　　interwar years and, 6, 157
　　resistance to Comintern, 143
Confederation Generale du Travail Unitaire
　　(CGTU), 75
Conference on Peace and Empire, 230–231
　　resolution on peace and collective
　　　security, 230, 231–232
Congress Bulletin, 132–133, 134, 137
Congress Socialist Party (CSP), 207–208
Cortright, David, 217
Cot, M. Pierre, 223
Cripps, Stafford
　　Conference on Peace and Empire, 230
Czechoslovakia, 228, 232, 235, 256

Davies, Stephen Owen, 35, 60
Delhi Manifesto, 169–171
Discovery of India (Nehru), 183, 184
dominion status or independence, 90–91,
　　104, 106, 107, 108, 110–111, *See also*
　　Delhi Manifesto; Independence for
　　India League; swaraj
　　Gandhi talks with Indian Viceroy on
　　　dominion status, 142, 163
　　INC question on Nehru Report, 135, 136
　　LAI and INC chasm, 154, 168
　　LAI support for independence, 118
　　Madras independence resolution, 120,
　　　121–122
　　second independence resolution, 112
Dover, Cedric, 198
Duong Van Giau, 134
Dutch East Indies. *See* Indonesia
Dutch Social Democratic Party, 88

Dutt, Clemens Palme, 129
Dutt, Rajini Palme, 155, 197
Dyer, Reginald, 26, 45

Edwards, Brent Hayes, 10, 201
Egypt, 56
　　British Empire and imperialism, 243
　　Indo-Egyptian solidarity, 271
　　Indo-Egyptian tension, 244
　　Nehru visit, 217, 241–243
　　Nehru's visit and views, 253, 254
Egyptian Nationalist Party (Watanist
　　Party), 56, 75
Einstein, Albert, 34
Engels, Friedrich, 72
Eurocentric worldview, 22, 23, 184

fascism and anti-fascism. *See also* Abyssinia;
　　British Anti-War Council (BAWC);
　　International Peace Campaign (IPC);
　　League against War and Fascism
　　(LAWF); Spanish Civil War
　　dilemma of peace activists, 217, 219, 224
　　Nehru invitation to Germany rejected,
　　　229
　　Nehru's views, 182, 214–216, 219, 225,
　　　234, 235, 237, 238, 240, 254–255
　　ties to imperialism, 230, 256
　　transition from anti-imperialism, 14, 234
Ferdi, Bekar, 160
Fimmen, Edo, 68, 69, 73, 74, 141–142, 144,
　　165–166
　　expelled from LAI, 175
　　INC-LAI relationship, 151, 193
　　Nehru correspondence, 74, 165, 172, 283
Ford, James, 149
Forward, 116
Forward Bloc, 252
Framke, Maria, 236
Frankfurt Congress (Second World
　　Congress), 16, 66, 67–69, 72–73,
　　78–79, 137, 141–143
　　Berlin agenda, 144–146
　　Brussels comparison, 152–153
　　Comintern and communists at, 142, 144,
　　　148–150, 151–152, 156, 158, 165
　　Comintern secret meetings, 147, 156–157
　　crisis in anti-imperialism, 150
　　divisions of opinion in, 162
　　ILP India Policy and Comintern, 155
　　India focus, 152–154, 155, 168

India resolution, 156, 157–158, 171
Padmore's role, 200
relations with AITUC, 148
reports of, 162
socialists and communists balance,
  144–145, 159–160
war danger resolution, Moscow drafted,
  152–154
French Communist Party, 68

Gandhi, Mohandas, 37–38, 58, 90, *See also*
  Civil Disobedience campaign;
  dominion status or independence
"Independence vs. Swaraj," 109, 111
assassination, 15
Baldwin's meeting to discuss Indian
  independence, 190–191
dispute with Bose, 252–253
imprisonment, 191
INC role, 26
opposition to independence, 123
Second Round Table Conference, 190,
  191
tension with Nehru, 91–93, 109–111,
  210–211
Ganguli, Kanailal, 167
German Foreign Office, 30
German Social Democratic Party, 72
Germany
  Berlin, interwar political activity, 29–30
  German Foreign Office, 29
  invitation to Germany rejected by Nehru,
    229
  postwar political unrest, 29
Gibarti, Louis
  Amsterdam peace conference, 220
  Comintern agent, 73, 76
  LAI role, 75, 76, 77
  League against War and Fascism (LAWF),
    221–222, 223
Glimpses of World History (Nehru), 182,
  183–186, 187–188, 193, 256, 279
  postscript on fascism, 234
Goebel, Michael, 9
Goldschmidt, Alfons, 68
Gopal, Sarvepalli, 103, 182, 184, 228
Gorki, Maxim, 34
Great War, 24, *See also* German Foreign
  Office
  Paris Peace Settlement, 26, 29
Greater India Society, 53

Gross, Babette, 222, 232, 260, 263
Guha, Ranajit, 2
Gupta, Shiva Prasad, Rashtra Ratna (Jewel
  of the Nation), 123, 141–142
  Frankfurt Congress, 154, 156, 157–159
  Frankfurt Congress report, 162–163, 171
  LAI letter of introduction to Chatto,
    Baldwin and Bridgeman, 143–144

Haig, Harry Graham, 163
Hatta, Mohammed, 55, 68, 83, 114, 134,
  141, 271, 276
Heckert, Fritz, 149
Hind Swaraj (Gandhi), 91, 110
Hindu, 116, 246
Hindustan Times, 116
Hindustani Seva Dal, 53, 115

Independence for India League
  anti-imperialism and independence, 120,
    121–122, 125
  Chatto's goals for, 124
  conflict with Motilal, 121–122
  creation of, 113
  Delhi meeting, 122–123
  goal to influence INC, 123
  importance of, 125
  Nehru, chief secretary, 113, 123–125
Independent Labour Party (ILP), 60, 85–86,
  87–88, 144, 161, 196
  Frankfurt Congress (Second World
    Congress), 150, 155–156
India, 29, *See also* Meerut Conspiracy Case
  (1929–1934)
  Communist party banned, 163
  Great War role, 26
  independence from Britain, 258, 265
  Jallianwalla Bagh massacre (Amritsar),
    19, 26, 45
  nationhood rights, 27
  partition and upheavals with Pakistan,
    265, 277
  political expatriates in Berlin, 30
  political prisoners and ICPP, 62
  self-rule and Simon Commission, 103
India and the World (Nehru), 197
India House, 30
India League (IL), 193, 195, 196
India Review, 196
Indian Committee for Food for
  Spain, 237

Indian National Congress (INC). *See also* Calcutta Congress; Delhi Manifesto; Lahore Congress; Madras meeting; Nehru report; purna swaraj declaration
"The War Danger" resolution, 107, 137
branded illegal with irregular meetings, 191
China independence resolution, 137
humanitarian aid to China and Spain, 215, 237–238
LAI association, 154
London branch critics of LAI, 194
organization moves left, 207
Pan-Asiatic resolution, 137
Swaraj Party and "no-changers," 38, 103, 108, 109–110, 171
Indian National Congress (INC), Nehru role
all correspondence with LAI to cease, 173
All-Indian Congress Committee (AICC) representative to Brussels, 33
anti-imperialism worldview for, 105
boycott of provincial ministries, 211–212
Brussels Congress, Nehru Report, 48–51, 58
delegate to Brussels Congress, 19
foreign department, 225–226, 237
foreign department resolution, 137
Johnstone resolution, 132
LAI association, 21, 79, 84, 107, 147
Madras meeting resolutions, 107
presidency of INC, 205, 211–212
presidential address on Indian nationalism, 206–207
resistance from right wing, 210
Indian National Congress (INC), Working Committee
Brussels Congress report to, 48
Delhi Manifesto, 169
foreign department resolution, 137
independence resolution discussed, 108
Nehru's argues for LAI association, 79, 80
right wing dominance, 210–211
Indonesia, 55
Dutch East Indies colonialism, 83
solidarity with India, 271
Indonesia Merdeka (Free Indonesia), 55
intelligence. *See* British Empire; German Foreign Office
International African Friends of Abyssinia, 203
International African Friends of Ethiopia, 200

International African Service Bureau (IASB), 200
International Committee for Political Prisoners (ICPP), 61, 82
International Federation of Trade Unions (IFTU), 128
International Labor Organization (ILO), 126
International Peace Campaign (IPC)
closure, 258, 259
communist and non-communist tensions, 224
coordinates smaller peace organizations, 223
INC membership, 214
INC support, 227, 228
India and anti-imperialist cause, 227, 228
League of Nations origin and support, 223, 228
Paris World Exposition in 1937 peace pavilion, 225
promotion of anti-fascism and anti-imperialism, 237, 243
International Peace Campaign (IPC), Brussels Congress, 224–225
Menon opening speech, 224
Münzenberg and Gibarti at, 223
Nehru message, 218–219
overwhelming support for, 223
International Peace Campaign (IPC), Nehru's role, 1, 216
ambiguities of internationalism in, 228–229, 235
encourages KMT to join, 250
Paris speeches, 232–234
promotion of anti-fascism and anti-imperialism, 14, 219, 233, 254
International Trade Union Committee of Negro Workers (ITUC-NW), 200
International Workers' Aid, 68
internationalism and interstate relations definition of, 13–15
Iyengar, Srinivasa, 117, 118, 123

James, Cyril Lionel Robert, 200, 203
Jansen, G.H., 267
Japanese Communist Party, 35
Jhabwala, Shavaksha H., 37
Jinnah, Mohammed Ali, 120, 244
Johnstone, J.W., 128–132, 163, 192
Joshi, P.C., 259

Karunovskaya, Eduardonvna, 259–260
Katayama, Sen, 35–36, 54
Kautsky, Karl, 96
Kennedy, John F., 280
Kenyatta, Jomo, 57, 192, 198, 268
  Conference on Peace and Empire, 230, 231
Khan, Noor, 242
Kirti Kisan Sabha, 115
Kishun, Suraj, 31
Kopf, David, 184
Kotewala, John, 276
Kouyaté, Tiemoko Garan, 200
Kuomintang Party (KMT), 31, 36, 52, 60, 68, 75, 241–242

Labor Socialist International (LSI), 72–73, 126, *See also* British Labour Party and labour movement
  retreat from LAI, 85, 86, 87
  truce with Comintern, 193
Labour Leader, 35, 48
Lahore Congress, 140
  independence question, 154
  Nehru president of, 140
Lansbury, George, 49, 70, 74, 85
  blending, 2
  Brussels Congress, 41–43, 60, 276
  chairman, LAI, 1, 67, 68, 73
  LAI resignation, 155
  resignation under pressure, 86–87
League against Colonial Oppression (LACO), 31
League against Imperialism (LAI), 9, *See also* Anti-Imperialist Review (AIR); Brussels Congress; Calcutta Congress; Frankfurt Congress (Second World Congress)
  anti-fascism in 1930's, 212
  attempt to counteract Comintern LAI takeover, 166–167
  Bandung Conference and, 14
  British intelligence view, 65
  China focus, 81
  closing announced, 258
  Comintern role, 67–68, 78, 141–143, 144, 145–150, 167, 174, 176
  disarray, 173, 175
  inaugural meeting, Brussels, 1, 15, 19
  INC support, 118, 137
  INC-LAI relationship, 48, 163, 167–168, 169–171, 193

  messages of solidarity to Calcutta Congress, 133
  national sections correspondence, 73
  primary objective, overthrow of imperialism, 106
  relations with AITUC, 126, 148
  response to treatment of colonials, 33
  socialists and communists balance, 106, 142, 144, 149, 150, 152, 166, 171–172, 173
  war danger theme, 220
League against Imperialism (LAI), British national section, 194
  affiliates with CPGB, 161
  affiliates with IPC, 223
  and Berlin Secretariat, 174–175
  Bridgeman resurrects LAI in London, 192
  Bridgeman, secretary, 60, 86, 87–88
  creation of British branch, 86
  Saklatvala influence, 84, 87
  socialists and communists in, 66
  support for Meerhut defendants, 164
League against Imperialism (LAI), Dutch section, 88
League against Imperialism (LAI), executive committee, 68
  Amsterdam meeting, 65, 67, 68–70, 71
  Brussels meeting, 105–106
  challenges of global organization, 73–74
  China protest, 70–71
  Cologne meeting, 83–84
  Communist influence, 85
  Indian independence discussed, 106
  membership, 71–72, 73
  propaganda of, 80–81, 113–114
  Soviet delegation, 149
League against Imperialism (LAI), Nehru role
  correspondence and communications, 125
  executive committee, 65–67, 74–75, 79–80, 84, 100–101
  LAI-INC relationship question to secretariat, 172
  Nehru–Baldwin letters, 74, 76–77
  relationship post resignation, 182, 188, 193, 194, 197
  resignation, 140–141, 142, 143, 147, 172–173, 182
  support ends, 175
  support for, 1, 21, 88, 100, 115, 168, 171

League against Imperialism (LAI),
  secretariat
  Chatto international secretary, 113
  Chatto role, 173
  Comintern agents added, 160
  Frankfurt Congress planning, 144–146
  linguistic departments, 73
  location, Berlin and Paris, 74–76, 77
  Manifesto publication, 47
  Münzenberg role, 67, 160, 173
  Nazi raid, 192–193
  non-communist purge, 141
  resistance to Comintern, 149, 176
  shift from Berlin to London, 192–193
League against War and Fascism (LAWF),
  223, 238, 265
  communists and non-communists,
  221–222, 231
League of Nations
  "collective security" on eve of World War
  II, 216, 219, 223, 228, 232
  Abyssinia request for support, 203, 204
  India status in, 27–28
  interstate diplomacy and, 13–14, 228
  tool for imperialist expansion, 8
Lenin, Vladimir Ilyich, 22, 72, 94, 96, 97,
  187, 202
  Leninist moment, 8
Liau Hansin, 36, 52, 68, 70, 81
  Comintern agent, 73, 76
  LAI role, 75, 77
Liberator, 120
Liberty under the Soviets (Baldwin), 95
Líster, Enrique, 239
Lloyd George, David
  Nehru response, 203
  speech on redistribution of colonial
  possessions, 203
Lohia, Rammanohar, 225–226, 237

Madras meeting, 103, 105, 107,
  108–110
Maier, Charles, 13
Manela, Erez, 26
Mao Zedong, 241, 247, 271, 279
Margueritte, Victor, 34
Marteux, Albert, 35
Marx, Karl, 72
Maxton, James, 87, 112, 117, 144,
  150–151, 155–156, 159–160
  expelled from LAI, 161–162

Meerut Conspiracy Case (1929–1934),
  147–148, 161
  Baldwin's support, 189
  defendants communist propaganda, 165
  Gandhi role, 164–165
  INC role, 164–165
  LAI named as a conspirator, 163
  Nehru role, 164–165
Melnitschansky, Grigorij, 149
Menon, K.P.S, 278
Menon, V.K. Krishna, 182, 188, 193
  anti-imperialist worldview, 196–197
  Brussels IPC meeting, 218
  friendship with Nehru, 195–196, 197
  IPC executive council and anti-imperialist
  cause, 227
  Spanish Republic humanitarian aid,
  237, 240
Mexico. *See* Brussels Congress
Miglioli, Guido, 40
Modern Review, 19
Münzenberg, Willi, 59, 84, *See also*
  Comintern (Communist International)
  AIR article, 119–120
  Amsterdam peace conference, 220
  and Nehru, 78
  anti-fascist role, 222
  Brussels Congress, 33, 35, 42–43
  Chatto relationship, 31, 148, 160, 166, 171
  death of, 258, 263–264
  flees Berlin to Paris, 175, 192, 222,
  259, 260
  Frankfurt Congress, 156, 157, 158,
  159–160, 165
  LAI and Comintern, 72
  LAI executive committee, 68–69, 75
  LAI role, 31, 67–68, 125, 142
  LAI-INC friction, 171
  Meerut Conspiracy Case (1929–1934), 163
  Moscow Comintern trip to defend
  LAI, 160
  organized against Nazis and fascists, 222
  resigns from Communist Party, 262–263
  resistance to Comintern over LAI, 149
  Workers International Relief (WIR), 32
Muslim League, 120, 244
Muslim minorities, 120

Naidu, Sarojini, 30
Nambiar, Arathil Candeth Narayanan
  (A.C.N.), 31, 115

Nasser, Gamal Abdul, 271
National Association for the Advancement
    of Colored People (NAACP), 57, 75
National Herald, 251
nationalism and internationalism, 2, 3,
    12–13, 21–22, 103, 106, 140, *See also*
    internationalism and interstate
    relations
    Brussels Congress, 21
    effect of World War II, 257
    Lansbury speech, 41–43, 276
    Nehru's endorsement, 15, 49, 84, 100,
        105, 113
nationalism and socialism, 100, 104, 208, 209
Nazi-Soviet Pact, 257, 258, 263, 265
Negro Peoples of the World
    Fifth Annual Convention, 40
Negro Worker, 200
Nehru Report, 120–122, 124, 127, 135–137
    government of India fails to act, 140
Nehru, Jawaharlal. *See also* League against
    Imperialism (LAI)
    "A Foreign Policy for India," 88–91
    All-Parties Conference secretary, 120
    blending of nationalism, socialism and
        communism, 126–127, 138–139, 208,
        254
    Britain, criticism of, 240
    China relationship, 52–55, 99, 100
    early politics, 25–26
    Egypt visit, 217, 241–243
    Europe trip prior to World War II,
        228–230, 232
    family and early years, 24–25
    imprisonment, 173, 181–182, 189,
        191, 265
    Indian-centric perspective, 11, 38–39
    Italian fascists encounter, 229
    League of Nations Geneva meetings, 27
    London visits, 188, 194–196, 197, 230
    Maxton expulsion opinion, 161
    Minister of External Affairs, 271
    Prime Minister of India, 195, 264,
        265–266
    socialism of, 23, 49–51, 93, 104, 184,
        208–209, 212
    Soviet Union trip, 66, 94–100
    United States and, 61–62
Nehru, Jawaharlal, Brussels Congress and,
    21, 33, 37–39, 63–64
    Africa and pan-Africanism, 57–58

British Left, 60
China plan, 53–54
    Egypt and, 56
    Indonesia and, 55
    pan-Asian solidarity, 54
    resolutions accepted, 46–47
    South Africa, 58
    Soviet Union and Communists, 58–60
    United States and, 62
Nehru, Kamala, 27, 191, 205
Nehru, Motilal, 24–25, 33, 97, 118
    All-Parties Conference chair, 120
    at LAI executive committee, 106–107
    dominion status, 105, 106
    letters, 91
Nkrumah, Kwame, 199, 275–276
Non-Aligned Movement, 269
    Nehru's role, 270, 277–278, 281
Non-Cooperation movement, 26, 38
North American Committee to Aid Spanish
    Democracy (NACASD), 238

Outline of World History (Wells), 184

Padmore, George, 182, 198–202, 275
    arrested by Nazis then fled to Paris, 200
    Conference on Peace and Empire, 230
    expelled from Comintern, 200
Pakistan, 120, 265, 277, 279
pan-Africanism. *See* Africa and pan-
    Africanism
Pennybacker, Susan, 10, 263
Perhimpunan Indonesia (PI), 55, 68, 75
Petersson, Fredrik, 20, 69
Pollitt, Harry, 60, 152
Popular Front, 193
purna swaraj declaration, 93, 140,
    170, 172

Quit India Campaign, 265

racism, 43, 58, 90, 129, *See also* black
    internationalism
Raza, Ali, 44
Review of Nations, 27
Rios, Fernando de Los, 238
Rolland, Romain, 34, 134
Rothstein, Theodore, 60
Roy, Franziska, 44
Roy, Manabendra Nath, 8, 30, 59, 94, 189
    Baldwin's support, 189

Sacco-Vanzetti trial, 83
Saklatvala, Shapurji, 142
    "British Imperialism in India: A World
        Menace," 117
    and Abyssinia crisis, 203
    and British LAI, 87, 156
    and LAI, 84, 85, 107, 157, 162,
        163, 194
    Brussels Congress, 60
    death of, 197
    London meeting with Nehru, 188
    Nehru's London visit and, 94
    on dominion status, 107
Sangh Parivar, 15
Sarkar, Sumit, 184
Schmidt, P. J., 83, 88
Scottsboro Defense Committee, 192
Second Round Table Conference,
    190, 191
Senghor, Lamine, 70
Senghor, Léopold Sédar, 68
Shaw, George Bernard, 25
Sikh League, 115
Simon Commission, 103, 120
Simon, John, 103
Sinclair, Upton, 34
Singh, Mangal, 115
Sinn Fein Irish Republican Movement, 75
Sluga, Glenda, 4
Smedley, Agnes, 82
Smeral, Bohumíl, 160
Society for Cultural Relations with the
    Soviet Union, 94
Soong Mei-ling (Mme. Chiang Kai-shek), 99
Soong Qingling (Mme. Sun Yat-Sen), 34,
    66, 117, 251
    Calcutta Congress, 133
    denied visa for Calcutta Congress, 134
    denied visa for Madras meeting, 99
    Nehru correspondence, 99
South African Trade Union Congress, 75
Soviet Union
    anti-imperialism of, 96
    dictatorship and tyranny, 98
    great experiment, 22, 36, 44, 95,
        97–98, 264
    invasion of Finland, 257, 265
    Nehru's defense of, 278
    non-aggression pact, 257, 258, 263
    Stalinization and power struggle, 95
    war scare of 1927, 44–45

Spanish Civil War, 214, *See also* Committee
    for the War Relief of Republican Spain;
    Indian Committee for Food for Spain;
    North American Committee to Aid
    Spanish Democracy (NACASD)
    Baldwin's views, 236
    Bridgeman's views, 221
    India's material support for Republican
        Spain, 237
    Nehru's views, 216–217, 236–237, 238
    Nehru's visit to Barcelona, 239, 240
    peace movement and Republican Spain
        support, 236–237
    refugee crisis, 256
    Soviet Union archives, 236
Stalin, Joseph, 95, 146, 187, 257, 263, 278
Stolte, Carolien, 53–55, 127
Sukarno, 14, 267, 271
Sun Yat-Sen, Mme.. *See* Soong Qingling
    (Mme. Sun Yat-Sen)
swaraj
    definition questioned, 90, 91, 97, 106,
        108
    Gandhi's view, 91, 110
    Nehru's view, 110, 111–112

Tagore, Rabindranath, 251
The Labour Monthly, 168
The New Leader, 161
Thögersen, Hans, "York," 173
Tilak, Bal Gangadhar, 26
Time and Tide, 203
Toller, Ernst, 34
trade union movement. *See also* All India
    Trade Union Congress (AITUC)
Treaties of Westphalia, 13
Trotsky, Leon, 95
Truman, Harry S., 279

U Nu, 276
Ugarte, Manuel, 68
Union of Soviet Social Republics. *See* Soviet
    Union
United Nations, 257
United States, 83
    British imperialism in India protested,
        189, 190–191
    imperialism of, 39, 83
    Nehru's relationship with, 279

Vasconcelos, José, 36, 39

Wadf Party, 253
Wafd Party, 75, 115, 241–244
  election defeat and waning influence, 245
  Nehru's secret anti-imperialist critique,
    245–246
  public blame to British, 246
Wallace, I.T.A, 203
Wang Jingwei, 71
Ward, Harry F., 221
Wells, H. G., 184
Wilson, Woodrow, 26, 33
Wilsonian Moment, 8, 26
Workers and Peasants Party (WPP), 115, 127
Workers International Relief (WIR), 31, 75
Workers' Welfare League of India, 155
World Conference for the Action on the
  Bombardment of Open Towns and
  the Restoration of Peace, 233
  Nehru speech anti-imperialism
    included, 234

World Congress of the Friends of the
  U.S.S.R, 98–99
World War I. *See* Great War
World War II
  anti-imperialist disillusionment,
    256–257
  Britain and Germany war danger, lack of
    understanding, 240
  decolonization and independence
    after, 257
  events leading to, 182, 212
  INC question of policy, 251
  Nehru visit with Münzenberg, 232
  non-aggression pact, 263

Yagnik, Indulal, 107
Young India, 109

Zachariah, Benjamin, 3–5
Zetkin, Clara, 34

CPSIA information can be obtained
at www.ICGtesting.com
Printed in the USA
LVHW112023161122
733301LV00003B/152